AN
ENCHANTING
DARKNESS

AN
ENCHANTING
DARKNESS

The American Vision of Africa in the Twentieth Century

Dennis Hickey and Kenneth C. Wylie

Michigan State University Press
East Lansing
1993

All Michigan State University Press books are produced on paper which meets the requirements of American National Standard of Information Sciences—Permanence of paper for printed materials ANSI Z23.48-1984

Michigan State University Press
East Lansing, Michigan 48823-5202

Printed in the United States of America

01 00 99 98 97 96 95 94 93 1 2 3 4 5 6 7 8 9 10

Library of Congress Cataloging-in-Publication Data

Hickey, Dennis.
    An enchanting darkness: the American vision of Africa in
    the twentieth century / Dennis Hickey and Kenneth Wylie.
        p.   cm.
    Includes bibliographical references and index.
    ISBN 0-87013-321-7 (alk. paper)
    1. Africa—Relations—United States. 2. Africa—Foreign
public opinion, American. 3. Public opinion—United States.
I. Wylie, Kenneth C. II, Title
DT38.7.H5   1993
960—dc20
                                            92-56916
                                            CIP

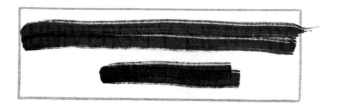

To my father, Charles Hickey, and in memory of my mother, Verna Hickey.

D.H.

To my children, Jennifer and Jared.

K.C.W.

Contents

Introduction

Most Americans only need to hear the word Africa and they instantly imagine a place dark and primitive, "tribes" living in jungles—and often at each other's throats—wild beasts dominating the landscape: a place without history, largely unchanged and untamed, and certainly uncivilized. Even the small percentage of Americans who know better, who can conjure up a simple map of a varied land of tawny savannahs, woodlands, vast deserts, old cities, and dynamic cultures, are typically influenced by the mythic Africa which lingers at the edge of consciousness. As historian Leonard Thompson has pointed out, people continue to make decisions based on mistaken historical images acquired when young, "even though scholars know those images to be false."[1] Why is this so? Why, after decades of painstaking historical and anthropological research, do so many Americans, including millions with college degrees, persist in such simplistic stereotypes? Why, as any historian of Africa can attest, does the slightest mention of "African History" cause such predictable skepticism—that dubious raising of eyebrows—even among professional historians who ought to know by now that Africa has a history quite distinct from these familiar images? Why is it that the slightest hint that Africa's role in world history has been underplayed so often evokes an irrational response, often phrased in negatives? Why is it that the biased overreaction known as "Afrocentricity" is the only approach to African history that most Americans have heard about?

Everywhere, it seems, we are bombarded with that mysterious Africa of yore, that realm made famous by Henry Stanley, Teddy Roosevelt, and Edgar Rice Burroughs, and solidified in our receptive minds by Hollywood: a place of jungle, mountain, and plain, peopled by naked primitives scattered across shadowed (or luminous) scapes; humans framed like museum-pieces within picturesque dioramas (grass huts, "kralls," cattle, drums, spears, and huge iron pots); an Africa preserved in amber despite centuries of intimate contact with the outside world; Africans who are never truly African unless they remain pristine, "unspoiled" by western education, western ideas, western creeds, and western corruptions.

Over time, it would seem, major change would occur. Hundreds, eventually thousands of Americans served in the Peace Corps beginning in the 1960s. Many of these made the study of Africa their profession. Many more, picking up on the established (albeit colonial) foundation of European scholarship, followed suit. At least from the late 1950s Americans had the opportunity to break away from the hide-bound European view which had served imperial purposes all too well. Certainly a handful of American scholars (several of these African Americans) had already pointed the way to a clearer vision. A number of European scholars had done the same. Certainly African scholars were doing so. Africa, these dissenters contended, was not outside history, was not that isolated "dark continent" beloved of the explorers and missionaries. Significant parts of Africa, including sub-Saharan Africa, had trading links to Europe and Asia and Africa possessed dynamic societies virtually unknown by most in the West. Africa, they pleaded, must be studied on its own account.

They were right, of course. In academia it was axiomatic among so-called "Africanists" that the reappraisal of Africa from a non-racist, non-judgmental, truly scientific perspective, was proceeding apace. In some cases this was demonstrably true, in others it was not. Monographs poured forth by the hundreds. Courses by the hundreds entered the curriculum. Some found reluctant acceptance in orthodox departments (History, Anthropology, Literature, Music, Art, etc.), some within newly established departments or within loosely organized centers. High schools and even elementary schools claimed an interest in the new curriculum. Decades passed. The quiet but hopeful fifties gave way to the violent but euphoric sixties. The seventies and eighties witnessed more specific, more data-oriented research, but this came amid setbacks, retrenchment, worsening civil and ethnic conflict, economic stagnation, irredentism and xenophobia.

Through it all this powerful imagery held, persistent and never far from consciousness, revealed again and again at every level of American public life, in popular culture (movies, television, magazines, newspapers, comics), in the fine arts, in literature (including the works of the best writers), and yes, in the ivy halls of academia.

Amid all this, for fifty years at least, scholars, journalists, open-minded travelers and observers attempted to counter this rooted image, the mindset that saw only dark and violent mystery.

Sometimes, and not surprisingly, the weight of hope (and the body of data) tipped the scale rather heavily in reverse. Though the idea did not originate in the U.S. it was mainly in the U.S. that another Africa emerged like a butterfly from its cocoon, equally fictional, unreal, and imagined as that dark wild place of the past. This "brightest" Africa was many things to many people: it was a lost Eden, it was golden shadows and flying hooves,[2] it was smoke-wreathed villages as old as time and as pure as diamonds, it was simple hunters who never knew patriarchy or hierarchy, it was gorillas in the mist and sunsets seen from shaded settler's veran-dahs, it was the noble savage fighting to preserve his ancient ways, it was that imagined Pleistocene where an adventuring American male could seek that grail (whatever it was, the biggest kudu, the fiercest lion, the lost or eroded manhood) no longer obtainable in Europe or America, or anywhere else. It was to some scholars an Africa where the truly primitive (now to become an ideology) was elevated to a level that even Rousseau might have envied.

Clearly, this reaction—however well-meaning—had the effect among some Americans of underlining the symbolic conventions noted above, rather than undermining them. Africa, traditionally viewed as a place of opposites, was thus seen in Manichean terms; it was all of one or all of the other. Most Africans, seen through this dichotomized prism, had to be "primitive," or else they were not properly Africans. Any part of Africa, any tradition, (urban, effi-cient, concentrated, complex, Byzantine) which did not fit this side of the Manichean view, was therefore not really African. If a writer or scholar illuminated the internal mechanisms of medieval Kano, or seventeenth-century Benin, or eighteenth-century Sennar, this was esoteric gobbledygook to a public which wanted only the primi-tive, which preferred only the savage, noble or ignoble. If an artistic practice or tradition was synthesized, borrowed, or compounded of some parts African other parts non-African, it could not be "African." By such a standard, of course, Christianity could not be a European tradition, nor Buddhism an Oriental one.

Of course, since Manichean views require opposites, extremes, and polarization, it would follow that some who revised African His-tory would feel compelled to produce not an alternative view, but rather a counter myth, a folkloric, magical past, as bogus and empty as the myth of darkness. In the process the legitimate recon-struction of Africa's past was itself called into question by those who remained, willfully or not, ignorant of Africa.

This, then, is the subject of this book, a joint effort by two schol-ars who between them have shared forty-five years or more of research and experience in and out of Africa. In the chapters which follow we have attempted a broad synthesis. Both authors, trained as historians, have backgrounds in anthropology as well, and both have taught writing and literature in an American Studies program. Our canvas, since we seek to illuminate a process that affects all disciplines, is necessarily interdisciplinary. We have chapters on fiction, ethnography, politics, and several other subjects, and in a second volume will cover film, the environment, afrocentric revisionism, and a number of regional cases-in-point. Our research, based on an analysis of the workings of these symbolic conventions across genres, is therefore cross-cultural, and we have not excluded research into the history of the Middle East, Islam, or the Orient, not to mention North America, which is, after all, the focus of this work. We have written with the general reader in mind as well as the specialist, the undergraduate as well as the graduate student. Careful readers will note that some of the more "academic" arguments, though no less significant, especially disputes among scholars within a single discipline, are included in the endnotes. We believe that jargon is the bane of modern scholarship, that it obscures clarity in thought and expression. We challenge reductionism whether it comes from the right or the left.

Having read, studied, and researched hundreds of books, magazines, journals, stories, films, and other materials (popular and controversial, famous and obscure) across the genres, both authors are firmly convinced that it is possible to "take apart" the neat, convenient, but often distorting frameworks (or constructs) into which the various disciplines too often place the study of Africa. The "real" Africa, the dynamic Africa of real people, we believe, is there to be seen and understood thanks to the sound work of generations of scholars who possessed a broader and less parochial vision. Africa can be, and must be, the subject of continuing scholarly endeavors, and thus it can be comprehended along with the rest of this complex world. Though it may be true that we make a special plea to reappraise our view of Africa in the pages which follow, and though we argue that Africa sometimes requires special treatment (to break through centuries of prejudice), we do not believe that Africa should be treated separately. Africa is not, as some would have it, a place apart.

Obviously we owe a debt beyond measure to scholars who have paved the way. Philip Curtin's *The Image of Africa* remains the foundation for research on Africa in this field, as is Carl Degler's *The Search for Human Nature* in the American sphere. *The Invention of Tradition*, edited by Eric Hobsbawm and Terence Ranger, is another seminal study without which the idea behind this book might never have germinated. Leonard Thompson's *The Political Mythology of Apartheid* provided learned insights, as did V. Y. Mudimbe's *The Invention of Africa.* Edward McKinley's *The Lure of*

Africa was helpful, and Michael McCarthy's *Dark Continent: Africa as Seen by Americans* was especially useful for its information on geographic texts, children's literature, and its perspective on the African American view of Africa. Sylvia Jacobs' *The African Nexus* is another vital work on African American perspectives early in this century, and Martin Staniland's *American Intellectuals and African Nationalists, 1955-1970* is equally important on more recent decades. Donna Haraway's *Primate Visions: Gender, Race and Nature in the World of Modern Science* provided a stimulating alternative to any unthinking sexist or orthodox discourse, especially on issues relating to scientific objectivity. Needless to say Edward Said's powerful *Orientalism* is central to any understanding of negative western bias. Among anthropologists the works of Clifford Geertz, James Clifford, and George Marcus proved central to the formulation of our own analysis. On a somewhat more personal note both authors feel a special identification (if not solidarity) with the great ethnographer Franz Boas, whose prodigious works reveal an extraordinary humanity which goes beyond science. Though Boas died before the time of either author, we both feel that he was our teacher as well.

Among the many who provided invaluable support in the preparation of this work we would like to thank Richard Hull, Professor of African History at New York University, who read and commented on significant parts of this manuscript. Professor Robert McKinley of the Department of Anthropology at Michigan State University provided useful insights, and Scott Whiteford, also Professor of Anthropology and director of MSU's Latin American and Caribbean Studies Center, and David Wiley, Professor of Sociology at MSU and director of MSU's African Studies Center were very supportive. John W. Eadie, Dean of MSU's College of Arts and Letters and the director of the Consortium for Inter-Institutional Collaboration in African and Latin American Studies, also provided vital support at a crucial juncture. We would also like to thank the late James R. Hooker. The list grows long, but Kenneth Wylie would especially like to thank Harold Marcus, David Robinson, Kenneth Harrow, and Pedro Maligo—all of whom helped in important ways. In the Department of American Thought and Language we especially thank Doug Noverr, Pat Julius, Larry Ziewacz, Gary Hoppenstand, and Kay Rout for their input and encouragement. Dennis Hickey would also like to thank the members of the Department of History at Ohio University, especially Suzanne Miers-Oliver, Gifford Doxsee, Richard Bradshaw, and Stephen Howard of the African Studies Program, the members of the Department of History at Edinboro University of Pennsylvania, and Dean Robert Weber of the School of Liberal Arts at Edinboro's School of Liberal Arts for their invaluable help and support. He would also like to express his deep appreciation to the graduate professors who helped him along the way—especially Harold Marcus and John Rowe.

Finally, since this book was written under the constant pressure of teaching undergraduates, in a department whose faculty normally teach a heavier load than is typical in most universities, we would like to thank our students for their patience and good will. We hope some of them make good use of this work.

Notes

1. Leonard Thompson, *The Political Mythology of Apartheid* (New Haven: Yale University Press, 1985),vii
2. George Schaller, *Golden Shadows, Flying Hooves* (New York: A Knopf, 1973).

1

Of Naked Apes and Noble Savages

In the April 1991 edition of *Harper's Magazine* Walter Russell Mead described the somber ordeal of a continent in crisis. Its political history was a chronicle of bloodshed and division, and its past was a burden which complicated the present and darkened the prospects of the future. A new generation of leaders had proclaimed a coming era of peace and unity, growth and prosperity, political and economic integration, but a cursory reading of the daily newspaper revealed that these predictions were little more than hollow rhetoric. Indeed, the actual situation provided little cause for optimism: old animosities were reemerging and ethnic and religious conflict was on the rise; civil war remained a constant danger in certain countries, threatening the very existence of fragile nation-states; and a number of governments were engaged in a dire search for development aid and emergency food assistance. Mead's essay was entitled "Dark Continent"; his subtitle: "A grand, grim tour of the New Europe."[1]

Mead's title included a familiar term which carried a familiar set of associations. Because of these expectations, his readership was obviously not prepared for the subtitle (and analysis) which followed. Indeed, ever since Henry Morton Stanley adopted this phrase as the title of one of his rousing traveler's accounts, Africa has been regarded as the "Dark Continent," the home of a hostile assortment of "natives" and "tribes" who were thought to live in timeless and primitive splendor. In constructing his textual vision of Africa Stanley himself was building on an existing set of themes, images and assumptions. As Philip Curtin demonstrated in his 1964 pioneering study of *The Image of Africa*, English traders, travelers, explorers and missionaries had developed a dramatic and distorted picture of the continent during several centuries of contact.[2] With the colonial "scramble for Africa" during the last quarter of the nineteenth century a new wave of European administrators, entrepreneurs and settlers expanded (and codified) this portrait for their countrymen who stayed at home. By 1878, Stanley's audience had been emotionally prepared for his dangerous journey *Through the Dark Continent*, and the commercial success of this book (and those which followed) confirmed that he was remarkably adept at fulfilling their expectations.[3]

Whatever the defects of his actions and his works, Stanley played a crucial role in acquainting the American public with the enduring reality that was Africa. Born John Rowlands in Wales, an illegitimate and unwanted child who was committed to a workhouse at the age of six, the story of his early years might have been fashioned by Dickens himself. Taking ship to America at the age of seventeen, Stanley landed in New Orleans and spent several years traveling the Mississippi as the agent of a cotton broker. With the coming of the Civil War he joined the Confederate army. He was taken prisoner by Federal forces during the carnage at Shiloh but promptly recouped his fortunes by volunteering for the Union Army. After his discharge Stanley enjoyed a brief adventure in Wales and Spain, and then, returning to America, he enlisted in the Federal Navy. In 1865, several months before the end of the war, he deserted ship and began the search for a more lucrative pursuit. After an interlude in Turkey and a stint as a journalist on the Great Plains he achieved a personal breakthrough in 1867 when he accompanied a British punitive expedition to Ethiopia as a correspondent for the *New York Herald*. This episode paved the way for further assignments in the "Dark Continent," and after his sensational "rescue" of missionary David Livingstone in 1871, his status as a celebrity—and popular authority on Africa—was assured.[4]

From an intellectual and emotional standpoint, no traveler arrives at his destination as a blank slate. The cultural "other"—the alien object of the narrator's scrutiny—is always perceived through the medium of previous experience and personal acculturation. For this reason, it should not be surprising that Stanley's perception of Africa and Africans was deeply affected by his American experience. The American image of Africa which emerged during this period was a fusion of two major sets of impressions: a vision of the continent derived from European (especially British) accounts, on the one hand, and a domestic inventory of texts and assumptions concerning the Amerindian and African American populations, on the other. This particular convergence is especially evident in the case of Stanley, whose works on Africa represent a relatively early (and extremely influential) expression of this process.

By the time of his celebrated search for Livingstone, Stanley had already received a thorough American grounding in the "character and nature" of non-European peoples and their expected place in the new imperial order. His first major assignment came in 1867 when he was hired by the *Missouri Democrat* of St. Louis. As Stanley described it, before this time he "had been only an Occasional Descriptist of battle scenes and important public events; but in my twenty-fifth year I was promoted to the proud position of a Special Correspondent, with the very large commission to inform the public regarding all matters of general interest affecting the Indians and the great Western Plains."[5] In this capacity he would witness the "exploits" of the U.S. Cavalry and he would sharpen his rhetorical skills within the bloody cockpit of their "savage war of peace." This interlude on the American frontier proved to be a valuable professional asset. While the military action he witnessed was limited, he nevertheless received a practical introduction to the philosophy and conduct of the "punitive expedition." Stanley discovered that a disciplined and well-supplied column armed with repeating rifles could defeat a numerically superior force which relied on traditional weaponry, a lesson which he later put to good use in his African campaigns. Also, the raids, reprisals, and "pow-wows" directed by Hancock, Sherman and Custer provided him with abundant raw material to sharpen his narrative skills. During this period he learned how to give form, coherence, and meaning to an uninspiring sort of episodic violence which bore little resemblance to the grander and more formalized slaughter which had characterized the battles of the Civil War.

Stanley's resounding success in the arena of American popular culture was a matter of style and calculation as well as experience. In describing his African adventures he was determined to entertain as well as enlighten, and his animated and immodest approach to the traveler's account was considered a vulgar departure in English literary and scientific circles. With the publication of *How I Found Livingstone* he became known as "a man who stopped at nothing, the product of the new 'blood-and-thunder' American journalism, which taught that action was what readers paid for."[6] As might be expected, the end of the Civil War had created something of a journalistic void. By 1865 the American public had come to expect their daily portion of the epic and the heroic, and perceptive editors and publishers clearly understood that Stanley's project in Africa—and the forceful prose which gave it life—was exactly the type of vehicle which could satisfy this demand and secure their position in an increasingly competitive marketplace.

Above all else, the Livingstone expedition was a commercial operation in pursuit of a salable text, and it is not surprising that its sponsor, the publisher of the *New York Herald*, would come to bitterly resent the acclaim which was lavished on his foreign correspondent. James Gordon Bennett Jr. "quite seriously believed that he deserved the major share of the credit because he conceived the idea of the expedition and put up the money to outfit it. His reward was the *Herald's* booming circulation, nothing more."[7] This reward, however, was not inconsiderable; and together, Bennett and Stanley had "discovered" a portrayal of Africa which was a profitable commodity, and developed a formula and fantasy which the American public was more than willing to pay for. Before this breakthrough, the readership of African travel accounts had been limited to a fairly select audience, and these works had commanded much greater attention in Britain (and continental Europe) than they attracted in the United States. With the appearance of *How I Found Livingstone* in 1872, Stanley established a popular and broad-based market for this genre on both sides of the Atlantic, a market which he, and others, were able to exploit. As Jeremy Bernstein has pointed out, this book, as well as *Through the Dark Continent* (1878) and *In Darkest Africa* (1890), was a major publishing event. "All three were an immense success, selling hundreds of thousands of copies and making Stanley a wealthy man."[8] From this point on, it was apparent that the textual construction of Africa would no longer be a European monopoly.

Stanley had mastered the art of captivating his audience during his earlier assignment in the American west. In his pieces for the *Missouri Democrat* "he worked in the beat of tom-toms, the war dances, a train ambush, and the fierce behavior of small Indian boys," deploying precisely the type of symbolic conventions which he would later use to great effect in his writing on Africa.[9] Unfortunately, his attitude toward his primary subject—the Indians themselves—is more problematic. In his biography of Stanley, historian Richard Hall suggests that he grew more sympathetic toward Amerindians as time went on, noting that he even referred to them in one of his later dispatches as those "'wronged children of the soil.'"[10] Admittedly, Stanley was strongly opposed to their extermination, but throughout his correspondence he made it abundantly clear that the Indians were a threat which needed to be contained, and he repeatedly criticized the responsible authorities for failing to bring them under effective military control. For Stanley, there was only one realistic solution to the problem: "set apart a sufficient territory, drive all the tribes within its limits, surround it with garrisons that none may leave it, and into which no white may enter without a special pass."[11] Once confined within the reservation, with the help of the missionary, the teacher, and the government agent, the Indian could gradually acquire the necessary elements of "civilization." To support his case he cited the example of the Cherokee, who had not only survived this process, but, in the opinion of many, had gone on to prosper as a direct result of it.

In his view, the Amerindians were not beyond redemption; nevertheless, Stanley saw little worth saving in their cultural universe. In 1895, in the retrospective introduction to his *Early Travels*, he rejected the notion that the whites were primarily responsible for "the red men's disappearance." He maintained that while there was "no doubt that the rifles and 'firewater' of the colonists have slain a great many . . . the principal causes of their disappearance have sprung from their own innate savagery. It was in their nature to destroy their own families, tribes, and each other."[12] His descriptions of the material life of the Indians tended toward the grim and judgmental, and, in his vision of their social life, "there were neither Hiawathas nor Minnehahas. Rejecting the romantic vision of the noble savage, he disparaged Indian women," arguing on one occasion that "'morality is hardly known among the Indians. . . . As a mother, the squaw ranks little above the lower animals.'"[13] In its essentials, his assessment of the daily life of Amerindians owed more to Hobbes than it did to Rousseau.

On the Great Plains, for the first time in his career, Stanley also confronted the obligatory task of historical and racial classification which was central to the enterprise of the nineteenth-century traveler. In fairness to Stanley, he never attributed the "backwardness" of the Indians—or the Africans—to racial or genetic factors. Instead, he explained their condition in terms of the vagaries of history and the destructive impact of cultural isolation. In one of his dispatches to the *Missouri Democrat* he offered several theories concerning the identity of the modern Amerindian. He first suggested that they were a segment of humanity which had fallen from a former state of greatness, an idea which allowed him to indulge in romantic speculation:

> If they were the builders of those ruined temples, the deserted cities, and the huge mounds . . . what astonishing degeneracy! Having no means of intercourse with other nations, we may suppose they gradually relapsed into barbarism—barbarism so profound that it will take a century to wean them back.[14]

However, in further considering the "majestic temples, standing solitary and alone, in Arizona and Mexico," he raised the question of whether the people who built them were "of a different race to the present Indians of the Plains." He then advanced the possibility that "the ancestors of these wild Indians," who were now the determined opponents of the U.S. Army, had been "the devastators of semi-civilised America."[15] Admittedly, Stanley never suggested that the Amerindians of the Plains, whatever their origin, were culturally equal to the white man: but neither did he argue that they were racially inferior. Stanley could be uncompromisingly brutal in his assessment of "savages" and their culture, but unlike many of his Victorian contemporaries, he never considered their deficiencies to be intrinsic or irreparable.

Although he had achieved his fame as a traveler and a writer, political matters, national loyalties, and issues of grand strategy held little appeal for Stanley. He pursued his immediate objective with a single-minded intensity, but he only reflected on its long-term consequences after the fact, if it all. His views on Africa were limited to a nebulous sort of paternalism, an attitude based on assumption and experience rather than considered analysis. The core of his approach can be traced back to his earlier dispatches from the American west: in particular, the notion that indigenous peoples needed to be protected from outside forces, and from each other, until they could adjust to the rigorous new demands of "civilization." His retrospective assessment of the African firearms trade is a case in point.

> To produce the same effects on the African aborigines as have resulted in the almost total destruction of the North Americans, all we need to do is freely permit the carriage of modern rifles and their ammunition into Africa, and in a few years we shall find the same rapid process of depopulation going on there. Savages have the minds of children and the passions of brutes, and to place breech-loaders in their hands is as cruel an act as to put razors in the hands of infants.[16]

Stanley had received his basic training in the means of conquest in the "Indian country" west of the Mississippi, and it was there he also mastered its rhetoric. In Stanley's

> later years, by which time he was a world-famous figure and General Sherman was retired, he astonished the old soldier by quoting extensively from a speech Sherman had made to the plains Indians when he was a member of the Peace Commission. "I have had occasion to repeat your speech almost verbatim more than once to the Negroes of Central Africa," said Stanley.[17]

Not surprisingly, his attitude toward Africans was also affected by his apprenticeship in the Deep South, where he had become personally acquainted with the "peculiar institution" and the racist ideology which supported it. While Richard Hall has suggested that Stanley demonstrated little "understanding and sympathy for the Negro slaves in New Orleans," in the course of his later travels the explorer did make a partial and halting attempt to come to terms with the persistent evidence of African humanity.[18] He could not afford friendship or familiarity with the "natives" who provided the backbone of his expeditions; the nature of his authority was too personal and fragile to allow for this, but his practical contact with black Americans and Africans seems to have immunized him against the more virulent forms of racial theory. In the pages of *Through the Dark Continent,* Stanley emphatically rejected the notion that Africans were "simply the 'link' between the simian and the European," and speaking of the "Wangwana" of Zanzibar, he concluded that

> they represent in their character much of the disposition of a large portion of the Negro tribes of the continent. I find them capable of great love and affection, and possessed of gratitude and other noble traits of human nature: I know too that they can be made good, obedient servants, that many are clever, honest, industrious, docile, enterprising, brave, and moral; that they are, in short, equal to any other race or colour on the face of the globe, in all the attributes of manhood.[19]

At the same time, he counseled his readers that they should, in fairness, remember "the condition of the Briton before St. Augustine visited his country." For, whatever their potential, the Africans he had encountered were "a people just emerged into the Iron Epoch, and now thrust forcibly under the notice of nations who have left them behind by the improvements of over 4000 years. They possess beyond doubt all the vices of a people still fixed deeply in barbarism, but they understand to the full what and how low such a state is."[20] Thus Stanley was confident that the Africans—like their counterparts, the Amerindians—could be led toward the benefits of a "higher civilization," although he was equally convinced that this task would be a long and demanding one for their European mentors.

Several decades after Stanley's final expedition, another famous adventurer made his entrance on the African stage. When Theodore Roosevelt "on March 23, 1909 . . . sailed thither from New York, in charge of a scientific expedition sent out by the Smithsonian, to collect birds, mammals, reptiles, and plants, but especially specimens of big game," the curious attention of the American public was assured.[21] Like Stanley, Roosevelt was a larger-than-life figure, a master of self-promotion, a traveler and author with a genius for capturing and manipulating the popular imagination. Roosevelt was more than this, however: he was also a statesman. A former President of the United States and a recipient of the Nobel Peace Prize, his words and persona carried an authority which a professional explorer, even a figure as celebrated as Stanley, could never completely equal. If Stanley was regarded as a borstal boy grown into working class hero, a fusion of Crockett and Kipling, Roosevelt more closely resembled the public school boy grown into maker of empire, the imperial proconsul who had retained his taste for the "strenuous life" and the virtues of the hunt. Both men were artists at adventure: what was a vocation for Stanley, however, remained a hobby for Roosevelt, who invariably approached his exploits as a moral and inspirational exercise and a useful means of instruction by example for the lower orders.

Unfortunately, Roosevelt's grand safari through Kenya, Uganda, and the Sudan did nothing to brighten the image of the "Dark Continent." The "hero of San Juan Hill" was never known for his subtlety nor could he be considered a devoted champion of the cause of racial equality. His African journey would do nothing to broaden his perspective. It was impossible for him to produce a more sensitive analysis. In the foreword to *African Game Trails: An Account of the African Wanderings of an American Hunter-Naturalist*, he noted that "the dark-skinned races that live in the land vary widely," the most backward being little more than "ape-like naked savages, who dwell in the woods and prey on creatures not much wilder or lower than themselves."[22] In contrast to Stanley, his approach to non-western peoples was both explicitly and ideologically racist, with the various families of humanity all fitting into their appointed niche. This basic tendency was fully consistent with his overall view of the continent itself. Indeed, for Roosevelt, East Africa had been a land beyond history, frozen in time, until the recent and fortuitous arrival of the white man. Speaking of the railroad which now linked Mombasa (on the Indian Ocean coast) and the Lake Victoria region, he noted that this artery, which was

> the embodiment of the eager, masterful, materialistic civilization of to-day, was pushed through a region in which nature, both as regards wild man and wild beast, did not and does not differ materially from what it was in Europe in the late Pleistocene. The comparison is not fanciful. The teeming multitudes of wild creatures, the stupendous size of some of them, the terrible nature of others, and the low culture of many of the savage tribes, especially of the hunting tribes, substantially reproduces the conditions of life in Europe as it was . . . ages before the dawn of anything that could be called civilization.[23]

Moreover, for Roosevelt, the general course of modern history was clear, since "again and again, in the continents new to peoples of European stock, we have seen the spectacle of a high civilization all at once thrust into and superimposed upon a wilderness of savage men and savage beasts."[24] Accordingly, he strongly approved of the British plan to reserve the highlands of Kenya for white settlement. He expressed his confidence that "at least part of the high inland region of British East Africa can be made one kind of 'white man's country,'" but he cautioned that "to achieve this white men should work heartily together, doing scrupulous justice to the natives, but remembering that progress and development in this particular kind of new land depend exclusively upon the masterful leadership of the whites."[25]

For Roosevelt, the "white man's burden" in East Africa was similar to the duty which had faced the settlers in the American west, that other "remnant of the Pleistocene" which had recently yielded to the genius of the European. As the author of a six-volume study on *The Winning of the West* he felt fully qualified to explain the obvious parallels.[26] In his estimation, however, there was one crucial difference between the two scenarios of conquest—the African would ultimately be an easier target than the Amerindian. Regarding Kenya, he concluded that

> there was much to remind one of conditions in Montana and Wyoming thirty years ago. . . . But the problem offered by the natives bore no resemblance to that once offered by the presence of our tribes of horse Indians, few in numbers and incredibly formidable in war. The natives of East Africa are numerous; many of them are agricultural or pastoral peoples after their own fashion; and even the bravest of them, the warlike Masai, are in no way formidable as our Indians were. . . . [27]

In his eyes, the Wakamba, the former masters of the "ranch country" he had traveled through, were little more than "primitive savages," but they were not without their uses. It surely was a positive sign that the settlers "much prefer to rely upon the natives for unskilled labor rather than see coolies from Hindostan [sic] brought into the country." Yet a firm hand and a proper perspective were required at all times, since "untold ages separated employers and employed."[28] There was no doubt whatsoever that the respective roles of ruler and subject must be clear and absolute, since the Africans were utterly incapable of managing their own affairs. "T. R." explained that

> the Wakamba [were] as yet not sufficiently advanced to warrant their sharing in the smallest degree in the common government; the "just consent of the governed" in their case, if taken literally, would mean idleness, famine, and endless internecine warfare. They cannot govern themselves from

within; therefore they must be governed from without; and their need is met in highest fashion by firm and just control, of the kind that on the whole they are now getting.[29]

Thus the author, who had also produced a majestic chronicle of "The Spread of English Speaking Peoples," could only approve of the fact that the Wakamba—and other peoples like them—would be spared the manifest danger of their own freedom.

In the course of his journeys, this eminent traveler had little time for sentimentality. From his particular vantage point the claims of the Wakamba were no more compelling than the claims of the Shoshone or the Sioux: in the final analysis, the imperatives of civilization and progress must always take precedence over aboriginal rights. Admittedly, Roosevelt also criticized the abuses of the white pioneers who had opened up the American west, and he reluctantly acknowledged that the romantic life of the cowboys, a life which he had glorified in shining prose, would soon be eclipsed by the pace of events. None, however, were exempt from the Darwinian logic of social progress: and, as for the Indians, he suggested that they "should be treated in just the same way that we treat the white settlers," a seeming concession to racial democracy which only referred to those stubborn white hunters and trappers who refused to adjust to the new economic realities. "Give each his little claim; if, as would generally happen, he declined this . . . let him, like these whites, who will not work, perish from the face of the earth which he cumbers."[30]

Roosevelt had come to Africa on the pretense of a scientific mission, and he managed to resist the urge to shoot at every animal that came within his gunsights. Nevertheless, whatever the motives (and merit) of its chosen instrument, this organized slaughter at the behest of the Smithsonian marked an important new departure in the American approach to Africa. As a "man of science"—by appointment, if not by training—Roosevelt would pave the way for more credible scholar-travelers such as Carl and Mary Jobe Akeley, natural scientists who would regard the continent as a laboratory as well as a field of personal adventure. By the turn of the century the American academy was beginning to realize that Africa represented a promising new theatre of operations, and the empirical assault on its mysteries would begin in earnest after the First World War. The "war to end all wars" would mark the end of the heroic age of Stanley, a widespread taste for the more militant forms of adventure being one more casualty of the trenches. In the decade after Versailles the popular discourse on Africa would require a more noble and rational charter, and, in light of this conceptual need, it is not surprising that the "scientific expedition"

Roosevelt's Thrilling Experiences in the Wilds of Africa (Chicago: n.p. c.1910)

HE'S COMING, BOYS—LET'S SKIDDOO.

came to serve as the most acceptable ideological passport to the non-Western world.

Roosevelt's agenda in traveling to East Africa went well beyond his mandate from the Smithsonian. Above all else, the former president had come to Africa as a committed advocate of empire, and he approached his mission as if he were a special plenipotentiary of the Anglo-Saxon world on an extended tour of inspection. Despite his domestic reputation as a political "progressive," his paternalistic concept of reform was totally consistent with an open and visceral admiration of the British colonial order. As Peter MacQueen made abundantly clear in his breathless account of the "Return of Col. Roosevelt from the Jungle"—a "jungle" which, incidentally, T. R. neither passed through nor approached—his trip to Africa had allowed him to indulge in some of his most cherished imperial fantasies:

> At Khartoum the Roosevelt party was received by the English government with the greatest and most distinguished honor. It was noticeable that the Sirdar of the Sudan, Sir Reginald Wyngate [sic], took Mr. Roosevelt first to the Gordon tree named after the famous Chinese Gordon whose lamentable death at Khartoum is part of the thrilling history of Egypt. The ex-president visited the battlefield of Omdurman and doubtless, in an honorable way, envied Lord Kitchener the brilliant glory of that famous victory. He doubtless showed the English officers just how he would have posted the Rough Riders at the fatal Donga where the lancers fell.[31]

Thus, just as Stanley had several decades earlier, Roosevelt—through word and deed—provided a vital symbolic link between the European conquest of North America and the ongoing European project in Asia and Africa. In time, his abiding role in championing this relationship would be enshrined. It seems only fitting that, in the American Museum of Natural History in New York, "to enter the Theodore Roosevelt Memorial, the visitor must pass by a James Earle Fraser equestrian statue of Teddy majestically mounted as a father and protector between two 'primitive' men, an American Indian and an African, both standing, dressed as 'savages.'"[32] In its guiding ideology and spirit, in its inherent tension between triumphal arrogance and paternalistic concern, the Fraser statue perfectly reflected the mainstream American attitude toward Africa during—and well beyond—the age of Roosevelt.

While it would be difficult (and misleading) to attempt to identify a wholly distinctive "American" image of Africa, by the 1920s the work of Stanley, Roosevelt and others had brought about a synthesis which might more accurately be described as an American variation on a European theme. This continuing correspondence with established European patterns was a product of inherited literary conventions and, perhaps more significantly, a parallel historical experience with indigenous Amerindians, and unfree African Americans who, even after their emancipation, were subjected to a form of civil and economic repression in the rural South which was every bit as comprehensive as the colonial systems imposed on the populations of the Third World. Nevertheless, while this dominant literary form would prove both durable and extensive, the American scene would also provide an opening for some important new trends and departures. By the time of the "Harlem Renaissance," black American voices were presenting an independent, anti-colonialist, and anti-racist perspective which was a clear departure from the norm, offering a range of original viewpoints which owed little to the "liberal" European and white American observers who had emerged to champion their cause. At the same time, an enterprising school of American anthropologists and social scientists—led by Franz Boas, and his students and disciples—began an intellectual assault on the scientific racism which was still the fashion in the American and European academies, mounting an effective challenge to a core of ideas which reinforced the notion of black—and African—inferiority. Finally, at another level, if Europeans had developed the symbolic and narrative conventions which continued to govern the western image of Africa, it was Americans—from Henry Morton Stanley to Edgar Rice Burroughs, from Ernest Hemingway and Robert Ruark to Sydney Pollack—who would turn this discourse into a commercially viable fantasy with a powerful and enduring appeal.

As we enter the twenty-first century, some might contend that the symbolic and ideological formulas which provided the basis of this appeal have been pushed off center stage by a more sophisticated, a more balanced, and a more informed approach to the continent. Such a conclusion can only be sustained if one ignores the daily evidence available in newspapers and books, speeches and editorials, films and television programs. A casual examination of these (and other) sources will quickly demonstrate that this basic array of themes, images, and ideas—what we will call the "symbolic conventions"—continue to play a central role in defining the western vision of Africa.[33] Moreover, these conventions regularly defy the expected boundaries of form and genre. Some might think that this complex of perception has been safely relegated to the imaginary world of film and fiction, but this is far from the case. Even today, three full decades after African independence, its logic can still influence an ethnographic monograph as well as a short story, and supply the content of serious journalism and commentary as well as a plot for a Hollywood adventure film. The Africa of myth and legend lives on.

It would be equally reassuring to think that the mindset which these images and attitudes represent is essentially benign, its influence limited to a harmless and occasional expression through the media of popular culture. Unfortunately, this is emphatically not the case: this distorted understanding of Africa continues to have a real impact on real people. As Leonard Thompson, the distinguished historian of South Africa, has reminded us, "everywhere, powerful people make decisions that affect human lives and prosperity in the light of historical images that they have acquired in their youth, even though scholars know those images to be false."[34] At a fundamental level, these images, or representations, are symbolic in the Jungian sense: that is, they are held at the level of emotion, felt rather than understood, persisting as an unconscious element in discourse and analysis. From their hidden station in the subconscious they remain an active factor in the decision-making process, and while their impact is not amenable to measurement or quantification, their practical importance should not be underestimated. Students of history, politics, and human relations may disagree on the significance of this factor in any given case, but they choose to ignore it at their own intellectual peril.

It should not be thought, however, that the popular vision of Africa is simply a fabric of reflexive prejudice and destructive stereotypes. From the time of Boas and Du Bois to the present, a small but growing number of Americans from many walks of life have gone beyond the symbolic conventions and helped to define a more rational perspective on the continent. Yet the distortions still persist, even among the educated and informed, and particularly within the highest councils of power where they continue to have their greatest practical significance. According to Seymour Hersh, the Pulitzer Prize-winning journalist, a racist and simplistic notion of Africa was very much in evidence in the Nixon White House where it regularly appeared in its crudest form. Hersh noted the difficulties faced by Roger Morris, a member of the National Security Council staff who was responsible for African affairs.

> NSC staff aides understood what was acceptable behavior and what was not. They would join the laughter at Alexander Haig's antics during the rare staff meetings that dealt with African issues. Morris recalls that when he would enter the Situation Room laden with briefing books, "Haig would begin to beat his hands on the table, as if he was pounding a tom-tom. It was all very manly—a locker-room mentality. Haig would make Tarzan jokes—'Where's your pet ape?' or, talking about blacks, say, 'Henry can't stand the smell.'"[35]

This basic attitude was not confined to Haig (whose casual racism would not debar him from serving as Secretary of State in the Reagan administration). During the Biafra secession crisis, "Ronald L. Ziegler, the White House press secretary, who knew and cared little about Africa and its civil wars, began a briefing by announcing he had a statement to read on the 'Niggerian' war."[36] Not surprisingly, this level of venality extended to the President himself. John Erlichman, in an interview with Nicholas Lemann, stated that "Nixon told him that he considered blacks to be less intelligent than whites. 'He thought, basically, blacks were genetically inferior' . . . 'He'd say on civil rights things, "Well, we'll do this, but it isn't going to do any good" . . . He thought they couldn't achieve on a level with whites.'"[37] This attitude was also apparent in his derisory approach to African affairs. In February 1970, when Henry Kissinger was preparing an important foreign policy statement, Nixon betrayed his deep concern for African issues by instructing him to 'Make sure there's something in it for the jigs.'"[38] During this period Kissinger was involved in a heated rivalry with Secretary of State William Rogers, and Nixon, on one occasion, offered a casual if telling suggestion to his National Security adviser. When Rogers

> received good press coverage during a trip to Africa, Kissinger had been distraught with jealousy and anxiety. There had been a soothing telephone call from Nixon, also overheard by one of the NSC aides: "Henry, let's leave the niggers to Bill and we'll take care of the rest of the world."[39]

It is painfully apparent that Leonard Thompson's warning applies with special force to the case of Africa. The arrogant dismissal of an entire continent cannot be written off as an aberrant attitude of an aberrant administration. The major actors in this cast have not entirely vanished from the arena of public policy, and, beyond this, it is extremely difficult to believe that the complex of attitudes and emotions which they expressed was strictly confined to their inner circle. In a real sense, the racism and ignorance betrayed by this behavior exceeds the rhetoric of Stanley and Roosevelt who at least made an effort, however flawed, to understand the continent and its people. Fortunately, within the Beltway there is a dedicated cadre of men and women with a genuine concern for Africa and its future; their task, however, is not an easy one. By most accounts, the "Dark Continent" has yet to be illuminated by "a thousand points of light."

From the earliest stages of contact, the western assessment of Africa was affected by two central (and related) biases: the prejudice of racism and the concept of the primitive. Racism, an irrational if formidable emotional reaction, would rapidly generate its own elaborate set of destructive myths and conventions, with the notion of black inferiority as its centerpiece. At the same time, the notion of the primitive, while firmly rooted in the conscious and the rational, would gradually acquire a host of regional and racial associations and steadily lose its value as a credible analytical instrument. Those who went to Africa in search of the "primitive" invariably found what they were looking for. This is certainly not surprising: their selective frame of reference meant that much would not be seen, and further ensured that much which would be seen would not be understood. Unfortunately, both racism and the notion of the primitive were mutually reinforcing, and it was the rare observer who could see beyond their collective distortions.

For the armchair travelers who stayed behind—the consumers of the texts produced by these observers—the very idea of "Africa" called forth a predictable assortment of dramatic expectations. It was seen, by turns, as a mysterious realm of jungle, mountain, and plain; a zoological Eden of infinite variety and appeal; a human museum of the primitive and picturesque; and a distant staging point for episodes of adventure and discovery. Ironically, at the very time that the continent was being "opened" by a measured application of western technology and firepower, the romantic aspect of its image was being reinforced by the consuls and the captains, the traders and explorers, the missionaries and the scientists who mediated its realities for the "outside world." Even today, decades later, the words and judgments of these earlier authorities still have force and power: a trip to the library will readily confirm that the Africa they described is still an active presence in our discourse and our dreams.

In approaching this problem the authors of this book do not presume a privileged insight. We question the ability of any observer, past or present, to produce a version of events that is wholly accurate and objective, a faultless mirror which reflects an indisputable reality. On the other hand, we reject the fashionable notion that all written accounts should be dismissed as fictional creations, inventions devoid of veracity or value, convenient textual corpses to be dissected (and discarded) in line with one or another political or intellectual agenda. Instead, we stubbornly hold the middle ground. We retain the belief that objectivity is, at the very least, a value to be aspired to; we argue that a critical awareness of personal and cultural bias, and symbolic and narrative convention, can provide the basis for a more credible level of analysis; and we are confident that scholars will ignore the advocates of intellectual surrender and continue to strive for a better understanding of their world—and each other.

Our goal in this study is limited but, we think, important. By examining the development of the American image of Africa we hope that we will help clear the way for a more reasoned and plausible discourse in the future. We are well aware that this broader project is already under way. Indeed, since the emergence of modern African studies—which achieved an institutional basis in American universities during the 1960s—a chorus of voices has taken the lead in restoring Africa, and Africans, to their rightful place in the dynamic of world history. Nevertheless, considerable work remains to be done. The old assumptions continue to appear in revised rhetorical form and new mythologies and varieties of reductionism have made their presence felt in both the popular and scholarly literature. Indeed, it may well be that the very "division of labor" (and intellectual fragmentation) which is characteristic of the academic world is contributing to a shortfall in perception which is every bit as problematic as the racist and ethnocentric paradigm which it is designed to correct. Admittedly, the battle has been joined, but it is still too early to declare a victory.

In approaching this question we do not intend to fabricate a "politically corrected" view of Africa since we see no merit in replacing one convenient set of exaggerations and distortions with another. African history is clearly not the story of "ape-like naked savages"; but neither is it an exclusive saga of great kingdoms and great kings, nor the awesome chronicle of a primary civilization to which every significant cultural achievement on the face of the earth can be directly and immediately linked. We find the picture which is gradually being pieced together to be much more complex, much more interesting, and ultimately much more satisfying than these polemical creations. We also see no point in discarding earlier documentary sources in a fit of self-righteous book burning. As historians, we are aware that useful information can still be gleaned from the works of Stanley, Roosevelt, and countless others like them if one allows for the cultural and intellectual framework in which they were produced. The work of oral historians is providing an exciting new perspective on the African past, and older written accounts can now be examined within a broader and more instructive context. Today, students of Africa are raising important new questions and using important new methods to answer them. At this point no one stands to gain if we choose the easier road and devalue the rational in favor of the rhetorical.

The time for viewing Africa in terms of Manichean absolutes is past. The continent is neither the "heart of darkness" nor the "mother of light," the source of all genius nor the refuge of all ignorance, the place of origin for an "inferior" or "superior" race. Instead, it is the home of millions of human beings whose fascinating story is finally being told to the rest of the world, and this history is fast becoming known to others. The symbolic conventions have been remarkably durable, but their influence on our intellect and emotions, while still substantial, is beginning to wane. As we move into the twenty-first century the way is now open to a more rational and dynamic vision of Africa, a vision which is firmly rooted in a diachronic (historical) approach and is fully alert to the complexity and diversity of the continent and its people.

Nevertheless, in terms of American popular consciousness, the transition to a more balanced appreciation of the continent has only just begun, a fact which thousands of African travelers have already discovered (at the cost of considerable embarrassment and unease). In 1974, the outstanding Nigerian author, Chinua Achebe, was serving as a visiting professor at the University of Massachusetts. During his stay in Amherst, a "progressive" college town, he was reminded on a daily basis that the American conception of his homeland was less than realistic, a fabric of assumption and mythology which bore little correspondence to contemporary reality. One "fine autumn morning," as Achebe was walking on campus

> An older man going the same way as I turned and remarked to me how very young they came these days. I agreed. Then he asked me if I was a student too. I said no, I was a teacher. What did I teach? African literature. Now that was funny, he said, because he knew a fellow who taught the same thing, or perhaps it was African history, in a certain community college not far from here. It always surprised him, he went on to say, because he never had thought of Africa as having that kind of stuff, you know.[40]

We begin our task with the earnest hope that Achebe's acquaintance—and the thousands upon thousands like him—will have less to be surprised about in the future. We are confident that, like Herodotus, they—or at least their children—will come to understand that "there is always something new out of Africa."

Notes

1. Walter Russell Mead, "Dark Continent: A grand grim tour of the New Europe," *Harper's* (April 1991): 45-53.
2. Philip D. Curtin, *The Image of Africa: British Ideas and Action, 1780-1850* (Madison: University of Wisconsin Press, 1964).
3. Henry Morton Stanley, *Through the Dark Continent*, 2 vols. (London: Sampson, Low, Marston, Searle and Rivington, 1878).
4. There is no shortage of biographies on Stanley. The most valuable recent works are John Bierman, *Dark Safari: The Life Behind the Legend of Henry Morton Stanley* (New York: Alfred A Knopf, 1990), and Richard Hall, *Stanley: An Adventurer Explored* (London: Collins, 1974).
5. Henry Morton Stanley, *My Early Travels and Adventures in America and Asia* (London: Sampson, Low, Marston and Co., 1895), 1: v.
6. Hall, 204.
7. Richard O'Connor, *The Scandalous Mr. Bennett* (Garden City, N.Y.: Doubleday and Co., 1962), 116.
8. Jeremy Bernstein, "The Dark Continent of Henry Stanley," *The New Yorker* (31 December 1990): 93.
9. Hall, 158.
10. Ibid., 152-58.
11. Stanley, *Early Travels* 1: 129.
12. Ibid. 1: ix.
13. Bierman, 48.
14. Stanley, *Early Travels* 1: 276-77.
15. Ibid. 1: 277.
16. Ibid. 1: x-xi.
17. Bierman, 52.
18. Hall, 153.
19. Stanley, *Dark Continent*, 46-47.
20. Ibid., 47-48.
21. Theodore Roosevelt, *African Game Trails: An Account of the African Wanderings of an American Hunter-Naturalist* (New York: Charles Scribner's Sons, 1919), 1: 4.
22. Ibid. 1: viii.
23. Ibid. 1: 3.
24. Ibid. 1: 1.
25. Ibid. 1: 9.
26. Theodore Roosevelt, *The Winning of the West*, 6 vols. (New York: The Current Literature Publishing Co., 1905).
27. Roosevelt, *African Game Trails*, 1:43-44.
28. Ibid., 45.
29. Ibid., 45-46.
30. Theodore Roosevelt, *Hunting Trips of a Ranchman: Sketches of Sport on the Northern Cattle Plains* (New York: G.P. Putnam's Sons, 1885), 19.
31. Peter MacQueen, "Return of Col. Roosevelt from the Jungle," in ed. Marshall Everett, *Roosevelt's Thrilling Experiences in the Wilds of Africa Hunting Big Game* (London: A. Hamming, c. 1910), 438. The subtitle of this book—which virtually runs a full page—is too long to repeat in its

entirely, but a portion is sufficient to reveal the author's general intent: "Exciting Adventures hunting the wild and ferocious beasts of the Jungle and Plain and mingling with the Savage People, studying their strange customs, their awful superstitions and weird beliefs, their curious marriage ceremonies and barbarous treatment of young girls and women. . . ." The publisher hastened to add, in an extended and laudatory preface, that "the fact that Theodore Roosevelt is the hero of our book is alone enough to secure it an introduction and hearty welcome in every American home" ("curious" marriage ceremonies and "barbarous" sexual practices notwithstanding). The author, in his own enthusiastic preface, promised that he would introduce the reader to "the primitive inhabitants of this mysterious continent, the brown and black savages, to whom civilization is a question mark and culture is as little known as snow in August." He further promised to acquaint his audience "with the strange habits, superstitious rites and religious ceremonies of these darkhued cousins of the apes and the monkeys, whose only right to bear the human name seems to be their poor and infantile jabbering."

32. Donna Haraway, *Primate Visions: Gender, Race and Nature in the World of Modern Science* (New York: Routledge, 1989), 27.

33. See Eric J. Hobsbawm and Terence Ranger, *The Invention of Tradition* (Cambridge: Cambridge University Press, 1983) for a fascinating series of essays which illustrate how such symbolic complexes played a supporting role in the rise of nineteenth-century European nationalism (and colonialism).

34. Leonard Thompson, *The Political Mythology of Apartheid* (New Haven: Yale University Press, 1985), vii.

35. Seymour M. Hersh, *The Price of Power: Kissinger in the Nixon White House* (New York: Summit Books, 1983), 110.

36. Ibid., 111.

37. Nicholas Lemann, *The Promised Land: The Great Black Migration and How it Changed America* (New York: Alfred A Knopf, 1991), 204.

38. Hersh, 111.

39. Ibid., It should not be thought that the exploitation of the symbolic conventions surrounding Africa was limited to the Nixon administration. During the Johnson administration—in 1964—a crisis in the Congo arose which prompted the United States, in November of that year, to provide the planes for a Belgian airdrop designed to rescue Europeans trapped in the city of Stanleyville. During this political upheaval, atrocities *were* committed—even as they had been during the bloody colonial reign of the Belgian king Leopold II. As Carl Rowan of the United States Information Agency—a distinguished black journalist—pointed out in a memo to the President, no effort was spared in stressing the savagery of the African rebel forces to the world at large. Rowan reported that "before the paratroop drop, the USIA Mission in Leopoldville had instructions on the press, motion picture, still picture, and radio coverage required to document this brutality . . . the Agency instructed its posts throughout the world to establish the essential facts and to 'play up evidence of rebel atrocities. . . .'" This

calculated portrayal of "the heart of darkness" was then disseminated far and wide. Indeed, "from November 24 to December 11, the Voice of America broadcast 360 newscasts in 38 languages describing the rescue operation and rebel brutality." Also, the Africa file of the USIA teletype service "carried 98 stories on the Congo crisis, of which 27 dealt directly with rebel outrages. The other files carried a total of 60 atrocity stories." Rowan to Johnson, 21 December 1964, as cited in William Minter, "Candid Cables: Some Reflections on U.S. Response to the Congo Rebellions, 1964," in ed. Nzongola-Ntalaja *The Crisis in Zaire: Myths and Realities* (Trenton, N.J.: Africa World Press, 1986), 286-87.

40. Chinua Achebe, "An Image of Africa: Racism in Conrad's 'Heart of Darkness,'" in Chinua Achebe, *Hopes and Impediments: Selected Essays by Chinua Achebe* (Garden City, N.Y.: Doubleday, 1989), 1-2. This piece also appears in *The Massachusetts Review* 18, no. 4 (Winter 1977): 782-94.

2

In Search of the "Other": Reflections in a Hall of Mirrors

1 0During the past decade the problem of the "other" has come in for serious analytical scrutiny in the scholarly literature. This concept, which refers to the alien cultural party in a given human encounter, is certainly not new. Indeed, as an enduring topic of interest and curiosity it can be traced back to the earliest stages of recorded history: while the terminology surrounding the "other" may be a recent development, the issue itself is of imposing antiquity. In recent years the examination of this question has proceeded along two basic lines: an inquiry into the nature of racism and ethnocentrism, with a primary focus on the western colonial encounter with the non-Western world; and a critical reassessment of the ethnographic enterprise, as anthropologists and other scholars continue to grapple with the possibility of meaningful observation and analysis across cultural lines. Both strands of this effort have played an important role in sharpening our understanding of the formation and persistence of the western image of Africa. Moreover, in addition to these areas of inequity, there is a growing body of historical studies which suggests that the West has not been alone in viewing the "other" through a distorted mirror of images and assumptions.

In addition to Curtin's classic work, the western image of Africa has also been considered in a number of other studies, the most recent and significant of which is the philosopher V. Y. Mudimbe's *The Invention of Africa*. Mudimbe argues that the basic western perception of Africa (as framed by anthropology) has been remarkably constant over the last several centuries. In his estimation, despite minor changes in strategy and emphasis "in accordance with changing trends within the framework of western experience," there were no meaningful developments in the nature and content of the symbolic conventions.[1]

We also stress the persistent nature of these constructs, although we disagree with Mudimbe on one essential point. The thematic continuity in these written portrayals is striking, but they did not, as he seems to suggest, reflect an extremely limited or internally consistent body of imagery and interpretation. The apparent dualities within this universe of texts are actually a logical consequence of "changing trends" (and differing agendas) which he, himself, accurately identifies. In nineteenth-century America, the idea of the "noble savage" had little rhetorical value for committed slavetraders and slaveholders; likewise, the notion of black inferiority was not especially helpful to ardent abolitionists (except for those who openly embraced the various colonization schemes). According to Mudimbe, "expedition reports only establish[ed] a very concrete, vivid representation of what paintings and theories of social progress had been postulating since the Baroque period."[2] This is rather too close to a "conspiracy theory" of cultural perception: admittedly, western observers tended to address the same issues, but they drew upon a set of assumptions and images which was not without its own contradictions. Even the works of Stanley and Roosevelt, when taken in their entirety, do not provide a consistent or monolithic view of their basic subject. We fully agree that the themes were predictable, that racial and cultural comparison was a basic starting point, and that the range of imagery was finite. We would also insist, however, that the resulting discourse was not as narrow or one-dimensional as Mudimbe suggests.

Mudimbe is also convinced that the colonial powers invariably pursued a strategy of "social and cultural conversion" as a basic means of controlling their subjects. In support of this point he presents an "ideological model of conversion" by which the colonial state, through the mediation of Christianity, education, and western social values, would transform the "primitive" into the "civilized," the "pagan" into the "Christian," and the "naked and childlike African" into the "civilized adult."[3] He further maintains that through this calculated process the European occupiers "broke the culturally unified and religiously integrated schema of most African traditions."[4] As he presents it, this approach was a premeditated, internally consistent formula which was universally applied by the masters of empire. To quote Mudimbe:

> in the first quarter of this century, it was clear that the traveler had become a colonizer, and the anthropologist, his scientific advisor, while the missionary, more vigorously than ever, continued, in theory as well as in practice, to expound the model of African spiritual and cultural metamorphosis.[5]

This argument has its attractions. Nevertheless, it tends to ignore a more complex political and cultural reality familiar to historians. In postulating a collection of "culturally unified and religiously integrated" African traditions Mudimbe comes dangerously close to reviving the "myth of Merrie Africa," the notion that precolonial African societies pursued their separate destinies in an ahistorical void, immune to the dynamics of change and growth and blissfully isolated from the "outside world" (and from each other).[6] To cite one exception, in a wide stretch of sub-Saharan Africa these "integrated schema" had already been "broken" by the coming of Islam. Moreover, the coastal regions of East Africa had been part of the Indian Ocean commercial system long before the onset of European colonialism, and the cultural and demographic exchange which ensued over a number of centuries makes the entire question of "tradition" highly problematic. Obviously, the "search for authenticity" is not without its dangers. All too often it is grounded in an oversimplified vision of the African past and ultimately reproduces, albeit in positive rhetorical form, the very paradigm which it is designed to refute.

There are other problems with Mudimbe's model of conversion. While it provides an appropriate description of French colonial practice, it does not account for those systems which linked the colonial state to existing African structures. The British method of "indirect rule," first implemented in India and then in northern Nigeria, is a prime case in point. Moreover, historians have established that in numerous instances the objectives and activities of missionaries were incompatible with the policies of governments. As for anthropologists, it is reasonable to argue that the materials they produced were sometimes useful to local officials. By the same token, however, it is extremely difficult to see how these social scientists could be logically regarded as agents of "conversion." Indeed, they can be accused with greater justice of attempting to preserve their individual areas of operation as field museums of the "anthropological present." Thus, while Mudimbe's formulation has a certain theoretical elegance, it is less impressive when considered against an adequate range of specific historical cases.

In recent years, no other work dealing with the problem of the cultural "other" has attracted as much attention as Edward Said's brilliant and controversial, if ultimately frustrating, study of *Orientalism.* From his dual perspective as a scholar of modern literature and an advocate of the Palestinian cause, Said described the emergence of the intellectual and institutional forces which shaped the European image of the Islamic world. Said's agenda was explicitly polemical: he was primarily concerned with the content and consequences of the

Orientalist paradigm, and he had no real interest in a comparative or theoretical exercise. Therefore, while his analysis is forceful and engaging, it suffers from the fact that he failed to consider his case as part of a broader and more universal problem of cross-cultural perception. In a passing reference to this question he simply notes that there is "nothing especially controversial or reprehensible about such domestications of the exotic; they take place between all cultures, certainly, and between all men."[7] For Said, then, in the majority of instances the process under examination was insignificant and benign. Apparently, it had only developed into a major cultural disorder within the European context, and then only as a result of the specific set of circumstances surrounding the age of imperialism.

If we are to believe Said, "Orientalism" is more than a complex and powerful ideological force; it is also a peculiarly western phenomenon, a complex of attitudes, texts and institutions with no obvious counterpart in the non-Western world. Indeed, he makes the case that such a comprehensive system for containing the "other" would not have been possible before the rise of European imperialism, a form of domination which (he maintains) had no historical parallel.

> Sheer scale and scope are only part of the difference. Certainly neither Byzantium, nor Rome, nor Athens, nor Baghdad, nor Spain and Portugal during the 15th and 16th centuries controlled anything like the territories controlled by Britain and France during the 19th century. The more important differences are first the extraordinary and sustained longevity of the disparity in power between Europe and its possessions, and second, the massively organized rule, which affected the detail and not just the large outlines of life, of that power.[8]

Apparently, when joined with Europe's industrial might, this new colonial order assumed the dimensions of a juggernaut in the eyes of its masters as well its victims, raising existing cultural differences between East and West, and North and South, to a whole new level of significance. Nevertheless, despite his confident (if casual) assertion of the uniqueness of the European case, Said is less than precise when it comes to defining the actual relationship between ideology and the practical projection of political, military, and economic power. Thus "Orientalism," in his view, was both predictive and supportive of the European conquest of the Third World. In one context he argues that "Orientalism reinforced, and was reinforced by, the certain knowledge that Europe or the west literally commanded the vastly greater part of the earth's surface," while in another he cautions that to simply assert "that Orientalism was a rationalization of colonial rule is to ignore the extent to which colonial rule was justified in advance by Orientalism, rather than after the fact."[9]

Mudimbe and Said are convinced that the European vision of the non-western "other" was more complete, more developed, and ultimately more destructive in its consequences than comparable portrayals of the alien conceived at other times, in other cultures. Their analyses require a significant leap of faith since their arguments are confined to the nature and severity of the European case, and their works are completely lacking in the comparative dimension which is essential to any logical appraisal of this broader issue. Still, their basic premise has some merit. Indeed, when one considers the combined expressions of literacy, technology, and political ambition which characterized the North Atlantic world during the age of imperialism, it is not surprising that the West led the way in the creation and application of such directed ideological systems. During this period, the ongoing European quest to construct a coherent vision of the social as well as the natural order was lent an added urgency by the pressures of a maturing capitalist economy. Whether deployed at home to fashion and mobilize support along lines of nation and class, as described by Eric Hobsbawm and Terence Ranger in *The Invention of Tradition*, or deployed overseas to "explain" and contain its unwilling alien hosts, as per Said's *Orientalism*, identities were regularly and systematically reshaped to fit a broad array of productive and political needs. This flexibility in the realm of ideas was matched by its material counterpart: without a doubt, the technology of domination was more sophisticated, more inclusive, and more diverse than anything that had gone before. Yet, at the same time, it should be equally apparent that the impulse to dominate, and with it, to reduce, or dehumanize, or, to use Mudimbe's term, to "convert" the objects of such domination, was not a radical new departure which made its debut with European colonialism. The means of global reach were now at hand: yet, as any schoolchild well knows, the ends of conquest and empire long predated them. When the expeditionary forces of the British and the French made their entrance into the cities of the "Orient," the statues of defeated rulers offered silent if compelling testimony to the actions—and the ideological charters—of the armies which preceded them.

Beyond the question of its scope and intensity, Said also suggests that European imperialism was unique in another respect: the virtually unanimous approval it received within the metropole. In addressing this issue he rises to new heights of indignation since he finds it embarrassing . . . that those elements of a society which we have long considered to be progressive were, so far as empire was concerned, uniformly retrograde. . . . I speak here of advanced writers and artists, of the working class, and of women, groups whose imperialist fervor increased in intensity and perfervid enthusiasm for the acquisition of and sheer bloodthirsty dominance over innumerable niggers, bogdwellers, babus, and wogs, as the competition between various European and American powers also increased in brutality and senseless, even profitless, control.[10]

However "embarrassing" this may be to Said and his "progressive" audience, it should not be especially surprising, since, from his perspective, the question at hand is relatively simple. At the heart of the problem lies "an undeterred and unrelenting Eurocentrism," an implacable and historically distinctive force which "accumulated experiences, territories, peoples, histories" and, not content with mere possession, "studied them . . . classified them . . . verified them; but above all . . . subordinated them to the culture and indeed the very idea of white Christian Europe."[11] Thus, through a convenient rhetorical expedient—by portraying European civilization as an elemental and unparalleled force, a "black hole" in the wider universe of cultures—Said avoids the bothersome necessity of meaningful and substantive comparison with other civilizations. Given the sheer power of the western capitalist colossus, such an approach is made to appear irrelevant (at best) and bourgeois, politically naive, and ideologically unsound (at worst). Begging the question, however, is not the same as answering it.

Admittedly, it may be comforting to argue that stereotypical images of the other—"domestications of the exotic"—were "not especially reprehensible" or harmful outside the temporal and political boundaries of European imperialism. Unfortunately, Said presents no specifics to support this sweeping and dubious assertion, and he fails to address the considerable body of evidence which would refute his case. Also, his passing comparison of imperial chronologies is not especially lucid or convincing. The "disparity in power between Europe and its possessions," far from being distinguished by its "extraordinary and sustained longevity," is actually more remarkable for its transience and limited life span. Ironically, Said gives the architects of the "white man's burden" far more credit than they deserve. From the standpoint of military technology—and crucial supporting sectors such as medicine and transport—it can be argued that Europe did not gain a substantial operational advantage until the middle of the nineteenth century, and even then its ascendancy was situational and far from absolute. Even if one is willing to push back this disparity in power to the age of

School of Oriental and African Studies, London University

Chinese actors made up to look like Africans perform a drama glorifying the African resistance to US intervention in the Congo-Léopoldville.

Columbus—and assume a position which would be extremely difficult to defend—the political and cultural hegemony of modern Europe, at least in terms of its duration, pales in comparison with some earlier imperial epochs, the most dramatic of which provided a full and abundant career for those very European Orientalists whom Said so ably critiques.

One need only examine the manner in which Chinese and Islamic Middle Eastern observers described Africans and their cultures to understand the complexity of the matter at hand. In neither case were travelers' reports, literary accounts and other portrayals consistent: the image of the African ran the gamut from the noble and heroic to the savage and inferior, with a textual middle ground which stressed description and detail over judgment and evaluation. Philip Snow, in *The Star Raft: China's Encounter with Africa*, takes the position that early "Chinese descriptions of African society are often clearer and more accurate than any surviving Islamic account,"[12] and he cites several texts which emerged from maritime voyages to the East African coast (between the ninth and thirteenth centuries) to prove his point. While "much they saw or heard seems to have struck them as barbaric," the members of these expeditions also "found a spirit of heroism" among some of the people they encountered.[13] The themes they addressed, however, were partially determined by narrative and symbolic convention. Indeed, in developing their subject, it is "possible . . . that the authors of these accounts wrote of African heroism because their readers expected Africans to behave heroically."[14] The comparative significance of this tendency should be obvious, and, beyond this, the Chinese depiction of the African "other" showed a number of conceptual similarities to the European case. Wang Dayuan, a fourteenth-century sailor who traveled along the Indian Ocean coast, must have touched a familiar chord when he noted that the East African "people of Zengbaluo 'have the uprightness of ancient times.'" According to Snow,

> cultivated Chinese, like cultivated Greeks and Romans, nursed a vague nostalgia for a golden age when men lived in harmony uncorrupted by knowledge and the desire for gain, and it seems they found something in the simpler African coastal communities which answered to that dream.[15]

Apparently, there are no logical grounds for regarding the idea of the "noble savage" as an exclusive product of the European sensibility: there were broader forces which influenced its construction.

The Chinese view of the African was not static, and domestic realities had an important impact on its evolution over time. In the earliest stages of the Afro-Chinese encounter, the few Africans who were brought back by returning Chinese fleets, or who found their way to China independently by means of overland trade routes, "excited in Chinese minds a mixture of admiration and awe. Possibly the Chinese hoped to harness their magic."[16] Nevertheless, by the end of the Song dynasty (960-1279 A.D..) the positive image of Africans had begun to change. African slaves had gradually become a fixture in the major Chinese ports. "Kunlun [African] slaves were kept, according to a record of 1119, by 'most of the rich people of Canton,'" with many of the slaveowners being "members of the Islamic trading colony which continued to flourish there." In this urban center, at least, they were no longer exotic curiosities since "the Chinese residents of Canton must have seen them daily."[17] Unfortunately, as blackness and African origin became equated with slavery, their popular identity assumed an increasingly negative cast:

> The Chinese tone has changed from awe to bleak realism. No longer either heroic or magical, Kunlun have turned into displaced nomads, tragically ill-adapted to their Chinese

surroundings. . . . In contrast to the Chinese-speaking Kunlun of fiction, "their speech and their desires are unintelligi-
ble. . . ." [Accordingly] Kunlun are not considered to be
human. They do not appear to be bound by the family ties
which for Chinese are the essence of humanity. . . . They are
called "savages" and "devil slaves," and their sexes are classified by Chinese terms used to denote the male and female
of animals and some birds.[18]

The parallels with the European experience are obvious, and
Snow, unlike Said, is quick to recognize them. As he notes, while
"Europeans in mediaeval and early modern times looked on
Africans respectfully as inhabitants of hazy but imposing lands,"
this initial perspective steadily eroded as "they saw at close quarters African victims of slavery, helpless and therefore contemptible;
and they extended their contempt in due course to Africans in general."[19] Thus, a critical examination of the Chinese case should
make it readily apparent that broader cognitive processes are at
work here—processes which can only be understood within a comparative and cross-cultural context. Moreover, the damaging impact
of these constructs on the humanity of their victims cannot be
summarily dismissed on the basis of a wishful ideological agenda. A
backward projection of the ideal of Third World solidarity has its
emotional appeal; unfortunately, such an approach has no logical
or empirical grounding in reality.

The historical relationship of the Islamic Middle East and
Africa—and the related question of racism in the Arab world—provides an especially vexing set of problems. In this instance, the
entangling factors of ethnicity and ideology complicate the task of
coherent analysis, and the tendency to oversimplify is a temptation
for partisans on every side of the argument. It is often argued that
Islam, in both theory and practice, presents a constructive ethic of
non-racialism which is clearly in advance of the other major faiths,
Christianity in particular. At one level this position is highly convincing: one need only witness the annual unfolding of the Hajj, the
pilgrimage to Mecca, to see people from every part of the world
joined in a common purpose and a compelling expression of their
faith. On the other hand, as any student of African history can
attest, the record of Muslims (from the Middle East) in sub-Saharan
Africa, while not without its positive side, is something less than an
extended litany of tolerance and brotherhood.

This controversial question was recently brought to the forefront
by the publication of *Race and Slavery in the Middle East* by
Bernard Lewis, Professor of Near Eastern Studies Emeritus at
Princeton University. While Lewis has often been praised for the

quality and rigor of his scholarship, his willingness to address the sensitive issue of race and ethnicity has done nothing to endear him to his critics. For example, Edward Said (speaking from experience) has characterized Lewis' approach as "aggressively ideological," and left the impression that he is the quintessential modern Orientalist Indeed, Said once denounced his intellectual labors as a "project to debunk, to whittle down, and to discredit the Arabs and Islam."[20] This particular work has also been criticized for its lack of attention to the African dimension of this problem.[21] Still, the very controversy which this work has stimulated is a basic testimony to its importance and timeliness.

This problem, however, is more than a subject of academic debate. A matter of far greater urgency is the ongoing incidence of religious conflict in Africa itself, with the civil war in the Sudan being the most destructive case in point. Among scholars and policymakers, and among African and Muslim intellectuals, there is a practical consensus that the resolution of these differences is an absolute prerequisite to peace, stability, and development in several crucial regions of the continent.

The proper relationship of Islam to Africa (and the African diaspora) has also been a matter of vigorous discussion within the African American community. Both the Black Muslim movement (including the writings of its most famous follower and apostate, Malcolm X) and more traditional expressions of Islam have attracted a significant following, and the decision of many African Americans to adopt Arabic and Swahili names, and to give such names to their children, provides some indication of the impact of Islam on African American popular consciousness. Nevertheless, despite these inroads, Islam (in its several American versions) has remained a minority faith within the African American community, and it continues to attract black critics across a broad intellectual spectrum. Most recently, Professor Molefi Kete Asante of Temple University, the author of *Afrocentricity* and the spokesman for the movement of the same name, has argued that "adoption of Islam is as contradictory to the Diasporan Afrocentricity as Christianity has been," and he warns that "Islam within the African American community has yet to come under Afrocentric scrutiny."[22] Asante's position provides further confirmation of the ambiguous standing of Islam within the African diaspora.

Within the scripture and tradition of Islam, the "other" has never been formally conceived in terms of a racial or cultural construct. Instead, the primary line of human demarcation has been drawn between the believer and the unbeliever, and between the *dar al-Islam* (the realm of Islam) and the *dar al-harb* (the realm of war). Islam did not emerge in a vacuum, and, according to Bernard

Lewis, there was a solid and well established precedent for this mindset in the social and intellectual history of the Middle East (and the Mediterranean world):

> Like every other society known to human history, the ancient Middle Eastern peoples harbored all kinds of prejudices and hostilities against those whom they regarded as "other." But the "other" was primarily someone who spoke another language (the prototypal barbarian) or professed another religion (the Gentile or heathen or—in Christian and Islamic language—the infidel). There are many hostile references to the "others"—among Jews about Gentiles and heathens, among Greeks about barbarians, among Romans about almost everybody.[23]

Lewis maintains, however, that the rapid expansion of Islam "created an entirely new situation in race relations."[24] While Said has argued that the territorial extent of the *dar al-Islam* was modest in comparison to that of nineteenth-century European imperialism, Lewis has stressed that the new Islamic order represented a radical departure in scale and inclusiveness over what had come before:

> Islam for the first time created a truly universal civilization, extending from Southern Europe to Central Africa, from the Atlantic Ocean to India and China. By conquest and by conversion, the Muslims brought within the bounds of a single imperial system and a common religious culture peoples as diverse as the Chinese, the Indians, the peoples of the Middle East and North Africa, black Africans, and white Europeans.[25]

In such a cosmopolitan setting it would have been more surprising if a growing awareness of racial and ethnic differences had not become a factor in the popular consciousness, especially among the Arabs, the people who had created this remarkable empire. While Islam, as a creed, remained color-blind, those who professed it and carried it to new lands developed an increasing consciousness of physical (as well as social and cultural) differences within the *dar al-Islam*, and the "other" began to be identified on several distinctive levels of practical significance. In *Race and Slavery in the Middle East* Lewis clearly establishes that the encounter between the Islamic Middle East and Africa (and Africans) was distorted by a persistent element of racism and ethnocentrism. As in the Chinese and European cases, racism was as much an effect as it was a cause, with the reduction of a particular group to servile status contributing to a widening range of commentary which solidified their identity as the "other." In this instance the slave trade between the East

African periphery and the Islamic heartland, a trade which claimed fewer victims than the Atlantic system but which extended over a much longer period of time, played a crucial role in establishing and reinforcing the notion of black inferiority. The equation of blackness and slavery assumed a more absolute character during the last several centuries as areas of supply in southern Europe and the Caucasus were cut off and sub-Saharan Africa became the primary source of new captives. Lewis maintains that

> the literature and folklore of the Middle East reveal a sadly normal range of traditional and stereotypical accusations against people seen as alien and, more especially, inferior. The most frequent are those commonly directed against slaves and hence against the races from which slaves are drawn—that they are stupid; that they are vicious, untruthful, and dishonest; that they are dirty in their personal habits and emit an evil smell. The Black's physical appearance is described as ugly, distorted, or monstrous.[26]

Other racist formulas are evident in the literature and oral tradition of the region. People of African descent were often described as "frivolous and lighthearted—that is, in other terms, cheerful and of happy disposition. Other positive stereotypes show the black as brave, generous, musical, and with a strong feeling of rhythm. Thus Ibn Butlan remark[ed] that 'if a Zanji [East African] were to fall from heaven to earth he would beat time as he goes down.'"[27] Black sexuality is also a subject of popular myth: "a common theme is [the] immense potency and unbridled sexuality" of the black man, and Lewis claims that "there is a good deal of Arabic poetry which shows the same kind of prurient interest in the Negress as one finds in European anti-Semitic writings about the Jewess."[28] Nevertheless, despite these attitudes, it has been argued that the consequences of slavery and racism were less severe in the Islamic world than they were in the Atlantic and European colonial contexts since most of the slaves in the former system were not directly involved in a system of production; that is, they were "domestic" slaves. Other variables, such as the extent of manumission and the immunities afforded by conversion to the faith, have also been advanced as extenuating factors. In the end, whether it was somehow more ennobling, or less degrading, to serve as a concubine, eunuch, or personal servant in the Middle East as opposed to being sentenced to a life of hard labor on a plantation in the Caribbean or southern U.S. is difficult to determine. In fact, this would seem to represent a pointless and futile line of analysis, though this school of thought has proponents. In both cases the African victims were exploited for their labor and their status value and, in both cases, their identity as the "other" was sanctioned and reinforced by a popular ideology of race.

The status and treatment of blacks—in particular, black slaves—within Islamic societies was obviously not uniform. This was also the case within Africa itself. For example, in Northern Nigeria the standing of an individual in relation to the orthodox version of the faith was far more important than any notion of ethnicity. Since there were no grounds for distinguishing believer from non-believer on the basis of physical difference, the question of "race" was peripheral to the major currents of social and intellectual debate, although it was not entirely absent from the discourse on the "pagan" peoples to the south. By contrast, in those areas where Islam was established and spread by a ruling expatriate community from Arabia or Persia, the situation was substantially different. In these regions racism would become a basic social reality, and the local notion of Islam would be adapted to accommodate, and even reinforce, its guiding premises.

The history of Lamu, an Islamic city-state off the coast of Kenya, would suggest that the philosophy and practice of racism (as described by Lewis) cannot be easily dismissed. The social dynamics of this island, which played an important role in the Indian Ocean commercial network, have been analyzed in detail by Abdul Hamid M. el Zein in his study *The Sacred Meadows: A Structural Analysis of Religious Symbolism in an East African Town*. Tradition holds that Lamu was originally settled around the eighth century A.D. by two groups of immigrants, one consisting of Arabs from the city of Yanbu and the other consisting of Syrians, Iraqis, and Persians. Much later, during the late eighteenth century, "the people of Lamu began to expand to the mainland of Africa. . . . the area was fertile, and they bought slaves to cultivate the land for them. . . . These slaves were mainly from what is now called Tanzania."[29] In all likelihood, this extension of slavery only reinforced an ideology of racism which was already in place. As el Zein notes:

> The people of Lamu thought that the slaves were uncivilized and therefore, of course, unequal. Since the core of civilization for the people of Lamu was Islam, and since the slaves were not Muslims, they were not considered civilized. For the Lamuans, Islam was the miracle by which the pre-Islamic Arabs, the barbarians, were transformed into civilized people. Thus astarabu, which means "civilization", refers exclusively to the Arabs and the Islamic civilization which they developed after converting. The slave was considered a human being, mwanadamu, a descendant of Adam; yet, unlike other children of Adam, he was thought to have forgotten the promise he made in heaven to obey God and be a Muslim, and was thus degraded.[30]

The slaveholders of Lamu also subscribed to a convenient theory which was familiar to their contemporaries and counterparts in the American South, as well as much of Europe: the "Hamitic hypothesis." According to "Lamuan creation myth, the slaves were believed to be descendants of Ham, the son of Noah, who disobeyed his father. Noah cursed his disobedient son by asking God to make the sons of Ham slaves and servants." This mythology was used to "demonstrate that the slaves were unable to support a civilization of their own. They could be taught, but they did not have the faculties to understand what they had been taught, because they could not escape from the curse that condemned them to a position lower than all other human beings."[31] Moreover, as "Wa Shenzi," "people of the bush," their obligatory and nominal conversion to Islam provided little in the way of rights and immunities.

> Because the slaves were to convert to Islam, they were given a minimal amount of Islamic theology. The people of Lamu considered it a waste of time to teach a slave all the finer points of their religion: he need only know that "there is no God but Allah," and that "Mohammed is His Prophet." Besides this he was given some instruction in how to pray. . . . The slave was taught neither the rules of marriage nor the rules of inheritance.[32]

The position of slave women was especially precarious. El Zein points out that they "were sexually accessible, without marriage, to the masters who owned them. If the owner liked a girl, he was able to take her as a *souriya*, or pastime girl."[33] These African women were further victimized by a prurient mythology which held that they "could not control their sexual desires, even when they reached old age. . . . they were described as jin or fire; they had to burn all the time in order to exist." The notion of inferiority also extended to the realm of death and the spirit world. "The dead slave had to be washed by other slaves. . . . his corpse was referred to by the word *mfu*, which in Lamu, is also used for dead animals."[34] As for the jin, those "inhabitants of the unseen world," it was thought that "the benevolent jin live in towns and imitate the Muslims; the malevolent jin live in dark places, outside of the towns, and are like the Wa Shenzi."[35] By any standard of analysis, it would be difficult to interpret this demeaning and wide-ranging vision of the "other" as either harmless or benevolent, and the numerous similarities between this particular Islamic case (which is certainly not unique) and the western expression of racism are both obvious and painful.

"The woman who discovered her maidservant having improper relations with an ass". Tabriz, Iran, ca. 1530.

Some would point to the obvious contemporary evidence of racial admixture in this and in comparable Muslim African societies to argue that day-to-day social realities were far more liberal than written records (or oral charters) would tend to suggest. This ignores the fact that race is a flexible ideological construct rather than an unambiguous physical reality: it is what people *believe* about race, and their *own* identity, that ultimately shapes their concept of the "other." An African American graduate student working in the Sudan was astonished when an informant whom he considered to be "black" began to lecture him on the nature of the "pagan" black peoples who lived near the equator. In presenting an analysis which could only be described as racist, he subscribed to the notion of the classical Arab travelers that the climate had adversely affected their skin color, intellectual capacity, and personal appetites.[36] There was little doubt whom this individual regarded as the "other." Moreover, realistically, the emergence of a class or caste of people of mixed race does not necessarily demonstrate a broader historical pattern of racial equality or toleration: one need only examine the social legacies of the American South and the Caribbean basin for confirmation of this fact.

Because of these parallels, which are not often discussed, the historical legacy of Islam has posed a difficult problem for African intellectuals outside of the faith. Mudimbe, in *The Invention of Africa*, has little to say about this question, which is unfortunate given the possibilities of comparison inherent in his critical analysis of the process of "conversion." In assessing the legacy and tactics of (European) Christian evangelism in Africa, he argues that

> missionary speech is always predetermined, pre-regulated, let us say *colonized*: Missionary orthodox speech, even when imaginative or fanciful, evolved within the framework of what, from now on, I shall call the authority of the truth. This is God's desire for the conversion of the world in terms of cultural and socio-political regeneration, economic progress and spiritual salvation. This means, at least that the missionary does not enter into dialogue with pagans and "savages" but must impose the law of God that he incarnates. All of the non-Christian cultures have to undergo a process of reduction' to, or—in missionary language—of regeneration in, the norms that the missionary represents. This undertaking is perfectly logical: a person whose ideas and mission come from and are sustained by God is rightly entitled to the use of all possible means, even violence, to achieve his objectives. Consequently, "African conversion," rather than being a positive outcome of a dialogue— unthinkable per se—came to be the sole position the African could take in order to survive as a human being.[37]

Again, we would argue that Mudimbe's model of conversion cannot be universally applied to the European colonial encounter with Africa. Nevertheless, in those particular historical cases where it can be advanced with a reasonable degree of accuracy, it still does not stand out as an entirely distinctive construct. Indeed, it would be difficult to maintain that the basic assumptions of this Christian strategy of conversion have been radically different from the guiding intellectual ethos of the Islamic project in sub-Saharan Africa. In both cases the "other" has been defined—or, more accurately, redefined—as those who retain their allegiance to a system of belief which predates "the coming of the book" (the "unregenerate," the "infidels," etc.) Moreover, at points of contact between alien bearers of the word and indigenous societies, in this case between the ideological "center" and the African periphery, this distinction has often been reinforced by a popular and non-scriptural discourse on racial and physical difference. In many instances, a practical recourse to syncretism—a creative fusion of old and new traditions—has helped to resolve the dangerous tension between the intrusive and the indigenous. Even then, the followers of these faiths who have not accepted the word in its orthodox form have run the risk of being perceived as a threat to the established (or ideologically desirable) order. On those occasions, repression—by missionary pressure and the intervention of the colonial state or alternatively through the declaration and unleashing of *jihad*—has been an all too common response to an implied challenge. Islam and Christianity have attracted their African adherents by the millions, winning most of their converts without recourse to force or compulsion, but despite the disclaimers of their apologists, neither faith has been free of hegemonic pretensions or openly accepting of traditional values and beliefs.

Mudimbe's commentary on Islam is largely confined to an analysis of the work of Edward Wilmot Blyden, a black intellectual and Christian minister from the West Indies, and a pioneering Pan-Africanist who eventually became convinced that Islam was the most appropriate tool for the economic advancement and political liberation of the continent. Blyden did not see any essential conflict between Islam and established African cultures: in *Christianity, Islam, and the Negro Race*, published in 1888, he argued that "none of the Nigritian tribes have ever abdicated their race individuality or parted with their idiosyncrasies in embracing the faith of Islam."[38] This conclusion was not without its contemporary appeal, but today, it can only be sustained by ignoring an important dimension of African social history, and Mudimbe is fully alert to its empirical limitations:

> According to Blyden, Islam is politically an excellent means of promoting an African consciousness and of organizing communities. Unfortunately, though the ideological assumptions can be accepted in principle, the historical facts badly contradict Blyden's belief in the positive capabilities of Islam. Throughout the nineteenth century in Central Africa, Islamic factions represented an objective evil and practiced a shameful slave-trade. And here, again, we face an unbelievable inconsistency in Blyden's thought: his naive admiration for Islam led him to accept the enslavement of non-Muslim peoples![39]

Furthermore, this ongoing "enslavement of non-Muslim peoples" was ultimately justified by a philosophical and legal definition of the "same" and the "other," primarily through a Manichean distinction between the "believer" and the "unbeliever" and secondarily through a significant element of racism within the popular consciousness of the Islamic heartland. Thus, both "the West" and "the Orient" (in the sense of Said's analysis) developed a reductionistic vision of the African "other," a vision which was linked to an intellectual program which justified their ideological, economic, and political penetration of the continent. Moreover, the historical record reveals a further level of complexity which must be fully considered. In parts of the continent, particularly West Africa, the antecedent (and dramatic) success of Islam would provide its African faithful with a powerful ideology of resistance to European imperialism, a force which would not emerge as a territorial threat until the mid-nineteenth century. Thus, over the long term, African identities and self-definitions have been notably fluid and dependent on the particular context, and African societies have proven to be remarkably adept at "reinventing" received ideologies for their own particular needs. Unfortunately, until the recent advent of the postcolonial era, the diversity and complexity of the African experience had escaped the notice of all but the most perceptive travelers and observers from Europe and the Islamic Middle East. This should not be surprising, however, even in retrospect. Those intent on imposing their own moral order tend to have little interest in the subtleties of the civilizations which they hope to contain or transform.

There are those who would argue for the essential cultural unity of the Middle East and Africa, and suggest that a discourse of "the same" and "the other" never really emerged in the historical interaction of these two particular regions. According to this position, racism and ethnocentrism—at least in their most damaging forms—have been a peculiarly European phenomenon, and the central dialectic of our age has been, in the words of the Nigerian writer

Chinweizu, an overarching and unequal struggle between the "West and the rest of us."[40] The record of European imperialism in the "Third World" over the last several centuries would suggest that this argument has its merits, although this one-dimensional perspective ultimately obscures as much as it explains. By the same token, the patterns of demographic, economic, and cultural exchange between Africa, the Arabian peninsula, and southwest Asia, from antiquity to the present, have been extensive and well-documented. This does not mean, however, that these regions can be regarded as a seamless cultural unit, nor does it demonstrate that perceptions across its ethnic and ideological boundaries have been of a qualitatively different—or less distorted—type than those which emerged out of the European contact with the non-Western world. While this rhetorical position provided a valuable rallying point during the anti-colonial struggle, it is much more difficult to sustain when it is evaluated on the basis of real evidence.

In this regard, it is crucial to understand that the "other" has always been a contemporary construct driven by immediate needs, a construct based on "differences" which are not only subjective, but situational. To suggest that this logic and process have been absent, or somehow rendered historically irrelevant, in the region broadly defined as the "Middle East"—a portion of the world that has been notable for its social and intellectual dynamism—is to carry the very "Orientalism" which Said has so rightly condemned to a new and baroque extreme. It is eminently reasonable to argue that, in a wide area of the *dar al-Islam*, a new threshold of inclusion and exclusion ("submission to God") achieved a greater social pertinence than constructions of identity based on language and culture, and race and ethnicity. This does not mean, however, that the expression of this tendency was uniform over time or constant throughout the entire length and breadth of the Islamic Middle East. For example, it is probable that the incidence and intensity of racism became more pronounced during the last several centuries as slave catchment areas in Europe and southern Asia were removed from the marketplace, and the link between blackness, African origin, and slavery was made more "obvious" and absolute. Likewise, it is equally probable that, in the ninth century A.D., the significance of race was much more pronounced in southern Iraq—where an intensive system of labor in the salt flats of Basra triggered a large-scale African slave rebellion[41]—than it was in those regions with a smaller slave population and a less egregious pattern of exploitation. The situation was no more monolithic within Africa itself, as the Islamic frontier extended south of the Sahara, and the drama of confrontation and accommodation was joined on a range of local and regional stages, producing a range of different results.

Thus, it should be obvious that the problem of "the same" and the "other," as it has manifested itself throughout the multilayered encounter between the Middle East and Africa, cries out for further systematic study. As the record stands today this complex issue cannot be addressed or dismissed by a convenient explanatory formula without a considerable sacrifice in historical precision.

Some scholars have been unwilling to take this step, however. A particularly interesting resolution of this question has been offered by the political scientist Ali Mazrui in his book, and in the companion television series, *The Africans: A Triple Heritage*. Mazrui's approach might best be described as geographical revisionism. Simply put, he regards the Arabian peninsula as an integral part of Africa, the victim of a false and arbitrary division at the hands of European mapmakers. Through this interpretation he is able to instantly transform Islam into an indigenous African belief system, thus obviating the problem of the "other" as it applies to the Arab (and Islamic) penetration of the continent. Apparently, a fortuitous rumbling of the tectonic plates provided an ideal opening for the machinations of European imperialism, and Mazrui is forced to conclude that "the most pernicious sea in Africa's history may well be the Red Sea":

> The problem goes back several million years when three cracks emerged on the eastern side of Africa. . . . Three cracks had occurred on the African crust—yet only the one which had resulted in a sea was permitted to "dis-African-ise" what lay beyond the sea. The other two cracks resulted in "rift valleys," straightsided trenches averaging thirty miles across.[42]

While one can understand the logic which is at work here, it is just as plausible—and ultimately, just as convincing—to argue that the Americas were unjustly separated from Asia by the disappearance of the Bering land bridge (an interpretation which would place the navigational skills of Christopher Columbus in a somewhat more favorable light). Mazrui goes on to argue that the final act in the tragedy of the Red Sea took place in the nineteenth century with that masterstroke of European imperialism, the construction of the Suez canal. "A cataclysm which had occurred several million years previously when the Arabian peninsula was torn off its continent was at long last completed at Suez, severing the physical umbilical cord between the Arabian peninsula and its maternal continent."[43]

Fortunately, history had provided an inspired solution to this untimely miscarriage. According to Mazrui, "The cultural effort to reintegrate Arabia with Africa after the geological divide . . . reached a new phase with the birth and expansion of Islam." Seen in this light, "the Muslim conquest of north Africa" was far from an act of aggression: instead, it "was a process of overcoming the divisiveness of the Red Sea."[44] The cartographers and intellectuals of Europe, however, were not willing to accept this development on its own terms, and they "dis-Africanised the Prophet Muhammad"[45] (by, one can only assume, a calculated attempt at "Asianizing" or "Orientalizing" Arabia). Given this strategy, it is not surprising that "African followers of Muhammad experienced their own crisis of identity," and Mazrui points to the fate of a Nigerian sect (led by Mohammadu Marwa, also known as "Maitatsine") to illustrate the full extent of this geographical and cultural conspiracy.[46] Maitatsine was killed in a clash with Nigerian authorities in 1980, and other outbreaks of violence took place in the years which followed. Mazrui offers a unique interpretation as to who should bear the ultimate responsibility for this tragic chain of events:

> The most distinctive yearning within [this] sect was a burning desire for the Africanisation of Islam, which later became a burning desire for an African prophet. It must remain an issue of conjecture and speculation whether the yearning for an African prophet would have been partly assuaged if Prophet Muhammad had himself been perceived as an African. . . . By drawing the boundary of Africa at the Red Sea, European mapmakers may have caused more havoc than we even realise. Many a life killed in the Maitatsine riots of 1980, or the riots of Maiduguri and Yola (Gongola State) and Kaduna in 1984, or in Gombe in 1985, conceivably could have been spared. . . . [47]

Thus, through an amazing act of projection, Mazrui is able to lay the "blame" for an African reinvention of Islam at the feet of medieval European cartographers. In his view, the continuing problem of the "other" along the African frontiers of Islam can be explained (or explained away) as a particularly ingenious achievement of western cultural imperialism. The matter is not so simple, however.

While the grossest forms of distortion have sometimes influenced European and American scholarship on Africa, the West possesses no monopoly on misrepresentation when it comes to the academic assault on the "Dark Continent." An anthology entitled *The Arabs and Africa*, published in 1985 by the Centre for Arab Unity Studies, provides a dramatic case in point. While some of the pieces in this collection are of obvious scholarly merit, others display a level of cultural chauvinism, ethnocentrism, and simple inaccuracy which is truly monumental. A particularly interesting perspective was offered by Izzud-din Amar Musa of the Department of History at Ahmadu Bello University in Zaria, Nigeria. Musa notes that "the racist conception is that the Arabs are Semites, while the Africans are Hamites." He accurately points out that "this nineteenth century European theory lost all its biological basis a long time ago," but he proceeds with the somewhat more partisan assumption that "its only remnants are found in the two racist entities of Israel and South Africa and the very existence of both depends on the external support of world imperialist powers." Having ascribed the contemporary persistence of the "Hamitic hypothesis" to a Zionist-imperialist plot, he then, in the next paragraph, goes on to stress the history of interaction between Arabs and Africans and argue that "the results of this interaction are so strong that it is extremely difficult in this age to tell who is of Semitic extraction and who is of Hemitic [sic] extraction," thus invoking the logic of the very paradigm which he has just consigned to oblivion.[48] An equally fascinating interpretation of the East African slave trade was offered by Abd Elrahman Abuzayd Ahmed, Secretary General of the National Council for Higher Education in Khartoum, Sudan. Ahmed's analysis of this trade revolves around a unique and personal reading of the documentary record; and it also focuses on the ultimate cultural (and racial) identity of one of East Africa's most notorious slavetraders:

> Taking East Africa as one of many examples of the deliberate confusion of "Arab" and "Muslim," it is possible to examine European travellers' remarks on slavery. Documents show the deep involvement of Europeans and Indians in this trade all along the east coast of Africa and Arabs were implicated in it by mistake. For instance, Tibotib was a Muslim who used to dress himself in Arab-Islamic dress but was not an Arab. Livingstone presented him as an Arab, and European historians built their theories on that assumption. I had the opportunity once to have a look into slave trade dealings in Zanzibar and to my great surprise I did not find a single Arab name in the list of major financiers and traders which included hundreds of French, Indian, and Portuguese names.[49]

While Ahmed rightfully points to the potential for "confusion" resulting from the multiple levels of identity in this instance, the estimate which follows is perplexing at best. He tells us who Tippu Tib is *not*; but he does not venture a guess as to who he *is*, or how his actual identity might best be described. He points to the records of "major financiers and traders" on the island of Zanzibar but he says nothing about the commercial (and coercive) networks which extended from the East African coastal city-states into the interior, ranging as far afield as eastern Zaire. Also, while he speculates about the agents of supply, he says nothing about the sources of demand: were the Arabs "implicated by mistake" in this respect as well?

Kathryn L. Green, in the *African Studies Review*, has presented a brief but highly effective critique of this volume. What is most disturbing is the recycling of reductionistic and, in certain respects, racist constructs which are justifiably condemned when they are advanced by western scholars and observers. Green concludes that *The Arabs and Africa*

> displays an appalling cultural chauvinism that only a few of the commentators seem to notice. Many of the authors insist on the civilizing mission of Arab culture in Africa. A few examples will serve to illustrate the tone of much of this work. "Islam played a major civilizing and social role in sub-Saharan Africa. . . . Islam introduced them to the outside world. The Arabs have a good record of conveying Islam and modern knowledge to the Africans" (p. 80). "The Sultanate of Zanzibar introduced civilization to the area" (p. 142). "All of Africa's cultural heritage is either Arab or written in the Arabic alphabet" (p. 454). . . . Mohamed Benaissa does comment on the danger of "bigoted and prejudiced attitudes" (p. 504) but such statements are few and far between.[50]

Certainly, it is not necessary to "Africanize" the Arabian peninsula (as per Mazrui), or to "Arabize" sub-Saharan Africa, in order to acknowledge the important role which Islam has played in the history of the continent. Like Christianity, it has become a vital and dynamic element in the life of the tens of thousands who have willingly embraced it. A scholarly or polemical insistence upon the exclusive authenticity of "pre-Christian" or "pre-Islamic" belief systems can all too easily degenerate into a "search for the primitive," and there is nothing to be gained by replacing one form of reductionism with another. It is equally necessary, however, to freely acknowledge the cultural diversity of the African landscape and to examine the myriad of ways in which Africans have not only accepted (or rejected) these "world religions," but how, in a variety of cases, they have gone on to interpret and adapt them in terms of their own particular needs and belief systems. Unfortunately, it is apparent that in addressing the subtleties of this problem, modern Islamic scholars cannot present a greater record of sensitivity or achievement than their western counterparts.

A particularly uncompromising approach to this question is taken by Ibraheem Sulaiman in his recent study of *The Islamic State and the Challenge of History*. This work focuses on the *jihad* of Usman dan Fodio and the series of campaigns and events which led to the creation of the Sokoto Caliphate in northern Nigeria in the early nineteenth century. The author, a research fellow with the Centre for Islamic Legal Studies of Ahmadu Bello University, makes no real pretense of scholarly objectivity. At the outset he establishes that "mankind is divided, in its beliefs and ideologies, into two distinct categories—the unbelievers and the believers," and his analysis proceeds from there.[51] The pursuit of *jihad* against a regime which has departed from the accepted norms of Islam is seen as a positive event: in such cases, "revolution, despite the bloodshed and destruction, can be seen as a blessing in its elimination of oppression, and its creation of a new world with definite values, moral and social commitments. People are given a new breath of life, a sense of direction after a long period of decay and aimlessness."[52] Sulaiman also makes it clear that such a situation had emerged in Hausaland at the time of Usman dan Fodio and that the time was ripe for action:

> There was no doubt that about the intellectual and moral superiority which Muslims enjoyed over the unbelievers; and Shehu Usman's intensive educational, spiritual and moral programmes helped to sharpen the social consciousness of those who were being mobilized for change. . . . Muslims gained the awareness that idol worshippers, corrupt and inept rulers and tyrants had no moral right to rule over them. . . . They had a duty, they were told, to seek the means to live as Muslims to secure their own dignity and the integrity of Islam—in short, to overthrow the unbelieving power and establish the dar al-Islam.[53]

In addition to the secular shortcomings of their rule, the Hausa rulers "paid homage to trees and stones, made animal sacrifices to them and turned to them for the fulfillment of their needs. Thus they were unbelievers, even if they prayed and fasted and performed other rites of Islam."[54] Thus, for Sulaiman—as for Usman dan Fodio in an earlier time—there is no acceptable scope for syncretism or spiritual creativity in the African cultural universe. In taking this position on an ideological issue, he gives his blessing to a Manichean notion of the "other" which is every bit as absolute and powerful as any comparable construct which is grounded on race or ethnicity.

It should be stressed that there is a cadre of Islamic scholars who are attempting to develop a more balanced and detached approach to the problem of the "other," social scientists who have begun the process of rethinking their own assumptions while maintaining a careful distance from the embattled paradigms of their western colleagues. In particular, this task of reassessment has been joined by Akbar S. Ahmed (in his book *Toward Islamic Anthropology*) and Saibo Mohamed Mauroof (in his article "Elements for an Islamic Anthropology").[55] Ahmed presents a plausible critique of his discipline and makes good sense in cautioning Islamic social scientists to avoid the simple emulation of discredited western models and methodologies. Both Ahmed and Mauroof point—with justice—to the pioneering contributions of the early Muslim traveler-scholars such as Ibn Batuta, Ibn Khaldun, and al Biruni. Ahmed presents the latter figure as the prototype of the rational ethnographer, and implies that his work—and the work of those in his tradition of scholarship—might provide an effective basis for a revitalized Islamic anthropology:

> perhaps al Biruni (973-1048) deserves the title of father of anthropology. . . . If anthropology is a science based on extended participant observation of (other) cultures using the data collected for value-neutral, dispassionate analysis employing the comparative method, then al Biruni is indeed an anthropologist of the highest contemporary standards. . . . His work on (Hindu) India—Kitab al Hind—remains one of the most important source books for South Asia. . . . almost a thousand years before Malinowski and Geertz, al Biruni was establishing the science of anthropology.[56]

A careful examination of these critiques would suggest, however, that Muslim scholars, like their western counterparts, are only in the earliest stages of redefining their approach to the problem of the "other." In the introduction to Ahmed's work, Isma'il R. Al-Faruqi, the President of the International Institute of Islamic Thought, adopts a position which condemns the West for its failure of vision but reveals a mindset which is every bit as limited and parochial:

> the Western social scientists and other professionals of many descriptions . . . [including] the new breed of western-trained Muslim scholars—are "anthropologists" who have mastered the art of absolutizing native provincial and popular cultures of the masses as the pre-Islamic founts of "national" existence.
>
> The pile of their blunders and prejudgements is colossal and, as Dr. Akbar Ahmed asserts, there is no escape from exposing their mistakes and recasting their knowledge after

purification. Whereas those who were unaware of the unconscious service they have been rendering to the neo-colonialist enemy may be excused as "useful simpletons" the others ought to be confronted, and their involvement in the fragmentation which colonialism has inflicted upon the Muslims of the world should be exposed.[57]

In fairness to Ahmed, nowhere does he call for the type of intellectual inquisition which Al-Faruqi seems to suggest. Also, while one can understand Al-Faruqi's criticism of an undue emphasis on, and romanticization of, "pre-Islamic" social formations, one is hesitant about the ultimate destination of any approach which invokes the need for a "purification" of knowledge. There are other difficulties as well. Ahmed defines Islamic anthropology "loosely as the study of Muslim groups by scholars committed to the universalistic principles of Islam—humanity, knowledge, tolerance—relating micro village tribal studies . . . to the larger historical and ideological frames of Islam."[58] What Ahmed ultimately suggests—and pursues throughout his book—is not so much the creation of an "Islamic anthropology" as the definition of a more acceptable "anthropology of Islam." Unfortunately, he has little specific to say about the construction of a new paradigm for understanding those peoples outside the temporal and geographical framework of the *dar al-Islam.*

For his part, Mauroof is far too confident in his categorical assertion of a tradition of tolerance within the Islamic world. In addition to condemning Lewis for equating the attitudes and conventions of Islamic literature with actual social behavior, he takes a dubious estimate of the present and applies it to the past:

> Its real consequences can be observed in any Muslim city today where most or all Muslim ethnic types parade on the streets in total unconsciousness of one another's ethnic differences. Evidently, intermarriage, colour-blindness, and ethnicity-unawareness have combined under Islamic law to create the present universalist configuration. Practically every Muslim city has seen countless waves of immigration by ethnically diverse peoples; but none is known to have had an ethnic ghetto for any length of time, and none has one today. Certainly Islamic religion, culture and law were the dissolving agents of ethnic differences.[59]

One can only assume that the operative phrase here is "*Muslim* ethnic types," and while Mauroof's estimate may have some limited validity for Cairo or Algiers it seems considerably more dubious when applied to Khartoum or Kano. Mauroof also (indirectly) addresses the crucial issue involved in the construction of a viable

Islamic anthropology. He condemns "the simplistic view of a University of Bombay anthropologist who . . . suggested that all Muslims ought to become cultural relativists and adopt the stance of an ethnographer so that they could overcome their cultural prejudices and thereby promote social harmony in the context of the plural society of the Indian republic." Mauroof responds that "none of this will do."[60] If this is, in fact, the case—if there is no room for a genuine and analytical cultural relativism within the Islamic social sciences—it is doubtful whether any redefinition of anthropology within the *dar al-Islam* will gain any acceptance, or have any practical utility, outside it. This issue is far from resolved, and Islamic scholars and intellectuals are the only parties who can resolve it.

It would appear from these examples of recent scholarship, and from a host of other evidence, that the Islamic Middle Eastern approach to sub-Saharan Africa is badly in need of its own Edward Said. This problem clearly warrants the type of extended critical analysis which he offered in his study of *Orientalism.* It is equally apparent that the European or "European imperialist" mindset has not been the only locus of racism in world history or, more particularly, the only external agent which has fabricated a racist and distorted concept of the African "other." The question at hand is not a matter of the relative "guilt" or the relative "innocence" of one cultural system either in relation to, or comparison to, another, and it cannot be resolved in terms of the tired political formulas through which it is usually approached. The immediate challenge is considerably more demanding: the need to search for broader processes behind the creation and definition of the "other," processes which manifest themselves within the context of a particular time and place but which can be traced across a broader spectrum of human interaction. As Leonard Thompson has warned us, this is more than an academic exercise. Indeed, a casual look at the world today suggests that the urgency of this task has never been more pressing. The time has come for scholars of the humanities and social sciences, whatever their allegiance, to go beyond "Orientalism"—in both senses of the term.

Notes

1. V. Y. Mudimbe, *The Invention of Africa* (Bloomington: Indiana University Press, 1988), 17.
2. Ibid., 16.
3. Ibid., (see figure 2, "Ideological Model of Conversion: Colonial Rule."), 50.
4. Ibid., 4.
5. Ibid., 44.
6. For the provenance of this phrase see Anthony Hopkins, *An Economic History of West Africa* (London: Longman, 1973), 10.
7. Edward W. Said, *Orientalism* (New York: Vintage Books, 1979), 60.
8. Edward W. Said, "Yeats and Decolonization," *Nationalism, Colonialism, and Literature,* Field Day Pamphlet no. 15 (Belfast: Field Day Theatre Co., 1988), 6.
9. Said, *Orientalism*, 39, 41.
10. Said, "Yeats", 7-8.
11. Ibid., 7.
12. Philip Snow, *The Star Raft: China's Encounter with Africa* (London: Weidenfeld and Nicolson, 1988), 13.
13. Ibid., 14, 16.
14. Ibid., 16.
15. Ibid.
16. Ibid., 18.
17. Ibid.
18. Ibid., 19.
19. Ibid.
20. Said, *Orientalism*, 316.
21. This issue was the subject of a stimulating discussion at the Thirty-fourth Annual Meeting of the African Studies Association in November 1991. (Panel IX-13, "Roundtable: Book Reviews: Bernard Lewis' 'Race and Slavery in the Middle East' from an African Perspective.") The panelists were (convenor) Janet Ewald, G. Michael LaRue, Dennis Cordell, and David Robinson.
22. Molefi Kete Asante, *Afrocentricity* (Trenton, N.J.: Africa World Press, 1988), 2.
23. Bernard Lewis, *Race and Slavery in the Middle East: An Historical Enquiry* (New York: Oxford University Press, 1990), 17.
24. Ibid., 18.
25. Ibid.
26. Ibid., 92.
27. Ibid., 93-94.
28. Ibid., 94.
29. Abdul Hamid M. el Zein, *The Sacred Meadows: A Structural Analysis of Religious Symbolism in an East African Town* (Evanston, Ill.: Northwestern University Press, 1974), 27.
30. Ibid.
31. Ibid.
32. Ibid., 27-28.

33. Ibid., 30.
34. Ibid., 78.
35. Ibid., 71.
36. Anthony Cheeseboro, interview by Dennis Hickey, East Lansing, Michigan, 4 December 1991.
37. Mudimbe, 47-48.
38. Edward W. Blyden, *Christianity, Islam, and the Negro Race* (Edinburgh: Edinburgh University Press, 1967), 122.
39. Mudimbe, 115.
40. Chinweizu, *The West and the Rest of Us* (New York: Random House, 1975).
41. Lewis, 56-57.
42. Ali A. Mazrui, *The Africans: A Triple Heritage* (London: BBC Publications, 1986), 29-30.
43. Ibid., 102.
44. Ibid., 32.
45. Ibid., 36.
46. Ibid.
47. Ibid.
48. Izzud-din Amar Musa, "Islam and Africa," in ed. Khair El-Din Haseeb, *The Arabs and Africa* (London: Croom Helm and Centre for Arab Unity Studies, 1985), 58-59.
49. Abd Elrahman Abuzayd Ahmed, "Comments on Izzud-din Amar Musa, 'Islam and Africa,'" in ed. Khair El-Din Haseeb, *The Arabs and Africa* (London: Croom Helm and Centre for Arab Unity Studies, 1985), 79.
50. Kathryn L. Green, "Review of *The Arabs and Africa*," *The African Studies Review* 32 (April 1989): 133.
51. Ibraheem Sulaiman, *The Islamic State and the Challenge of History: Ideals, Policies, and Operations of the Sokoto Caliphate* (London: Mansell Publishing Ltd., 1987), 1.
52. Ibid., 2.
53. Ibid., 3-4.
54. Ibid., 4.
55. Akbar S. Ahmed, *Toward Islamic Anthropology: Definition, Dogma, and Directions* (Herndon, Va.: International Institute of Islamic Thought, 1986); Saibo Mohamed Mauroof, "Elements for an Islamic Anthropology," in ed. Isma'il R. Al-Faruqi and Abdullah Omar Nasseef, *Social and Natural Sciences: The Islamic Perspective* (Jeddah: Hodder and Stoughton and King Abdulaziz University, 1981).
56. Akbar Ahmed, 56.
57. Isma'il R. Al-Faruqi, Foreword, in Akbar Ahmed, *Toward Islamic Anthropology: Definition, Dogma, and Directions* (Herndon, Va.: International Institute of Islamic Thought, 1986), 8.
58. Akbar Ahmed, 56.
59. Mauroof, 130-31.
60. Ibid., 133.

3

In Search of the Primitive:
Reflections on a Lost Crusade

Within the western intellectual tradition, Africa has rarely been considered on its own terms. Instead, the continent and its peoples have been interpreted according to the immediate ideological needs of its beholders. Nevertheless, our modern image of Africa has emerged through the prism of two dominant and persistent constructs—the theory of race and the notion of the "primitive." While the guiding assumptions within these constructs have been far from constant, Eurocentric racism has been a much more stable and predictable factor in this equation than the vision of the primitive. In point of fact, the latter paradigm has assumed an assortment of divergent, even contradictory forms over the last several centuries. For this reason, the changing attitude toward the "primitive" has been especially significant in shaping the western perception of Africa: its particular definition at any given time has interacted with the element of racism, producing differing images of its people. At another level, the "search for the primitive" has also had much to say about the crisis of confidence in the West, a phenomenon which has asserted itself with increasing frequency and urgency since the holocaust of the First World War.

The European enlightenment saw the birth of the "noble savage," a mythical creation which achieved its fullest expression in the work of Rousseau. The *philosophes* who developed this abstract world of simplicity and harmony from the earlier observations of Montaigne had no substantial knowledge of the peoples they described. This critical omission made little difference to their intended audience, however, since their depiction of the "primitive" was ultimately designed to function as a counterpoint and commentary on the failures of their own society. In any case, the reign of the "noble savage" would not be a long one: by the middle of the nineteenth century it was apparent that he had outlived his usefulness. By this time, the conquest and expropriation of the indigenous peoples of the Third World and the Americas had entered its final and most intensive stage. What was needed was a social charter for aggression, not a litany of the virtues of its victims. The portrayal of "primitive man" as violent, anarchic, and hopelessly degraded was far more compatible with the guiding ethos of the colonial enterprise. Not surprisingly, scientific racism, social Darwinism, and a strict and unilineal version of cultural evolution achieved widespread acceptance among proconsuls, soldiers and intellectuals alike. Collectively, they provided the European world with a convenient apologia for bringing "the lesser breeds" within their law.

In the United States in particular, and the Western world in general, the rapid spread of industrialism and urbanism ultimately inspired a reaction to this trend. Blighted cities, rows of tenements, an agricultural crisis in the South and Midwest, an intensification of racial oppression and violence, the perception of a growing gap between rich and poor, and a devastating depression during the 1890s all suggested that America's "golden age" had come to an end. America was incredibly rich, but many Americans were distressingly poor. Across the Atlantic, fin de siecle Europe also presented a vista of corruption and excess beneath its glittering imperial facade. British "concentration camps" in South Africa (during the Boer War), the anti-Semitic hysteria of the Dreyfus affair in France, and the "red rubber" scandal in Leopold's Congo provided an inkling of a future which seemed as dangerous as it was uncertain. To those who chose to heed the warnings it was painfully apparent that the "white man's burden" was becoming increasingly more difficult to bear, both at home and abroad.

Despite the popular triumph of the notion of "progress," the legacy of Rousseau had not been forgotten. Darwinian formulas had served as Magna Chartas for the ruling class; but a revival of the notion of the "noble savage" promised a ray of hope for the common man. "Primitive Peoples"—domestic or foreign, past or present, real or imagined—could be presented as paragons of equality, civility, and brotherhood, in dramatic contrast to the modern captains of industry and finance and the political and military hirelings who did their bidding. With the crucial assistance of the emerging discipline of anthropology, which provided the charter and method to compile a growing inventory of celebratory texts, the "search for the primitive" was renewed in earnest in the early stages of the twentieth century. As the French social critic Pascal Bruckner has argued, this movement had much to offer to the discontented intellectuals of Europe and North America, as it carried a potent romantic attraction which persists to this day.

> Whereas, in the nineteenth century, the savage was nothing
> but a crude human sketch intended for protection by civi-
> lized peoples, at the beginning of the twentieth century, he
> became the original man, man without sin, and the West
> was called to renew itself through contact with him. . . . We
> have the misfortune of living with debilitating values and
> preoccupations, while they have symbolism, happiness, and
> simplicity, all functioning together with the wonder of some
> social magic. Without fail, in contrast to the frigid monsters
> of the Northern hemisphere, the great beauty of the primi-
> tive world is praised, as is the revival of deceased identities
> and the rise of religion, fidelity to oneself, [and] the ceaseless
> recapitulation of the cultural past. . . .[1]

Fortunately, the revival of interest in the "primitive" was not strictly
limited to a futile and reductionistic pursuit of vanished Edens.
Anthropology itself produced a school of thinkers who took the first
halting steps toward restoring the indigenous peoples of the Third
World to their particular historical contexts. These scholars avoided
the temptation of transforming non-western societies into a *tabula
rasa* for their personal theoretical agendas concerning the "nature
of man" or the imagined sequence of cultural evolution. Instead,
when examining particular cases, they were careful to consider the
impact of the past as well as the broader social and political
environment which critically affected the present. If one allows for a
predictable degree of anachronism, their work can still be read with
benefit.

Despite this breakthrough, the movement toward a more balanced and realistic understanding of small-scale, non-western societies has been far from even. For many scholars, even in the
present, it has remained more convenient to regard these societies
as peoples without history (that is, without a coherent recorded
past), the raw material of preemptive speculation and abstraction.
The intellectual tension between these two approaches has been
very much in evidence since the turn of the century, and it continues to have a highly significant influence on the modern image of
Africa. Along with more rational and productive studies, the "search
for the primitive" has continued with undiminished intensity. For
the devotees of "cultural authenticity," Africa, indeed the entire
Third World, has continued to function as a "vast empirical hunting
ground, where intellectuals from advanced countries can search for
confirmation of what they already know—that somewhere along the
banks of the Amazon or in the wastes of Mali or in the snows of
Bhutan they will find a purity their own societies lack."[2] Obviously,
these romantic expeditions into the realm of the "other" pave the
way for highly distorted portrayals of those societies unfortunate

enough to be the final destinations of their ideological caravans. Nevertheless, the quest goes on and the textual stockpile continues to mount, with predictable effect on our current understanding of Africa and other target regions.

The American contribution to the twentieth-century discourse on the primitive has been substantial, and some prominent figures have nourished its enduring controversies. In 1899, Thorstein Veblen published his iconoclastic masterwork of social and economic theory, *The Theory of the Leisure Class*. The Wisconsin son of Norwegian immigrant parents, Veblen produced a withering critique of the "lifestyles of the rich and famous" that was all the more devastating for its apparent intellectual detachment. Veblen's critique of the modern condition was rooted in a variety of instinctual anthropology in which an abstract concept of "primitive man" served as a basis for comparison and a model for reform. Admittedly, these speculations on the primitive were neither systematic nor empirical. On the one hand, John Kenneth Galbraith has maintained that "before writing this work Veblen had read widely on anthropology. He has a great many primitive communities and customs at his finger tips, and he refers to them with a casual insouciance that suggests . . . that he had much more such knowledge in reserve."[3] However, Don M. Wolfe is more to the point when he notes that Veblen "posed assumptions rather than evidence of the nature of primitive man, projecting conditions and attitudes in his imagination rather than assembling facts by sensory verification."[4] This latter task would be left to the ethnographers—both American and European—who would increasingly turn to Africa (and distant locales such as the Pacific Islands) for the "case studies" which would reveal the "primitive" in all of his glory. Veblen's theory may have been born in Chicago but it would truly "come of age" in Samoa and achieve its full maturity in places as removed from each other as the Arctic north, the Australian outback, the Kalahari desert and the Ituri forest. While the ethnographers of the 1920s and 1930s may not have "studied" Veblen they pursued their work within an intellectual climate which his theoretical adventure had helped to encourage and create.

Like Rousseau's "noble savage," Veblen's "primitive man" was an admirable version of humanity. Central to his theory was the conclusion that "the conditions under which men lived in the most primitive stages of associated life that can properly be called human, seem to have been of a peaceful kind." Tragically, this state of grace proved ephemeral, since, as "the struggle for existence changed in some degree from a struggle of the group against a nonhuman environment to a struggle against a human environment," behavior and culture increasingly assumed a predatory character.[5]

Nevertheless, even in the earlier phases of this transition man still displayed some crucial characteristics which would set him off from his "barbarian" descendants. Fortunately, these redeeming tendencies would not be completely lost: in later stages they would continue to appear in certain individuals, and thus, to a greater or lesser extent, within particular cultures as well. Veblen argued that "among these archaic traits that are to be regarded as survivals from the peaceable cultural phase, are that instinct of race solidarity which we call conscience, including the sense of truthfulness and equity, and the instinct of workmanship."[6]

As prehistory shaded into history, the "archaic" and constructive elements of the human personality became more and more of a liability for the individual who possessed them. This apparent paradox was explained by the intrinsic nature of "barbarian culture." According to Veblen, the "salient characteristic" of this stage of human development was "an unremitting emulation and antagonism between classes and between individuals." Apparently, social evolution had reached a point where "this emulative discipline favors those individuals and lines of descent which possess the peaceable savage traits in a relatively slight degree."[7] Admittedly, this basic insight into the human condition was not surprising given Veblen's practical experience in the political mores of an American graduate school. More significantly, while his theory implied that mankind was poised on the brink of another basic transformation, its current state provided little cause for celebration. In characteristically direct fashion, Veblen made the sweeping (and unsubstantiated) assertion that "the ethnic types of today . . . are the variants of primitive racial types." Accordingly, he was able to conclude that "the man of the hereditary present is the barbarian variant, servile or aristocratic, of the ethnic elements that constitute him."[8] In sum, a material victory had been won but at an appalling cost to the spiritual and ethical potential of mankind.

By the time the "feudal stage" was reached—or, as Veblen defined it, "the higher stages of the barbarian culture"—a "leisure class" had emerged. Exempt from manual and industrial occupations, he argued (with considerable insight) that their basic "occupations may be roughly comprised under government, warfare, religious observances, and sports."[9] The resemblance between these "higher barbarians" and the wealthier citizens of end of the century America was not coincidental. Indeed, Veblen had deliberately laid the groundwork for an adversarial anthropology which trained its gunsights on the rich and privileged of his own society. Through an explanation of "pecuniary emulation," "conspicuous leisure," and "conspicuous consumption" he detailed the means by which these latter-day barbarians perpetuated their own legitimacy, and, in so doing, frustrated the advancement of peace and social justice. In pursuing this analysis he gave no quarter, and his matter-of-fact prose style made his irony all the more devastating. As Galbraith suggests, in Veblen's estimation

> The effort to establish precedence for one's self and the yearning for the resulting esteem and applause are the most nearly universal of human tendencies. Nothing in this respect differentiates a Whitney, Vanderbilt or Astor from a Papuan chieftain or what one encounters in "for instance, the tribes of the Andamans." Indeed, it is inconceivable that the affluent should be viewed with indignation. The scientist does not become angry with the primitive tribesman because of the extravagance of his sexual orgies or the sophistication of his self-mutilation.[10]

As the First World War drew to a close, Veblen's appraisal of the human condition offered an attractive ideological platform for American intellectuals intent on defining a "new world order." His theory had the great advantage of being free from the taint of "Bolshevism," but like Marx's "primitive communism" it offered an encouraging "concept of Neolithic man not only as using the materials around him imaginatively and constructively toward the end of life, but also as possessing the dominant traits of impulsive brotherhood and a strong preference for a peaceful way of life."[11] In other words, in order to go forward man first had to look backward and eliminate the cultural and institutional barriers which divorced him from his basic nature. As Hartwig Isernhagen has pointed out, Veblen's speculative anthropology had a significant influence on the polemicists who shaped the "reconstruction program" of *The Dial*, an influential journal of opinion which addressed the crisis (and opportunity) of the postwar world.[12] It was not coincidental that Franz Boas, Robert Lowie, and Edward Sapir made a notable contribution to this dialogue: indeed, a piece by Lowie entitled "Anthropology Put to Work" suggested the pivotal role that an emerging "science of man" might play in reordering the values of a civilization which had lost its bearings.[13] Ironically, at the very time that the territories of Africans—and the homelands of other supposedly "primitive" peoples—were being reallocated at the conference table of Versailles, the real and imagined virtues of these colonial subjects were being dusted off as a promising model for "civilized" behavior in the postwar world, and scientists were sharpening the tools which would be needed to examine the gears and pulleys of their intriguing social machinery.

In April 1918, Veblen himself weighed in with a piece which optimistically predicted "The Passing of National Frontiers." In his estimation, man had come full circle: the demands of the new industrial age required that archaic notions of territoriality and nationalism be swept away and "primitive" values of cooperation and craftsmanship restored to center stage. Since national frontiers served no purpose other than "obstruction, retardation, and a lessened efficiency"[14] they were better relegated to Marx's "dustbin of history." Although the existing order lay in ruins there was cause for hope, since it seemed that a new internationalism, a nonviolent "revolution without frontiers" might be achieved if man could once again recapture the essential qualities of his primitive nature.

Veblen's concept of the primitive had an enduring impact well beyond the First World War and its immediate aftermath. The alienation of modern man from his primitive past—and his quest to recapture that past, and the existential meaning which it promised—became a guiding vision of the "lost generation" which transformed American literature during the 1920s and 1930s. Isernhagen has argued that "the anthropological concept of human instincts" is at the core of "much of the American modernist fiction of the Twenties, notably in the works of John Dos Passos, William Faulkner, F. Scott Fitzgerald, and Ernest Hemingway."[15] This driving force is at the heart of Faulkner's "enduring figures, predominantly black, and (above all) the primeval hunters like Sam Fathers in 'The Bear'"; it is also evident in Fitzgerald's lost "American Adam," Jay Gatsby; and it achieves its fullest realization in Hemingway's most primal characters, in particular his "hunters, fishers, and bull-fighters."[16] Indeed, it is not surprising that Hemingway would ultimately turn to Africa for his most vivid evocation of this quest. Still, there is a basic problem with Isernhagen's analysis: while he accurately identifies the significant role of the search for the primitive in these texts, he fails to realize that the American modernist analysis offered a far more pessimistic vision of the future than was ever hinted at by Veblen. For these writers the new technological era, far from opening a vista of liberation, simply promised a deeper descent into the emptiness of materialism and a more agonizing and baroque development of those very obsessions which Veblen most deplored. Gatsby, indeed, was a "lost Adam," but he was also a case of conspicuous consumption gone mad, the realization of Veblen's worst nightmare, a banished innocent who is hopelessly incapable of finding his own way and is ultimately sacrificed on the altar of his own possessions. Sadly, it appeared that Veblen's "barbarian" had emerged from the war as the ultimate victor, and the virtues of the primitive had become all the more elusive and distant.

By the 1890s, another prolific scholar had embarked on a long and distinguished career which helped to shape the American vision of the "primitive world." Franz Boas would give the fledgling discipline of anthropology coherence and form, and he would produce a generation of students who would carry on his legacy of intellectual rigor and his commitment to social and political justice. His lifelong concern with issues of tolerance and equality was not coincidental: as Marshall Hyatt has observed, "from early on in his university days in Germany, and throughout his life, Boas experienced anti-Semitism firsthand. These incidents left a lasting impression and molded his behavior and consciousness."[17] It was therefore understandable that in addressing the problem of "primitive man" he avoided the temptation of simplistic formulas and reductionistic paradigms. Boas brought an intellectual openness to this question which was not always evident in the work of his contemporaries. Through his emphatic rejection of an absolute (and unilineal) vision of cultural evolution, in his notable refusal to denigrate or idealize the peoples whom he studied, and in his basic willingness to challenge the conceptual dimensions of the "primitive," he set a standard of scholarship which has not always been equalled by his successors.

In his 1911 study, *The Mind of Primitive Man*, Boas did identify some general differences between the thought processes of "savage" and civilized man. For example, he argued that while, in the case of primitive man, "the perceptions of his senses are excellent, his power of logical interpretation seems to be deficient." He was quick to point out, however, that this phenomenon "was not based on any fundamental peculiarity of the mind of primitive man, but lies, rather, in the character of the traditional ideas by means of which each new idea is interpreted,"[18] a cultural context which was fully amenable, indeed, highly vulnerable, to forces of change and development. Boas also attacked the recently proclaimed notion of the French philosopher Lucien Levy-Bruhl that "primitive thought" was "prelogical,"[19] that man at the earlier stages of cultural development is "unable to isolate a phenomenon as such, that there is rather a 'participation' in the whole mass of the subjective and objective experience which prevents a clear distinction between logically unrelated subjects."[20] In his estimation, Levy-Bruhl had made the crucial mistake of examining "traditional beliefs and customs" rather than individual behavior. Boas further maintained that if we pursued this line of analysis in our own society we would

> reach the conclusion that the same attitudes prevail among ourselves that are characteristic of primitive man. The masses of material accumulated in the collections of modern superstitions proves this point and it would be a mistake to assume that these attitudes are confined to the

uneducated. Material collected among American college
students . . . shows that such belief may persist as an emotionally charged tradition among those enjoying the best of
intellectual training.[21]

Thus, while Boas continued to distinguish between the "primitive" and the "civilized," he explained the difference in terms of a
continuum rather than a dichotomy, and he began a process of
"demystifying" the primitive which would be radically reversed after
his death.

Because of his staunch opposition to "scientific" racism and its
practical justification of the oppression of African Americans he
also undertook the task of demystifying the African continent and
pointing out the virtues of its much-maligned cultural heritage.
Admittedly, he did agree that the behavioral patterns of "our poor-
est Negro population" were less than desirable or constructive, a
conclusion which might itself be regarded as an overt expression of
racism.[22] Such an interpretation would be hard to sustain, however, since he categorically denied that these tendencies were in
any way determined by racial or biological factors. To prove his
contention of black intellectual potential he pointed to an impressive (if neglected) record of African achievement in *The Mind of
Primitive Man*:

> the blacksmith, the wood carver, the weaver, the potter-
> these all produce ware original in form, executed with great
> care. . . . No less instructive are the records of travelers,
> reporting the thrift of the native villages, of the extended
> trade of the country, and of its markets. The power of orga-
> nization as illustrated in the government of native states is
> of no mean order, and when wielded by men of great
> personality has led to the foundation of extended empires.
> All the different kinds of activities that we consider valuable
> in the citizens of our country may be found in aboriginal
> Africa.[23]

Boas was convinced that African Americans would derive an important psychological benefit from a tangible display of African cultural
accomplishments. In 1906 he began a campaign to secure funding
for "an African museum that would present to the public, 'by
means of exhibits and by means of publications, the best products
of African civilizations.' The museum would also sponsor a scientific study of that civilization"; and it would contain separate
departments devoted to physical anthropology and the collection of
"statistical data" on African Americans, a research center which
could pursue the empirical refutation of racist ideology and

assumptions.[24] The important fact is that this project was *not* conceived as a visual inventory of "primitive" art and culture: instead, it was designed to serve as a concrete tribute to a dynamic and complex civilization. Boas appealed to the Carnegie Institution and to John D. Rockefeller for support, stressing the value of this proposed institute for the progress of the American Negro. Unfortunately, "the foundation heads did not agree, and the African Museum remained a dream."[25] Nevertheless, despite this setback, Boas would continue his lifelong crusade against the distortions of racism, romanticism, and reductionism in the study of the peoples of the Third World. Moreover, through the training of students such as Melville Herskovits he helped to prepare a generation of scholars who would begin to forge a more rational and balanced vision of the African past.

For scholars who were less fastidious than Boas the concept of the "primitive" provided an open invitation to theoretical excess. A number of intellectual avenues presented themselves as logical lines of advance, and among them the discipline of analytical psychology seemed especially promising. Unfortunately, the earliest efforts in this direction produced a retrograde (and rather bizarre) result. In 1931, when Charles Roberts Aldrich offered his analysis of *The Primitive Mind and Modern Civilization*, Carl Jung felt able to endorse "his sane and balanced opinions" and praise his "book as one of the most vivid and clear presentations of the primitive mind in its relation to civilized psychology."[26] A closer reading, however, might tend to repudiate his judgment. In framing his subject Aldrich came down on the side of Boas (as opposed to Levy-Bruhl), although his emphasis on the role of the evolutionary process in shaping human behavior placed him in a notably different school. Also, like Veblen's "earliest man," his prototypical "savage" displayed a natural tendency toward peaceful and cooperative behavior.[27] His paradigm of the primitive, however, ultimately attributed more to instinct than to intellect, and his savage, while noble, was also notably ineffectual.

In tracing "the course of man's psychic evolution," Aldrich placed great weight on the concept of "biomorality." This principle was based on the rather astonishing premise that "subconscious urges to cooperation are found among various animals, and plants, which are mutually helpful."[28] His "savage," like Veblen's "barbarian," was destined to pass through a stage in which his healthy primal impulses are eclipsed by baser tendencies. In this case, however, the man who emerges from this psychic divide is a man who is utterly transformed. He has not rediscovered an earlier behavioral heritage: instead, he has evolved to a higher and distinctive level of consciousness. As Aldrich explained it, man begins with unconsciousness, when he is biomoral simply because the instinct to cooperate is stronger than any other instinct: he becomes imperfectly conscious, whereupon anti-social, egotistical urges appear, and make it necessary for the group to establish and enforce norms of conduct, or conventions; and more and more he will approach full consciousness, full individuation, and full individual self-control and responsibility. As he does this—as the race itself becomes adult—the necessity for being morally controlled from without will progressively disappear.[29]

Whether "consciously" or "unconsciously," Aldrich provided a psychological variant of Marx's "withering away of the state." The analytical road to this utopian conclusion was an uneven one, however, especially in terms of the portrayal of his hypothetical primitives. Aldrich found much in the behavior of "savages" which was laudable: indeed, the instinct of "biomorality" was very much in evidence in their daily affairs.[30] Nevertheless, they were notably lacking in the instinct of workmanship and industriousness which was so prominent in Veblen's formulation. In fact, Aldrich maintained that "people of low culture have a most enviable capacity for being completely idle, a divine laziness that many of us have lost. They do not fatigue themselves with thought when they can avoid it (and they usually find some way to avoid thinking)."[31] The male of the species was especially given to idleness, his efforts largely being confined to "tasks that require much strength to be exerted during comparatively brief periods—fighting, hunting dangerous beasts and the like." Aside from this, he engaged himself in activities "such as making things with his hands and decorating them—weapons and the like," toolmaking apparently being little more than a recreational exercise for the whimsical primitive. Aldrich also suggested that "a very great element of amusement enters into many savage religious ceremonies," their capacity for entertainment being developed to a remarkably high degree.[32] It was painfully apparent that Aldrich, with his sweeping generalizations and minimal recourse to specific cultural examples, was content with an approach which was diametrically opposed to the more rigorous strategy of Boas.

There were other difficulties with his "psychological" approach. In explaining the concept of "biomorality" he sometimes resorted to the crudest sort of analogy between animal and human behavior. While direct references to Africa were few and far between in *The Primitive Mind and Modern Civilization*, those which did occur were casual and predictably reductionistic. In attempting to explain the evolutionary roots of "good manners" he noted that

> Even animals have their ritual ways of approaching each other. This is very obvious in the case of dogs. The wagging tail and lifted leg disarm suspicion and are an assurance of friendly intentions. When two savages belonging to different African groups draw near to each other each stops, lays his weapons on the ground, and squats. . . . Savage salutations are very courteous.

> Just as the dog ritualizes an action that contains the seeds of combat and danger so does the partly conscious savage.[33]

Such analogies obviously did nothing to advance a rational, historically based appreciation of the African experience. Taken literally, Aldrich's statement might suggest that, in certain non-Western colonies, notices in public facilities barring the presence "of dogs and natives" were inspired by a scientific understanding of implicit evolutionary relationships. Clearly, *The Primitive Mind and Modern Civilization* did convey an important (if inadvertent) message to the reader who was perceptive enough to recognize it. In the final analysis, Aldrich had succeeded in demonstrating the extent to which a psychological and ahistorical study of "primitive" societies was fraught with intellectual danger.

While Boas had demonstrated the essential role of history in the study of particular societies, the persistent belief in a universal process of "cultural evolution" had not been banished from the anthropological field. It would be revived (albeit in confusing form) by Leslie White, who, "in agreement with cultural evolutionists of an earlier period," accepted "the thesis of the evolution of human culture and of natural laws of cultural development through fixed stages."[34] Unfortunately, his particular contribution to this theoretical school, an attempt to distinguish "culture history" from "cultural evolution," did nothing to clarify the issues under debate. "History," as he defined it, was a subordinate and secondary means of understanding the human experience.

> History is concerned with particular events, unique in time and place. Evolution is concerned with classes of things and events, regardless of particular time and place. To be sure, the evolutionist process always take place somewhere and in a temporal continuum, but the particular time and the particular place are not significant. It is the temporal sequence of forms that counts.[35]

Such an approach was particularly congenial to an abstract concept of the primitive as a particular "stage" in a "temporal sequence of forms."

Indeed, since White himself boldly proclaimed in *The Evolution of Culture* that "the *theory* of evolution set forth in this work does not differ one whit in principle from that expressed in Tylor's *Anthropology* in 1881,"[36] it certainly was not surprising that he found no real need to challenge the terminology which had informed this earlier work. The survival of the "primitive"—in this case, as a convenient category for social scientists—was not in serious doubt when White assumed the offensive in the 1940s and 1950s. Nevertheless, it is safe to say that his efforts gave its enthusiasts a new lease on life in the period following the Second World War.

According to White, life in the "earlier" phases of cultural evolution was far from nasty and brutish. Admittedly, for many, life was short, but there were collective compensations: in fact, "the elimination of the weak and the biologically unfit by sickness and disease tended in many instances to produce a stock that won admiration and praise from European travelers for its physical excellence and even beauty."[37] For the (surviving) primitive, life was gloriously free from the social burdens which characterized the American experience at midcentury:

> warm, substantial bonds of kinship united man with man. There were no lords or vassals, serfs or slaves. . . . There were no mortgages, rents, debtors, or usurers. . . . Food was not adulterated with harmful substances in order to make money out of human misery. There were no time clocks, no bosses or overseers, in primitive society, and a two-week vacation was not one's quota of freedom for a year.[38]

Despite their technological limitations, our distant ancestors basked in the warmth of social systems "characterized by liberty, equality, and fraternity" (with nary a Robespierre in sight). When viewed in its totality, their daily existence was "unquestionably more congenial to the human primate's nature, and more compatible with his psychic needs and aspirations, than any other that has ever been realized in any of the cultures subsequent to the Agricultural Revolution, including our own society today."[39] In White's view, cultural evolution and psychological alienation had proceeded hand-in-hand: effectivity had been gained but authenticity had been lost, a rather dubious exchange for mankind.

White was not especially concerned with the survival of the primitive in the present, since his major interest was the process of cultural evolution itself. In his scheme, particular historical instances, however interesting, were merely secondary details, a diversion from his primary theoretical agenda. Nevertheless, certain (unspecified)

African cases did retain an explanatory value since they represented "transitional stages between primitive and civil society." From his evolutionary perspective, the biological was a more suitable idiom than the historical when approaching African civilization:

> a monotreme is an animal that, in the course of biological evolution, acquired the mammalian faculty of suckling the young while at the same time it has retained the old reptilian faculty of laying eggs. In the same way, some of the Negro nations of Africa have acquired, in the course of sociocultural evolution, some of the institutions of civil society, such as a king, while at the same time they have retained some of the institutions of primitive society, such as clan organization.[40]

Apparently, the cultural anthropologist from the University of Michigan was suggesting that acolytes venturing to Africa in search of "authentic" primitive societies might be in for a disappointment. It appeared that the devoted western scholar was more likely to encounter an African who was suspended in the limbo of an evolutionary moment, the bearer of traditions neither fully lost nor fully realized, the involuntary resident of a cultural halfway house. Obviously, such "transitional" societies were no longer "authentic"; having partially evolved within their African embryo they were slouching toward Ann Arbor, struggling to be born. Regretfully, with setbacks to the spirit such as the invention of agriculture and the emergence of "civil society," the golden age of primitive brotherhood—in Africa, and throughout the world—had been forever lost.

During the 1950s, the social issue of race became far more urgent than the abstract question of the primitive. Nevertheless, the following decade witnessed a dramatic resurgence of interest in the utopian promise of a more fulfilling and humane way of life. With the onset of war in Southeast Asia and domestic racial violence at home a "new left" joined the old in launching an impassioned attack on the evils of American capitalism and materialism. Thus engaged, it was not surprising that some would turn to an invented vision of the "primitive" for an alternative social charter. William R. Beer, in his introduction to Pascal Bruckner's *The Tears of the White Man*, has identified the essentials of this quest, a point of departure which has not disappeared from the contemporary intellectual scene.

> Peasants and primitives are seen as somehow closer to nature and to one another then we are. The frippery and complexity of our modern societies contrast with the noble simplicity of their lives. To redeem ourselves as individuals,

we must try to be like them; to redeem our societies, we must try to make them pre-modern, more organic. This involves pilgrimages—the word is Bruckner's and precisely appropriate—to somewhere appropriate in the Third World, where one picks up a little savvy, and perhaps a costume or artifact.[41]

Not all of these spiritual journeys were undertaken by laymen, however. Anthropologists, with their intellectual focus on preindustrial society, were especially well qualified to invest this crusade with an aura of scientific legitimacy. While many resisted this temptation, a dedicated minority within the discipline eagerly embraced its pursuit. "Committed" social scientists were anxious to join the battle, and, with a wealth of symbolic conventions to draw upon, it was not surprising that Africans emerged as their primary models in a determined search for the contemporary "noble savage."

This movement certainly had its eloquent spokesmen. In 1974, the anthropologist Stanley Diamond published a collection of essays entitled *In Search of the Primitive*. To his credit, he insisted that this project was "not, and cannot be, a question of grafting primitive forms on civilized structures or . . . of retreating into the past." It was also "not a question of regaining lost paradises or savage nobility, neither of which ever existed in the manner imputed to their authors." Instead, the objective was to "conceptualize contemporary forms that will reunite man with his past, reconcile the primitive with the civilized, making progress without distortion theoretically possible, or, at least, enabling us to experience the qualities that primitive peoples routinely display."[42] Although he was careful to qualify his agenda, the ultimate direction of his analysis was apparent. By embracing the "primitive-civilized" dichotomy he opted for the assumptions and passions of Rousseau over the cautious and measured approach of Boas. In this interpretation the "primitive" was real and absolute and distinctive, and its empirical pursuit was transformed into an inspired celebration of the human spirit.

For Diamond, the "primitive" was a concept which was capable of concrete definition. In approaching this problem he was careful to consider its historical dimensions, if in a rather cursory fashion.[43] He also outlined the general criteria for this stage of development which, broadly and partially stated, included the presence of communalistic economies, a kin or tribal (as opposed to "political") form of social organization, traditional (rather than "political" or "secular") leadership roles, the primacy of "custom" in the absence of codified law, a high degree of cultural integration, an extended range of individual participation in the overall "social economy,"

and an inherent tendency toward systemic stability and "social con-
servatism." Moreover, at the level of the individual psyche, the
authentic "primitive" was supposedly distinguished by his "concrete, existential, and nominalistic" mode of thinking as well as by
a personality that was remarkable for its effective degree of "individuation" and "personalism."[44] Unfortunately, while this comprehensive set of characteristics and dichotomies may have seemed
plausible in the abstract, it would prove somewhat less convincing
when applied to specific societies at specific times.

Predictably, Africa would be the laboratory in which this paradigm would be tested. Since Diamond was himself an Africanist, it
was understandable that the continent would serve as his primary
analytical arena. However, when deployed as a framework for interpreting an earlier field experience, the conceptual limitations of his
"primitive-civilized dichotomy" became painfully apparent. In his
case study of the "primitive," a portrayal of the Anaguta of the
Nigerian plateau, he freely acknowledged that his subjects lived in
close proximity to the city of Jos, an important mining center.
Undaunted, he then resorted to the dubious expedient of describing
their society as "a sort of suburban primitive culture, buried in its
rocky habitat, difficult of access, yet only a few miles as the crow
flies from the most Europeanized city in Northern Nigeria."[45] However "difficult of access" from this local urban center, it was less
than credible to suggest that this people could have continued to
subsist in a state of splendid isolation in the waning days of the
British colonial state. This does not deny that the Anaguta may
have been only marginally integrated into the regional economy and
the colonial political system. Nevertheless, Diamond's interpretation was disturbingly reminiscent of the popular vision of "mysterious tribes" living in "remote jungles" or "extinct volcanoes" that had
been favored in the adventure fiction of an earlier era. By any realistic standard, the Anaguta could not have been living in a social,
economic, political, and historical void, a "no man's land" of the
anthropological imagination.

Despite this obvious complication, Diamond, who was convinced
that "there are profound qualitative distinctions between primitive
and civilized peoples," felt able to proclaim their total and positive
realization within his "primitive suburban" culture.[46] He noted that
the Anaguta elders possessed "the most expressive, most fully
human faces I have ever seen. They made me feel pity and shame for
the cosmetic, contrived, acquisitive, vain, uniform, despairing and
empty faces that are familiar even among the elderly in the cities of
the West."[47] Likewise, he was able to celebrate the physical constitution of the Anaguta who, unselfconsciously, "most of the time . . .
exposed most of their bodies." Admittedly, "their uncovered bodies

were not pretty, either cosmetically or in the sense of having achieved the Greco-Roman ideal of physical perfection. But they were tough, graceful, and used. There were no gross, distorted, or repellent bodies among them; each displayed a natural proportion of working parts and no withered functions."[48] Even if these assertions—and the ideology which informed them—could be accepted in a literal sense, they raised a host of questions about the intervention (or nonintervention) of the state which were never addressed by the author. Apparently, what had withered was the author's sense of scientific detachment and his prior disclaimer of romantic intent. Embedded in his text was a vocabulary of imagery, assumptions, and stereotypes which would have been congenial and familiar to the reader of (the more liberally inclined) nineteenth-century traveler's accounts. Apparently, the varied tides of cross-cultural contact and conflict, regional commerce, *jihad*, the colonial state, and the proximate influence of international finance capital had passed the Anaguta by and left them to flourish, undisturbed, in the pristine fastness of their primitive Shangri-la, a fitting exhibit in the museum of the ethnographic present.

Even as an earlier generation of novelists was attracted by the romance of the primitive, a number of contemporary American poets have taken their inspiration from Diamond and his impassioned quest for primal authenticity. In 1986, Sherman Paul offered a volume of criticism entitled *In Search of the Primitive*, a "rereading" of the poetry of David Antin, Jerome Rothenberg, and Gary Snyder which was also a tribute to the anthropologist who had reinvigorated that search. Diamond's influence on their work had been substantial: indeed, as Paul noted in his preface, "his thought has directly contributed to the work of Antin, Rothenberg, and Snyder—in fact, *Alcheringa*, the magazine with which all have been associated, reprinted a portion of Diamond's title essay in its second issue." Paul stressed that Diamond's objective was not to return to an imagined past but "to teach us to spare the primitive and incorporate what we may still learn from it in our present way of life."[49] Nevertheless, it was obvious that the "contemporary" primitive was to be the teacher and host for western pilgrims intent upon a symbolic journey of enlightenment. Ironically, "primitive" men and women had been elevated to the role of missionaries in reluctant service to the alienated intellectuals of the West. From an artistic standpoint this was not surprising since, as Paul explained, "the search for the primitive has become one of the notable projects of recent poetry—poetry since World War II—though the primitive, a legacy of Romanticism, has been a conspicuous element of the avant-garde arts throughout this century."[50] Indeed, the dramatic impact of the "primitive" on the "modern" (in the world of art) has been forcefully illustrated by Marianna Torgovnick in her recent study of this phenomenon, *Gone Primitive.*[51]

The concept of the primitive has also persisted in the arena of literary criticism, most notably in the work of Fredric Jameson. In his seminal work, *The Political Unconscious*, Jameson proclaims that "only Marxism can give us an adequate account of the essential *mystery* of the cultural past, which, like Tiresias drinking the blood, is momentarily returned to life and allowed once more to speak, and to declare its long-forgotten message in surroundings utterly alien to it."[52] Jameson presents an intriguing estimate of the relationship between art and society, although he does so in language which is hard going for anyone not versed in the jargon of his particular field. Yet, within this same work, Jameson goes beyond this level of interpretation since, for him, even Marxism is ultimately a "strategy of containment." In his study, *Jameson, Althusser, Marx: An Introduction to the Political Unconscious*, William Dowling describes these strategies as "a means at once of denying those intolerable contradictions that lie hidden beneath the social surface . . . and of constructing on the very ground cleared by such a denial a substitute truth that renders existence at least partly bearable." Individual works of art and literature, ideological acts in and of themselves, are seen to offer a measure of "structural limitation and ideological closure on the aesthetic level," thus constituting an "attempt of art as such to shut out or deny the intolerable reality of History."[53] From this perspective, then, these abstract creations of the human intellect function to "contain," distort, or obscure reality rather than illuminate it, and to alleviate, at least in part, the trauma of an individual consciousness cast adrift in the sea of alienation which is the modern world.

Nevertheless, from the imposing barricade of his own particular "strategy of containment," Jameson is able to look back to a happier era of human existence. Indeed, he reserves a significant role in his theory for what he refers to, with a notable lack of precision, as "preclass society (what is called tribal or segmentary society, or in the Marxian tradition, primitive communism)" or alternatively, "primitive communism or tribal society (the horde)."[54] As Dowling observes, what is especially crucial about this concept "for Jameson as a student of culture is the mode of *perception*, the way of being in the world, that primitive communism may be imagined to represent."[55] For it was only within the context of such an "unfallen social reality"—whose structural and experiential base corresponded to the earliest stages of prehistory—that the collective mind was able to function in lieu of a purely individual consciousness. Moreover, it was only within such "primitive" societies that the phenomenon of "interior fragmentation" had yet to take place, "a process through which the senses become estranged from one another and begin to function autonomously."[56] Jameson can only lament the consequences of this relentless force, which achieved an irresistible momentum with the onset of capitalism. Indeed, the end result of this process of rationalization, or "reification," as he calls it, is the contemporary state in which "the quantifying, 'rational' parts of the psyche are . . . developed, indeed overdeveloped, while the more archaic functions—the senses, or certain types of thinking—are allowed to vegetate in a kind of psychic backwater."[57] Realistically, given the global reach of modern capitalism and the complex currents of cultural and economic contact which long preceded it, it seems less than credible that any society on the face of the earth (even if one accepts Jameson's analysis) could have escaped a significant level of "reification" and persisted on a course outside the bounds of history, within the practical boundaries of prehistory. Nevertheless, there is always the ready human inventory of Africa, and in a reference which is all the more telling for its cursory, even casual, nature, Jameson is able to point to Colin Turnbull's study of the BaMbuti pygmies of the Ituri forest as "the most powerful contemporary vision of primitive communism."[58]

Jameson's cryptic reference to *The Forest People* is rife with ambiguity. In positing a sort of proto class consciousness, with the natural world as a sort of primal class enemy, he maintains that Turnbull's work "suggests that the culture of prepolitical society organizes itself around the external threat of the nonhuman or of nature, in the form of the rain forest, conceived as the overarching spirit of the world."[59] While he accurately echoes Turnbull in asserting the centrality of the forest in BaMbuti cosmology, his implication that this environment was perceived as a threatening or adversarial force is both misleading and inaccurate. In point of fact, Turnbull asserts that the BaMbuti "believe in a benevolent deity or supernatural power which they identify with the forest. To this they owe as much respect and affection and consideration as they owe to their own parents, and from it they can expect the same in return."[60] Moreover, a closer reading of this English anthropologist reveals that the concerns of these eminently political people have long extended well beyond the confines of their immediate physical environment.

Turnbull waxes lyrical in his description of the forest and the people who inhabit it, and, like Diamond, he might be accused of abandoning science in favor of sentiment. There is a crucial difference, however: Turnbull does not attempt to divorce his subjects from their historical and social context, and his narrative is informed by a constant tension between the ideal and the actual, the romantic vision he would like to recreate and the disappointing reality he feels obligated to report. The reader soon discovers that the BaMbuti did not possess a culture unsullied by external contacts and influence: far from it, since they spoke "dialects of three major Negro languages. The Pygmies seemed to have lost their own language, due to the process of acculturation, though traces remained."[61] Accordingly, it is not surprising that Turnbull's portrait is as much an analysis of the BaMbuti's long-standing, complex and extensive relationship with the settled agriculturalists of the forest fringe as it is an ethnological chronicle of their life in the Ituri.

Indeed, for the adventurous reader who has come to Turnbull's Congo "in search of the primitive" there are further disappointments in store beyond the bend in the river. The author had been especially anxious to witness the "molimo" ceremony, a central and recurrent episode in the BaMbuti's spiritual life. In the glossary, he describes the molimo as a "ritual performed at times of great crisis . . . consisting primarily of songs sung nightly by the men. It is also the name given to the musical instrument, a long trumpet, usually of wood, that plays an important part in the ritual."[62] Unfortunately, Turnbull was in for a great shock when the critical ethnographic moment finally arrived and the sacred molimo trumpet was taken from its hiding place.

> I do not know exactly what I expected, but I knew a little about molimo trumpets and that they were sometimes made out of bamboo. I suppose I had expected an object elaborately carved, decorated with patterns full of ritual significance and symbolism, something sacred, to be revered, the very sight or touch of which might be thought of as dangerous. I felt that I had a right, in the heart of the tropical rain forest, to expect something wonderful and exotic. But now I saw that the instrument which produced such a surprisingly rude sound, shattering the stillness as it shattered my illusions, was not made of bamboo or wood, and it certainly was not carved or decorated in any way. It was a length of metal drainpipe, neatly threaded at each end, though somewhat bent in the middle. The second trumpet was just the same, shining and sanitary, but only half the length.[63]

Turnbull wondered "how it was that for the molimo, which was so sacred to them, they should use water piping stolen from roadside construction gangs, instead of using the traditional materials." Their response was practical and direct: "What does it matter what the molimo is made of? This one makes a great sound, and, besides, it does not rot like wood. It is much trouble to make a wooden one, and then you have to make another."[64] Turnbull, an honest and open-minded observer, was not dissuaded by this revelation. Had he come to the Ituri with the sole objective of finding a people who had preserved their "primitive authenticity," a people who had escaped the currents of the modern world and maintained their prehistoric integrity, he would have been forced to abandon his quest in despair (or alter his findings to fit a preconceived script). Admittedly, his central implication that his subjects were able to shed the cultural influence of the outside world and assume their true persona when they returned to the forest is less than credible in light of his actual evidence. Nevertheless, in spite of this wishful concession to the romantic, he went on to produce a perceptive account which did justice to the complexities of his subject.

Had he examined the subject more closely, Jameson might have been amazed at the extent to which his primitive communists of the Ituri had lapsed from their state of Edenic grace. Turnbull was familiar with the region from a previous trip, and when he returned to the site of Camp Putnam in the late 1950s he discovered "an ugly modern motel, built by an enterprising Belgian who had hoped to attract tourists," as well as a government hunting station.[65] Camp Putnam, the nucleus of this expanded settlement, possessed an important history of its own. In a footnote, Turnbull explained that

> Patrick Putnam first went to the Belgian Congo in 1927 to do field work for Harvard University. Apart from one or two brief return visits to the United States he remained there until his death at the end of 1953. At Camp Putnam he established a dispensary and a leper colony, turning his home into a guest house to help pay the expenses of his hospital work.[66]

In his medical work, Putnam has left an honorable legacy. Nevertheless, devoted advocates of the "primitive-civilized" dichotomy might be less than enamored with the social and cultural consequences of his activities among the BaMbuti. In 1939, *American Magazine* published an account of "The Great White Chief of the Congo." In this piece, Jerome Beatty breathlessly announced that "way down there to Hellangone in Darkest Africa, 60 miles north of the equator, among cannibals, witch doctors, and leopard-men, is the darnedest Dude Ranch and Adventure Factory in the world . . . conducted by Patrick Tracy Lowell Putnam of Boston and New York." Putnam's neighbors were described as "rare, raw, black, fascinating, and usually friendly specimens of savagery," and "some of the most interesting whites in the world—millionaires and missionaries, anthropologists and authors, explorers and elephant hunters—[came] to visit them."[67] For Beatty, "the exciting part of Africa [was] not its animals, which are familiar to every child who ever went to a zoo, but its hundreds of thousands of wild and weird people," and Camp Putnam served as a magnificent theme park for those select devotees of "primitive humanity" who could afford to pay the fare.

> For $12 a day, to pay for their food, Putnam brings 50 to 75 pygmy men, women, and children to live at the edge of the forest, 200 yards from your guesthouse. As easily as though you were walking from the 18th hole to the locker-room, you join them and learn more about these wild people than you know about your next-door neighbors at home. They build their huts, invite you to crawl into them, gather wild honey in the top of trees 100 feet high, shoot passing monkeys with poisoned arrows.[68]

If this was not enough, Putnam's camp was also invaluable to filmmakers who needed a cast of "untouched" pygmies for an "authentic" backdrop in their tales of African adventure. Apparently, many BaMbuti had been reduced to willing extras in a fictionalized version of their own culture. Beatty reported that "for additional bribes of chicken and cloth, hundreds will come to work for a moving-picture director like the best troupers in Hollywood." Citing the example of "a recent movie of an explorer's death-defying adventures in Darkest Africa," he noted that "like almost all good pygmy shots, those scenes were made at Putnam's, well rehearsed before they were photographed."[69]

It would seem that filmmaking was becoming something of a growth industry in the "remote and uncivilized" Ituri. In 1946, when the American explorer and producer Lewis Cotlow arrived in the region to shoot some of the scenes for his latest exercise in cinematic understatement, *Savage Splendor*, he found a large potential cast that was ready to do his bidding. With scrupulous (and predictable) regard for the symbolic conventions, Cotlow noted that on the night of his arrival he "heard the drums, and knew that the message was going out that the *bwana bukuba* had arrived, the white man bearing many gifts. . . . By the fifth day at least five hundred Pygmies had established themselves in and near the big clearing—far more than I could possibly use. . . ."[70] While filming "routine Pygmy activities" did not demand any special arrangements, Cotlow had "a few more exciting events specially staged," a "fight between Pygmy clans" being the most dramatic.

> The forest people, especially the older men who remem-
> bered, seized on the idea eagerly and set about planning the
> "war". . . . The acting of the Pygmies was almost frightening
> when we shot the sequence. The happy, carefree little folk of
> the forest suddenly became vicious and savage warriors,
> bent on spilling blood . . . they tore at each other, shooting
> their arrows with what looked like fair accuracy. But not an
> arrow hit a man; they all sailed cleanly over everyone's
> head—although a couple came rather near me.[71]

On his return in 1954-55 to film *Zanzabuku*, Cotlow, armed with
"an assistant producer and four other cameramen [and] a Dodge
Power Wagon and truck," diligently arranged some further spontaneous expressions of Pygmy culture for his potential American
audience. He was particularly determined to film the construction
of a genuine Pygmy bridge made of vines. Again, the cast was willing if a bit bemused:

> Pygmies were assembled, given pay, and briefed on the pro-
> ject. They seemed agreeable, but I heard a few of them mut-
> ter, "bumbafu! bumbafu!" while shaking their heads. Bill
> Spees [a resident missionary] explained it. "When someone
> tries to do something that is difficult and daring and not
> very sensible, he is bumbafu. These pygmies don't need a
> bridge here, because their camp and the village of their
> Negro masters and their hunting ground are all on this
> side. . . . So you are bumbafu—'a crazy white man.'"[72]

Cotlow was perhaps not aware of the long (and increasingly
extensive) experience of the Pygmies with such *bumbafu*, which
stretched as far back as the 1880s when Henry Morton Stanley
slashed his way through the Ituri during the Emin Pasha relief
expedition. In self-defense, by this time they surely had developed
their own particular version of cultural anthropology.

Turnbull should not have been surprised at his BaMbuti hosts
when, in a debate over whether the elima ceremony should be held
in the village or the forest, a "wily old grandfather" argued that "the
village was better as they might be able to make money out of
tourists who would pay to see them dance."[73] Apparently, the concept of the primitive had become a valuable commodity on the
Epulu River a full decade before Turnbull's first arrival; and Jameson's "primitive communists" had adopted a New Economic Policy
long before the literary critic encountered the anthropologist's
inspirational work. Still, the ideological market which focused on
the Ituri, and places like it, would persist, and expand, as the western need for an alternative vision of humanity grew even more
acute after the Second World War.

Along with the pygmies, the "bushmen" of the Kalahari assumed a special place in the western vision of primitive Africa. In this instance as well, popular and scientific interest were far from mutually exclusive: the boundaries between ethnography and travel account and reality and imagination were less than absolute. The work of Isaac Schapera (particularly his 1930 survey of *The Khoisan Peoples of South Africa*) brought these forgotten peoples to the attention of social scientists and suggested their value as a compelling object of study.[74] In 1958 the South African writer Laurens Van Der Post attracted a significant audience with his romantic portrayal of *The Lost World of the Kalahari*, an image which was reinforced a year later by the publication of *The Harmless People*, an interpretation of the world of the San by an American observer, Elizabeth Marshall Thomas. The titles of these books were revealing in themselves: in their suggestion of timelessness and isolation (Van Der Post) and the survival of a distinctive and exemplary social order (Thomas) they announced the central themes which constitute the western mythology of the "bushman."[75]

By this time the scientific community had already rediscovered the "bushmen." As hunters and gatherers who managed to subsist in a harsh and forbidding environment they held a special fascination for social anthropologists and students of prehistory. In a 1966 symposium at the University of Chicago on "Man the Hunter," George Peter Murdock voiced the common concern that there were only a precious few peoples on the face of the earth who still followed this economic pattern, "nearly all of them under markedly altered conditions." Murdock urged that "it is time—indeed, long past time—that we take stock of these dwindling remnants, for it is only among them that we can still study at first hand the modes of life and types of cultural adjustments that prevailed throughout most of human history."[76] In his global inventory of these scattered survivors he noted that the majority of the Bushmen had "undergone intensive acculturation" and were no longer viable candidates for such a survey. On the other hand, he reported that "about 5,000 of them still pursue essentially their aboriginal nomadic mode of life" and that recent studies had suggested that "field work of the highest quality is still possible among them."[77] Richard B. Lee of Harvard University had already done an intensive study of the !Kung Bushmen of the Dobe region of Botswana and, over the next decade, a succession of other researchers would follow in his wake. The quest to unravel "the lessons of the bushmen" had begun in earnest.

While the students of this enterprise offered obligatory words of caution, most were convinced that the !Kung (and related peoples) could provide some important hints regarding man's social and economic behavior during the distant stages of prehistory. Crucial to this assumption was the notion that these "archaic" people retained a way of life that had defied the dramatic forces of change which swept southern Africa during the last three centuries. Nothing could be further from the truth, as Edwin N. Wilmsen has demonstrated in his brilliant reconstruction of the history of the Kalahari, *Land Filled with Flies*. In an examination of the archaeological and linguistic record, he establishes that the "isolated" San had actually been in contact with Bantu-speaking immigrants from the time of their arrival in the region, and it was these newcomers who emerged as the ultimate beneficiaries of the ensuing cultural exchange with their "primitive" hosts. Wilmsen notes that "several independent lines of evidence agree that proto-Herero-speaking Bantu peoples entered the western part of southern Africa roughly 2,000 years ago, where they found Khoisan-speaking herders." Moreover, he reminds us that the linguist Christopher Ehret made the case "twenty years ago that these Bantu-speakers obtained cattle, or at least a cattle-keeping vocabulary, from Khoisan herders in this region."[78] In sum, the notion that the Kalahari San had been confined to hunting and gathering "from time immemorial" has no real basis in fact. Moreover, he points to nineteenth-century traveler's accounts which confirm that many of the people who later would be classified as "bushmen" still possessed substantial herds of cattle. Obviously, something was missing from the equation: a closer look had revealed that an "ancient way of life" was actually a recent historical development.

Wilmsen provides the answer to this puzzle. The San of the Kalahari had been subordinated and dispossessed. The emergence of the Tswana as a dominant regional force during the nineteenth century initiated this process and the intrusion of the colonial state (in Botswana and Namibia) had carried it to its logical conclusion. For a brief period the San played an important role as hunters and guides during a commercial boom which began in the 1850s, a development which allowed them to preserve a limited degree of autonomy. However, by 1890 the wildlife resources of the region had been decimated by an uncontrolled slaughter and the European market for the Kalahari's primary exports—ivory and ostrich feathers—had experienced a significant decline.[79] The ensuing transformation was rapid and dramatic. As Wilmsen explains, "during the previous decades the entire region had pulsed with activity; everybody had had a piece of the everyday action, no matter how that worked against long-term interests. Now the region seemed as empty and remote as it was later conceived to be."[80] Also, by this time, accounts of cattle-holding San had ceased to appear: Tswana expropriation (and a rinderpest epizootic at the end of the century) had brought that chapter of their history to an end. Some of these people found work as herders for their Tswana overlords, but

> the remainder—those whose labor was not immediately needed, and these were not only San peoples—were now without direct means to participate in regional economies. They were relegated to the more inaccessible and difficult ecological zones of the Kalahari, falling deeper and deeper into foraging, which had become a condition of poverty in the overall structure of society.[81]

By 1900, the San had been forced to the physical and economic margins of the Kalahari—and their "primitive" and "primeval" way of life, the "world of the 'bushman,'" had assumed the appearance which would be celebrated by a later generation of writers and anthropologists.

For American social scientists, the 1960s and early 1970s was a period of revision and renewal, a time when racial conflict at home and a pointless war abroad intensified the quest for a new social order. The American dream seemed to be dying a natural death in places like My Lai and Watts, Kent State and Khe Sanh. Anthropology, as a warehouse of cultures and an incubus of theory, assumed a greater relevance as the search for an alternative vision of humanity once again emerged as an urgent intellectual pursuit. In such a climate, it was not surprising that, like "the forest people," the "harmless people" of the Kalahari would be thought to hold some answers—even, perhaps, *the* answer—to the dilemma of modern man.

In 1963, Richard Lee began his field research among the !Kung Bushmen of the Dobe area of Botswana. Noting that this region only received "six to nine inches of rainfall a year," he maintained that "it is precisely the unattractiveness of their homeland that has kept the !Kung isolated from extensive contact with their agricultural and pastoral neighbors." In the next paragraph, however, he points out that the 466 Bushmen in the district "share the area with some 340 Bantu pastoralists largely of the Herero and Tswana tribes," a fact which brings his definition of "isolation" into serious question.[82] During his ensuing research Lee went on to make what appeared to be a remarkable discovery. In spite of their modest level of technology and the foreboding environment of the region the Dobe !Kung lived a life of relative ease which was largely free of material (or least nutritional) want. According to his calculations, these accomplished hunter-gatherers devoted only "twelve to nineteen hours a week to getting food." This allowed a generous and well-balanced pattern of "steady work and steady leisure" which was "maintained throughout the year." Moreover, the productivity of this system was more than adequate: his research established that individual daily "food output exceeds energy requirements by 165 calories and 33 grams of protein." From this, he suggested that "one can tentatively conclude that even a modest subsistence effort of two or three days work per week is enough to provide an adequate diet for the !Kung Bushmen."[83]

Apparently, poverty was indeed relative, and forceful relegation to the most marginal of environments ironically had its advantages. For Lee, the story of the !Kung contained an important moral for modern man: the reassuring notion that "a truly communal life," which was "often dismissed as 'a utopian ideal,'" was clearly possible. There was room for hope since "a sharing way of life . . . [had] actually existed in many parts of the world and over long periods of time."[84]

In recent years, Lee's evaluation of the !Kung San economy has been called into question by his fellow anthropologists. In a summary and critique of his work, Barry Isaac has noted that the prevailing cultural climate helped to ensure a positive response to his initial findings. "Peace, Prosperity in Food, Ease of Life, Equality of the Sexes—this was an ethnographic case tailor-made for the late 1960s and the 1970s."[85] Not surprisingly, Lee's conclusions had a significant impact on the assumptions of other ethnologists:

> During the 1970's, in fact, many archaeologists eagerly followed ethnologists in their concerted San-itizing of our thinking about nomadic hunter-gatherers—wiping both subdisciplines almost clean of thinking and models that were at variance with the !Kung San case as reported by Richard Lee. . . . The San-itation phenomenon would not have been seriously harmful . . . if we had exercised better judgment. Lest I appear to be pointing only at others, let me confess that my own thinking and teaching were San-itized during the 1970's, too. (To make a clean breast of it, I had previously been Nanook-ed—but that's another story).[86]

Lee's early work was soon followed by an even more ambitious vindication of the foraging way of life. In 1972, in his treatise on *Stone Age Economics*, the anthropologist Marshall Sahlins proclaimed that the hunter-gatherers of the Paleolithic should be recognized as "the original affluent society." Apparently, prehistoric societies had anticipated the wisdom of later Oriental sages—they had adopted "a Zen road to affluence, departing from premises somewhat different from our own: that human material wants are finite and few, and technical means unchanging but on the whole adequate." The moral was inspiring if somewhat inconsistent: by "adopting the Zen strategy, a people can enjoy an unparalleled material plenty—with a low standard of living."[87] Sahlins readily admitted that the conditions in which modern hunter-gatherers were forced to live were not directly comparable with those of their economic ancestors. He freely acknowledged that "the surviving food collectors, as a class, are displaced persons. They represent the Paleolithic disenfranchised, occupying marginal haunts untypical of the mode of production." Nevertheless, from a theoretical standpoint at least, he was encouraged by the existing evidence. Considering that these peoples had been banished to the world's harshest environments, their "current circumstances" amounting to a "supreme test, all the more extraordinary, then, [were] the . . . reports of their performance."[88]

The record of the "Bushmen" as reported by Lee (and others) was especially impressive. Severed from their recent history, rendered "affluent" by their very disenfranchisement, the !Kung displayed, according to Sahlins, "that characteristic Paleolithic rhythm of a day or two on, a day or two off—the latter passed desultorily in camp."[89] In reviewing the cultural achievements of the !Kung—and those few surviving peoples like them—he did not hesitate to offer a dramatic conclusion. In Sahlins' opinion, "this much history can always be rescued from existing hunters: the 'economic problem' is easily solvable by paleolithic techniques. But then, it was not until culture neared the height of its material achievements that it erected a shrine to the Unattainable: Infinite needs."[90] In a time of troubles the social scientist had gone "back to Africa" and discovered that poverty and powerlessness were not only virtues to be admired but alternative visions of the human condition to be celebrated, even emulated. Sahlins also underscored the !Kung's satisfaction with their hunting-gathering way of life by citing an observation by one of Lee's informants: "'Why should we plant, when there are so many mongomongo nuts in the world?'" a statement which conjured up a vision of Edenic contentment.[91]

Unfortunately, the historical process which led them to this rhetorical decision was somewhat less attractive and certainly more complex. As Wilmsen explains, at the end of the last century "the peoples of the Kalahari, except for a few families who became elites, were left with a travesty of what they had previously possessed in their land." Moreover, not all the so-called "Bushmen" were as enthused as Lee's informant with their current plight. For example, a Zhu man named Gcaunqa had reached the tragic metaphysical conclusion that "'God made whites with everything; he made blacks with cattle; but he made Zhu with fuck-all.'"[92] Upon further reflection it seems quite likely that "Paleolithic economies"—or their supposed modern counterparts—were more popular with American anthropologists than with the people who had been condemned to practice them.

For their students and admirers in the 1960s, the exceptional social virtues of this invented "traditional" people were even more compelling than their economic genius. In 1969, Marjorie Shostak traveled to the Dobe area of Botswana to join the Harvard project (which was then in its final stages). Her objective was to study the role of women in the !Kung society and economy. The subject, indeed, was a promising one. As Isaac has noted, "the !Kung San ethnography brought Woman the Gatherer to our attention in such a way as to make us feel like so many sexist pigs (or dupes of them) for ever having thought in terms of Man the Hunter." As he remembers it, "the big-game animal that attracted the most attention in certain anthropological circles during the 1970s was the Male Chauvinist Pig Anthropologist who voiced doubts about the generalized foraging model of band-level economy *a la* !Kung San or its applicability to prehistoric cases."[93] Shostak explained that

> My initial field trip took place at a time when traditional values concerning marriage and sexuality were being questioned in my own culture. The Women's Movement had just begun to gain momentum, urging re-examination of the roles western women had traditionally assumed. I hoped the field trip might help me to clarify some of the issues the Movement had raised. !Kung women might be able to offer some answers; after all, they provided most of their families' food, yet cared for their children and were lifelong wives as well. . . . A study revealing what !Kung women's lives were like today might reflect what their lives had been like for generations, possibly even for thousands of years.[94]

Shostak's account of this expedition, *Nisa: The Life and Words of a !Kung Woman*, is refreshing both for its honesty about her explicit feminist agenda and her willingness to challenge preconceived notions when confronted with a starkly different reality. Her analysis of the life of !Kung women is ambiguous and radiates a certain sense of disappointment. She struggles to maintain that in a society of (supposedly) "ancient traditions, men and women live together in a nonexploitative manner, displaying a striking degree of equality between the sexes—perhaps a lesson for our own society." At that same time, however, she acknowledges that !Kung men "do seem to have the upper hand."[95] Given the sensitive nature of her inquiry her task was not easy one. In particular, it could not have been encouraging to learn that the !Kung had described her "in one of their amusing (and often scathing) character portrayals as someone who ran up to women, looked them straight in the eye, and said, 'Did you screw your husband last night?'"[96] Although Shostak stresses the egalitarian and compassionate aspects of the !Kung's social universe she is equally candid in reporting the exceptions to her hypothesis. For example, her suggestion that the limited available evidence "points to a rate of violence among the traditional !Kung that is comparable to that found in American cities" does not do much to sustain the appealing image of a "harmless people."[97] Also, her frank admission that "nearly 50 percent of children die before the age of fifteen; 20 percent die in their first year. . . . Life expectancy at birth is only thirty years, while the average life expectancy at age fifteen is fifty-five"[98] is clearly not designed to advance the misleading notion of a prehistoric utopia.

While it may not have been her original intention, Shostak ultimately portrays a people who are striving to overcome a legacy of poverty, a people who are in no way content with an imaginary "Paleolithic" prosperity. Ironically, she discovered that the Harvard project itself had provided the Dobe !Kung with a limited and short-term means of improving their material condition. She was realistic enough to accept the fact that they were more concerned with their immediate future than with the "authenticity" of the "anthropological present." She was also willing to admit that, in a comedy of manners and a reversal of roles, her colleagues had themselves been reduced to an object of empirical study:

> as time passed we became aware that we had also inherited serious problems. The !Kung had been observing anthropologists for almost six years and had learned quite a bit about them. Precedents had been set that the !Kung expected us to follow. That was difficult, because we were critical of much we saw: a separate elaborate anthropologists' camp, tobacco handouts, payment for labor and crafts in money, and occasional excursions by truck to the nut groves.[99]

In a valiant attempt to deal with this problem Shostak abandoned her tent and moved to a hut in the neighboring village. Despite her best intentions, however, this measure did not suffice, since the Harvard project had by now become the most important local industry:

> Once we were on our own our romanticism was attacked by the !Kung themselves. They wanted us to give them jobs as the others had; they wanted money; they wanted to stop relying on their traditional [sic] way of life, which was becoming impossible to sustain. With money, they said, they could buy goats, clothing, and blankets. They wanted seed to plant crops, to have fields just as the Herero and Tswana had.[100]

In short, they wanted to recover their dignity, and they wanted to struggle for a better life for themselves and for their children. Whatever its immediate benefit, there was no long-term future in serving as fictional creations in an ongoing anthropological drama, and, unlike the photogenic BaMbuti who had frequented Putnam's camp, they had no intention of being reduced to extras in a script penned in Hollywood, Harvard, or Ann Arbor. The time had come for the men and women of science to fold their tents: the mongomongo nuts had obviously lost their savor.

In F. Scott Fitzgerald's *The Great Gatsby*, Nick Carraway can look across Long Island Sound and dream about another time, an idyllic era when the natural world still stood triumphant, as yet unscarred by the intentions and instruments of modern man:

> as the moon rose higher the inessential houses began to melt away until gradually I became aware of the old island here that flowered once for Dutch sailors' eyes—a fresh, green breast of the new world. Its vanished trees, the trees that had made way for Gatsby's house, had once pandered in whispers to the last and greatest of all human dreams; for a transitory enchanted moment man must have held his breath in the presence of this continent, compelled into an aesthetic contemplation he neither understood nor desired, face to face for the last time in history with something commensurate to his capacity for wonder.[101]

For Fitzgerald and his generation, this vision of America was a distant memory: that fresh green breast of land was now a valley of ashes, its earlier custodians broken and scattered on the wheel of progress. Yet other shores remained, and Africa still beckoned to the seekers of that "last and greatest of all human dreams."

Notes

1. Pascal Bruckner, *The Tears of the White Man: Compassion as Contempt* (New York: The Free Press, 1986), 101.
2. William R. Beer, "Introduction," in Pascal Bruckner, *The Tears of the White Man: Compassion as Contempt* (New York: The Free Press, 1986), xii.
3. John Kenneth Galbraith, "Introduction," in Thorstein Veblen, *The Theory of the Leisure Class* (Boston: Houghton Mifflin, 1973), xvii.
4. Don M. Wolfe, *The Image of Man in America*, 2nd ed. (New York: Thomas Y. Crowell, 1970), 306.
5. Thorstein Veblen, *The Theory of the Leisure Class* (Boston: Houghton Mifflin, 1973), 220.
6. Ibid., 150.

7. Ibid., 151.
8. Ibid., 148.
9. Ibid., 21.
10. Galbraith, xvi.
11. Wolfe, 302.
12. Hartwig Isernhagen, "A Constitutional Inability to Say Yes: Thorstein Veblen, the Reconstruction Program of *The Dial*, and the Development of American Modernism after World War I," *REAL: The Yearbook of Research in English and American Literature* 1 (1982): 153-90.
13. Franz Boas, "The Mental Attitude of the Educated Classes," *The Dial* (5 September 1918): 145-48 and "Nationalism," *The Dial* (8 March 1919): 232-37; Robert H. Lowie, "Anthropology Put to Work," *The Dial* (15 August 1918): 98-100; Edward Sapir, "Civilization and Culture," *The Dial* (20 September 1919): 233-36; and Anonymous, "Review of *Primitive Society* by Robert H. Lowie," *The Dial* (November 1920): 528-33.
14. Thorstein Veblen, "The Passing of National Frontiers," *The Dial* (25 April 1918): 387-90. Veblen had already produced a book-length analysis of the prospects for a "new world order": see his *An Inquiry into the Nature of Peace and the Terms of its Perpetuation* (New York: Augustus M. Kelley, 1964 [1917]).
15. Isernhagen, 185.
16. Ibid., 187.
17. Marshall Hyatt, *Franz Boas, Social Activist: The Dynamics of Ethnicity* (New York: Greenwood Press, 1990), x.
18. Franz Boas, *The Mind of Primitive Man* (New York: Macmillan, 1938 [1911]), 220.
19. Lucien Levy-Bruhl, *Primitive Mentality* (Boston: Beacon Press, 1966).
20. Boas, *Primitive Man*, 135.
21. Ibid., 135.
22. Ibid., 268-69.
23. Ibid., 269.
24. Hyatt, 92.
25. Ibid., 92-93.
26. Carl G. Jung, Foreword, in Charles Roberts Aldrich, *The Primitive Mind and Modern Civilization* (New York: AMS Press, 1969), xvii.
27. Charles Roberts Aldrich, *The Primitive Mind and Modern Civilization* (New York: AMS Press, 1969), 227-28.
28. Ibid., 228.
29. Ibid., 232.
30. Ibid., 228.
31. Ibid., 45.
32. Ibid., 123.
33. Ibid., 119-20.
34. David Bidney, *Theoretical Anthropology*, 2nd ed. (New York: Shocken Books, 1967), 268.
35. Leslie A. White, *The Evolution of Culture: The Development of Civilization to the Fall of Rome* (New York: McGraw-Hill, 1959), 30.
36. Ibid., ix.

37. Ibid., 277.

38. Ibid.

39. Ibid., 278.

40. Ibid., 302.

41. Beer, xi.

42. Stanley Diamond, *In Search of the Primitive: A Critique of Civilization* (New Brunswick, N.J.: Transaction Books, 1974), 174-75.

43. Ibid., 126-27.

44. Ibid., 129-50.

45. Ibid., 58.

46. Ibid., 61.

47. Ibid., 60.

48. Ibid., 62.

49. Sherman Paul, *In Search of the Primitive: Rereading David Antin, Jerome Rothenberg, and Gary Snyder* (Baton Rouge: Louisiana State University Press, 1986), vii.

50. Ibid.

51. Marianna Torgovnick, *Gone Primitive: Savage Intellects, Modern Lives* (Chicago: University of Chicago Press, 1990).

52. Fredric Jameson, *The Political Unconscious: Narrative as a Socially Symbolic Act* (Ithaca, N.Y.: Cornell University Press, 1981), 19.

53. William C. Dowling, *Jameson, Althusser, Marx: An Introduction to the Political Unconscious* (Ithaca, N.Y.: Cornell University Press, 1984), 54.

54. Jameson, 290, 89.

55. Dowling, 22.

56. Ibid., 24.

57. Jameson, 220.

58. Ibid. 290.

59. Ibid.,

60. Colin M. Turnbull, *The Forest People* (New York: Touchstone Books, 1968), 145.

61. Ibid., 19.

62. Ibid., 286.

63. Ibid., 75.

64. Ibid., 76.

65. Ibid., 29.

66. Ibid., 20.

67. Jerome Beatty, "Great White Chief of the Congo," *American Magazine,* July 1939, 20.

68. Ibid., 152.

69. Ibid.

70. Lewis Cotlow, *In Search of the Primitive* (Boston: Little, Brown, and Co., 1966), 52.

71. Ibid., 55.

72. Ibid., 80.

73. Turnbull, 156.

74. Isaac Schapera, *The Khoisan Peoples of South Africa: Bushmen and Hottentots* (London: Routledge, 1930).

75. Laurens Van Der Post, *The Lost World of the Kalahari* (New York: William Morrow, 1958); Elizabeth Marshall Thomas, *The Harmless People* (New York: Alfred A Knopf, 1959).
76. George Peter Murdock, "The Current Status of the World's Hunting and Gathering Peoples," in eds. Richard B. Lee and Irven DeVore, *Man the Hunter* (Chicago: Aldine, 1968), 13.
77. Ibid., 15.
78. Edwin N. Wilmsen, *Land Filled with Flies: A Political Economy of the Kalahari* (Chicago: University of Chicago Press, 1989), 71.
79. Ibid., 115-29.
80. Ibid., 127.
81. Ibid., 133.
82. Richard B. Lee, "What Hunters Do For A Living, or, How to Make Out on Scarce Resources," in eds. Richard B. Lee and Irven DeVore, *Man the Hunter* (Chicago: Aldine, 1968), 30-31. Also see Wilmsen, 159. It should be noted that Lee did his work on the nortern periphery of the region analyzed by Wilmsen.
83. Ibid., 37-39.
84. Richard B. Lee, *The !Kung San: Men, Women, and Work in a Foraging Society* (Cambridge: Cambridge University Press, 1979), 461.
85. Barry L. Isaac, "Economy, Ecology, and Analogy: The !Kung San and the Generalized Foraging Model," in eds. Kenneth B. Tankersley and Barry L. Isaac, *Research in Economic Anthropology: A Research Annual*, supp. 5, *Early Paleoindian Economies of Eastern North America* (Greenwich, Conn.: JAI Press, 1990), 325.
86. Ibid., 323-24.
87. Marshall Sahlins, *Stone Age Economics* (Chicago: Aldine-Atherton, 1972), 2.
88. Ibid., 8-9.
89. Ibid., 23.
90. Ibid., 39.
91. Ibid., 27.
92. Wilmsen, 128.
93. Isaac, 324-25.
94. Marjorie Shostak, *Nisa: The Life and Words of a !Kung Woman* (New York: Vintage Books, 1983), 5-6.
95. Ibid., 237.
96. Ibid., 350.
97. Ibid., 308.
98. Ibid., 15.
99. Ibid., 26.
100. Ibid., 27.
101. F. Scott Fitzgerald, *The Great Gatsby* (New York: Collier, Scribner Classic, 1986), 182.

4

Finding Cultures, Reinventing Tribes: American Ethnography in Africa

Americans in the nineteenth century, when they considered Africa at all, had virtually no experience of their own to fall back on except the distorted legend of slavery and second-hand accounts of British or European exploration and conquest. Images of the terrible "Guinea Coast" and its shackled cargoes lingered at the periphery of New England's seafaring literature and in the gruesome tales of slave and slaver. Nonetheless, even as vivid an account as Olaudah Equiano's *Narrative*, first published in 1789, which described the life of an African captured in his youth, enslaved and sold to the Americas, who later purchased his freedom and moved to England, had small impact outside England—though American abolitionists generally knew his work. Even then, Equiano's own account of an African childhood was sketchy at best.[1] The American experiment in Liberia had increasing impact as the century wore on, but most white Americans—beyond the immediate circle of repatriated slaves who sought their destiny in that obscure West African colony—knew next to nothing of it, and apparently cared less. The great works of W. E. B. Du Bois , Carter Woodson, and other black scholars were still in the future.[2] Indeed, right up to World War I very few Americans had personal experience of Africa. True, there was a growing, and in time, significant American missionary effort in Africa, but there was very little available to counter the popular images made available through British traveler's accounts and adventure fiction *a la* H. Rider Haggard, not to mention the enormously popular works of Henry Morton Stanley.[3]

Therefore, even for the most intrepid of America's intellectuals, Africa remained a great unknown, its peoples, history, even its geography, a huge blank. To paraphrase Graham Greene, Africa remained an enormous void the shape of the human heart. Indeed, it was into this void that the works of Henry Morton Stanley intruded with such force. Even then, American scholars, when finally they began to consider Africa on their own terms early in the twentieth century, had but one legacy to fall back on; that of their own frontier, and of the Native Americans—however misunderstood—who, until recently, had inhabited and dominated it.

It is difficult to discern a clear watershed in all this, that is, to clearly define the beginnings of a particular *American* perspective on Africa, one distinct from that of the British or French, for example. And, when it comes to a specific branch of scholarship, the task is even more daunting. Nevertheless some patterns do emerge in silhouette, especially when one looks closely at the popular writing on Amerindians, whether in the form of fiction or supposedly true narrative accounts, or whether in the guise of early ethnographic description. One need only mention a few examples wherein the noble (occasionally ignoble) savage of the American frontier is celebrated against a backdrop of green forests, rocky peaks, or vast plains. Cooper's enormously popular *The Last of the Mohicans* and others of his famous "Leatherstocking Tales,"[4] "best-sellers" in the middle of the nineteenth century, remained hugely popular well into the twentieth century. So did Henry Wadsworth Longfellow's turgid epic *The Song of Hiawatha.*[5] Popularized accounts of the Lewis and Clark Expedition of 1803-1806[6] blossomed throughout the nineteenth century, and works like Francis Parkman's *The Oregon Trail* provided bedtime reading in thousands of homes.[7] Novels of the American frontier had earned a deserved place at the heart of "American" consciousness even before the Civil War, as did hundreds more thereafter, especially as the Amerindians put up their heroic last resistance on the western plains.[8] Shortly before his death at the hands of his "enemies" the Sioux and Cheyenne, Custer had written an adventure book called *My Life on the Plains,* which, like his wife's later best-seller, *Tenting on the Plains,* was a national success, and to some of the better-read citizens of the time it must have seemed that every army officer above the rank of major had written his memoir about fighting the Indians.[9] Similarly nearly every frontier scout from Jim Bridger to Buffalo Bill published something that claimed to accurately portray frontier life.[10] Such widely read works as John Charles Fremont's *Report of the Exploring Expedition to the Rocky Mountains*[11] had helped prepare the track, and that extraordinary mythic universe of the "West" was on its way long before Owen Wister wrote that "first" true Western, *The Virginian,* in 1902.[12] It is no accident, for example, that James Gordon Bennett, the editor of the *New York Herald* who bankrolled Stanley's expedition to "find" Livingstone in Africa in 1870-71, had apotheosized William Cody (Buffalo Bill) in his newspaper after a brief visit to one of General Phil Sheridan's hunting camps on the plains, and later invited him to dinner in New York.[13] Nor is it accidental that even before he penned his massive (and popular) history, *The Winning of the West* (1889-1896), Theodore Roosevelt had published a personal memoir of his life as a youthful rancher in the Dakotas, entitled *Hunting Trips of a Ranchman.*[14]

Educated Americans around the turn of the century could also look to more serious works which purported to document the facts of Amerindian culture, frontier realities, and the folkways of a "vanishing" culture. American anthropology, still largely an amateur science (the first American Ph.D in Anthropology was awarded in 1892) had nonetheless found in the Amerindians its essential subject, one which would dominate the field for decades to come. Unlike Europeans who had to turn to Africa or Asia to study "native" folk, American ethnographers could claim that the native peoples of America, despite the recent passing of their "ancient ways," the loss of their lands, and their removal to reservations, could be studied *in situ* as traditional peoples, with some claim at least to an accurate portrayal of how things were before European civilization intruded. Modern scholars might question this assumption, or any assumption which presumes the superiority of the studier over the people studied, but it was a fact that scholars could actually interview persons who had been at the Little Big Horn, or had lived out their lives in hogans on the southwestern desert. Indeed, as the career of Lewis Henry Morgan (1818-1881) illustrates, contact even with remnant groups like New York's Iroquois, long since left behind by the frontier, could ignite a romantic quest for the realities of Indian life strong enough to last a lifetime.

Morgan, perhaps the greatest amateur ethnographer of them all, had published his ground-breaking *League of the . . . Iroquois* in 1851, and like his later book, *Ancient Society* (1877), it was much read throughout the century. Proclaimed in its time as the first "scientific" study of the Amerindian, Morgan's work on the Iroquois certainly deserves its place as one of the first ethnographies to attempt objective analysis of a non-western society. This was a considerable achievement, and despite the fact that Morgan categorized the Iroquois at the "barbarian" middle stage, half way between "savagery" and "civilization," his brilliant—if somewhat romanticized—description of Iroquois culture paved the way for the next generation of American ethnographers who would in turn claim a far more rigorous objectivity based on a new methodology.[15]

Morgan's far more ambitious work, *Ancient Society*, represents one of the most far-reaching attempts by any American scholar to place all societies, throughout history, into a systematic and comparative perspective, and it had a profound impact on both American and European thought that lingers to this day. Much of the

popular language pertaining to what was called "savage," "barbarian," "civilized" etc., can be directly attributed to this book. Though
rather judgmental by late twentieth-century standards in his classi-
fying Amerindians as "barbarians"—for he subscribed to the generally held evolutionary theory of progress common to his era—Morgan,
nonetheless, was a bold and original thinker. His well-known influence on Marx, and especially on Engels, is legendary, and, despite
the fact that his claim to a far-reaching scientific ethnography has
long since been debunked, Morgan is altogether representative of a
quintessential nineteenth-century American philosophy which took
for granted that, in an America where no nobility ruled and each
man was free to pursue his destiny, progress among all humans
was attainable, even inevitable. Robert E. Bieder, in *Science
Encounters the Indian, 1820-1880*, points out that early American
ethnography, represented especially in the works of Albert Gallatin,
Samuel G. Morton, Ephraim George Squier, Henry Rowe School-
craft, and Lewis Henry Morgan, was more distinguished than is
generally recognized by historians of anthropology, and he suggests
that Morgan's work is best seen as the culmination of a century-
long tradition of American scholarship which, perhaps mistakenly,
but understandably, placed the Amerindian at the center of the
evolutionary model.[16]

Amerindians therefore provided a model, but, as we shall see,
even as a new "science" of anthropology emerged, another problem
intruded, for it was apparent by 1890, less than a decade after
Morgan's death, that the American frontier had ended.[17] Hence a
crisis loomed for ethnographers. Amerindians might be found in
appreciable remnants within isolated regions—the southwestern
plateau, Michigan's Upper Peninsula, northern Wisconsin and Minnesota, the extreme Northwest coast beyond Vancouver, the Arctic—but they were assuredly rare elsewhere. Franz Boas was able
to do ethnographic research during his youth, among Eskimos or
Northwest Coast peoples, but even by the time he emigrated to the
U.S. in 1887 the "raw material" for anthropological enterprise in
America was increasingly limited.[18] Neither he nor his students
could easily find peoples as yet "untouched" by western civilization,
a tactical problem for some, but a serious strategic barrier for others since ethnography then claimed, and for a long time sustained,
the idea that only "traditional" societies were worthy subjects of
anthropology.[19] In time, indeed within approximately twenty years
of Boas' arrival in America, a significant part of American ethnographic enterprise had been redirected toward the peoples of Asia,
Africa and Latin America.

To put it simply, and fairly, Franz Boas probably did as much as
any scholar to advance the cause of a more scientific, non-racist

anthropology, especially regarding Amerindians. Suffice it to say here that the German-born Boas, immediately upon his arrival in the U.S. in 1887, embarked on a long career dedicated to several ideas which remain to this day a primary focus of much American ethnography. First, that each people studied should be studied on its own terms, in relation to its culture as a whole, and not—as was common at that time—in terms of comparisons with other cultures. Second, as Boas himself put it, that "ethnological phenomena are the result of the physical and psychical character of men, and of its development under the influence of the surroundings."[20] Third, that such guidelines, applied with precise and scientific methodology in the field, ought to yield certain universal "laws" about the basic development of mankind as a whole, both physiological and psychological.[21] Though Boas himself later repudiated the search for universal laws of human development, all of this—radical then, commonplace now—lent itself perfectly to another of Boas' central contributions to twentieth-century American anthropology, namely that it was the dynamic interplay between humans and their constantly changing environment which created most of the "cultural" distinctions made so much of in the past, indeed that it was this process, not race, which largely determined most of the differences between human groups.

No doubt some of this insight came from his personal experience with the growing anti-Semitism within Europe especially in his native Germany, since this anti-Semitism invariably fell back on the most egregious doctrines of genetic traits. As his biographer, Hyatt, clearly points out, Boas was deeply suspicious of the grand "generalizers" and "theory builders" like Edward B. Tylor, Lewis Henry Morgan, and Emile Durkheim, not to mention Herbert Spencer, since so much of their theory lacked particular and quantifiable scientific evidence. Boas, according to Hyatt, favored the "particularists" like William James who were bothered by the fact that, invariably, certain particulars did not fit the theory.[22] In arguing, successfully, for a more professionally trained cadre of field ethnographers who would adhere to a thorough, university-based, fiercely empiricist standard, Boas anticipated the course his profession would take for the next one hundred years. Though he fought hard battles with such gifted "amateurs" as John Wesley Powell, enormously influential within the Smithsonian, and Otis Tufton Mason (also of the Smithsonian), both of whom subscribed to Morgan's "evolutionary" theory of progress,[23] Boas, in freeing the fledgling discipline from the pervasive biases of caste, class, and race, helped set the stage for the future. As a Jew he was hardly a spokesman for the predominant belief in Anglo-Saxon supremacy and, as we shall see, his influence on another generation of American anthropologists who took the peoples of Africa as their subject, was for the most part benign.

But of course, Boas was for long decades very much a minority influence in ethnography in America. The dominant theory of the age, both racist and patronizing, held that human societies, like biological orders, could be understood best along an ascending line of "evolutionary" complexity, from the most simple to the most complex.[24] Amerindians in this scheme were near the bottom, usually held somewhere above Africans, though well below Asians. Indeed within this scheme, "civilization," invariably defined by Europeans, was "synonymous with European society" while the "lower" races were "primitive" or "savage," more especially those with darker skins.[25]

American ethnography, coming of age around the turn of the century when sweeping generalizations about human groups were commonplace, found a ready and obvious focus in the study of Amerindians. As Carl Degler has shown in his brilliant work, *In Search of Human Nature*, Boas and his views triumphed in time.[26] Certainly the race-centered comparative approach lost ground in the 1930s because it was so favored by the Nazis. In the meantime, even by the late 1920s, some of Boas' best students turned their attention away from America and toward Africa.

Obviously, then, when American ethnographers turned to Africa, they carried with them a considerable legacy. Americans, no less than Europeans, uncritically accepted the interpretations of the comparative evolutionists who generally believed, given much of the evidence then at hand, that civilization as it was understood in the West had diffused outward from the Mesopotamian (or possibly the Egyptian) hearth.[27] Hence American anthropology mirrored (and in fact exaggerated) the split between those who believed in comparative cultural and historical development—usually with an attached belief in racial superiority—and those who were increasingly convinced that the distinctions between societies could not be reduced to formulas, to race, or to allegedly inherent traits. A leading proponent of the former view was Comte Joseph de Gobineau, whose four-volume work, *The Inequality of Human Races* (1853-1855) is an extreme example.[28]

This dichotomy was exacerbated as cultural anthropologists, early in this century, collected data which seemed to substantiate the universality and constancy of human physiology, and the "almost universally malleable" capacity, which, according to Margaret Mead (a Boas Ph.D. in 1929), made it possible for human groups to "condition" almost any kind of behavior, so long as the conditioning began in early childhood.[29] In this seemingly modest and allegedly empiricist assumption we can see the entire thrust of American ethnography through its "golden age" roughly from 1925 to 1975, an era marked by anthropological relativism advanced to the nth degree.

As far as Africa is concerned American ethnography made perhaps its most original contribution—via its early focus on Amerindian societies—in the concept of the "Cultural Area" first suggested by Clark Wissler,[30] and brilliantly refined by Boas' former student, and his first Ph.D. at Columbia, Alfred L. Kroeber, in an important article "The Culture-Area and Age-Area Concepts of Clark Wissler" (1931) and in his seminal work *Culture and Natural Areas of Native North America.*[31] Here, in a sweeping attempt to classify "systemic" patterns, particularly among Amerindians, which could only be understood in reference to historical processes, Kroeber set the stage for much of the Africa-centered work which followed. Reduced to its essence Kroeber's idea was elegant and compelling: first it postulated that peoples who lived in certain environments, regardless of ethnic or linguistic affinity, often developed widely shared traits which transcended their kin-based or societal distinctions, and second, that in such "cultural regions" there was a powerful tendency toward similar modes of production, principles of exchange (trade), ritual practices, and often a common *lingua franca*. Clearly, groups as originally various as the Cheyenne, Sioux, Arapaho, Blackfeet, Kiowa, and Comanche, had come to share a great deal over time (primarily via the adaptation of the horse to a mobile bison-hunting life), even to the point that contemporary white observers, aware of language differences between these peoples, spoke of the "Plains Indians" as one cultural group. Likewise the peoples of the Lake-Forest environment—encompassing the Great Lakes and much of the Northeast—shared a great deal: summer horticulture (growing corn, squash, beans, etc. in small plots), extensive fishing and gathering along lakes and streams, fall and winter hunting in transhumanic patterns, and the use of the birchbark canoe for hunting and gathering as well as for trade.[32]

In the face of the prevailing racist and hierarchical classifications which dominated western research at least through the 1920s, and which are perhaps best demonstrated by the Harvard African Expedition of 1926-27,[33] those who argued for any kind of cultural "relativism"—based on assumptions of scientific objectivity in viewing the "other," yet allegedly free of value judgments—were certainly progressive if not radical. For one thing the idea of cultural areas did not easily play into the hands of contemporary colonial administrators who sought to emphasize ethnic (tribal) distinctions.[34] Furthermore it offered a historical or time-focused dimension at a time when the anthropological "present" was gaining force from the South Pacific to South Africa. The latter presumed studying a society as if it was frozen in amber. Kroeber, we must remember, was among the first to directly challenge the lingering "Lamarckianism" which permeated much of Social Science well into the twentieth century: the still powerful (though mistaken) assumption that peoples inherited their primary characteristics via *acquired* characteristics passed on by their parents, and that "race" and "culture" were inextricably linked.[35] Any method which postulated larger "cultural" patterns that transcended obvious "tribal" categories and which seemed to conform to common-sense observations—Africa's vast savannas supporting widespread pastoral complexes, Africa's vast forests supporting massive "swidden" complexes—seemed compelling indeed.

It is no accident, therefore, that Melville J. Herskovits, another Boas student, when he began his Africa-centered research, suggested in a 1924 paper entitled "A Preliminary Consideration of the Culture Areas of Africa" that Africa could be logically divided into nine culture areas.[36] These areas arbitrarily divided the continent so as to reduce the "chaos" faced by the anthropologist when confronted by "the paucity of scientific studies of African groups," and among Americans they held sway for many decades.[37] One of the authors of this book recalls being introduced to Herskovits' African culture areas while in training for the Peace Corps at Columbia University in the autumn of 1961, and while many anthropologists had by that time come to reject the scheme—despite its conceptual elegance—such doubts had barely surfaced in the classroom. Like the Amerindian culture areas, these African culture areas[38] were based primarily on the idea that "trait-distributions"—such things as dependence on particular foods, types of markets, musical patterns, related myths and tales, religious practices, patterns of descent via kin-group or lineage, artistic expression, kinds of implements, etc.—could be accurately mapped for each region. Thus, for example, in the Guinea Coast region would be found widespread commonalities in folklore (trickster tales, moralistic fables, riddles, proverbs and the like), in agricultural modes (the swidden system, growing yams, rice, plantains, greens, etc.), in economics (especially the periodic markets), in music (tonal structures, melodic lines, rhythmic structures, even musical instruments), in sculpture and other art forms (including the use of sculpture in dance), and in a bewildering array of religious syncretisms (belief in powers that control the souls of the dead, divination practices, spirit-possession complexes, pantheons of gods, and so on). Herskovits was too careful a scholar not to caution that such categories inevitably "shaded" one into the other, that they decreased at the outer edges of each zone, and that anomalies abounded, and he took pains to explain that the traits he so laboriously compiled were in no way to be confused with hereditary or linguistic affinities; thus race was not a factor, while *culture* most emphatically was. Furthermore, he always insisted that any data reflected only a particular point in time, thus historical dynamics had to be taken into account.[39]

Certainly in the 1920s, and 1930s, and even into the 1950s, Herskovits' scheme was nothing if not challenging, especially when linked to another of his postulates: that an ethnohistorical approach was vital to all field work.[40] Perhaps no anthropologist of his generation was more insistent on rigorous field techniques. Applied to Africa, with its assumption—so typical of American ethnography—that *culture* was a scientifically definable phenomenon, Herskovits' theory was immediately attractive to scores of younger anthropologists. Preliminary analysis—based on the standard made famous by Bronislaw Malinowski[41] that one must do extensive field research before generalizations of any kind could be made—seemed to indicate that in Africa as well as in North America there were several regions which could be scientifically objectified on ecological, social, and cultural grounds.[42]

Leading American ethnographers, suspicious of the emerging British school of functionalist social anthropology with its emphasis on discreet "tribes," like the Nuer or the Tallensi, whose societies seemed to exist in isolation from neighbors, removed from history, began to look beyond the convenient indices of ethnographic convention, especially those presuming a typology of fixed systems like those proposed by Radcliffe-Brown at Oxford.[43] These American anthropologists were especially distinguished from their European (particularly British) colleagues, by their insistence on the so-called "diachronic" dimension, based upon the assumption that a culture is always undergoing change however stable it may appear. Of the many legacies of Boas this was to prove among the most lasting and potent. Many also shared Herskovits' belief—inherent in the idea of the culture area—that, the borrowing of traditions by one people from another is commonplace, and that the charting of this process could be carried out scientifically.[44] Furthermore, almost to a person, they rejected the deterministic idea that culture is inborn rather than learned. We should point out here that this theory of the centrality of culture is not to be confused with the diffusionist *Kulturkries Schule* originating in Germany and Austria, which postulated "core cultures" or "spheres" which aggregated through time in a consistent fashion, whether among preliterate peoples or among advanced cultures with written records.[45]

In all this Herskovits and his colleagues remained true, for the most part, to the Boasian credo. Africans, no less than Europeans, Asians, Amerindians, or any other people, would therefore be brought—via rigorous description and relentless analysis of the *dynamics* of their cultures—into a broader notion of "the family of man."

This, at least prior to World War II, was no small matter. Clearly some far-seeing British, French, and other European ethnographers also sought a less deterministic, less racist schemata by which to explain Africa and its peoples. Certainly the structuralists looked to an alternative mode, less insidiously comparative.[46] Nonetheless, the bulk of European ethnographic publication, confined for the most part to journals and institutions inevitably biased by their connection to colonial regimes, only reinforced pre-existing conventions—i.e., that Africans could be classed from "top" to bottom," from complex to simple, from civilized (or nearly so) to savage, based on such criteria as blood, polity, and above all, linguistic or cultural affinity with "advanced" North African societies. Thus whether a people were considered "pure" Negro, or whether they were allegedly mixed with "superior" Caucasoid stock, counted for everything.

C. G. Seligman, whose influential and seemingly comprehensive 1930 work *The Races of Africa* was reprinted until 1966, is a case in point.[47] Seligman, longtime professor of Anthropology at the University of London, while progressive in his psychological insights, contended that the guiding principle in distinguishing Africans by group was their genetic heritage. According to Seligman the "true Negro" (a phrase he used for the titles of two chapters) was by his definition confined to the Guinea Coast and the Zaire basin (the Congo) and characterized by both physical and social traits quite distinct to "type."

> Culturally they possess some characteristic features. They build gable-roofed huts; their traditional weapons include bows tapering at each end, with bowstrings of vegetable products, swords, and plaited shields, but no clubs or slings.[48]

Where Seligman got his information he does not say, but one of the authors of this work lived for several years among certain of the groups classed by Seligman as among the "true Negroes" of West Africa (including the Temne, the Susu, and the Mende of Sierra Leone), and for extended periods among others (including the Hausa and the Gwari of Nigeria), and he witnessed slings in common use among boys who were detailed to protect crops from crows, though he never saw a bowstring made of vegetable products, indeed never saw a plaited shield (and bows only once or twice), though firearms were in common use and had been so in each of the regions mentioned for several hundred years. Seligman might be forgiven such language since the first edition of his book appeared in 1930, but it seems amazing in retrospect that the same passage appears in the later editions. Describing any settled West African people in this ahistorical fashion is akin to suggesting that Eskimos still live in igloos. It might satisfy a certain romantic image of pristine Africans living as their ancestors had for millennia, but it bears little resemblance to reality.

In another passage Seligman, while admitting to West Africa's "confused" political map, writes that the "true" Negro of West Africa characteristically "shows a skill in plastic art that is rarely found elsewhere in Negro Africa" and he specifically refers to the magnificent bronze heads of Ife and Benin as prime examples.[49] While praiseworthy on the one hand—even in Seligman's day no one could long pretend that the sculpture of Benin and of the Yoruba in the "classical" period was *not* magnificent—this statement is also egregiously dismissive of dozens of carving traditions and other African artistic expressions which stretch across central Africa, not to mention East and Southern Africa. Most blatant of all is the following passage from chapter 5 of *Races of Africa*,

> Apart from relatively late Semitic influence—whether Phoenician (Carthiginian) and strictly limited, or Arab (Muhammadan) and widely diffused—the civilizations of Africa are the civilizations of the Hamites, its history the record of these peoples and of their interaction with the two other African stocks, the Negro and the Bushman.[50]

It was exactly this kind of unsupported generalization that Herskovits and his students sought to allay.

Of all the commonly held misconceptions beloved of the late nineteenth and early twentieth century perhaps none was so widespread or accepted as this "Hamitic hypothesis" which held, roughly, that infusions from the north and northeast in the form of so-called "Hamitic" peoples (like the Berbers of North Africa, or the Somali of the Horn) had heavily impacted on "Negroid" tropical peoples of Africa, producing more "refined" mixed populations, and that these peoples were clearly superior. According to Seligman, the Fulani, or Fulbe, also called the Fula or Puel, are such a people, with "a preponderance of non-negroid physical traits—straight hair, straight nose, thin lips, slight physique . . ." and he adds that "the women are distinguished by their beauty of countenance and graceful carriage."[51] While common sense dictates that peoples from North Africa and the eastern Horn certainly mixed extensively over time with peoples from the savannah and forest regions of Africa, the assumption that one group was more advanced (or more beautiful) than the other, by virtue of color, is a purely judgmental one. One of the authors of this work remembers a beauty pageant to choose "Miss Port Loko" as a contestant in the "Miss Sierra Leone" contest in 1962. The winner of the national round would attend the Miss World contest. The "Fula" contestant was not chosen, while a far darker woman—and far more beautiful in the unanimous opinions of the several judges—won the contest. Perhaps there was nothing in this, but the lesson that beauty is in the eye of the beholder (and is culture-bound for the most part) seems self-evident. The bias which associates Caucasian characteristics with superiority, whether in matters of intelligence or matters of esthetics, is racism pure and simple.

In 1969 Edith R. Sanders published one of those unforgettable debunking articles in the *Journal of African History* which come to mark the end of one era in academic theory and the beginning of another. In this article Sanders critiqued the blatant racism behind the idea that so-called Hamitic peoples, as well as occasional Semitic infusions (Arabs in particular), when mixed with "pure" Negroes, produced a "superior" stock. Not only did she demolish the "scientific" basis for the Hamitic hypothesis by showing its origins in bogus Biblical exegesis, she also linked the whole idea to the emergence of colonialist racism.[52]

One must acknowledge that many of the younger European ethnographers, especially the contemporaries of Herskovits who studied under Malinowski at the London School of Economics or under Durkheim at Paris, had come around to a method which prescribed rigorous field work, and which avoided this old-fashioned biological reductionism. Like Malinowski, the young Evans-Pritchard, or Meyer Fortes, or Claude Levi-Strauss could claim, "I was there," and would attempt to see the peoples they studied in their own context. Nonetheless, Seligman's book remained standard fare through the 1960s. Indeed, as we shall see in the next chapter, most travel literature and not a few popularized scientific accounts, adhered to the debunked Hamitic hypothesis right up to the 1990s.

For the non-specialist all of this was dimly perceived at best, if not invisible. Most educated Americans from the opening decades of this century up through World War II viewed Africa through the larger, and more distorted, prism of what we today call, rather cavalierly, "the media." When scholars and their works intruded at all it was usually in the form of popularized reports or texts by reputable naturalists like Carl Akeley, or in the form of the early film documentaries such as those produced by Martin and Osa Johnson. More typically, even among the intelligentsia, Africa was realized through the popular travelogue or through works of fiction. We have noted the enormous popularity of Theodore Roosevelt's two volume book on his much-publicized African trek of 1909-10, and we have elsewhere noted the impact of travel literature, of fiction and of film, but how deeply the better-known ethnographic works impacted on the American consciousness is a difficult question.

Assuredly, the work of Herskovits had a growing impact within social science, if to a lesser extent among the general public. Herskovits was prominent in that distinguished lineage—the students of Boas—through which we trace so much of mainstream American anthropology. Studying under Boas at Columbia—after graduating with a B.A. in history from Chicago in 1920, where he was also deeply influenced by Thorsten Veblen—Herskovits rubbed shoulders and tested his mind with a powerhouse of young talent which had also gravitated to Boas and his cohorts; the youthful Margaret Mead, Elsie Parsons, Ruth Benedict, and Malcolm Willey, to name some of the more famous. His dissertation, awarded in 1923, was published in 1926 as "The Cattle Complex in East Africa" in the *American Anthropologist*.[53] His first serious field work began in Surinam in 1928, where he began to shape his hugely influential ideas about acculturation (i.e., the whole question of African cultural influences within the diaspora of African peoples in the New World). Ironically, it was not until 1931 that Herskovits, with his wife Frances, first traveled to sub-Saharan Africa, which was to remain his primary interest for four decades. Dahomey, then a French colony on Africa's west coast (sandwiched between Togo and Nigeria) was the site; the extraordinary culture of the long-time, once enormously powerful African kingdom of that name, was the subject. Herskovits and his wife, a talented researcher in her own right, were jointly able to make excellent use of their previous experience in Surinam, quickly winning the confidence of informants of both sexes, and publishing in 1938 their *magnus opus* of hands-on field research, *Dahomey: An Ancient West African Kingdom*.[54]

One can scarcely exaggerate the impact this book had regarding the scientific study of Africa's peoples, a field which Herskovits dominated for more than two decades. Here, in two dense volumes, replete with descriptions, canopied with elegant propositions, and buttressed by pages of data, was the model of a culture seen whole, in its own context, that the Boasian discipline expected. Indeed, as Herskovits himself wrote in the preface, the study was specifically intended for students of anthropology who wanted to know more about the cultures of Africa, whence had come the ancestors of millions upon millions of "the Negroes who inhabit the Americas."[55] Throughout the two volumes the emphasis was on religion and art—more specifically, to detail and explain the hitherto unknown (and speculative) connection between these phenomena, essential ingredients of any developed culture. Elegant explanations of the established priesthoods, the complex systems of theology, the linkage between song, dance, sculpture, ceremony, and belief, the elaborations of political systems and agricultural practices, and the intricacies of social organization and cults of ancestors, did much to lay to rest any idea (perhaps still lingering in the mind of the reader) that these Africans lived in a primitive society, rude, barbarous, and crude. Also, Herskovits clearly considered the history of Dahomey—including its well-documented involvement with the slave trade—as significant in his analysis.[56] In doing so, nevertheless, he was not about to fall into the trap of other contemporary scholars who saw only barbarism. As he put it,

> Unfortunately the native cultures of West Africa have far too often been written of in a deprecatory tone, so that the 'savage' African background has become stereotyped in reference to the ancestral traditions of the Negro peoples of the Americas to a degree that it has attained almost universal currency in the United States, and is today accepted by Negroes no less than by whites. But a consideration of this Dahomean culture, with its excellence in technology and art, its complex political and social structure, its profoundly integrated world-view and its mythology rich in elaborate conceptualization may prove of help toward a truer and more realistic view of how far removed from the popular idea is the actuality of the cultural heritage of the New World Negro.[57]

Furthermore, in this extraordinary work, Melville and Frances Herskovits revealed—really for the first time—something of the richness of African culture (in its larger sense) and something of the power with which aspects of that culture had been carried over from the Old World to the New. This was a theme, at least in the 1930s, of tremendous importance, not only to African Americans, dispersed in vast numbers from Brazil to Canada, from Surinam to Costa Rica, but among all persons interested in the dynamics of acculturation. No European scholar had produced a work of equivalent scope.

It is no accident, of course, that Herskovits had already published articles on acculturation among Americans of African descent before he worked in Dahomey, nor that he published a major work on this subject, *Acculturation: The Study of Cultural Contact* in 1938 (after his Dahomeyan field work but before *Dahomey* appeared), nor that he continued to published seminal works on this subject (including *The Myth of the Negro Past*) in later years.[58]

At such a distance in time it is not easy to reconstruct events within a larger culture let alone within a single academic field, but there can be little doubt that Herskovits deserves the lion's share of the credit for establishing a respectable basis in the United States for the ethnography of Africa. In this he was up against still powerful racist trends in American social science, and in science generally. Roland Dixon, author of *The Racial History of Man* (1923) was Professor of Anthropology at Harvard for many years, and though he corresponded with Boas, he subscribed entirely to the prevailing view that the cranial or cephalic index—which included alleged "scientific" measurements of the face, nose, skull and palate—when added to volume of the brain capacity, produced a scientific measure of significant racial distinction. Furthermore, Dixon certainly made no apologies when equating race with culture.[59] A later proponent of long-term, evolutionary racial distinction based on physical anthropology was Harvard's Carleton S. Coon, author of *The Races of Europe* (1939), *The Origin of Races* (1962), and within months of his death, *Racial Adaptations: A Study of the Origins, Nature, and Significance of Racial Variations in Humans* (1982).[60] Essentially Coon argued for the separate evolution of the modern races, as branches, as it were, off the very early *Homo erectus* grade. He believed that these separate races were actually subspecies.

THE FIGHT WITH THE AVISIBBA CANNIBALS

Reprinted with permission of Charles Scribner's Sons, an imprint of MacMillan Publishing Company from IN DARKEST AFRICA by Henry M. Stanley (Charles Scribner's Sons. New York. 1890)

While it would be wrong to say that any particular institution was associated with such views—certainly Harvard reflected the ferment in the nation as a whole—biological determinism had its adherents in many other institutions, including the Field Museum in Chicago, whose resident anthropologist, Wilfred Hambly, toured large parts of Angola and Nigeria in 1929, collecting exotic film, measuring adult males with "anthropometric calipers," gathering artifacts, stumbling (so he reported) on some cannibals, and recording various ceremonial cults.[61] Though he later edited a *Source Book for African Anthropology*, for the Field Museum, Hambly's largely single-handed expedition contributed little to the understanding of Africa and Africans. As Edward McKinley has pointed out in his excellent work, *The Lure of Africa*, Hambly's expedition was in some ways akin to the well-publicized zoological expeditions of that era, which catered to the public's interest in the colorful and the exotic. Certainly, despite the fact that Hambly published little of what he "found" on his wide-ranging expedition, he was representative of a familiar type.[62] "Scientists" who toured Africa in search of the exotic represent an interesting variant on the theme of the dilettante traveler (the art collector, the filmmaker, and in some cases, the hunter) whose primary interest was the unusual, the off-beat, anything out-of-the-ordinary. We must remember that twenty years earlier, Theodore Roosevelt's grand hunting tour, chronicled in his best-selling *African Game Trails*, was officially designated as a scientific collecting expedition for the Smithsonian.[63] Obviously much of ethnography is the collection of a culture (and the ethnographer is, of course, the arbiter of what should be "preserved" for the purposes of science), but any concentration on the exotic for its own sake hardly seems a defensible task.

In retrospect it is important to recognize that Herskovits, like so many of Boas' students, remained faithful to the principles behind Boas' ethnography: namely that people can be properly understood only in relation to their own culture and not in comparison with other, allegedly "superior" societies, that, however different, ethnological phenomena are for the most part consequences of environment, and that there is an endlessly changing dynamic (an interplay between humans and their surroundings) within any culture that can only be understood in diachronic terms. This credo seems to have stood Herskovits in good stead for decades, and it provided his own students with a common underpinning for research when they, too, went out to Africa.

Herskovits's students, many to become distinguished themselves, certainly took up the challenge with energy. Many of their names will be familiar to anyone educated in the U.S. since 1960 who has taken an introductory anthropology course. Among some of the better known are William Bascom, Alan Merriam, Joseph Greenberg, Simon Ottenberg, Harold Schneider, Daniel Crowley, J. Gus Liebenow, Robert Lystad, James W. Fernandez, Warren d'Azevedo, Vernon Dorjahn, Igor Kopytoff, Johnetta Cole, and Nancy Schmidt. The lineage from Boas to Herkovits to the above generation, and even to the next, is extraordinary, perhaps unmatched in any discipline in this century.[64] Zaire and its ethnomusicology, for example, are known today largely through Merriam's work. Without Greenberg's far-ranging reconstructions, linguists might still be writing about "Hamitic," "Nilo-Hamitic," and "Bantu" languages with only the slightest comprehension of their true relations. For those who hope to understand African art—in particular the complex relationships between art and culture—Bascom is essential. Students of the Temne, and in fact, anyone interested in the workings of "secret" societies, must begin with Dorjahn. Leibenow has produced a lifetime of work on Liberia and its peoples. Moreover, d'Azevedo's research on acculturation in the Central West Atlantic Region stands after three decades as the best work of its kind.[65] Undoubtedly, any scholar interested in the African "frontier" and its significance in the formation of societies must deal with Kopytoff's brilliant and controversial research.[66]

Furthermore, it is a tribute to Herskovits and the intellectual rigor that he demanded that several of these students (particularly Schneider, d'Azevedo, and Kopytoff) have long since challenged certain of Herskovits' more sweeping assumptions. These include the delineation and application of his cultural regions, exactly how acculturation occurs within groups who live within certain environments, and his understandable misconceptions about how cattle people *use* their cattle.[67] Some have carried ideas which were mere germs in his works to unexpected fruition. Greenberg's work on linguistics, while revealing much about the "Bantu migrations" that populated so much of equatorial Africa, also showed conclusively that linguistic "affinity" is not linked to race. His work undermined the foundation of the Hamitic hypothesis—with its unspoken assumptions that "admixtures" of Caucasian blood accounted for "higher" or more complex cultures.[68] It is noteworthy that Greenberg in later life has turned his attention to the New World and its languages, with attendant consequences to our understanding of possible migration patterns into and within North, Central and South America.[69]

It is certainly no exaggeration to say that without Herskovits and his American school the ethnographic "landscape" of Africa, as we know it today, would be very different. Having said as much, however, we must acknowledge some of the inherent limitations in the

Boasian cultural approach. For one thing there is the almost reflexive tendency, perhaps less evident in Herskovits' work as in that of many who followed, to assert "truths" based upon what James Clifford calls the "experiential authority."[70] Roughly, this is defined as the idea that only the ethnographer can properly interpret the society in question, through "a kind of accumulated savvy." This the ethnographer knows not because of any specific (or scientifically repeatable) hypothesis, but because he or she alone can assert "I was there." Thus the anthropologist casts himself as the insider, whose arcane and special knowledge (based as much on intuitive experience as on quantifiable data) separates him from the outsider, and by implication, armors him against criticism. This, of course, was also a weakness inherent in the British social anthropology of the Malinowski, Radcliffe-Brown school.

Margaret Mead, for many years perhaps the most eloquent defender of this proposition, took on all comers (and all criticism of her work, implicit or explicit) by arguing as if from scripture (her own). Thus what she had discovered about sex among the Samoans, for example,[71] was not merely an observation of customs among one "primitive" oceanic folk; it was, she argued, of universal application, and could henceforth provide the foundation of a thoroughgoing critique of America's "repressed" sexuality.[72] While much that Mead wrote stands as a triumphant example of how ideas can liberate people from constricting mythologies, much of what she proposed, especially about the Samoans and other South Pacific peoples, has been subjected to a rigorous criticism. According to Derek Freeman, the author of *Margaret Mead and Samoa: The Making and Unmaking of an Anthropological Myth*, even her basic data has been rendered questionable. While it may be true, as Lowell D. Holmes has pointed out, that Freeman's criticism is "biased" on the side of biological determinism, the cavalier dismissal of Freeman's decades-long research in Samoa is scandalous. If one can level the charge of bias against Freeman, is it not also obvious that Mead's work represents a classic example of "culturalism" elevated to the level of determinism?[73]

Clearly, even in an era when so many invidious (mostly racist) misconceptions still held force, there was also a danger in elevating culture, *per se*, through ethnographic reconstruction, so as to demonstrate the existence of integral primitive societies whose workings were perfect examples of unity and harmony. Perhaps this was nowhere more evident than in the work of several American anthropologists who in the sixties and seventies took on the task of unraveling the lessons of the !Kung and related peoples (usually called bushmen), who were ostensibly representative of a prehistoric hunting-and-gathering mode, perhaps a final relic of the Pleistocene wherein was shaped the nature of mankind.[74]

Looking back over the past half century or so, one can understand why so many social scientists—despite adherence to the methodical collation of empirical data—have been susceptible to the idealization of traditional African systems. There were all these wonderful new worlds being "discovered" via the new ethnography, especially in the 1920s and 1930s, but with plenty more to come, and certainly there was a revival of this sense during the halcyon days of independence when Africans began to control their own destinies. Reading through the literature one frequently gets that sense of having found some kind of Lost Paradise. Like the philosopher Kant, who imagined that all ambition, greed, miserliness, all asocial and antisocial characteristics were "historical prerequisites for man's emergence from his original state of savagery,"[75] several American ethnographers seem to have postulated a better, albeit more primitive, world not corrupted by things European (or American for that matter), and above all not corrupted by any of the egregious divisions of labor, wealth, power, and authority so typical of the civilized societies of the West. As indicated elsewhere in this book, here was a foundation for a renewed search for the primitive which in time would take on unmistakable neo-Rousseauean overtones.

Perhaps an even greater weakness in applied American anthropology, at least as it developed in subsequent decades, was the assumption that Africa, even more than "native" America, was a sort of "museum" of cultures, held in amber for the investigator to unravel in all its elemental glory. Although Herskovits himself, like Boas before him, emphasized *historical* patterns as well as each ethnic group's particular societal rhythm (the integrity of its lasting systems), all too often Africa's siren call proved too much for the field investigator, bent on his or her personal adventure into the unknown. Here, seen in hindsight, is one of the more evident "failures" of anthropological practice, if not of theory. How could any young American, of whatever sex, religion, or race, avoid that inevitable rush of adrenaline when he or she heard the first drum across the river on his or her first night in the "bush"? It was true that Africa possessed "tribal" (i.e., pre-industrial) peoples, many of whom lived in romantically round thatched dwellings, amid circling forests or hills, and sometimes, though rarely, amid vast game herds. The idyllic settings of a thousand novels and a hundred movies had some basis in reality. But of course, even in the 1920s, an urban Africa existed and was rapidly expanding, not to mention an Africa of dynamic social and cultural transformation where, if anything, little of the old was preserved if anything of the new could be acquired. In this respect Africans differed not at all from Asians, Amerindians, or Europeans for that matter. This Africa—far more "typical" than that of the idyllic village unchanged by time—was rarely considered by anthropologists until the decade of the 1970s. We noted in the previous chapter that as intrepid an ethnographer as Stanley Diamond could postulate that the Anaguta, who, in his own words, lived only "a few miles as the Crow flies" from the large mining town of Jos, existed in a kind of splendid isolation, a worthy example of the "primitive" at its best.[76]

It is true, when faced with widespread urbanization throughout the African continent, that some American anthropologists sought continuities in urban settings which could be directly traced to the "traditional" society from which the urban settler came, but few were prepared to consider the urban environment in its larger (historical) context, or to consider Africans as urban peoples, whether of ancient or recent derivation. Daniel F. McCall of Boston University was one of the first American ethnographers to do so. In a prescient article in 1955 he pointed out the fact that urban life tended to destroy larger kin groups, replacing them with unstable nuclear families. Although William Bascom, for years the leading expert on Yoruba cities and the complexities of the segmentary lineage organizations within these cities, had documented the deep historicity of Yoruba cities and towns (noting that the specialization necessary to urban development was an equally developed Yoruba tradition), his analysis put renewed emphasis on the vitality—at least in the classic Yoruba cities—of the bonds of kinship which characterized traditional Yoruba social organization. He noted almost in passing (this was in 1955) that such bonds were, however, rapidly weakening.[77] Though a few social scientists, and some of the better journalists, had also begun to examine the disintegration of traditional social systems, for some reason it has taken mainstream anthropology nearly forty years to acknowledge this unwelcome fact. The emphasis on collection of data within traditional structures, in its drive to provide a "science of the concrete," had led to an almost willful neglect of internal narrative. Historians knew this, but their work typically (until the 1970s at least) focused on the documented record of colonial or pre-colonial societies, stratified societies, larger economic and diplomatic networks and systems, and the struggle against colonialism. Rarely did historians deal with the so-called "small-scale" societies, to which perhaps the majority of Africans belonged as the era of independence began. Some historians, in the 1960s, had begun to consider the loosely-organized yet vital amalgamations (economic and social, as well as political) which Africans had created even before the colonial era—as d'Azevedo suggested in his seminal piece on the West Atlantic Cultural Region.[78] But most remained bound to the larger more visible entities: traditional, colonial, or post-colonial.

Terence Ranger, beginning with his 1975 work on the effect of dance (across ethnic lines but within the context of colonialism), and later with his brilliant work on the invention of ethnicity, seemed to steal a march on anthropology by focusing his formidable analysis on the very meat of ethnography, the "traditional" small-scale, linguistically divergent, "tribal" peoples. His compelling evidence that the "ethnicity" of the Shona, in modern Zimbabwe, was a construct of white missionary activity, colonialism, and most important, of African participation in peasant agriculture, labor migration, and education (usually within one or the other church mission), seems far more pertinent than the turgid reductionism of so many pure ethnographies.[79]

The broader historical view, which Boas emphasized from the start, thus only began to gain ground as the gap between present reality and anthropological theory grew so deep it could no longer be ignored. Eventually, in the 1970s and 1980s, several anthropologists began to address some of these real problems, especially urbanism. Sandra Barnes, another in the third generation of the Boas-Herskovits lineage, was one of the younger ethnographers who turned to the daunting environment of urban Africa. Her 1986 book, *Patrons and Power: Creating a Political Community in Metropolitan Lagos*, addresses some of the real (and largely historical) problems of urbanization, especially in the much-neglected realm of politics.[80] It is interesting that her work, which owes much to Bascom and his previous work on Yoruba urban life, is also "Boasian" in the larger sense. Where a narrow synchronic study might find only disintegration—the timeless "aboriginal" system irretrievably broken and seemingly dysfunctional—Barnes finds a Herskovitsian continuity.

One could carry this too far, of course. Anthropologists are not the only academics in recent decades who have fallen victim to "pie in the sky" fantasies. Two decades ago Anthony Hopkins pilloried the "myth of merrie Africa" which seemed to captivate some historians with its comfortable assumption that "the pre-colonial era was a Golden Age, in which generations of Africans enjoyed congenial lives in well-integrated, smoothly-functioning societies."[81] As he further pointed out, this myth presumed that African peoples had it easy, plucked fruit from the trees at need, and danced and drummed away to their heart's content, and that only with colonialism did Europeans disrupt this harmony with their ruthless exploitation, backed by force. Needless to say this is exactly the kind of *reductio ad absurdum* which has in recent years come under attack from within anthropology. As we shall see, the critique from within can be the most withering of all.

None of us can pretend immunity to the conventions and stereotypes which undergird our own society. Is there a young researcher who has not known that feeling—having first experienced Africa via a teeming, noisome city (Freetown, Lagos, Kinshasa, Accra, Zaria, Nairobi, it does not matter)—of disjointed disaffection upon first arriving: "Where is *Africa* in all this, where the quiet cone-shaped huts, the silent herdsman, the women pounding at the mortar, the kitchen-smoke wreathing the golden thatch, the elders in council, the distant hidden grove of ceremonies as old as time?" In time, one can eventually find some of these, if not quite in the pristine state expected. Is the teeming shantytown, the sprawling suburb, the crowded roadway, the noisy metropolitan night, any less African because it is so depressingly familiar?

A highly trained ethnographer, conversant in the latest field techniques, armored for culture-shock, prepared to handle the emotional burden of living within a culture very different from his own, might be able to see far more clearly than a newly arrived missionary expecting to "better" the peoples among whom he will work, but such a person is bound to be affected deeply by the "baggage" of his own society. The field researcher who is seeking a "pristine" African society of placid villages and mellowed clans, where every practice, no matter how terrible, has its larger purpose, will no doubt find it.[82]

Which brings us to a difficult point. It is relatively easy to accept the image of a Stanley or a T. R., finding his proverbial Africa wherever he traveled. Roosevelt, whatever the scientific pretensions of his large African "expedition," was completely comfortable in his "big-game" hunter's role, observing Africans as if they were another variety of game, just as it would never have occurred to Stanley to question the motives of his adventuring. The latter, after all, had written "We are of the blood which furnishes the world with its Daniel Boones, its Francis Drakes, its Cecil Rhodes."[83] However, as indicated at the beginning of this chapter, it is not so easy to accept the idea that conscious or unconscious conventions affected even the best ethnographers, since their works claim a scientific objectivity. As Laura Bohannan reveals in her anthropological novel *Return to Laughter*,[84] the ethnographer cannot escape the values of her own culture and is invariably influenced by the *Weltanschauung* of her own society, despite the most rigorous training.

James Clifford, in *Writing Culture*, describes the typical layman's image of the anthropologist in-the-field, deeply immersed in his work among some little-known people, as if anonymous. We invariably think of Margaret Mead amid the palms of one of the South Seas archipelagoes, "going native," as it were, in order to find out exactly how the Samoans viewed, and practiced, sex. Or, perhaps we think of Colin Turnbull observing the BaMbuti pygmies of

Zaire, watching this gentle people as they hunt and gather amid the greenery of the great rainforest. Some might think of Levi-Strauss among the Bororo of the Amazon basin, recording elaborate rituals and interpreting myths which unveil the unity beneath that people's lore. Clearly, as Clifford reminds us, this idealized view is not entirely accurate: for even as we read of Colin Turnbull's adventures among the BaMbuti "running along jungle paths," Turnbull mentions "that he lugged around a typewriter."[85] Left unsaid is the question about the "other" baggage which the researcher already has in his head. Obviously, it is the *process* by which the author intrudes within the text which is all-important. George E. Marcus, Clifford's co-editor, adds the somewhat disturbing idea that the new "literary consciousness" (i.e., the focus on the text) of current ethnography is a healthy thing since the theoretical underpinnings of anthropology are in disarray.[86] Although this is an attitude which Boas or Herskovits would have found puzzling (one can surmise that both would have concluded that contemporary ethnography has lost its grounding in empiricism), Marcus's observation reflects a tentativeness among modern scientists of all kinds, and nowhere has that tentativeness been more evident than in the social sciences.

Clifford Geertz goes further yet in his 1988 book, *Works and Lives: The Anthropologist as Author*, suggesting, for example, that the marvelously self-confident, self-assured, and apparently straightforward certitude of the British anthropologist E. E. Evans-Pritchard, whose classic work *The Nuer* is standard reading in hundreds of introductory Anthropology courses, is itself evidence of that author's cultural bias.[87] The result is what Geertz calls "magic lantern" anthropology, a captivating slide-show full of unforgettable visual images.[88] At least implied in Geertz' critique is the possibility that these images largely reflect Evans-Pritchard's own ordered, reasonable, English university world.[89]

A close look at *The Nuer* within the framework of our book reveals further, somewhat disturbing insights. It is, as we explain in chapter 5, a time-honored convention of the popular travel story to begin the account with a brief list of difficulties encountered. This is done in order to set the reader up for the truly exotic environment being described. As Percy Adams has written in a book called *Travellers and Travel Liars*, the more distinct the adventure is from the reader's experience (or the author's previous experience) the more exotic, indeed the more "other worldly" is the place and its people.[90] Though certainly no invidious comparison between a fine anthropologist like Evans-Pritchard and your garden variety travel writer is intended, here is Evans-Pritchard himself describing his arrival in Nuerland in 1930:

> My carriers dropped tent and stores in the centre of a tree-
> less plain, near some homesteads, and refused to bear them
> to the shade about a half mile further. Next day was devoted
> to erecting my tent and trying to persuade the Nuer, through
> my Atwot servant who spoke Nuer and some Arabic, to
> remove my abode to the vicinity of shade and water, which
> they refused to do. Fortunately a youth, Nhial, who has
> since been my constant companion in Nuerland, attached
> himself to me and after twelve days persuaded his kinsmen
> to carry my goods to the edge of the forest where they lived.[91]

In the meantime Evans-Pritchard's servants, "terrified of the
Nuer" had fled the camp, leaving the author to fend for himself with
the aid of the young Nhial, as he does with admirable pluck. Several pages more of this kind of description follow, providing the
reader with apparent evidence of the remarkable integrity of Nuer
cultural norms, as well as that people's stubborn resistance to
change. As Evans-Pritchard puts it when explaining Nuer obsti-
nacy, "I defy the most patient ethnologist to make headway against
this kind of opposition."[92] Nevertheless, before we finish Evans-
Pritchard's introduction we are happily informed that in time these
untrammeled folk had come to accept their visitor, treating him "as
an equal."[93] No doubt the tenacious Evans-Pritchard had earned
the grudging respect of these now-famous Nuer, the subject of his
brilliant, indeed courageous analysis. No doubt his classic ethnography will continue to inform (and entertain) students for years to
come.

Nonetheless, readers familiar with travel literature will recognize
the formative western conventions which frame the presentation of
travel literature.[94] Prominently included among these traditions is
the evocation of symbols of wildness: having to live in a tent, for
example, without the normal amenities of civilization, cut off amid
"intractable" country, deserted by one's bearers and servants. There
is the evocation of symbols of unmistakable differentness, i.e., the
"other" clearly defined: the named, unpredictable, intractable, suspicious, perhaps dangerous natives, who might at any moment
revert to type. There is the classic paradigm of the "outsider" looking in; though of course the reader instinctively knows that he or
she (like the author) is really the insider gazing at images—provided
by the author's magic lantern—of that other world, which is truly
outside. Finally, at least in Evans-Pritchard's case, there is the
alien—that same dangerous "other"—who, once we get to know
him, becomes the paradigmatic *familiar*, a kind of mirror reflection
(sans clothes, sans the corruption of civilization) of us. Indeed what
we seem to have, beneath the cogent analysis, is that familiar of the
Enlightenment, the noble savage.

This, of course, is the triumph of Evans-Pritchard's work. He convinced us, with good observation, with lists and evidence and coherent arguments, that these strange Nuer—despite their at-first seemingly incomprehensible behavior—are brothers under the skin, perhaps what we might once have been. Even thirty years after the first reading, one cannot read this excellent work without feeling that Evans-Pritchard, the clear-eyed social scientist, sought his Eden too.

It is interesting, as Adam Kuper points out in *The Invention of Primitive Society*, that Evans-Pritchard's book, *The Nuer*, postulates an almost perfect model of a kin-based primitive society, one which could be discovered again and again (if the correct methodology was used) all over the world. Evans-Pritchard was hardly a utopian, nor was he guilty—like Montaigne or Chateaubriand—of constructing the classic Eden filled with innocents. Yet for him the primitive society in question, at least the society in his book, seemed to provide dazzling confirmation that, however simple their economy and technology, the Nuer had a complicated, systematic, intrinsically sophisticated kinship system, one which was at one time or another (if not in evolutionary terms) or one place or the other, shared by all mankind. In that sense at least he *had* found his Eden.[95]

The more recent work of Douglas Johnson, *History and Prophecy Among the Nuer of the Southern Sudan*, goes beyond the scope of an internal anthropological critique, since historian Johnson casts doubt on many of Evans-Pritchard's basic assumptions, especially in matters of religion. Furthermore, Evans-Pritchard, according to Johnson, seemed to be unaware of recent major events in the history of the Sudan which had temporarily "isolated" the Nuer from their neighbors, the Dinka in particular.[96] Perhaps we shall never know exactly how much of Evans-Pritchard's work was influenced by external (colonial) considerations and how much of what he published represents a kernel of hard truth. Recent scholarship suggests that, as in the case of Margaret Mead, theoretical considerations played a significant role.

In a section of his book *In Search of the Primitive*, called "Entering the Field," Stanley Diamond also succumbed to the prosody of the traveler in a passage which might have been written by a nineteenth-century explorer,

> I wandered, also, through the introverted alleys of the old town [Kano]. . . . But even here, in northern Nigeria, one could sense the body of Africa throbbing under the cloak of Islam, like a great bird under a hood. I was familiar enough with the Middle East; it was Africa I was after, in order to

quicken an academic specialty, and we were not sorry to leave Kano. But first I was able to arrange, by lucky circumstance it seemed then, for a Hausa- and English-speaking Igbo cook, steward, interpreter and general factotum to join us at a later date at Jos.[97]

It is no accident that another of the world's famous anthropological works, *Tristes Tropiques* by Claude Levi-Strauss, also fits rather neatly within these conventions. It, too, is essentially a kind of literary travelogue. As Geertz notes, this wonderful ethnographic tome, "founding yet one more *scienza nova*," is also an attempt to "rehabilitate" Rousseau.[98] What Levi-Strauss accomplishes in his justly notorious travelogue is essentially the creation of a mythic world of exotica and adventure, whereby the author takes the reader on a trek into Brazil that is both physical and metaphysical. Indeed when viewed from the perspective of the symbolic conventions, Geertz's charge seems modest. Interestingly, at the beginning of *Tristes Tropiques*, Levi-Strauss himself warns the reader against the falsehoods common to popular travel literature:

> When I open one of these travel books, I see, for instance, that such and such a tribe is described as savage and is said still to preserve certain primitive customs, which are described in garbled form in a few superficial chapters; yet I spent weeks as a student reading books on that tribe written by professional anthropologists either recently or as much as fifty years ago, before contact with the white races and the resulting epidemics reduced it to a handful of pathetic rootless individuals.[99]

Levi-Strauss, after roundly condemning such literature, and pondering the "naive credulity" with which it is received by the public,[100] posits his own rather elaborate system, which, we are assured in a chapter called "The Making of an Anthropologist" is both intensely personal and intellectually rigorous. Nonetheless, as one reads on, it becomes evident that Levi-Strauss routinely pulls the reader into the very paradigm which he scorns. First, there is no false modesty about his role. He is there, we are informed, to explore things anew, to formulate a fresh perspective, to promulgate a heretofore unexamined synthesis. Early in the book he describes the nature of his own intellect:

> I have a neolithic kind of intelligence. Like native bush fires, it sometimes set unexplored areas alight; it may fertilize them and snatch a few crops from them, and then it moves on, leaving scorched earth in its wake.[101]

What can one say? Can any of us measure up to such an inferno?

Regarding his discovery of Robert Lowie's *Primitive Society*,[102] which he claims rescued him from the sterile disputations of philosophy and opened him to the spontaneity of anthropology, Levi-Strauss continues,

> My mind was able to escape from the Turkish-bath atmosphere in which it was being imprisoned by the practice of philosophical reflection. Once it got out into the open air it felt refreshed and renewed. Like a city-dweller transported to the mountains, I became drunk with space, while my dazzled eyes measured the wealth and variety of the objects surrounding me.[103]

It would seem that Levi-Strauss is deliberately setting himself up as the supreme outsider. He attempts no subtle influence but imposes himself on the text as the new ethnologist with a new world to discover. Regarding his "American" gurus, Lowie, Kroeber, and Boas, he writes,

> They seem to me to be as far removed as possible from the James or Dewey kind of American philosophy which has been out of date for so long, or from what is now called logical positivism. Since they were Europeans by birth and had been trained in Europe or by European professors, they represent something quite different; a synthesis which Columbus had made objectively possible four centuries earlier; the synthesis of a strong scientific method with the unique experimental field offered by the New World at a time when American anthropologists [could] visit native communities as easily as we could go to the Basque country or the Riviera.[104]

At best this is exaggerated. As Hyatt, Boas' biographer points out, Boas was suspicious of the generalizers and took a "particularist" stance when it came to ethnographic method. In this, says Hyatt, Boas was side-by-side with William James.[105] Further, just in case we don't get the message, Levi-Strauss takes us back to the era of Columbus, with a marvelous discussion on the shortcomings of "observation" in the fifteenth and sixteenth centuries. Through this juxtaposition of how things were, when "men . . . were not sensitive to the harmonious arrangement of the universe,"[106] versus how they are (in the mid-twentieth century) when science has all kinds of rational tools, Levi-Strauss not only shows us the range of his education, but quite clearly sets himself up as a new Columbus, one superbly equipped to explore this New World, which he assures us, is indeed still unique.

> The impression of enormous size is peculiar to America, and
> can be felt everywhere, in town and country alike: I have
> experienced it along the coast and on the plateaux of central
> Brazil, in the Bolivian Andes and the Colorado Rockies, in
> the suburbs of Rio, the outskirts of Chicago and the streets
> of New York.[107]

This travel boasting, which certainly cannot be claimed as a reliable mode of anthropological investigation, seems to be, like the other admittedly superfluous passages that fill *Tristes Tropiques*, intended for another purpose. Certainly such romantic asides help set the reader up for Levi-Strauss's own discoveries among the Bororo, Nambikwara, and other unknown tribes of the Brazilian rainforest. Disdaining travel books and their lies (easy enough to expose), Levi-Strauss lays the groundwork for his new scientific mode, what Geertz aptly calls "a formal metaphysics of being."[108] Yet, throughout *Tristes Tropiques* Levi-Strauss does exactly those things for which he condemns the travel writers: he paints a marvelous and intensely subjective picture of a new and exotic world. Frankly, this is an intrusion of Gallic ego similar to the kind of balderdash found in the "award winning" film *The Sky Above: The Mud Below*, a work voyeuristically obscene in its assumption of superiority.

Repeatedly in *Tristes Tropiques*, we find passages, which, though of high literary merit, reveal the essential romantic quality of the text,

> Nothing now remains along this coast, which has reverted to
> its paradisal state, except a few lonely and majestic build-
> ings in front of which the galleons used to moor. . . .[109]

Why, one wonders, did Levi-Strauss neglect to mention the land-stressed population immediately inland of this "paradisal" coast with its endless empty beaches? Even fifty years ago Northwest Brazil was overpopulated, though its littoral was empty.

Perhaps one of the most telling passages in *Tristes* is Levi-Strauss's literate and innovative description of a Brazilian rainforest, where "As in the Douanier Rousseau's paintings of exotic landscapes, living entities attain the dignity of objects."[110] This is by clear contrast—via a wonderful series of Cartesian balances and paradigms—with the woodlands of the West "where the landscape is subservient to man."[111] By the time we have read several hundred pages of this fabulous stuff, we might be forgiven if we find Levi-Strauss's disclaimer, that certain Amerindian civilizations also mastered the landscape and turned it to their needs, a little disingenuous.

It might seem too glib to quote Levi-Strauss himself about the dangers of the exotic; "I therefore mistrust superficial contrasts and the apparently picturesque; they may not be lasting. What we call the exotic expresses an inequality of rhythm."[112] Yet, one finds in his magnificent prose a mirror of the romanticism in us all.

> Dreams, "the god of the savages," as the old missionaries used to say, have always slipped through my fingers like quicksilver. But a few shining particles have remained stuck, here and there. At Cuiaba, perhaps, where the gold nuggets used to come from? At Ubatuba, now a deserted port, but where the galleons used to be loaded two hundred years ago? In the air over the Arabian deserts, which were pink and green with the luster of ear-shells? In America or Asia? On the Newfoundland sandbanks, the Bolivian plateaux or the hills along the Burmese frontier? I can pick out at random a name still steeped in the magic of legend: Lahore.[113]

A truly great writer, certainly an original in his creation of new ethnographic modes, Levi-Strauss gives himself away in these passages. When he quotes that most romantic of romantics, Chateaubriand, we know what really moved him in all his researches: "'Every Man', wrote Chateaubriand, 'carries within him a world which is composed of all that he has seen and loved, and to which he constantly returns, even when he is travelling through, and seems to be living in, some different world.'"[114]

Our criticism of Levi-Strauss—in an era when nearly every textual critique has highlighted the romantic weaknesses in the works of this great scholar—does not mean that all of his work is therefore invalid. Through his exhaustive studies of the myths and rituals of preliterate peoples Levi-Strauss revealed certain underlying structures (ideas, mental properties, symbols) which are (allegedly) as coherent as many systems of modern philosophy. But this news, once disseminated via his scores of publications, was not essentially superior to the similar news, available in Herskovits' magnus opus, *Dahomey*, that religious practices, once dismissed as dark and violent rites, were in reality integrated pieces of a sophisticated and coherent system.

In his powerful book *Paths Toward a Clearing*, anthropologist Michael Jackson—when confronted with the anxiety that affects so many ethnographers "who want to ditch the positivist notion of a value-neutral social science, yet cannot accept the relativist, solipsistic kind of anthropology they imagine will follow in its wake"—dares to suggest a closer look at John Dewey's idea about the "troubling contrast between the seen and unseen."[115] Jackson quotes Dewey as follows:

> We may term the way in which our ancestors dealt with such contrast superstitions, but the contrast is no superstition. It is a primary datum in any experience. . . . Our magical safeguard against the uncertain character of the world is to deny the existence of chance, to mumble universal and necessary law, the ubiquity of cause and effect, the uniformity of nature, universal progress, and the inherent rationality of the universe.[116]

Bemoaning "the loss of our empirical field" Jackson calls for a return to the kind of "radical empiricism" (i.e., the uncompromising openness to raw evidence) originally defined by another pragmatist, William Bateson, and before that the great William James.[117]

As Karl Mannheim pointed out six decades ago in *Ideology and Utopia* the idea that objectivity resides in the eye of the beholder is an ancient one.[118] More important, Mannheim showed how belief in a system can skew any view of reality.[119] In time, any theory, no matter how brilliantly conceived, can become distorted by its adherents and by what appears to be a logical, coherent, analytical framework, leading to the "truth." For example, the thrust of Immanuel Wallerstein's corrective in *The Capitalist World Economy* has frequently led to another type of distortion. In the last two decades many studies of Africa (especially histories) are microstudies so reductionistic that no one but a specialized Ph.D. committee would be interested; this is the sort of thing one scholar called "Mud-Pie Production among the Ba-X and its Linkage to the World Economy." Whatever the discipline, few possess the larger vision of Wallerstein or Eric Wolf, whose *Europe and the People without History* is as challenging in concept as it is sweeping in scope.[120]

So where does that leave us?

One thing seems clear. The focus on larger cultural interactions and groupings among traditional societies which began in American ethnography and was applied (via Herskovits and his students) to Africa, did much to liberate ethnography from a pseudo-scientific, often racist, comparative approach, which still dominated much of anthropology well into this century. By midcentury the Boasian view prevailed among the majority of American ethnographers, especially Africanists. The best work over the middle decades of this century, much of it carried out by Herskovits' own students, emphasized the dynamics of cultural change and adaptation over time, although the emphasis on the collection (and analysis) of empirical data remained central to most anthropological endeavors. In the post-colonial era, increasing numbers of British and Continental ethnographers, once freed from the restraints of colonialism, also sought a more objective approach. Some, like Daryll Forde and

Evans-Pritchard, remained as influential in their own spheres as was Herskovits or Turner in the U.S., or Levi-Strauss in France.[121] Others remained hide-bound, refining outmoded "evolutionsist," sometimes racist, views long after their supposed basis in science had been demolished.

On the one hand, with its grand success in Africa, in Oceana, in North America, indeed wherever the Boasians traveled, came a danger for the culturalist mode—perhaps inherent in any successful school of thought—noted by Karl Mannheim in the 1930s. Taken to extremes, the cultural approach, with its focus on borrowed or shared characteristics, over time, could lead to a dangerous determinism, a preoccupation with the "primitive," and a worshipful neo-Rousseauianism whereby the simpler the people (i.e., the less socially differentiated, the more economically primitive, the less stratified, etc.) the "better" they are. It could also lead, as Derek Freeman has pointed out in his critique of Mead, to a cultural determinism every bit as restrictive in its focus on a single process as the biological determinism of the early-twentieth century was wedded to hereditary principles.[122]

On the other hand, once more hearkening back to Boas, American anthropology generally maintained a healthy skepticism regarding any ethnographic mode which celebrated the isolated "tribe," which seemed to exist in a perfect anthropological present, and which, in the more extreme examples of "functionalism" seemed to exist—at least in ethnographic tomes—in isolation from all others. This led to a healthy search for broader commonalities extending beyond the original concept of the "cultural zone." In some instances noted in this chapter this resulted in a focus on empiricism—at least among some ethnographers—so rigorous that Boas himself would approve. Nevertheless, as is so often the case when a thesis becomes a theorem, some anthropologists, in the commendable desire to seek a parallel complexity among the simpler societies which they studied, succumbed to the blandishments of a relativism so extreme that the magical lore known to the "savage mind"—as explicated in Levi-Strauss's book of that name—could be construed as a distinct but analogous mode of scientific thought.[123] In this re-created romantic world, traditional superstitions and mystical and religious beliefs were rationalized as exhaustive observations of the natural world, different from those of the West, perhaps less precise, but equally valid for all of that. The consequence in some ethnographies was a nether-nether world (one beloved of the disciples of structuralism) wherein prescientific ideas of the supernatural were elevated to a philosophical plane. If one is to believe Levi-Strauss, though the modes of thought among "savages" were different, the consequent reality was every bit as reasonable. Under this influence many social scientists began to question the entire notion that there is a marked distinction between what is rational and irrational within any "system" of beliefs. Obviously social science had long-since proved that the rational and irrational operate within all societies, and that there is no clear distinction regardless of the level of social development. Nonetheless, among these neo-Rousseauians the differences between "western science" and non-western mythology were blurred, reduced to questions of emphasis. A sorcerer's incantations had as much meaning, therefore, as the diagnosis of a physician. In this schemata formal education and the accumulated knowledge of generations of literate investigation apparently would count for little or nothing. Theoretically, the lore and practice of a clever shaman could equal the wisdom accumulated during a western scholar's lifetime. Even Levi-Strauss would not go this far, of course, but the ensuing reductionism and exaggerated relativism of much ethnography in the 1970s and 1980s was a direct consequence.

One of the authors recalls a conversation around 1970 with a young anthropologist, just beginning his field work in Africa, who was convinced that no one except other specialists would read his work, "Margaret Mead, Evans-Pritchard, Herskovits, Lucy Mair, Turnbull, everyone with a decent education has read them. But who reads anything published by anthropologists now, except other anthropologists?" What could one say? It was already apparent in 1970 that any work written for the general public would be suspect to begin with, so minutely specialized and reductionistic had much ethnographic literature become. Furthermore, the discourse within the discipline was increasingly arcane, the language dense, the focus narrowed. As we suggested above, the same could be said for other disciplines, but since anthropology had from the beginning purported to interpret the particulars of any given society so as to make them meaningful to all of humanity, this lament seemed especially poignant.

Obviously, there are many whose work has found a significant audience, including the works of Victor Turner, Johannes Fabian, Sandra Barnes, Igor Kopytoff, and the former New Zealander, Michael Jackson.[124] The latter's studies of the Kuranko, when seen in connection with his fiction and poetry, only serve to underline the significance of the creative text in the best contemporary anthropology. In ethnography, as in history, the success of a work would seem to come down, in the final analysis, to the author's capacity to explain and convince.

Finally it would be unfair to say that the infamous "anthropological present" and the obviously distorted portraits which it produced was limited to the various structuralist schools noted above. Plenty of American anthropologists went out to find their romantic Africa; where every animal killed helped preserve a balance of nature, where every child reared was evidence of mutual interdependence and equality between the sexes, where every rite and ritual held a deeper and unifying meaning to all participants, indeed an Africa quite as uncorrupted by the West—and all its unnamed evils—as was ever imagined by any Stanley, any Roosevelt. Nor have we suggested that the celebration of the exotic—all marvelously disguised within an elegant Cartesian structure of perfect logic, which, in retrospect, seems to have colored so much of the work of the structuralists—did not captivate any number of American ethnographers. Examples of both have been presented here in some detail. Africa was simply irresistible to such romantic souls. Nonetheless, there were dedicated anthropologists who pushed their work in new directions. Not satisfied with ideas which seemed tainted by imperial links or purposes, or which seemed only to further the isolation of Africa and Africans, or which seemed to place Africans in some Edenic time-warp, these Americans sought modes which illuminated real problems and real people.

Notes

1. Olaudah Equiano, *The Interesting Narrative of the Life of Olaudah Equiano or Gustavus Vasa, The African* (London: Dawsons, 1969 [1789]). Other similar accounts, such as Venture Smith, *A Narrative of the Life and Adventures of Venture* (New-London, Conn.: A Descendant of Venture, 1835 [1798]) and Ukawsaw Gronniosaw, *A Narrative of the most remarkable particulars in the life of James Albert Ukawsaw Gronniosaw, An African Prince* (Millwood, N.Y.: Kraus-Thompson Organization, Ltd., 1972 [1780]), typically written long after the events they describe, are equally sketchy on Africa.

2. W. E. B. Du Bois, *The World and Africa* (New York: The Viking Press, 1947) and *Black Folk Then and Now* (Millwood, N.Y.: Kraus-Thompson Organization, Ltd., 1975 [1939]); Carter Woodson, *The Negro in Our History* (Washington, D.C.: The Associated Publishers, 1962) and *African Background Outlined* (New York: Negro Universities Press, 1936). Earlier works such as George W. Williams, *History of the Negro Race in America* (New York: Putnam's Sons, 1883), and Booker T. Washington, *The Story of the Negro* (New York: P. Smith, 1940) are not very informative about Africa.

3. Henry Morton Stanley, *How I Found Livingstone*, 2 vols. (New York: Gilberton, 1954 [1872]), *Through the Dark Continent*, 2 vols. (London: Sampson, Low, Marston, Searle and Rivington, 1878), and *In Darkest Africa*, 2 vols. (London: Sampson, Low, Marston, Searle, and Rivington, 1890).

4. James Fenimore Cooper, *The Last of the Mohicans* [1826] and *The Deerslayer* [1841] were two of the most popular of the five novels collected as *The Leather-Stocking Saga* (New York: Pantheon Books, 1954 [1823-1841]).

5. Henry Wadsworth Longfellow, *The Song of Hiawatha* (New York: Gilberton, 1949 [1855]).

6. Milo M. Quaife, ed., *The Journals of Captain Meriwether Lewis, etc, kept on the expedition of western exploration, 1803-1806* (Madison: The State Historical Society of Wisconsin, 1916).

7. Francis Parkman, *The Oregon Trail* (Garden City, N.Y.: Garden City Books, 1959 [1847]).

8. Including Cooper's, scores of frontier novels were written before the civil war and hundreds after. Many of these were first serialized in popular magazines. See Henry Nash Smith, *Virgin Land* (New York: Alfred A Knopf, 1950), 90-125 for a useful analysis of the genre. Though some scholars lump these works together with the classic "western" novel, they actually constitute a separate category.

9. George A. Custer, *My Life on the Plains* (New York: Sheldon, 1876); Elizabeth Bacon Custer, *Tenting on the Plains* (Norman: Oklahoma University Press, 1971 [1887]). Among the better-known memoirs of ranking officers are Martin F. Schmitt and Dee Brown, eds., *General Crook: His Autobiography* (Norman: Oklahoma University Press, 1946); Nelson Miles, *Personal Recollections* (New York: Werner, 1896); and Anson Mills, *My Story* (Washington, D.C.: The Author, 1918).

10. Few of these men wrote their own works, but their stories (often largely fictionalized) were printed in many collections, including George Frederick Ruxton, *Life in the Far West* (London: Blackwood and Sons, 1849) and Frances Fuller Victor, *The River of the West* (Hartford and Toledo: R. W. Bliss and Co., 1870). Many books have been published about the great "mountain men" and scouts, but the best remains Bernard DeVoto's masterpiece, *Across the Wide Missouri* (Boston: Houghton Mifflin Co., 1947).

11. John Charles Fremont, *Report of the Exploring Expedition to the Rocky Mountains* (Washington, D.C.: Gales and Seaton, 1845). Much of this work was carefully edited by Fremont's gifted wife Jesse. Its style is largely hers, its content, his.

12. Owen Wister, *The Virginian* (New York: Macmillan, 1902).

13. Henry Nash Smith, 117.

14. Theodore Roosevelt, *The Winning of the West* (New York: The Current Literature Publishing Co., 1905) and *Hunting Trips of a Ranchman: Sketches of Sport on the Northern Cattle Plains* (New York: G. P. Putnam's Sons, 1885).

15. Lewis Henry Morgan, *League of the Ho-de-no-sau-nee, Iroquois* (Rochester, N.Y.: Sage and Brothers, 1851) and *Ancient Society: Or Researches in the Lines of Human Progress from Savagery, through Barbarism to Civilization* (New York: World Publishing Co., 1963 [1877]).

16. Robert E. Bieder, *Science Encounters the Indian, 1820-1880: The Early Years of American Ethnology* (Norman: University of Oklahoma Press, 1986), 194-246. This assessment of Morgan challenges mainstream historians of anthropology, including Marvin Harris and Fred W. Voget.

17. The end of the American frontier occasioned one of the most influential articles ever published by a historian, Frederick Jackson Turner's

celebrated "The Significance of the Frontier in American History" (*The Frontier in American History* [New York: Holt and Co., 1921 (1893)]). Turner's thesis, that the frontier environment of America had shaped the American character, has been noted by virtually every historian of anthropology from George Stocking to Marvin Harris.

18. Marshall Hyatt, *Franz Boas, Social Activist: The Dynamics of Ethnicity* (New York, Greenwood Press, 1990), 9-14. Boas was still officially a geographer when he worked among the Eskimos and Northwest Coast peoples, but as Hyatt and others (see Melville J. Herskovits, *Franz Boas: The Science of Man in the Making* [New York: Scribners, 1953]) have pointed out, these expeditions marked his conversion to the new science.

19. Margaret T. Hodgen, *Anthropology, History, and Cultural Change* (Tucson: University of Arizona Press, 1974), 1-32. The debate between the "functionalists" (who generally opposed any study of the cultural experiences of dated peoples) and those who favored a more diachronic approach (including Kroeber, Lowie, and others of the Boas school) has never been resolved among anthropologists. Also see Adam Kuper, *The Invention of Primitive Society* (London: Routledge, 1988), 126-51.

20. Hyatt, 18-19.

21. Ibid., 19.

22. Ibid., 21. This fact is especially interesting, since Claude Levi-Strauss specifically claimed that Boas, as a European-trained scholar, was "as far removed as possible from the James or Dewey kind of American philosophy."

23. George W. Stocking Jr., ed., *The Shaping of American Anthropology 1883-1911: A Franz Boas Reader* (New York: Basic Books, 1974), 57-58. Also, Kuper, 130-31.

24. George W. Stocking Jr., *Race, Culture, and Evolution: Essays in the History of Anthropology* (New York: The Free Press, 1968), 111-32. Also see Carl N. Degler, *In Search of Human Nature: The Decline and Revival of Darwinism in American Social Thought* (New York: Oxford University Press, 1991), 59-83. Chapter 3 of the latter is a brilliant exposition of Boas's historical and relativistic challenge to prevailing racist theory.

25. Stocking, *Race, Culture, and Evolution*, 131.

26. Degler, 59-101.

27. Fred W. Voget, *A History of Ethnology* (New York: Holt, Rinehart and Winston, 1975), 136-64. Also see Degler, 3-18.

28. Comte Joseph de Gobineau, *The Inequality of the Human Races*, 4 vols. (New York: Putnam, 1915 [1853-1855]). Gobineau (1815-1882) linked national history specifically with race and class, and argued in favor of Nordic superiority (and against miscegenation which he believed would weaken that superiority) long before Hitler and his minions made it popular.

29. Margaret Mead, *Cooperation and Competition Among Primitive Peoples* (New York: McGraw-Hill, 1937), 558-59.

30. Clark Wissler, *Man and Culture* (New York: Crowell, 1923) and Alfred L. Kroeber, "The Culture-Area and Age-Area Concepts of Clark

Wissler" in ed. Alfred L. Kroeber, *Methods in Social Science: A Case Book* (New York: Harcourt, Brace and Co., 1931). Also see Alfred L. Kroeber, *Culture and Natural Areas of Native North America* (Berkeley: University of California Press, 1939).

31. Kroeber, *Culture and Natural Areas*, 248-50.

32. Marvin Harris, *The Rise of Anthropological Theory* (New York: Crowell, 1968), 375, has pointed up the weaknesses of this concept.

33. Richard P. Strong, ed. *The African Republic of Liberia and the Belgian Congo, Harvard African Expedition, 1926-1927*, 2 vols. (Cambridge: Harvard University Press, 1930). Though there was no anthropologist among the eight scientists who made up this expedition (three were experts in tropical medicine, one a medical entomologist, one an ornithologist and photographer, one a botanist, one a zoologist, and one a mammalogist) they did not hesitate to make egregiously judgmental statements about the native peoples. For example, the porters "would call to one another by baying as hounds do. They are a savage people and sometimes would beat their drums furiously throughout the entire night" (82).

34. British social anthropologist Lucy Mair, *An African People in the Twentieth Century* (London: Routledge, Kegan Paul, 1965 [1934]), argued from her work among the Baganda, that Indirect Rule was to be preferred in the African colonies because traditional society was thereby protected from unnecessary changes, and thus preserved as a base for the future. Nothing mitigated more in favor of Indirect Rule than the concept of the discreet "tribe." Indeed in some parts of Africa where distinct tribal entities were not easily discerned, anthropologists helped hard-pressed administrators to so define local populations. One of the more interesting books on this subject is Talal Asad, ed., *Anthropology and the Colonial Encounter* (New York: Humanities Press, 1973), especially the chapter by Helen Lackner, "Social Anthropology and Indirect Rule. The Colonial Administration and Anthropology in Eastern Nigeria: 1920-1940," 123-51. The creation of the infamous "Warrant Chiefs" in Iboland (where there had been no chiefs) by the Colonial Administration, relying on the dubious ethnography of Northcote Thomas, is a case in point.

35. Stocking, *Race, Culture, and Evolution*, 259-60.

36. Melville J. Herskovits, "A Preliminary Consideration of the Culture Areas of Africa," *American Anthropologist* 26 (1924): 50-63. Herskovits later refined this idea in *Man and His Works* (New York: Alfred A Knopf, 1948), 183-200.

37. Herskovits, *Man and His Works*, 191.

38. These areas were detailed as follows: (1.) Hottentot (2.) Bushman (3.) East African Cattle Area (4.) Congo (5.) East Horn (6.) Eastern Sudan (7.) Western Sudan (8.) Desert Area, and (9.) Egypt. Herskovits later renamed the first two Khoisan a and Khoisan b, and divided the Congo and Guinea Coast into two separate areas.

39. Herskovits, *Man and His Works*, 198.

40. George Eaton Simpson, *Melville J. Herskovits* (New York: Columbia University Press, 1973), 101-3.

41. Bronislaw Malinowski, *Argonauts of the Western Pacific* (New York: Dutton, 1966 [1922]).
42. Simpson, 100-4; Kuper, 190-92.
43. Though few anthropologists were hide-bound by any overarching theory, many in the British school adhered to a structural-functional model which presumed, as Radcliffe-Brown put it, "stability, definiteness, and consistency in the social structure" (Harris, 534). Harris correctly notes that Radcliffe-Brown advocated three sociological "laws" all of which, according to his thesis, led to social cohesion.
44. Melville J. Herskovits, *Acculturation: The Study of Cultural Contact* (New York: J. J. Augustin, 1938), 1-32.
45. Regarding the *Kulturkries Schule*, see Margaret Hodgen, 30-31.
46. French structuralism owes much to Emile Durkheim, who founded a highly theoretical school of sociology and anthropology which dominated ethnography in France for more than seventy years. Essentially structuralism postulated that social facts are entities (more mental than material, but no less powerful for all that). See Emile Durkheim, *Emile Durkheim: Selections from his Work* (New York: Crowell, 1963). Durkheim's ideas found a progressive (and prodigious) response in Claude Levi-Strauss, whose constructs are discussed later in this chapter. Although Harris argues that French structuralism, like American culturalism, did much to emancipate social science from biological reductionism (464-65), the authors of this work (while agreeing with this proposition) also contend that Levi-Strauss' structuralism, in some of his works, could lead to neo-Rousseauianism. It should be noted that British "functionalist" anthropology likewise avoided biological determinism.
47. C. G. Seligman, *Races of Africa* (London: Oxford University Press, 1930).
48. Ibid., 45.
49. Ibid., 45-46.
50. Ibid., 85.
51. Ibid., 135-36.
52. Edith R. Sanders, "The Hamitic Hypothesis: Its Origin and Functions in Time Perspective," *Journal of African History* 10, no. 4 (1969): 521-32.
53. Melville J. Herskovits, "The Cattle Complex in East Africa," *The American Anthropologist* reprint/monograph s.1: s.n. (1926).
54. Melville J. Herskovits, *Dahomey: An Ancient West African Kingdom*, 2 vols., (Evanston, Ill.: Northwestern University Press, 1967 [1938]). Also see George Eaton Simpson, 10-14.
55. Herskovits, *Dahomey* 1: i.
56. See Melville J. Herskovits, "The Significance of West Africa for Negro Research," in George Eaton Simpson, *Melville J. Herskovits* (New York: Columbia University Press, 1973), 127-40.
57. Herskovits, *Dahomey* 1: ii.
58. Melville J. Herskovits, *Acculturation* and *The Myth of the Negro Past* (New York: Harper and Row, 1941). Also see Simpson, 25-31.

59. Roland B. Dixon, *The Racial History of Man* (New York: Scribners, 1923). Also see Stephen J. Gould, *The Mismeasure of Man* (New York: Norton, 1981), 73-145.

60. Carleton S. Coon, *The Races of Europe* (New York: The Macmillan Co., 1939), *The Origin of Races* (New York: Alfred A Knopf, 1962) and *Racial Adaptations: A Study of the Origins, Nature, and Significance of Racial Variations in Humans* (Chicago: Nelson-Hall, 1982). While physical anthropologists agree that racial distinctions which can be "measured" physiologically exist among humans, strictly speaking what we call "race" is nothing more than the minor geographical adaptations known as "clines" among zoologists. Where Coon differs from most is in his theory that modern races actually evolved separately, from distinct branches off *Homo erectus*.

61. Edward H. McKinley, *The Lure of Africa: American Interest in Tropical Africa, 1919-1939* (New York: Bobbs-Merrill Co., 1974), 150.

62. McKinley, 151-52. Hambly's film, *Journey in Southern Angola*, 1929-1930, is still available. This film is summarized in Steven Ohrn and Rebecca Riley, eds. *Africa from Real to Reel* (Waltham, Mass.: African Studies Association, 1976), 52.

63. Theodore Roosevelt, *African Games Trails: An Account of the African Wanderings of an American Hunter-Naturalist* (New York: Charles Scribners Sons, 1910).

64. The excellent collection, *Continuity and Change in African Cultures* (William R. Bascom and Melville J. Herskovits, eds. [Chicago: University of Chicago Press, 1959]), remains one of the best examples of the range of Herskovits' students' interests. Several of his distinguished students are represented here early in their careers.

65. William R. Bascom, *African Art in Cultural Perspective* (New York: Norton, 1973); J. Gus Liebenow, *Liberia: The Quest for Democracy* (Bloomington: Indiana University Press, 1987); Alan P. Merriam, *The Anthropology of Music* (Evanston, Ill.: Northwestern University Press, 1964); Vernon Dorjahn, "The Changing Political System of the Temne," *Africa* 30 (1960): 110-40; Warren d'Azevedo, "Some Historical Problems in the Delineation of a Central West Atlantic Region," *Annals of the New York Academy of Sciences* 96, no. 2 (1962): 512-38. Greenberg's work has transformed our understanding of African linguistics.

66. Igor Kopytoff, ed. *The African Frontier: The Reproduction of Traditional African Societies* (Bloomington: Indiana University Press, 1987).

67. Harold K. Schneider, "The Subsistence Role of Cattle among the Pakot and in East Africa," *American Anthropologist* 59 (1957): 278-301; d'Azevedo, "Some Historical Problems"; and Kopytoff, *The African Frontier.*

68. Joseph H. Greenberg, *Studies in African Linguistic Classification* (New Haven: Compass, 1955) and *The Languages of Africa* (Bloomington: University of Indiana Press, 1963).

69. Joseph H. Greenberg, *Languages in the Americas* (Stanford, Cal.: Stanford University Press, 1987).

70. James Clifford, *The Predicament of Culture* (Cambridge: Harvard University Press, 1988), 35.

71. Margaret Mead, *Sex and Temperament in Three Primitive Societies* (New York: New American Library, 1950 [1935]) and *Coming of Age in Samoa* (New York: Morrow, 1928).

72. Margaret Mead, *Male and Female: A Study of the Sexes in a Changing World* (New York: Morrow, 1952).

73. Derek Freeman, *Margaret Mead and Samoa: The Making and Unmaking of an Anthropological Myth* (Cambridge: Harvard University Press, 1983). Freeman's criticism has been under attack (for the most part) as a renewed manifestation of biological determinism. See Lowell D. Holmes, *Quest for the Real Samoa: The Mead/Freeman Controversy* (South Hadley, Mass.: Bergin and Garvey Publishers, 1987).

74. See previous chapter, and Edwin N. Wilmsen, *Land Filled with Flies: A Political Economy of The Kalahari* (Chicago: University of Chicago Press, 1989).

75. Henri Baudet, *Paradise on Earth: Some Thoughts on European Images of Non-European Man* (Westport, Conn.: Greenwood Press, 1965), 59.

76. See previous chapter, and Stanley Diamond, *In Search of the Primitive: A Critique of Civilization* (New Brunswick, N.J.: Transaction Books, 1974), 176-202. It should be noted, especially in "Plato and the Definition of the Primitive," originally printed in *Culture in History* (ed. Stanley Diamond [New York: Columbia University Press, 1960]), but included in this latter work as well, that Diamond does not attempt to construct a utopia, indeed he warns against this tendency, "some utopias face backward to a sometimes fantastic image of the primitive, others face forward to the complete triumph of the rational state" (118). Nonetheless Diamond is a leading thinker among those who clearly see the primitive (that is to say societies without hierarchies, stratifications, specializations, classes, etc.) as possessing superior humanity.

77. Daniel F. McCall, "The Dynamics of Urbanization in Africa," *The Annals of the American Academy of Political and Social Science* 292 (1955): 150-60; William Bascom, "Urbanization Among the Yoruba," *American Journal of Sociology* 60 (1955): 446-54.

78. Warren d'Azevedo, 512-38. Also see Alan Howard, "Big Men, Traders and Chiefs: Power, Commerce, and Spatial Change in the Sierra Leone-Guinea Plain" (Ph.D. diss., University of Wisconsin, 1972); Adam Jones, *From Slaves to Palm Kernels* (Weisbaden: F. Steiner, 1983); and Kenneth C. Wylie, "From the Fountainheads of the Niger: Researching a Multiethnic Regional History," in eds. John P. Henderson and Harry A. Reed, *Studies in the African Diaspora: A Memorial to James R. Hooker* (Dover, Mass.: The Majority Press, 1989), 67-86.

79. Terence O. Ranger, *Dance and Society in Eastern Africa: 1890-1970* (Berkeley: University of California Press, 1975) and "Missionaries, Migrants and the Manyika: The Invention of Ethnicity in Zimbabwe" in LeRoy Vail, ed. *The Creation of Tribalism in Southern Africa* (Berkeley: University of California Press, 1989), 118-49.

80. Sandra T. Barnes, *Patrons and Power: Creating a Political Community in Metropolitan Lagos* (Manchester: Manchester University Press, 1986), is a case in point. Barnes' methodology, as well as her subject, takes for granted the urban setting (ancient as well as modern).

81. Anthony G. Hopkins, *An Economic History of West Africa* (London: Longman, 1973), 10.
82. This model, which cannot be confined to any of the "national" schools, is nonetheless usually associated with the "British" social anthropology of Malinowski and his students, particularly Radcliffe-Brown and Evans-Pritchard. In fairness none of these sought "pristine" societies untouched by time, but the impression often given by the functionalist social anthropologists, indeed by much anthropological work in general, that only the "primitive" (in lay terms) is of real interest to the discipline, persists to this day. See, A. R. Radcliffe-Brown, *The Social Anthropology of Radcliffe-Brown* (London: Routledge and Kegan Paul, 1977) and *Method in Social Anthropology: Selected Essays* (Chicago: University of Chicago Press, 1958). Also see E. E. Evans-Pritchard, *Essays in Social Anthropology* (New York: Free Press of Glencoe, 1963).
83. Quoted in Martin Green, *Dreams of Adventure, Deeds of Empire* (New York: Basic Books, 1979), 258.
84. The extraordinary anthropological novel *Return to Laughter* by Elenore Smith Bowen (Laura Bohannan) (Garden City, N.Y.: Doubleday and Co., 1964) is exceptional in its candor in dealing with this issue.
85. James Clifford and George E. Marcus, eds., *Writing Culture: The Poetics and Politics of Ethnography* (Berkeley: University of California Press, 1986), 1.
86. Clifford and Marcus, 263.
87. Clifford Geertz, *Works and Lives: The Anthropologist as Author* (Stanford, Ca.: Stanford University Press, 1988), 61.
88. Ibid., 64-65.
89. Ibid., 70.
90. Percy Adams, *Travelers and Travel Liars, 1660-1800* (Berkeley: University of California Press, 1962), vii-xii.
91. E. E. Evans-Pritchard, *The Nuer* (Oxford: Oxford University Press, 1969 [1940]), 10.
92. Ibid., 13.
93. Ibid., 15.
94. The essential ingredients of this analysis are the authors' own, though works on travel literature cited here, and in chapter 4, have influenced this.
95. Kuper, 233.
96. Douglas Johnson, "History and Prophecy Among the Nuer of the Southern Sudan" (Ph.D. diss., University of Michigan Microfilms, Ann Arbor, 1980). Johnson's criticism of Evans-Pritchard, especially regarding the limitations on Evans-Pritchard's research on Nuer religion (the prophets in particular), underlines the dangers of the synchronic approach (38-50). Also see Raymond Kelly, *The Nuer Conquest* (Ann Arbor: The University of Michigan Press, 1985).
97. Stanley Diamond, *In Search of the Primitive*, 54-55.
98. Claude Levi-Strauss, *Tristes Tropiques* (New York: Antheneum, 1974 [1955]); Geertz, 44.
99. Levi-Strauss, *Tristes Tropiques*, 39.

100. Ibid., 39.
101. Ibid., 53.
102. Robert Lowie, *Primitive Society* (New York: Boni and Liveright, 1920).
103. Levi-Strauss, *Tristes Tropiques*, 59.
104. Ibid., 59.
105. Hyatt, 21-22.
106. Levi-Strauss, *Tristes Tropiques*, 77.
107. Ibid., 78-79.
108. Geertz, 41.
109. Levi-Strauss, *Tristes Tropiques*, 90.
110. Ibid., 91.
111. Ibid., 93.
112. Ibid., 51.
113. Ibid., 42.
114. Ibid., 44.
115. Michael Jackson, *Paths Toward a Clearing* (Bloomington: Indiana University Press, 1989), 181.
116. Ibid., 181.
117. Ibid., 183-86.
118. Karl Mannheim, *Ideology and Utopia* (New York: Harcourt, Brace, and World, 1936), 70.
119. Ibid.,, 92.
120. Immanuel Wallerstein, *The Capitalist World Economy* (Cambridge: Cambridge University Press, 1979); Eric Wolf, *Europe and the People without History* (Berkeley: University of California Press, 1982).
121. Daryll Forde, ed., *African Worlds* (London: Oxford University Press, 1976) and *The Context of Belief* (Liverpool: Liverpool University Press, 1958); Victor W. Turner, *Schism and Continuity in an African Society* (Manchester: Manchester University Press, 1957) and *The Forest of Symbols* (Ithaca, N.Y.: Cornell University Press, 1967).
122. An article by Louis A. Sass, "Anthropology's Native Problems" (*Harpers* [May 1986]: 49-75) is especially pertinent to this. Also see Derek Freeman regarding—at least by his definition—the excesses of cultural determinism. Also see chapter 2 of this work, and Wilmsen, xi-xviii, 16-38.
123. Claude Levi-Strauss, *The Savage Mind*, translated from *La Pensee sauvage* (Chicago: University of Chicago Press, 1966), 11-16.
124. Michael Jackson, *The Kuranko: Dimensions of Social Reality in a West African Society* (London: C. Hurst, 1977), *Latitudes of Exile* (Dunedin: McIndoe, 1976), and *Barawa and the Ways Birds Fly in the Sky* (Washington, D.C.: Smithsonian Institution Press, 1986); Victor Turner, *On the Edge of the Bush: Anthropology as Experience* (Tucson: University of Arizona Press, 1985); Johannes Fabian *Time and the Other: How Anthropology Makes its Object* (New York: Columbia University Press, 1983); Barnes, *Patrons and Power*; Kopytoff, *The African Frontier*.

5

The Perpetual Adventure: Travelogues and Traveler's Accounts

In an address to the National Geographic Society on February 16, 1906, Herbert L. Bridgman, who had just returned from the newly pacified Anglo-Egyptian Sudan, said

> Great Britain, applying the same principles which have made her the great colonial power of the world, goes on developing the industrial and commercial resources of the countries which have fallen under her influence, establishing law and order, schools . . . and pouring in upon the places which have for centuries been shrouded in darkness the light of modern civilization.

In this speech Bridgman added, "Since the capture of Khartum [sic] and the conquest of the Egyptian Sudan barely seven years have passed, but peace, plenty, and prosperity reign everywhere."[1] Included in the article, in the fashion that had already made *The National Geographic* by far the most popular travel-oriented periodical in the United States, were several striking black-and-white photographs. One reveals imposing "Shillook" warriors (grouped around a be-ribboned *askari* wearing a fez), intended to show, as the author indicates, how the natural military propensities of that people are now being utilized for peaceful purposes. Another titled "Nearing the Equator: A Village Scene at Bor" shows a cluster of naked women surrounded by their equally naked children, hunkered in front of a small grass hut. The only visible artifact, besides the hut, is a half-calabash. The image of savagery at the heart of darkness, now to succumb to the benign influence of British administration, is unmistakable. Another photograph, "The Mail Leaving Lado for Stations in the Congo Free State," shows a dozen half-naked carriers, boxes on their heads, led by two uniformed *askaris* armed with rifles. Again the intended message is obvious.[2]

Fifty years or more were to pass before this basic image—framed within the symbolic conventions which filled the travelogue canvas of Africa—was to appreciably change. The literature of travel, already well-established as a standard form in Europe by the seventeenth century,[3] had by the twentieth century become thoroughly familiar to Americans. Most of those who wrote about Africa conformed, often in a self-conscious fashion, both in the presentation of their work and in mimetic structure, to this hallowed tradition. That is, the majority of travel accounts, whether they appeared in a reputable magazine like *The National Geographic*, or whether they took the form made famous by Sir Walter Raleigh and, much later, Herman Melville,[4] constituted a *genre* whereas the author attempts to provide vicarious but factual knowledge of a foreign or alien world.

As noted elsewhere in this book, Christopher Miller, in *Blank Darkness*, argues convincingly that Africa was Europe's "other" far more than any other region,[5] and surely by the nineteenth century books and other publications which dealt with Africa tended to emphasize the differences, the strangeness, the exotica, of that continent. Thus, the more exotic the traveler's experience, the better. The intrepid traveler who wanted his or her works to sell, therefore, was aware of the need to establish credentials with the reader as one who is exploring—or observing—the "other." Therefore, American travelers, like their European counterparts, did their best (and as we shall see many still do) to evoke symbols of wildness, of intractability and unpredictability, of the "natives" as both subjects of scrutiny, (perfect examples of the "other") and as objects of wonder. Africa, with its ready inventory of symbolic conventions clearly provided American writers with the perfect canvas for their creations.

In 1929 Merian D. Cooper, with photographer Earnest B. Schoedsack, wrote an article for *The National Geographic* entitled "Two Fighting Tribes of the Sudan." The co-authors—who had earlier published "The Warfare of the Jungle Folk" in the same magazine—were obviously impressed by the efficiency and aplomb of a young British Assistant District Commissioner, and they wrote, "it was hard to realize that the millions of wild men who inhabit this great, savage Sudan are ruled to-day by a few score of just such young Englishmen."[6] The photographs begin with a striking image of two Nuba boys, members of "one of the wildest tribes of the Sudan" standing next to a towering pet ostrich. The juxtaposition of semi-tamed ostrich and "savage" folk is characteristic. Another photo of a Nuba village is equally striking; a begowned Nuba sentinel leaning on his spear, four men around a fire, the clustered huts "made of mud which has dried to concretelike hardness . . . thatched with pointed roofs" across the distant hillside. This luminous scene is highlighted with shadows in glorious tropic light.

Shilook Warriors

Nearing the Equator. A village scene at Bor.

The mail leaving Lado for stations in the Congo Free State.

Another photograph shows a circle of fierce warriors, round hide shields strapped to their naked backs, watching two men squared off with massive five-foot swords, with the caption, "From boyhood the fuzzy is taught to use the sword."[7]

The question is not whether these images of 1906 and 1929 were accurate reflections of real life. Just as the 1990s photographs of any exotic tribal group might reflect some extraordinary divergent culture, so the 1926, "fuzzy-wuzzy" warriors could mirror a significant African lifestyle. But this is beside the point. What counts is the imagery itself. In 1906, as in 1929, *The National Geographic*, this most American of magazines, knew exactly what to emphasize. The "fuzzies" with their wild hairdos, great swords, and razor-sharp spears, represented an Africa of lore and legend already expected if not clarified in the minds of readers. In the twenties the Sudan, then as now, abounded in itinerant merchants, richly dressed and often learned, amid their camels and wares, but such things (as one might expect in 1991) were ignored. The Africa of ancient trade routes, of organized kingdoms, of venerable Koranic schools, was hardly imaginable to the American traveler early in this century. The geographer, the adventurer, the photographer, the hunter-tourist (for the latter made up the most important category of Americans who ventured into Africa in the opening decades of this century) already knew what to expect.

The vision of Africa as a dark place filled with primitives living in ways unchanged since the emergence of the species was well established in European (and in American) consciousness by 1906. One of the greatest problems faced by the Scots explorer James Bruce, following his epic journey to Ethiopia over a century before (1771-1773), was the disbelief he faced back in England when he described the splendor of Sennar.[8] Few of the polished and skeptical wits of that era of supreme rationalism believed that a kingdom could exist in Africa so well organized as to field a magnificent contingent of horsemen in chained-mail (the legendary "Black Horse" of Sennar) that was feared from the Red Sea to Kordofan. The great man-of-letters, Samuel Johnson, who had penned a wholly fanciful novel set in Abyssinia and entitled, *Rasselas, Prince of Abyssinia* (a place that coffee-shop adventurer had assuredly never visited), said he doubted Bruce had ever been to Ethiopia. Though Bruce's published account has been generally praised by twentieth-century scholars, Bruce himself suffered lifelong humiliation because of the skepticism of Johnson and others.

Ironically, readers of Herodotus in the fifth century B.C. would have had no reason to doubt the author when he described his sojourn in Egypt, well up the Nile (he traveled "as far as Elephantine," near Aswan, on the Nile),[9] nor would his descriptions of legendary Kush, still a considerable distance beyond Elephantine, have roused the slightest skepticism. This was despite the fact that Herodotus did not travel there. Well-traveled Greek merchants in Herodotus' time made visits to Kush and beyond, to trade for the ivory, gum, slaves, and other products of that region. The markets of Ethiopia, even then, were known. And, despite the disruptions of Empire (Alexandrian, Roman, Byzantine, Arab, etc.) well into the late Medieval period, a similar situation prevailed in parts of the African Horn, and well down the eastern coast. One is not aware that any Johnson-like skeptics assailed the veracity of great Arab travelers like Ibn Batuta (who traveled in Africa in 1325-1354). Neither did the fifteenth-century Portuguese doubt Vasco de Gama's description of luxurious Sofala (in present-day Mozambique) in 1498, nor did they question his somewhat bloody adventures along the lush East African coast that same year, before he sailed on to India.[10]

In the meantime, however, much had happened to bolster the negative image; so that, while the romantic Africa of "noble savages" might find, for reasons we have already explained, a strange rebirth in the twentieth century, the Africa of savagery and darkness, the Africa of the slaver's narrative, the Africa of remote and isolated tribes, was never more alive.

History played the central role, of course, since England, France, Germany, Belgium, and Portugal, had in the final years of the nineteenth century, embarked on the most rapid and most extensive conquest—that is, the conquest and partition of Africa between about 1875 and 1905—since the Islamic conquest. In the process virtually every significant African polity (with the exception of Ethiopia) was either defeated outright in battle (the Fulani Emirates of Hausaland, the Sudanic Mahdist state, a resurgent Zulu kingdom, Great Benin, a recalcitrant Ashanti confederation, the Futa Jallon, Samori's vast but fragile empire) or expropriated through the clever treaties wrought by imperious proconsuls (the Sultanate of Zanzibar, The Yoruba Kingdoms, Buganda, Toro, etc.)[11] Less centrally-organized systems, from the Temne of Sierra Leone to the Gwari of northern Nigeria were either conquered outright at the least sign of resistance or brought under imperial rule by the threat of force. Some "stateless" societies like the Tiv and the Ibo offered far more effective long-term resistance, mostly because there were no "authorities" with whom the conquering Europeans could negotiate, but, with minor exceptions, they too succumbed by 1910 or so.[12] Every resistance, however heroic it may be cast in the revised histories of recent decades, seemed at the time further evidence of the irredeemable barbarism of Africa's peoples. Like Romans or Greeks confronted with a peripheral "barbarian" society, Europeans could not imagine any justification for the death of even one European missionary, soldier, or administrator at the hands of Africans. Believing, like the ancients, that all civilization centered in their own world (though this was compounded by a racism that went far beyond anything in ancient Greece or Rome) the conquerors wrote racy accounts of their adventures. It is no accident that some of the most rousing adventure tales of the era were written by the conquering soldiers and proconsuls, men like Sir Frederick (later Lord) Lugard, Sir Harry Johnston, Carl Peters, and General Joseph Gallieni.[13] Likewise, even the most obscure colonial bureaucrat, if possessed of the requisite skill with pen, could produce a tale of adventure among the "dark inhabitants" of his particular district. This is not to disparage the mostly lonely and sometimes laudatory activities of isolated district commissioners or *prefects*, trying to bring order amid apparent chaos, but it is interesting that such "I was there" accounts as *The Sherbro and Its Hinterland*, by J. T. Alldridge, and *Nigerian Days*, by A. C. C. Hastings, were sought by a European public avid for sensation.[14] Perhaps a contemporary parallel might be found in the hundreds of novels and memoirs of the Vietnam War, a senseless conflict seemingly more chronicled in its endless horrors than the far more bloody, and infinitely more significant World War II. Another factor, at least for the Victorian readers of the time, was that the chronicle of Africa in its final stages of conquest (and its earliest phase of imperial administration) echoed the theme of a final frontier, one which the Americans, as well as the French, the Germans, and the British could readily identify with.

In the United States the works of colonial conquerors, governors, and administrators were certainly less widely read than in Europe. America after all had no formal empire beyond its own shores until 1898, and a relatively small one in Asia and the Caribbean after that. Still, the images projected by popular writers like Stanley (who, after all, retained his "American" identity, even while he served King Leopold of Belgium in the Congo) and Harry Johnston were immediate and powerful. Africa was, by all accounts, populated largely by remote and isolated villagers, many under the authority of powerful chiefs or chiefly clans, many without any visible government whatsoever, some under traditional kings—with hierarchical systems of government—and others in systems that seemed to mix a variety of these. But even the greatest kingdoms, save Ethiopia, had been readily conquered by Europeans in far inferior numbers, who, using the most advanced technology then available (the Maxim gun, repeating rifles, gunboats, the telegraph, etc.) had simply pulverized any organized opposition. If, on the one hand, the relentlessly methodical Germans were criticized for their brutal repression of the Herero in Southwest Africa (Namibia), the British could argue, on the other hand, that, as in Northern Nigeria, or Nyasaland, the firm hand of the military commander was a necessity in the midst of barbarism, where the slightest misstep could rouse violence. This, of course, was the credo of Empire, the justification and slogan of every imperialist from Savorgnan de Brazza to Rudyard Kipling.[15]

This then was the setting as American travelers, like Bridgman, began to visit the vast colonial domains which stretched from the Cape to Cairo, from Dakar to Zanzibar. The reasons that Americans visited Africa—if one excludes the obvious motives of the mostly Protestant missionaries who began to pursue their callings in Africa—varied a great deal, but one thing seems constant in the accounts up to about World War II, and that is an almost universal acceptance that Africa was thoroughly outside the pale of civilization. The few exceptions, including a handful of African Americans like William Leo Hansberry and W. E. B. Du Bois, often possessed a sentience with regard to Africa that seems remarkable in retrospect. Du Bois, while professing all his life that Africa had little emotional impact on him from childhood (and his scholarly career provides evidence of this), could still record the African past without the blinders of racism, and coolly appraise past glories and present humiliations. Yet, upon first landing in Liberia, he could write romantically, in *Dusk of Dawn,*

> Here darkness descends and rests on lovely skins until brown seems luscious and natural. There is sunlight in great gold globules and soft, heavy-scented heat that wraps you like a garment. And laziness, divine, eternal, languor is right and good and true. I remember the morning; it was Sunday, and the night before we heard the leopards crying down there. Today beneath the streaming sun we went down into the gold-green forest. It was silence—silence the more mysterious because life abundant and palpitating pulsed all about us and held us drowsy captives to the day.[16]

What a contrast between this paean and the following passage, written by the American millionaire George Eastman (inventor of the celebrated Eastman Kodak camera and the huge company of the same name) when he went on hunting safari in the Sudan in 1928 at the age of seventy-four. In this passage he is attempting to describe the end of a conflict between the "warlike" Nuer and the "peace-loving" Dinka.

> That night, we tied up at Shambe, the headquarters of the Neuer war, and got all the news from the Syrian doctor. It seems the natives were driven into the swamp with their

cattle and bombed from the ten planes. Forty or fifty natives and several thousand cattle were killed and three ringleaders captured, one escaping. The man who actually killed Ferguson (an Englishman) tried to escape and they had to kill him, much to their regret, as they wanted to execute him with some ceremony. The fourth is still at large, but they expect to get him. In the meantime, the whole tribe became terrified, and men, women, and children scrambled for headquarters, begging for mercy. This was what the authorities were after, and they probably won't kill any more of them until they see how they behave after this scare. They are, however, a thoroughly bad lot and may have to be wiped out before the district can be cleaned up.[17]

The idea that any people fighting against colonial rule, or any subgroup of any "tribe" involved in what Eastman called a "nativist" rebellion, might have to be "wiped out" may not have seemed unusual to white Americans in 1928, since it echoed a sentiment which, a mere generation earlier, had justified the wiping out of whole groups of Native Americans, though it rings a discordant note in the 1990s. We might reason that Eastman, who was seventy four in 1928, was in his twenties when the Sioux were fighting their last-ditch war on the plains, but it is clear that the sentiments recorded in Eastman's letters are as much those of the British officials who arranged his safari as they were his own.

Like Theodore Roosevelt who in 1909 had "shown his countrymen that the British colonies south of Ethiopia and Egypt offered a return to the conditions of the American West before the Civil War" (seemingly endless game, magnificent landscapes, and the strenuous outdoor life),[18] Eastman seemed incapable of forming his own opinions about the Africans he encountered. If British officials characterized the Nuer resistance to their rule as "nativistic" and claimed that the leadership was in the hands of that archetype of colonial "history," the witch doctor, who was there to say them nay? Like most Americans of his generation—indeed of the next generation as well—it is understandable that Eastman saw only the Africa that his hosts wished him to see.

In 1925-1926, well before Americans grew accustomed to detailed reports on Africa, Raymond Leslie Buell, a Harvard Political scientist, visited Africa over fifteen crowded months. His voluminous report, published in two volumes in 1928, was remarkable for its objective and critical (yet hopeful) analysis of the political and social currents of the time. Buell believed that in 1920s Africa it was "not too late to adopt policies which will prevent the development of the acute racial difficulties which have elsewhere arisen."[19] This optimism was, however, largely misplaced.

Another *National Geographic* article published in 1938, just ten years later, by Lawrence Copley Thaw and Margaret Stout Thaw, entitled, "A Motor Caravan Rolls Across Sahara and Jungle Through Realms of Dusky Potentates and the Land of Big-Lipped Women," provides clear proof that little had changed in the thirty years since Bridgman visited Africa in 1906,

> Here [at Fort Archambault on the Ubangi River] both the upper and lower lips of girl babies are pierced and small wooden plugs inserted into the holes. As they grow up, these plugs are gradually increased in size until they reach the dimensions of large soup plates. The effect is amazing.
>
> Tom (the photographer) was enchanted, photographically with what he termed the "platter pusses."[20]

Again the reality of this portrait is not in question; it is rather the choice and emphasis in such pieces that gives away the mindset we are exploring; a mindset which assumes that there was no rational response to the rampant slave-raiding in the Ubangi region only short years before. A photo in the same article taken "near the edge of the Belgian Congo" is captioned as follows, "Huge Trumpets Sound Eerie Notes as the Mangbettu King, With His Favorite Long-Headed Wives, Presides at Court." These words effectively set up the reader or viewer so that the significance of the potentate in question is diminished. One's eye is inevitably drawn to the "long-headed wives," whether or not this was a conscious intention of the authors. One of the authors of this book recalls a photograph taken by himself in 1966 of the Emir of Abuja, showing that ruler and his brother the *Dallatu,* standing side-by-side at the entrance to his palace. When shown to classes in African History, along with other slides of the Abuja emirate, students invariably asked questions about the radiant cloth-of-gold gown, the resplendent turban, etc., worn by the Emir (the *Sarkin Zazzau*), and inquired about the powers and prerogatives of such an impressive figure. On the other hand, a photo of a village chief with several of his wives, taken in the Temne region of Sierra Leone in 1963, would invariably occasion questions not about the chief's role or position, but about polygamy. Sometimes the expected impression, fully supported by the preconceived symbolic connection, is inadvertently conveyed.

The year 1960 was one of enormous change in Africa. Kwame Nkrumah had guided Ghana (the former Gold Coast) to self-government only three years before, the first British colony in Africa to achieve that goal. Much of the vast region called French West Africa and French Equatorial Africa became independent in 1960, as did Nigeria, the Sudan, and other countries within the British sphere.

Belgium was negotiating to leave its enormous colony in the Congo to its own devices. That same year *The National Geographic* weighed in with a beautifully illustrated article by Ann Eisner Putnam, the widow of the Harvard-trained anthropologist Patrick Tracy Lowell Putnam who had lived much of his life on the Epulu River, deep within the Ituri forest. Entitled "My Life with Africa's Little People," the article might have been written in a vacuum as far as the "winds of change" were concerned. The lead photo, for example, showing a dozen Pygmies drumming in the forest, bears the following caption:

> The start of a dance finds a Pygmy elder intently coaxing provocative rhythms from a skin-covered drum while other performers exchange jokes. To show their hearts are gay, the younger men wear girdles of leaves over bark-cloth breech-cloths. Ituri Forest Pygmies often dance far into the night.[21]

As we pointed out earlier in this book, by 1960 serious research on the "Pygmies" of the Ituri, particularly the work of Colin Turn-bull—who was fully aware of the massive changes which affected the BaMbuti—was readily available. Certainly the larger signifi-cance of a dance such as that described by Putnam was known, and surely that reporter (who had by her own account lived among the Pygmies with her anthropologist husband for eight years) had access to such information. But the impression conveyed would have fit perfectly within the mindset of 1938, 1928, or 1906. Near the end of her article Mrs. Putnam—having revisited her former friends, the forest people, for a few weeks—wrote,

> As Christmastime approached, I decided I had had my fill of witchcraft, superstition, and pagan rituals. I wanted to share the holiday joy with my white neighbors, and so I invited them to Camp Putnam for a party. My boys under-stood and helped me decorate.
>
> For dinner we had guinea hens the Pygmies had killed for me with bows and arrows. It was good to sing the old famil-iar Christmas carols instead of trying to join in the Pygmy chants.[22]

A trained ethnographer might wonder if there is anything less "superstitious" about the essentially pagan rituals of a Christmas celebration in the European tradition (based as it is on the Roman "Saternalia") than those of the BaMbuti pygmies described. One might find Mrs. Putnam's honesty refreshing—her willingness to state her preference for an ancient Christian ritual over that of a people not her own is understandable, even admirable—but the ethnocentrism here is both self-evident and characteristic.

In fairness, one must note that in the 1960s *The National Geographic* made a genuine effort to deal with the changing African scene. In an extensive and (as usual) lavishly illustrated September 1960 article by Nathaniel T. Kenney, entitled "Africa: The Winds of Change Stir a Continent," with photographs by W. D. Vaughn, the magazine attempted a region-by-region update on the new nations and the changing ways. In some respects this piece tried to provide a capsule of the history that colonialism had denied for three quarters of a century, yet with ample servings of old stereotypes. Portraits of Kwame Nkrumah and Emperor Haile Selassie alternate with more traditional photos of Masai herdsmen and bare-breasted maidens. A photo of the article's author, Kenney, with the aged Dr. Albert Schweitzer, showing the two men watching a "playful chimpanzee, baby gorilla, and dog wrestle at the philosopher's jungle hospital at Lambarene," was still entirely commonplace in 1960.[23] One of the authors of this book recalls the article vividly, since, having graduated from college that same spring, he was seeking ways to travel and study in Africa. The idea that anyone might object to Dr. Schweitzer's paternalism and the thinly disguised racism in the way his hospital was run (and had been run for forty years) certainly did not spring to mind, nor, one suspects, did it enter the minds of ninety-nine percent of the magazine's subscribers in that eventful year. Reading through this lavish article more than thirty years later, however, one is struck by the incongruities—though some of these are inherent in any sweeping view of Africa. Only a few pages apart are magnificent photos of the pomp and pageantry of an Ashanti "paramount chief" with his "silk-and-cotton robe" and gold-encrusted diadem, and a Fanti fisherman drumming "in ecstasy." The caption explains, "'A veil mists African faces in such moments of trance,' says the author. 'No alien can hope to understand it.'"[24]

The three illustrated *National Geographic* articles that accompany this extended article include a seminal piece by L. S. B. Leakey, "Finding the World's Earliest Man."[25] This piece, which illustrates Leakey's discovery of *Zinjanthropus boisei* at Olduvai Gorge, along with other Leakey articles in *National Geographic,* helped make its author world famous, and firmly established Africa as the original birthplace of humanity. Of course, through surely without any such intent, the juxtaposition of such an article with the above-mentioned travel narrative would serve to reinforce the idea of Africa as a museum of things primitive, pristine and primeval.

American journalism, Henry Morton Stanley aside (and unless one considers the *National Geographic* kind of article a form of journalism), paid only passing attention to Africa in the early years of

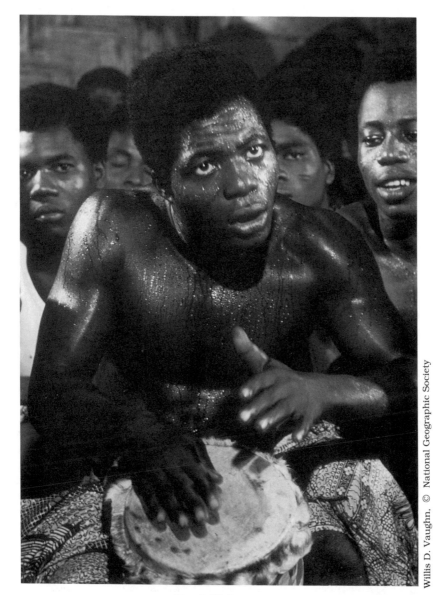

Fanti Fisherman

Willis D. Vaughn, © National Geographic Society

this century. Exploration was completed and the colonies were demarcated before World War I. The events of that war, covered extensively in the European press, reached America's shores as a dim echo of distant conflict. The exploits of Von Lettow-Vorbeck in the five-year battle for the "Bundu" were of little interest outside Germany and England. It might be news a few years later when Carl Akeley died of fever, deep within the central African rain-forest which he so loved, but for most Americans it was hardly newsworthy when Simon Kimbangu, following his vision, curing the sick and lame, and preaching his prophetic word, was imprisoned in the Belgian Congo for treason in 1921.[26] Even in the thirties little had changed. The Ethiopian Emperor Haile Selassie, fighting Mussolini's invading Italians in 1936, might warrant brief stories in major newspapers, (his remote kingdom, after all, held a peculiar fascination for Americans, white and black), yet, as the editors of black newspapers knew only too well, the larger American public scarcely blinked. Things changed somewhat when the Lion of Judah spoke desperately before a helpless and toothless League of Nations and momentarily captivated the European and American public. However, even as headlines blazed their indignation at Il Duce's rape of this ancient kingdom, there was no rush of volunteers from the forty eight states, as there was, for example, to Spain in that same year. Most Americans continued blissfully unaware of the violence unleashed in this last gasp of a dying colonialism (the other colonial powers, deploring what Mussolini was doing, nonetheless allowed him to continue doing so). Certainly few in America saw Italian fascism in Africa as a prelude to a far more expansive and dangerous fascism within Europe.

World War II, of course, changed things forever. Americans had to pay attention to the larger world, even that African part, remote yet deeply bothersome since so many African Americans themselves had once come from there. As Americans began to take up the "burden" of the new American imperium (one not so much conquered as inherited, one not formal but informal), as they found themselves forced to look at events in Asia, South America, and Africa, American journalists also began to pay closer attention to places like South Africa where something called *apartheid* had been promulgated, to Kenya where a violent uprising called Mau Mau was raging, to Central Africa where Congolese openly resented Belgian paternalism, and to West Africa where Nkrumah's Convention Peoples Party was sharing power with the British as early as 1954. The fifties were a decade of eye-opening revelations. Educated Americans, forced to look beyond convenient symbols, began to realize that Africa was more than a huge liana-draped jungle, the home of Tarzan and the refuge of cannibals; it was various, complicated, and above all, interesting.

It was no surprise, then, when the premiere travel-journalist of that generation, the celebrated John Gunther, author of the best-selling books, *Inside Asia, Inside Latin America, Inside Europe,* and *Inside U.S.A.* turned his attention to Africa in 1953. *Inside Africa,* which was reprinted in several editions through the fifties, ran to just under one thousand pages, crammed with facts and figures. Like his other guides, this was something of a "tour de force" with its handy—though slanted—country charts with the following headings: "area, capital, political status, description, population, racial composition, principal tribes, religion, chief problems, principal products, political parties, and leaders." This was exactly designed to appeal to Americans with their affection for statistics and their penchant for simplistic explanations, including an immutable belief in separate and intact African tribes. Gunther, though not by any means an "old Africa hand," had been there. To write his fifth "inside" book he traveled over forty thousand miles, largely by air, crisscrossing the continent which he had first visited in 1926, traveling (with his wife) through forty-four countries, 106 towns and cities, and in the process producing the kind of book in which journalist (and arm-chair travelers) delight, but which historians despise. Some of his reportage is stereotypical:

> They [Black Africans] are much warmer, gentler, more relaxed, than Arabs or the scornful, arrogant Ethiopians. An allied point is their volatility, their physical effervescence (no matter how lazy they may be) and gregariousness and delight in music, art, and spectacle.[27]

Some of it is perspicacious:

> One thing remarkable about their [the Kikuyu] tribal orga-nization is that, like the Ibos in Nigeria—whom they resem-ble in other respects—they had no chiefs. The British, trying to make Indirect Rule work, improvised chiefs and sought to impose them on the Kikuyus, but the effort was a failure. The Kikuyus were too democratic, too individualistic, too suspicious of western influence, and too deeply devoted to their anciently entrenched institutions.[28]

Some absurdly exaggerated:

> A case can be made for slavery and even for the slave trade. It is that tribal wars took place in the African interior without cessation, and that it was better for a man to be taken pris-oner and made a domestic slave, or even sold into slavery,

than to be killed and perhaps eaten. On a slave raid the object was to get the prisoner alive, and, with luck, he might survive the trip to America or Arabia. On balance, the slave trade (despite its inferno-like horrors) may have saved more lives than it cost. In any case it is the origin of a great many healthy, useful and progressive Negro communities in the United States and elsewhere in the Western world.[29]

And some prescient:

What the government [of South Africa] wants is to make the present system [apartheid] work, and pretend cynically that it is "good" for Africans. Native labor will live in "buffer areas" near the towns, and will be pumped into industry as needed. But this system has already produced intolerable friction, and will produce more. For instance, Africans are, at the moment, forbidden to hold skilled jobs, but it is rapidly becoming impossible to draw the line in secondary industry between jobs skilled and unskilled. More and more Africans will, in time, be getting better and better jobs, unless industry chooses to commit suicide. This means that more Africans will inevitably get more earning power, which in turn will mean that they will demand more education and political advantages. Full industrial development can, in other words, only come at the steadily increasing risk of racial clash, which means that the government will necessarily have to become more (instead of less) repressive and totalitarian as time goes on.[30]

The picture of Africa produced by Gunther's massive compilation was both paradoxical (as Africa itself is) and, for anyone who knew even a small part of that continent even modestly well, infuriating. *Inside Africa* suffered from the inherent weakness of many (by no means all) journalistic accounts; it rose at moments to trenchant observation at its best, but all too often it merely reflected the latest (and most shallow) contemporary wisdom, and as indicated by some of the passages above, sometimes it descended into a kind of schizophrenic and contradictory melange. The symbolic conventions clearly dominate here. Gunther, though he could report the African struggle for self-determination with sympathy and compassion, could not seem to avoid repeating every bloody tale ever hatched by grousing colonials at their sundowners from the Cape to Cairo. Beyond this, he romanticized Haile Selassie, he stigmatized Muslims, he excoriated Mau Mau, he admired Kenyatta, and in the final analysis his book seems to reflect the same Manichean contradictions that cluttered the works of another journalist, Henry Morton Stanley, three quarters of a century before.

Hundreds of American journalists have since visited Africa, though few could afford to travel quite so widely or freely as Gunther in 1952-53. The best, like David Lamb and Blaine Harden, have lived in Africa for extended periods (four to five years or more), the worst—whose names are legion—typically fly in and out for visits of a few days or weeks and write their dispatches from the bars of luxury hotels. Harden, who apparently came to love Africa during his long stay as a correspondent for the *Washington Post*, nevertheless pulled no punches when he wrote of bloody civil wars, famine, irredentism, environmental deterioration, economic collapse, political corruption, and the tyranny of "big men" such as Zaire's Mobutu and Samuel Doe of Liberia:

> Doe's sweet talk about democracy attracted American aid dollars in ever larger amounts. In the time-tested tradition of African Big Men, Doe used the money to shore up the loyalty of people capable either of undermining his rule or killing him. He doubled the size of the government work force and raised salaries. He ordered the construction of new, multi-million-dollar army barracks. At the same time, he started to enjoy the perquisites of power. Doe's camouflage fatigues gave way to three-piece suits. His Honda Civic (which he drove himself) gave way to a bullet-proof chauffeur-driven Mercedes limousine.[31]

Needless to say, despite despicably passive American support, Doe went the way of so many tyrants of his stripe (he was caught, tortured and dismembered by thugs under the leadership of Prince Johnson, who overthrew him in September 1990). Liberia was then plunged into even greater civil conflict from which it has not yet emerged.

In a quite different passage, however, Harden describes the unexpectedly bloodless end to the awful Nigerian Civil War (1967-1970), which most pundits assumed would result in endless recriminations, and at the very least, the kind of exploitation that followed the U.S. Civil War:

> It turned out differently in Nigeria because of exemplary leadership. When the war ended, General Yakubu Gowan, supreme commander of the military government that crushed Biafra, was feared by the Ibo people as a leader with "genocidal" tendencies.

However, on the day the war ended, Gowon delivered a nationwide radio address that Ibos still point to as the reason why they are still alive.

"I solemnly repeat our guarantees of a general amnesty for those misled into rebellion. We guarantee the personal safety of everyone who submits to federal authority," Gowon said. The general insisted that the war would produce "no victor and no vanquished."

> Gowon's authority and the discipline of his senior officers prevented the revenge that many . . . wanted to visit on the Ibos. Under Gowon's orders, no war reparations were demanded of the Ibos, nor were any medals granted for war service. Many Ibos returned to their former jobs in the national army and the civil service. Much of their property in the north and west of Nigeria was restored to them. "In the history of warfare" wrote John de St. Jorre in what is regarded as the foremost history of the Biafran war, "there can rarely have been such a bloodless end and such a merciful aftermath."[32]

Harden's approach here is entirely reasonable. Occasionally, African critics like Ali Mazrui and Chinweizu condemn any reportage—particularly by Americans—that reveals anything negative about Africa. By this standard, because it is so bleak and bloody, Harden's vivid description of Doe's tyrannical regime should not be mentioned at all. Sometimes the charges of "unfair" or biased coverage are echoed by Africanists in America whose politically correct agenda requires a knee-jerk supportive response to every charge against the press leveled by any African, however absurd. Fortunately, without falling into the trap of the symbolic conventions, as Gunther so clearly did in the 1950s, reporters like Harden have attempted a balanced coverage that is scrupulously documented as to fact. The truth is that the dark and savage image of Africa, however exaggerated in the past, does not diminish in direct proportion to official denials—by government officials or anyone else—that nothing bad is happening. The double standard which says that everything evil that happens (or has ever happened) in Africa is the result of a western racist plot requires, of course, a totally racist assumption that Africans one and all are subject to such invidious manipulation.

Unfortunately, this conspiracy theory is gaining ascendancy in America, particularly among African Americans, and in various forms is already widely believed in Africa. Fomented, perhaps unwittingly, by works such as Walter Rodney's powerful but tendentious book, *How Europe Undeveloped Africa* and Chinweizu's eloquent but ahistorical *The West and the Rest of Us*,[33] the essence of this theory is both simplistic and appealing, and, of course, historically insupportable. Essentially this theory goes far beyond the early twentieth century critique of colonialism and imperialism (based on the works of Marx, Lenin and other Communist theoreticians), which suggested that European hegemony was largely a consequence of capitalism at a certain stage in its inevitable development. The Marxist analysis, after all, was an economic one, not a racist one. Rather, the new theory postulates a conscious and continuous conspiracy by Europeans and Americans which extends right back to the early days of the Atlantic Slave Trade, to deliberately undermine, manipulate, exploit, enslave, and dominate Africans. Though the exact details of this Caucasian conspiracy are never revealed (beyond the well-known history of colonialism), this has apparently been accomplished by a combination of means so devious and complex—even as the Europeans were fighting each other in colonial wars, and killing each other off by the millions in two world wars—that only the satanic whites themselves can understand them. This is the kind of demonology which is the centerpiece of Minister Louis Farrakhan's impassioned appeal.

The work of David Lamb, another American journalist who lived and traveled much in Africa during the early 1980s is sometimes unsettling and often controversial. His book, *The Africans*, which some believe to be unnecessarily "negative," is indeed blunt and unblinking, yet, like Harden's work, it is based on solid journalism. In fact Lamb's writing often reflects a strong disdain for the colonial regimes of the past, as for example, in the following passage condemning the "partition" of Africa at the 1885 Berlin Conference:

> The effect of the Berlin Conference was to divide, not unify. The colonial boundaries were artificial and illogical. They ignored the cultural cohesion of tribal Africa and separated the peoples of ethnic mini-nations held together for centuries by their common heritage and language. No sensible groupings of people remained.[34]

In another characteristic passage he questions the belated and timid criticism of Idi Amin within Africa, as well as the outside's world's dirty connivance.

> Tragically, Amin would not have lasted as long as he did if Africa had had the courage to isolate him, and if the East and West had cared less about their own interests and more about Uganda's. But Libya helped train Amin's army and sent military advisers and civilian technicians. Saudi Arabia promised Amin $2 million in the dying days of his regime in the name of Islamic brotherhood. The Palestine Liberation Organization provided personal bodyguards as a reward for Amin's anti-Israeli ravings. Egypt, Pakistan and Bangladesh sent university professors for Makerere, doctors for Mulago,

engineers and other professionals. The Soviet Union gave sophisticated weapons, East Germany trained the secret police.

The West's interests were economic. The United States . . . was for years the biggest purchaser of Uganda coffee. Western companies supplied the country with petroleum. Britain, Uganda's largest trading partner, sold Amin everything from radio technology to drugs to military uniforms. It was not until Amin ordered the murder of Uganda's Anglican archbishop and two senior cabinet ministers in 1977—Amin said they died in a car accident—that world opinion turned solidly against the man who had once seemed such a good-natured oaf.[35]

One can see how such direct language might offend some people. But of course, traveler-journalists like Lamb do not write to please, they are assigned by their home newspapers in order to inform. Lamb's charge, well-substantiated by subsequent research, that it was not Amin's murderous treatment of his own countrymen (they died in numbers running into the scores of thousands) which brought him down, but rather his stepping over the line that—in much of Africa—kept whites isolated and protected from such rampaging thugs, is altogether unpleasant. It is also true. The accuracy of such reporting, always subject to challenge, depends on essentially the same factors that characterize solid academic research; the depth and breadth of reading and background preparation, and the ability to dig beyond what is obvious, beneath stereotype and image. Lamb does not, for example, attempt—as some traveler-journalist still do—to lay the blame for Africa's awful economic condition on any of the classic conventions such as "lazy" Africans, or traditional superstitions (though he reveals in other places how ancient practices can impair efficiency). Instead he provides a foursquare and terse analysis of international inequity.

> When Europe ran the continent, African peasants were forced to produce export crops to satisfy the import needs of Europe and to pay the colony's bills. The colonial economy—and later the national economy of individual African countries—was more often than not based on a single commodity such as cashew nuts or cocoa and was deprived of the cushion that diversity provides. Each country, in effect, had all its eggs in one basket. If disaster struck, in the form of drought, famine, crop failure or mismanagement, the fragile economy shattered.[36]

Such unpleasant realities, like those in contemporary Eastern Europe, have nothing to do with racism or bias. Few people, East or

West, North or South, would agree that it is defensible to suppress the news of government-supported violence, ethnic conflict, high-level corruption, or repression on the part of an East European government, for example. Honest reporting of the bloody conflict in the former Yugoslavia is not seen as racist or biased simply because it reveals a dark side which all of us fear might surface at any time in our own society. Yet to report, as Sanford Ungar does below, on a tyrant like Zaire's Mobutu, is all too often condemned by African officialdom, and not a few intellectuals, as evidence of "western" bias.

> Mobutu's political and personal behavior is eccentric and contradictory. In the process of "Zairianizing" his country to make it more authentically African, he gave himself a new name (complete with connotations of sexual prowess) and created an elaborate mystique surrounding his origins and his achievement of power; Zairian children can read all about it in comic-book form. Yet he has actually remained more aloof from the common people of his country than most leaders in Africa. Mobutu has complained often about the corruption in his society, but he has been its most corrupt member; indeed during his time in power, he has become one of the richest men in the world, with a personal fortune estimated to be worth upward of $3 billion. (His properties include several chateaus in Belgium and other homes in France, Switzerland, Italy, Senegal, and Ivory Coast.)[37]

Actually Ungar's reporting is balanced, and indeed exceedingly critical of the United States, which for decades had been Mobutu's primary supporter. If anything, according to Ungar, it is the U.S. which has acted badly in this sordid and ongoing tale of ignorance and greed.

> Mobutu has played his American connection with great skill, alternately biting the hand that feeds him (even to the point of expelling American ambassadors whom he accused of meddling in his country's internal affairs) and gently stroking it. He seems to have a keen sense of American domestic political trends. Thus, while he temporarily improved his record on human rights during the years of the Carter administration, he began to arrest and jail more of his opponents within days of Ronald Reagan's inauguration in Washington. . . . At another particularly tense moment in the standoff with his U.S. congressional critics, Mobutu made the dramatic gesture of resuming Zaire's diplomatic relations with Israel (having been the first of many African leaders to break them off during the Middle East crisis of the

early 1970s). That step delighted the United States at the same time that it somewhat diluted American leverage in Zaire; Israel would now be an alternative supplier of military aid and training for Zaire. By keeping up a fairly steady stream of anti-Soviet remarks, Mobutu has also maintained the friendship of China, which seems willing to ignore his domestic record.[38]

One wonders how the conspiracy theory deals with all this? But, of course, even when scholars labor to reveal the deeper roots of bias, or when observers expose racial and other stereotypes, there is always that all too human predilection (which seems to be developed in its highest degree in officialdom, regardless of nation or race or creed) to "control" and manage the flow of information. The history of the totalitarian regimes of Eastern Europe (particularly the Soviet Union) and of other so-called "Socialist Democracies" in Asia, the Caribbean, Africa, etc., provides the most perfect examples of this (though the West is not exempt). The ultimate failure of such attempts at mind-control, particularly in those nations where it has been most widely practiced, should act as a deterrent. Few should be surprised, however, that in Africa, as in Asia or parts of Europe, it has not.

Despite the enormous appeal of *The National Geographic*, and the sporadic popularity of travel journalism, American travel literature which took Africa as its subject is probably best represented over time by the safari story, usually penned in the 1920s and 1930s by a hunter-traveler or naturalist-adventurer of considerable experience. Wealthy and well-connected Americans formerly content, if the spirit moved them, to explore the sites of old European glories, or still "pristine" New World backlands, or an occasional New World ruin, had begun to look to Africa for the kind of adventure once available only beyond the frontier. Francis Parkman, had he been born half a century later, would have been unable to find in the American West the relatively unspoiled conditions that made *The Oregon Trail* (1847) among the most readable and satisfying works of its time.[39] Theodore Roosevelt was but one of many Americans, coming to maturity after the "Old West" was tamed, who found a hunter's Valhalla, a naturalist's paradise, an adventurer's Nirvana in the sun-drenched plains, rugged scarps and highlands of Africa, particularly East and Southern Africa.

It will come as no surprise, therefore, that this genre is represented early on, and in its purest sense by Theodore Roosevelt's famous book *African Game Trails*. Suffice it to say here that former President Roosevelt, fully aware of the tradition already well-established by such British adventurers as Frederick Courteney Selous,[40] and with similar works of his own behind him,[41] fully understood the norms when he penned the following in 1909:

> In these greatest of the world's great hunting-grounds there are mountain peaks whose snows are dazzling under the equatorial sun; swamps where the slime oozes and bubbles and festers in the streaming heat; lakes like seas; skies that burn above deserts where the iron desolation is shrouded from view by the wavering mockery of the mirage; vast grassy plains where palms and thorn-trees fringe the dwindling streams; mighty rivers rushing out of the heart of the continent through the sadness of endless marshes; forests of gorgeous beauty, where death broods in the dark and silent depths.

He knew that the reader sought not only stories of the hunt for dangerous game but other challenges as well.

> There are regions as healthy as the northland; and other regions, radiant with bright-hued flowers, birds and butterflies, odorous with sweet and heavy scents, but, treacherous in their beauty and sinister to human life. On the land and in the water there are dread brutes that feed on the flesh of man; and among the lower things, that crawl, and fly, and sting, and bite, he finds swarming foes far more evil and deadly than any beast or reptile; foes that kill his crops and his cattle, foes before which he himself perishes in his hundreds of thousands.

It is, of course, a wholly romantic world, timeless, dreamlike, and mysterious beyond description.

> These things can be told. But there are no words that can tell the hidden spirit of the wilderness, that can reveal its mystery, its melancholy, and its charm. There is delight in the hardy life of the open, in long rides rifle in hand, in the thrill of the fight with dangerous game. Apart from this, yet mingled with it, is the strong attraction of the silent places, of the large tropic moons, and the splendor of the new stars; where the wanderer sees the awful glory of sunrise and sunset in the wide waste spaces of the earth, unworn of man, and changed only by the slow changes of the ages through time everlasting.[42]

Few writers have so unabashedly celebrated romance in a setting so exotic (even the stars, so near the equator, are "new"). There is nothing here of Hemingway's restraint—understated, minimally described, yet ferociously felt in suspended emotion. Roosevelt, true to his muse, is all purple prose, and his quest is framed within a place "unworn of man," although Roosevelt surely knew that humans had been there for ages. His license, of course, is a literary one, if not a poet's. Though he might not have understood, in 1909, that Africans framed the landscape as much as they were framed by it, he expresses the view, for the reader's sake (and perhaps his own), that the landscape of his quest is wholly pristine. After all, the only convention one needs, in order to accept this, is the commonly held belief that the Africans themselves are little more than beasts, a view which T. R. himself repeated often enough in this work.[43] Thus, Roosevelt's "Pleistocene" landscape with its great herds, great beasts, great expanses, and its great opportunity for strenuous hunting adventure, can be pristine only insofar as the people native to it are also of that Pleistocene.

It is, of course, one of the most tried and true notes in the long tune of the travel story, not to pay too much attention to "the natives." A deeper concern for "tribal" societies, a human interest in the other—such is not for the hunter-traveler, this is for anthropologists, or perhaps missionaries. Roosevelt was an accomplished popularizer himself, and he certainly understood that the armchair adventurer who read his book typically wished to know only as much about "the natives" as was needed to provide the appropriate backdrop for adventure. The days of "rampaging tribes" were past, so it was assumed, and the *Pax Brittanica* was now triumphant. Thus for the would-be hunter the Africans were relegated to a supporting role; they were extras to provide local color. Nothing so disturbing as genuine history must intervene; that might require thought about what the great white hunter (or naturalist, photographer, whatever) was doing there, supported by so many. It might even require thought about the whole system of colonialism then at its apogee.

It should be at least of passing interest that Colonel Roosevelt, as his hosts called him (and as he himself preferred), was one of the better-known amateur American historians of his time. His multi-volume work, *The Winning of the West*, published over the period from 1889 to 1896, and much reprinted through his Presidential years, was filled with the rousing history of the white conquest of North America. And, though modern scholars find much to criticize in that rather heady work, with its celebration of Manifest Destiny and the triumph of the Anglo-Saxon over "lesser" breeds, at least Roosevelt attempted a narrative of events.[44] It is difficult to discern, however, in Roosevelt's equally famous *African Game Trails*, a historian's interest in events. Here the hunter predominates, with the amateur naturalist taking a close second. We might recall that in the corpus of his work Roosevelt wrote first and last about his greatest love, hunting and the chase. True, ornithology ranked high among his life-long pursuits, and there is much bird-listing (after the bird was bagged and identified) in *African Game Trails*. Likewise, Roosevelt indulged in a kind of elementary zoology (the length, breadth, estimated weight, etc., of rhino, buffalo, elephant, kudu, giraffe, hippo, etc.). He might wax eloquent—within the limited range of what was known to his generation—about the environment surrounding a particular species, like the leopard or the ostrich. Yet, his deep interest in the Native American, albeit expressed in the rather condescending fashion common to his era, does not seem to have been transferred to Africa's native populations. The curiosity about cultures and societies one might expect of a historian does not seem to have survived his travel across the Atlantic, through the Mediterranean, down the Red Sea, along the Indian Ocean, and into the East African interior. Perhaps because he had arrived only after the great "pacification" was accomplished, he left that saga to others. But this omission does seem curious. Why did this polymath not take greater interest in the extraordinary legends, already known and so close about him, of the great "Interlacustrine Kingdoms," or in the heroic struggles—so akin to those of certain Amerindians which he had attempted to chronicle—of Africans against the juggernaut of white expansionism? When he so much as mentions Africans in reference to the past, he does so only to underline his thesis that Africa (the Africa he wanted, the Africa he found) was outside the pale of civilization, and that the only civilization worthy of note in Africa was that brought by Europe. Indeed, he believed that even in their most warlike state no Africans could really be compared to American Indians.[45]

The extensive East African travels of Martin and Osa Johnson, whose safari stories were very popular among Americans through the 1920s and 1930s, represent a significant variation on this theme. Martin's 1928 book, *Safari: A Saga of the African Blue*, filled with photographs (sixty six in all) which made him famous, might be taken as a model for its kind. Johnson and his wife Osa (with whom he co-authored later works), claimed that British East Africa was their real home, a paradise of thrills, sunshine, flowers and laughter. As Martin put it, explaining the daily life that he and Osa had created in northern Kenya at their "Lake Paradise" home, up near the Ethiopian border:

> There are no frills to our regime. We dress to keep warm and eat to live. Simple pleasures stand out in their true values unsullied by the myriad artificial entertainments of civilization. Our diet is plain; our costume unadorned; we rise

with the sun and labor while it lasts. As a result we find life more savory than ever it was amid the conveniences of hot hotels and traffic-jammed streets.[46]

The Johnsons had a clear objective during the extended expeditions from Lake Paradise, namely to "film more completely than it had ever been done before, a record of Africa's fast vanishing wildlife."[47] Though this might seem quaint today, with thousands of tourists clicking away at every water hole from Amboseli to Ngorongoro, it was then a new field. Already a small number of pioneering photographers had "invaded" Africa, influenced by England's great bird photographers, the brothers Richard and Cherry Kearton, and especially by the Americans, Frank Michler Chapman (of the American Museum of Natural History), A. G. Wallihan, and George Shiras, whose magnificent photos of white-tailed deer and other animals at his Whitefish Lake camp in Northern Michigan proved that night photography was not only possible, but often superior in results. Shiras apparently never visited Africa during his career which stretched from the 1890s to the late 1930s, but in his day he was the most celebrated of *The National Geographic's* many fine photographers. Perhaps the best of the early photographers of African wildlife was the German Carl Georg Schillings, who began his work in East Africa in 1896-97 and continued into the new century. Schillings, like Shiras, learned to use the trip-wire to great effect, and his night photos of hyenas, jackals, leopards, lions (and their prey) caused a minor sensation.[48] Among other innovations he pioneered the use of telephoto lenses.

Probably the best known before the Johnsons was the Englishman A. R. Dugmore (who teamed with the American Museum's taxidermist James L. Clark). Dugmore's famous photo (in 1909) of a charging rhino, taken head-on at a mere fifteen yards, remains one of the most famous pictures of its kind. Dugmore, perhaps influenced by Carl Akeley's pre-war cinematography experiments, also made a few movies in East Africa after World War I.[49]

Carl Ethan Akeley, ever resourceful, had almost as much influence in this arena as he did in taxidermy, or in the burgeoning specialty of museum design and display. His "natural" backdrop settings for wildlife displays at the American Museum in New York remain a model for similar displays to this day throughout the world. Dissatisfied with the equipment then in use, he created the Akeley Panoramic Camera, a far more manageable tool, with which he filmed (in 1921) wild gorillas at Mount Mikeno.

The Johnson's had a dual aim: to record wildlife not only in still photos within a natural habitat, but extensively in cinema (using the Akeley Panoramic Camera), and in such a way as to entertain and inform audiences back home. They had already achieved a modest success showing filmstrips of travels in the South Pacific; now Africa beckoned. Their route, beginning in 1923, was typical; England, Suez, Mombasa, Nairobi, then the vast "bush" around Marsabit in Kenya, which became their home for the next several years. The Johnson's were well-equipped for their adventure. Martin had begun his career as a youngster, signing with Jack London as a cook for a South Seas cruise on the writer's yacht, the *Snark*, where he discovered a gift with the camera. After marrying Osa, the two filmed illustrated travelogues throughout the Solomons, the New Hebrides, and Borneo, saving funds for their great African adventure. A meeting with Carl Akeley, which elicited the support of the American Museum, also attracted the sponsorship of George Eastman. Several Willys-Knight vehicles (forerunners of the famous "jeep) made them far more mobile than previous expeditions, and the consequence, by the mid-thirties, was several hundred thousand feet of film—mostly of animals but frequently including various "wild" tribes—whose influence on the pre-war generation can hardly be exaggerated. One of these films, *Simba*, released in 1928, featuring the behavior and actions of the lion, rhino, and elephant, was still shown in American schools into the late 1940s. One of the authors remembers *Simba* from that period, including a rousing lion hunt by, as he later learned, Lumbwa warriors.[50] Could anyone who had read even one of the popular Tarzan novels (whose author, Edgar Rice Burroughs, used common Swahili nouns for the larger animals) forget that title, or the adventure implied in the filming?

Other portions of the Johnson's filmed record, like the later work of Clyde Beatty, were widely viewed in the era before the Disney studio began to make feature films on well-known wildlife species. They undoubtedly did much to reinforce the stereotypes of Africa and Africans already deeply rooted in prose. And, though Martin and Osa both avoided the romanticized exaggeration common to so many safari stories, Martin repeatedly expresses conventional colonial attitudes toward the "natives,"

> Except for wages sometimes, fresh meat or a cigarette the white man has nothing that the black man desires.
>
> [Swahili] is a sort of African Esperanto understood by the native tribes which roam Tanganyika, British East Africa, and even Abyssinia far to the North. . . . It is made up of native dialects and Arabian terms, first stirred into a lingual goulash by the old Arab slaver traders who used to range these parts.[51]

Perhaps Johnson can be forgiven for not knowing that this so-called "lingual goulash" has ancient linguistic roots in the Bantu languages spoken across half of Africa. He obviously did not learn enough of that lovely tongue to even begin to appreciate its marvelous poetry, its rich descriptive vocabulary, or its extraordinary capacity to adopt useful terms from other languages. He can only make fun of "new" words like "statione" or "officey" (actually these should end in "i"), perhaps unaware that one of the strengths of another lingua franca, English, is its ready borrowing from other languages. One wonders what he might have thought had he known that the common Americanism "okay" had roots in Africa, and came to North American whites via enslaved Africans. Perhaps this lingual "goulash" was too much trouble, except in its "bastard or cockney" form?

Regarding white-black relations in 1928, the following statement by Johnson tells volumes: "We had learned to handle natives on our previous visit and during our years in the South Sea Islands; to like them also."[52] In keeping with this mindset, one could only respect "natives" if they also understood their role.

All of this is not to say that wild Africa, the Africa of endless vistas, of great game herds, of magnificent game reserves and unexpected natural beauty, should not have its chroniclers, its praise-singers, its photographers and story-tellers. The simple fact that this Africa is the Africa most craved by and most dreamed of by millions of readers or viewers in Europe and America cannot be denied. In this tradition, still within the general definition of the safari story, are the more recent works of several American writers, who, building on the solid record of Carl Akeley, Mary Jobe Akeley, and others, have continued to entertain us, and sometimes to enlighten us.

Premier among them, probably the most prolific and inimitable of contemporary American naturalists, is Peter Matthiessen. His first major work on Africa, *The Tree Where Man Was Born*, published in 1972 with photographs by Eliot Porter, remains one of the most beautiful books ever written on Africa and its wildlife. Matthiessen, when he traveled to East Africa in the early 1960s to research this book, was already known for *Wildlife in America* (still, several editions later, a standard reference) as well as his chronicle of adventures in New Guinea, *Under the Mountain Wall*, and the extraordinary novel set in Amazonia, *At Play in the Fields of the Lord*.[53] Having co-founded the respected *Paris Review* with George Plimpton in the early fifties, Matthiessen brought a literary sensibility to his travels which was unusual, if not unexpected. Add to this his exceptional talent for descriptive prose and the result is some of the most vivid and informed writing of our time.

Here is Matthiessen, describing in 1961, a flight over the Sahara while en route to the upper Nile, a desolate but magnificent landscape:

> In the old millenniums of rain during the Pleistocene and after, much of this waste had been well-watered grassland. Years later, flying at dawn from Rabat on the Atlantic coast and drifting southeast over endless red infernal reaches of gravel, windspun sand, and smokey sky, I would see the ancient rivers of the Ice Age, like fossil tracings in the sands of the Sahara.[54]

Here it seemed was a new kind of American writing, owing little to the British (or French) tradition of naturalist prose which had until then dominated this genre. To be sure this work borrowed lightly from the best of American naturalists—Aldo Leopold and John Muir are echoed here, as well as Carl Akeley—with perhaps a touch of Hemingway in it, especially in the plain sentences as clear as spring water. Matthiessen, however, was willing to plunge more deeply into the past. This book was clearly influenced by ethnography, archaeology, and paleontology, by a careful reading of solid zoological tracts, as well as the better-known histories. If, in the early sixties, Matthiessen had not apparently read Ngugi wa Thiong'o or B. A. Ogot, he knew the works of Jomo Kenyatta, E. E. Evans-Pritchard, Basil Davidson, Roland Oliver, Sonia Cole, Joseph Greenberg, and Colin Turnbull, not to mention the obvious writers that anyone writing on East African wildlife would know—the great ethologist George Schaller, Iain Douglas-Hamilton, Peter Beard, I. S. C. Parker and R. M. Laws, and Desmond Vesey-FitzGerald. Matthiessen also, and necessarily, read the earlier wanderer-hunters like Frederick C. Selous, and the white settler writers like Elspeth Huxley, whose work faithfully played to the symbolic conventions. The result, therefore, is a classic safari book which rises above the symbolic conventions that cloud so many of the works of other naturalists, and sometimes (because of egregious ethnocentrism) render even the most careful ethological or zoological report rather difficult to stomach. Near the end of *The Tree Where Man Was Born*, Matthiessen describes his feelings after many days in close proximity with African guides and companions, with whom he admits he shares very little.

> Lying back against these ancient rocks of Africa, I am content. The great stillness in these landscapes that once made me restless seeps into me day by day, and with it the unreasonable feeling that I have found what I was searching for

without ever having discovered what it was. In the ash of the old hearth, ant lions have counter-sunk their traps and wait in the loose dust for their prey; far overhead a falcon—and today I do not really care whether it is a peregrine or lanner—sails out over the rim of rock and on across the valley. The day is beautiful, my belly full, and returning to the cave this afternoon will be returning home. For the first time, I am in Africa among Africans. We understand almost nothing of one another, yet, we are sharing the same water flask, our fingers touching in the common bowl. At Halanogamai there is a spring, and at Darashugan are red rock paintings—that is all.[55]

What a contrast, this, to the thunderous Rooseveltian descriptions of charging rhinos, to the breast-beating and the boastings of new kills, which so mar *African Game Trails* (a book once hugely popular, now so dated and out-of-date). Matthiessen, though he visited Africa for only a few months during this and later visits, managed to drink in something of that experience wherein small and often unnoticed things count most. Reading his work one senses that Matthiessen witnessed more of Africa in the ant lions at his feet than Roosevelt could ever have comprehended with a score of dead lions, bagged and measured.

In 1979 Matthiessen returned to tour the enormous Selous Game Reserve in southern Tanzania, this time with famed wildlife photographer Hugo van Lawick. Another book on Africa entitled *Sand Rivers*, published in 1981, was the result. Though the book is outwardly the chronicle of an extended foot safari—with dazzling verbal and photo portraits of the great game encountered—it is also a safari of the mind, an investigation of the "inner spaces" that Matthiessen has sought in all his work (particularly in *The Snow Leopard* which won the National Book Award in 1978). The following passages from *Sand Rivers* are hardly typical of safari literature. The first is a segment from a diary kept by Kazungu, the African safari cook.

> We saw elephants [wrote Kazungu] where we wanted to pass. We went upwind of them to give them our smell, and this makes me understand that no matter how dangerous an animal is, if he is not familiar with a smell, he will run.
>
> We went up and down the hills and met some different animals.

Matthiessen continues:

> Behind the elephants is a large grove of borassus palms, with their graceful swellings high up on the pale boles; from each palm, or so it seems, a pair of huge griffons violently depart, their heavy wing beats buffeting the clack of

wind-tossed fronds. At this season, the borassus carries strings of fruit like orange coconuts, which are sought out by the elephants; here and there in the dry hills, far from the nearest palms, lie piles of dried gray borassus kernels, digested and deposited, from which the last loose dung had blown away. The mango-like kernels remind Brian [Nicholson] of the elephant habit of gorging on the fallen fruits of the marula tree. "Used to ferment in their stomachs, make them drunk or sleepy, they'd just lie down on their sides and snore. Ever hear an elephant snore? Oh, you can hear that a *hell* of a long way!"[56]

And, regarding the "old hand" white warden who leads the foot safari:

> I suspect Brian Nicholson of liking Africans, despite all the conventional prejudices he displays. If I had any doubts about this, most of them would be resolved by the evidence of my own eyes and ears that Africans, from the simplest of these porters to an urbane, well-educated man such as Costy Mlay, seem fond of Brian, whose fluent Swahili must convey subtleties of understanding and even concern that are absent in most whites. Unlike Ionides [C. J. P. Ionides, who almost single-handedly founded the Selous Reserve], Brian was born in East Africa and has known and worked with Africans since he was a child. It is true that he has usually been in a superior's position with these people, which goes a long way to explain his preference for country Africans over those in the city, and no doubt he would agree with Ionides that western civilization has reduced many first-rate Africans to third-rate Europeans; I no longer bother to point out that, forced to adapt suddenly to an African culture, a first-rate European would certainly be thought of as a third-rate African, at least for the first few hundred years.[57]

Or this lament about the passing of the great game, so much on Matthiessen's mind, as on the mind of anyone disturbed by the terrible environmental degradation and destruction of natural habitat one sees throughout Africa:

> Beyond the kongoni five elephants, dusted the red color of the Tsavo elephants of Goa's [the African guide's] youth, stand peacefully in the sun-bloodied water, and downriver a solitary bull feeds in a meadow just behind the bank. Like all the bulls that we have seen this is a young one, with small ivory, and reading my thoughts, Brian says, "Where are the big bulls, Peter? I can't pretend to myself much longer that all those elephants seen from the air are back up

in the thickets, or the big herds of buffalo, either; we've *been* back in the thickets, and they're just not there."[58]

A third work, *African Silences*, written by Matthiessen over several years, is a chronicle of separate travels in Senegal and the Ivory Coast in the late 1970s and in The Central African Republic, Gabon, and Zaire in the late 1980s. Matthiessen was seeking evidence of the state of the smaller "forest" elephant (a subspecies of the larger "bush" elephant, *Loxodonta africana*) which allegedly survived in great numbers throughout the equatorial rainforests.[59] Matthiessen, with ecologist (and pilot) David Western, discovered something quite the contrary in their journeys through these equatorial regions. First there are very few wild elephants left alive in West Africa, except scattered (and theoretically protected) remnants in Senegal and the Ivory Coast, and a tiny number in Nigeria. Cameroon, whose eastern forests are contiguous with the great equatorial rainforest of Central Africa might provide an exception. Clearly the picture of wildlife in West Africa, as reported by Matthiessen into the late 1980s, is appalling. As observers have long noticed across the entire region from Mauretania to Nigeria, virtually nothing that moves seems safe from the relentless search for food, a situation which Matthiessen fears is rapidly obtaining for all of Africa. Equally appalling, because it was not understood, is the incontrovertible fact that the smaller forest elephant, once widespread in the equatorial forest extending from the borders of Zaire in the east all the way across to Cameroon in the west, survives only in greatly reduced numbers because of hunting and loss of habitat. What might appear from the air to be endless virgin rainforest, unaffected by man, is, on closer examination, often second-growth forest or older forest so impacted by human use that its flora is degraded and its fauna depleted. In this book, as in his previous African books, Matthiessen avoids the trap—so typical of certain naturalists and popularizers of safari-style environmentalism—of simplistically blaming Africans for this sad state of affairs. Nevertheless, he does not hesitate to excoriate the governments responsible, who pretend to environmental programs and policies, while in fact doing little or nothing to alleviate the condition of their populations. *African Silences*, though as eloquent and sensitive as Matthiessen's earlier works on the continent, is a sad book, with almost nothing of the euphoria and the celebration that fired the pages of *The Tree Where Man Was Born*. A quarter of a century after his first visit to Africa, its author can find no reason for optimism.

Travel literature of the more typical kind defined in this chapter—that is, the sort of work not specific to wildlife or hunting safaris—is perhaps best represented in the U.S. in recent years by the widely-praised work of Edward Hoagland and Alex Shoumatoff. The former, author of an excellent travel book on British Columbia, *Notes from the Century Before*, and several works of almost Thoreauvean celebration of the natural environment, *Red Wolves and Black Bears* and *The Edward Hoagland Reader*, set off to the Sudan in 1977 (his second trip to Africa) for a three month journey which resulted in a book called *African Calliope: A Journey to the Sudan.* As can be seen here, Hoagland has a highly personal journalistic style:

> After one has read dozens of explorer's journals, with the books of contemporary wilderness enthusiasts thrown in, it isn't hard to reach the conclusion that the search these individuals have made to find the wildest areas left on earth—a kind of relay race, at best, but a long compulsion in many cases—was really an attempt, itself, to start over.[60]

He can also write with admirable self-restraint about his own role as a reporter from the U.S. "not utterly untypical of all the white people who had roamed Africa before."[61] In this respect he is actually more atypical than typical. *African Calliope* is refreshingly free of travel boasting about hardships encountered and obstacles overcome—though he had his share—and likewise free of ethnocentrism. It is clear from the start that Hoagland, though—like virtually all travel writers—he seeks the unusual and different, is not aiming his words at the armchair adventurer who wants exotica and thrills however contrived, but at a more select audience who prefer an informed and balanced view of the "other." As Hoagland says regarding the vital question of objectivity:

> Unlike a novelist, a journalist is dependent upon where he has stationed himself and what happens to him—what he stumbles upon—and so he is likely to put himself into adventurous situations occasionally, or will push out into the current of a different geography to see where he is carried. Let me see what I run across here, he says, and sometimes has the sense when he gets home—like stepping off an airplane after a shaky landing—of *having walked away from another one.* My discovery may have been obvious that, far from learning something new about the black-white torque that is such a misery in America, here I was freer of it. But the other reason why I had come to Africa, instead of to another southern continent, was that on the contrary, it was not a clean slate, not neutral ground The myth of blackness, darkness, this "land of sorrow," might be a sounding board. "Before the Congo I was just a mere animal," Joseph Conrad said.

And:

> Almost any white man traveling in Africa floats close to
> the surface, but one realizes that the administrative class
> drifts close to the surface too. A swift, perhaps cursory
> observer, touching down only briefly, as I did, has his uses
> in reporting upon such a rapidly changing scene.[62]

And describing a village near Juba:

> All that water [during the rains], but the local people were
> short of food, and lacked wood to keep warm. From many
> villages it was an all-day expedition to the nearest copse of
> trees, so during pneumonia season it was a hero's job for
> them to forage for fuel. Now, however—in the midst of the
> dry spell—the Africans could be told to wash their children's
> fly-sucked eyes (the flies were thirsty too), but they did not
> have even enough drinking water.[63]

Clearly Hoagland, in the grand tradition, is emphasizing things
here that the typical American reader will never have experienced.
Some of this might be called exotica; nonetheless Hoagland's report
is on target. Throughout the work (though Hoagland does not pretend to any special insight) is this refreshing perception, however
framed within the symbolic conventions, presented with the humil-
ity of the observant outsider looking in. Reading an illuminating
book like this one sometimes wishes that more visiting scholars,
with academic goals in mind, could be so modest about the illusory
nature of so much of what they observe (with their full panoply of
empirical data) as well as what they write.

Alex Shoumatoff, longtime nature writer for *The New Yorker* and
recent correspondent for *Vanity Fair*, is the author of two travel
books on Africa: *In Southern Light: Trekking Through Zaire and the
Amazon* (1986), and *African Madness* (1988). The former, a brilliant
examination of ancient legends and modern realities in Amazonia
and in modern Zaire, is, at least on the surface, within the grand
travelogue tradition. Here, both in the rainforests of the Amazon
and amid the vast Ituri, Shoumatoff seeks and finds practically
everything that is considered exotic and extinct in the humdrum
protected American world. Certainly, in the African half of the book,
he seeks (and finds) everything in Zaire that most Americans associate with Africa, especially in the rainforest itself.

> After a while, we came to a smoky clearing with half a
> dozen domes of mangungu thatch in it. They were the
> smallest dwellings I had ever seen, like tropical igloos or

nests of some gregarious ground creature. I could not quite have stretched out in one. Two Efe women, squatting before a little fire that smouldered at the meeting point of three logs, got up and, without daring to look at me, bravely took my extended hand. A man and another woman came out of one of the huts. The man was very muscular, like a wrestler, and his arms and legs looked slightly long in relation to his torso. He stood about four feet nine, and except for a rag tucked through a vine belt, he was naked. The women, who were a few inches shorter, wore similar loin-cloths. They had black circles of plant juice painted on their arms and legs and black lines on their faces, much as some Amazonian women have, and their teeth were chipped to points.[64]

Though it is obvious that such writing plays unabashedly to the conventions of the African travelogue, Shoumatoff is, nonetheless, an observant naturalist and reporter.

We were sitting in a grove of hundred-and-fifty-foot strangler figs. The species *Ficus* thonningii, is partial to high, well-drained sites. Each tree had started as a seed dropped by a bird in the crotch of a different species of tree which had originally occupied the site. Like wax melting down the side of a candle, the roots had descended from the seeds, mingled and merged, and eventually smothered the host tree out of existence. At the same time, usually about thirty feet from the ground, a trunk had ascended from the seed and shot up for a hundred feet or so before finally branching into a crown. Gamaembi cut into a huge buttress of anastomosed fig root with the edge of an iron arrowhead, and a sticky white latex bubbled out. "Along the rivers, we line traps with the milk of this tree and bait them with seeds," he said. "Birds walk in and get stuck." He said the tree was called *popo* and was one of those whose inner bark the Efe and some of the older BaLese pounded into loincloths.[65]

For the reader, having already learned, in the Amazonian section of *In Southern Light*, how vital is the complicated reproduction and distribution of distinct and numerous species, this paragraph reveals much. Good writers can do this: good nature writers need to do this. One learns, without having to be told outright, many things: that the trees cannot reproduce themselves unless various birds survive to place the seeds; that the local human population makes several uses of the tree; that all are intricately interconnected, and that the scientific identification of a species (in its taxonomic naming and placing) is only half the story in understanding the workings of this natural world.

This is what makes Shoumatoff's work worthwhile, despite the overt sensationalism of title and subject. *African Madness*, though outwardly a work purely redolent of the symbolic conventions, is *between* its covers a searching and often disturbing book. Chapter headings such as "The Emperor Who Ate His People" and "The Woman Who Loved Gorillas" are excessive. The allusions to cannibalism—that ancient shibboleth of Africa—and to "love" between woman and gorilla, serve the author as a kind of signal. Having originally written these pieces for *The New Yorker* and *Vanity Fair*, he admits (in his preface) that his vision is a romantic one.

> I was, and am swept away by these worlds of ecstatic light and color and overwhelming beauty, by the birds, flowers, and butterflies, by the seething, radiant life of the rain forests and the markets, by the generosity and gentleness of the people, by the music and the slow, delicious rhythm of life.[66]

Yet, Shoumatoff seems determined, reporter as he is, to educate his readers in the elements of nature behind the romance of wilderness, and behind the sensational headlines of blood and darkness . For example, the emperor referred to in the chapter title, Jean-Bedel Bokassa of the Central African Republic (which Bokassa briefly renamed an Empire), has been previously and luridly described with all his atrocities. Shoumatoff reveals little that is new in 1988. What he does offer is a narrative which exposes the mindless support for that tyrant on the part of the French (especially the former French President, Giscard d'Estaing, who had often visited Bokassa's "empire" to shoot elephants) and he reveals a callousness among French officialdom that borders on criminality. In circumstances which almost exactly echo the case of Amin in Uganda, it was not until Bokassa had executed over a hundred school children (some of whom, apparently, had dared to stone his official car as it passed) and, indeed, only after Amnesty International had verified the massacre, that the tyrant was removed forthwith.

> A thousand crack French paratroopers known as *barracudas*—red berets, camouflage fatigues tucked into combat boots, automatic weapons—took Camp de Roux, the presidential residence, seized the radio station, and proclaimed the end of the empire.[67]

Though Shoumatoff does not dwell on this obvious point, one leaves the tale fully aware of the reality of continued French involvement with (and control over) this particular African nation, nominally "independent" for decades, but still subject after all these years to the caprice not only of a mad tyrant, but to the goodwill of the metropole (Paris).

Likewise, the chapter on Dian Fossey is outwardly sensational and romantic in the extreme. The narrative of her extraordinary vigil to save her beloved gorillas, her heroic struggle against the evil of environmental destruction, and her almost Hollywood-style demise—hacked to death with a machete—could hardly have been concocted by a dozen pop screenwriters. This, however, belies Shoumatoff's deeper investigation into the heroine's persona, indeed into the whole disturbing question of how the white world works its will in Africa, especially when animals are involved.

"'I only knew the person I had to deal with for eight years'" Shoumatoff quotes a long-time associate of Fossey's,

> and this was a sad person. She was riding on some kind of dedication she once had . . . . Dian could have had all the accolades in the world for what she did during the first six years. It would have been natural for others to build on her work, but she didn't have the self-confidence or the charac- ter for that to happen. . . . She invented so many plots and enemies. She kept talking about how nobody could take it up there, how they all got 'bushy', but in the end she was the only one who went bonkers. She didn't get killed because she was saving the gorillas. She got killed because she was Dian Fossey."[68]

The story behind this rather unpleasant fact, particularly Fossey's relentless assumption that Africans living in the vicinity of the Parc des Volcans were invariably enemies (and never potential allies), is the core of Shoumatoff's account. It therefore provides a necessary corrective to the image presented in the Hollywood version of her career and especially her death. Whatever he thinks of this com- monplace European and American assumption that Africans are the primary antagonist in the struggle to preserve wild places and wild species Shoumatoff does not shy away from presenting the his- tory of Fossey's troubled relations with Africans, indeed with any- one with whom she had close association during her legendary career. Though Shoumatoff's admits his romantic preoccupations, and though these obviously reflect the standard archetypes associ- ated with Africa throughout this century, he reveals a larger truth. Perhaps this is because he retained a critical and analytical sense in spite of the "exotic" setting of his travels.

Perhaps in the final analysis the traveler is not really different than the ethnographer or scientist whose goals are precise and lim- ited. As Levi-Strauss observed, the traveler may find "our own filth" strewn across the unfamiliar terrain he seeks, but that is no less true of the anthropologist, the zoologist, the historian.[69] The garbage of which Levi-Strauss speaks is as much cultural as physical. The Neo-Rousseaueans invariably search for "authentic" experience. The variety and complexity of Africa assures that they will find, sooner or later, what they seek. All travel is in some respects through time as well as space. In Africa today, as in the time of Herodotus, the experience of the traveler almost inevitably leads to powerful indicators and even remnants of the remote past (somehow in Africa this always comes through with more force than in Europe, for example). Industrialization in Africa, for instance, seems more a veneer than an entirely new construction. Village life, in spite of mass urbanization, lingers with its ancient roots exposed. What was once known to all humanity—the daily cycles of extended family and clan within environs close to nature—has for the Westerner become exotica. For millions of Africans it is mundane. Perhaps it is true, as certain anthropologists have argued, that the only sure way to demythologize (or de-exoticize) those romantic images of people supposedly living in ways unchanged for millennia, is to live so closely among them as to adopt their point of view. This, Michael Jackson seems to say in his novel, *Barawa and the way birds fly in the sky*,[70] is a worthwhile endeavor, even if we only partially succeed in the attempt. The attempt, however, confirms our humanity.

Few travelers—in Africa or anywhere else—linger long enough to approximate this goal, no matter how observant, no matter how thorough their preparation. It is a rare travelogue, therefore, which breaches the gulf of culture and history, bringing real insight to the task. Though some of the works noted here have clearly done so, most have not, indeed cannot.

Scorn for the traveler can be misleading. Great writers can transcend the limitations of space and of time. Over half a century ago W. E. B. Du Bois (entering his seventieth year) wrote a thoughtful book, part travelogue and part personal memoir. Its subtitle was An Essay Toward an Autobiography of a Race Concept; its title was *Dusk of Dawn*. In this book he said,

> The problem of the future world is the charting, by means of intelligent reason, of a path not simply through the resistances of physical force, but through the vaster and far more intricate jungle of ideas conditioned on unconscious and subconscious reflexes of living things: on blind unreason and often irresistible urges . . . of which the concept of race is today one of the most unyielding and threatening.[71]

Indeed, in his own personal odyssey, as he penned this book, Du Bois the traveler described Africa as he saw it the first time. Here he is the "sixth generation in descent from forefathers who left this land," arriving at the coast of Liberia:

> On beyond flowed the dark low undulating land quaint with palm and breaking sea. The world grew black.
>
> And there and elsewhere in two long months I began to learn: primitive men are not following us afar, frantically waving and seeking our goals; primitive men are not behind us in some swift foot-race. Primitive men have already arrived. They are abreast, and in places ahead of us; in others behind. But all their curving advance line is contemporary, not prehistoric. They have used other paths and these paths have led them by scenes sometimes fairer, sometimes uglier than ours, but always toward the Pools of Happiness.[72]

Notes

1. Herbert L. Bridgman, "The New British Empire of the Sudan," *The National Geographic Magazine* 17, no. 5 (May 1906): 241

2. Ibid., 259, 264, 266.

3. Mary B. Campbell, *The Witness and the Other World: Exotic European Travel Writing, 400-1600* (Ithica: Cornell University Press, 1988), 5-7.

4. Walter Ralegh, *The Discoverie of the Large, Rich, and Bewtiful Empire of Guiana with A Relation of the Great and Golden City of Manoa (which the Spaniards call El Dorado . . .* (London: Printed for the Hakluyt Society, 1848 [1596]); Herman Melville, *Typee: a Peep at Polynesian Life* (New York: Wiley and Putnam, 1846) and *Omoo: a narrative of adventures in the south seas* (New York: Harper, 1847). Also see Dennis Porter, *Haunted Journeys: Desire and Transgression in European Travel Writing* (Princeton: Princeton University Press, 1991) for an interesting interpretation of the literature of travel.

5. Christopher Miller, *Blank Darkness: Africanist Discourse in French* (Chicago: University of Chicago Press, 1985).

6. Merian C. Cooper, photographs by Earnest B. Schoedsack, "Two Fighting Tribes of the Sudan," *The National Geographic Magazine* 56 (July-Dec. 1929): 465.

7. Ibid., 470, 475.

8. James Bruce, *Travels to Discover the Source of the Nile*, 5 vols. (New York: Horizon Press, 1964 [1790]). Bruce did not publish this extraordinary record until sixteen years after his return and humiliation. Scholars have since given Bruce high praise, despite his somewhat lurid style.

9. A. R. Burn in Herodotus, *The Histories*, trans. Aubrey de Selincourt (Harmondsworth, Middlesex: Penguin Books, 1972), 30.

10. Alan Moorehead, *The Blue Nile* (London: Hamish Hamilton, 1960) may be the best single account of Bruce's travels and his travails in

England after his return. Also see Elspeth Huxley, "The Challenge of Africa," in Elspeth Huxley *Africa and Asia: Mapping Two Continents* (London: Aldus Books, 1973), 181-82.

11. Robert I. Rotberg, *A Political History of Tropical Africa* (New York: Harcourt, Brace, and World, 1965), 244-86. Also see Philip Curtin, et al., *African History* (Boston: Little, Brown, and Co., 1978), 445-71. A recent comprehensive study of the scramble, though seen almost entirely from the European perspective, is Thomas Pakenham, *The Scramble for Africa* (New York: Random House, 1991).

12. Kenneth C. Wylie, *The Political Kingdoms of the Temne* (New York: Africana Publishing Corp., 1977) and "The Politics of Transformation: Indirect Rule in Mendeland and Abuja, 1890-1914," Ph.D. diss., University of Michigan Microflim, Ann Arbor, 1967.

13. Frederick D. Lugard, *The Rise of Our East African Empire* (London: W. Blackwood and Sons, 1893) and *The Story of the Uganda Protectorate* (London: H. Marshall and Son, 1900). Henry Hamilton Johnston, *British Central Africa: An Attempt to Give Some Account of a Portion of the Territories under British Influence North of the Zambezi* (New York: Arnbold, 1897) and *The Story of My Life* (Indianapolis: Bobbs-Merrill Co., 1923). Carl Peters, *New Light on Dark Africa* (London: Ward, Lock and Co., 1891). Joseph Simon Gallieni, *Deux campagnes au Soudan francais, 1886-1888* (Paris: Hachette, 1891).

14. J. T. Alldridge, *The Sherbro and Its Hinterland* (New York: Macmillan and Co., 1901); A. C. C. Hastings, *Nigerian Days* (London: John Lane, 1925). Alldridge's work is widely considered to be fairly accurate anthropologically, for the time, and is relatively free of cant and sensationalism. Hastings work is altogether typical.

15. Pierre Paul Savorgnan de Brazza, *Conferences et lettres de Pierra Savorgnan de Brazza sur se trois explorations dans l'Ouest African, 1875-a-1806* (Paris: M. Dreyfous, 1887); Rudyard Kipling, *Rudyard Kipling's Verse Definitive Edition* (Garden City, N.Y.: Doubleday, 1940).

16. W. E. B. Du Bois, *Dusk of Dawn: An Essay toward An Autobiography of a Race Concept* (New York: Harcourt, Brace and Co., 1940), 125-26.

17. George Eastman, *Chronicles of a Second African Trip* (Rochester, N.Y.: Friends of the University of Rochester Libraries, 1987). The letters and photographs printed in this volume are collected from those written and taken by Eastman on his safari in 1928. As Elias Mandala states in the forward, Eastman was "denied . . . any meaningful contact with Africans living outside the society of colonizers" (71-72).

18. Kenneth M. Cameron, Introduction, in George Eastman, *Chronicles of a Second African Trip* (Rochester, N.Y.: Friends of the University of Rochester Libraries, 1987), xvii. For further information on Eastman and his earlier safari in British East Africa, see Kenneth M. Cameron, *Into Africa: The Story of the East African Safari* (London: Constable and Co., 1990, 88-89).

19. Raymond Leslie Buell, *The Native Problem in Africa*, 2 vols. (New York: The Macmillian Co., 1928).

20. Lawrence Copley Thaw and Margaret Stout Thaw, "A Motor Caravan Rolls Across Sahara and Jungle Through the Realms of Dusky

Potentates and the Land of Big-Lipped Women," *The National Geographic Magazine* 74 (July-Dec. 1938): 327-64.

21. Anne Eisner Putnam, "My Life with Africa's Little People," *The National Geographic Magazine* 117 (Jan.-June 1960): 269.

22. Ibid., 302.

23. Nathaniel T. Kenney, photographs by W. D. Vaughn, "The Winds of Change Stir a Continent," *The National Geographic Magazine* 118 no. 3 (Sept. 1960): 324.

24. Ibid., 307.

25. L. S. B. Leakey, "Finding the World's Earliest Man," *The National Geographic Magazine* 118, no. 3 (Sept. 1960): 421-35.

26. Rotberg, 339.

27. John Gunther, *Inside Africa* (New York: Harper and Brothers, 1955), 294-95.

28. Ibid., 365.

29. Ibid., 753.

30. Ibid., 536-37.

31. Blaine Harden, *Africa: Dispatches From a Fragile Continent* (Boston: Houghton Mifflin, 1990), 243.

32. Ibid., 286-287.

33. Walter Rodney, *How Europe Undeveloped Africa* (Washington, D.C.: Howard University Press, 1982); Chinweizu, *The West and the Rest of Us* (New York: Random House, 1975).

34. David Lamb, *The Africans* (New York: Methuen, 1985), 104.

35. Ibid., 90-91.

36. Ibid., 283.

37. Sanford J. Ungar, *Africa: The People and Politics of an Emerging Continent* (New York: Simon and Schuster, 1985), 359-60.

38. Ibid., 362-63.

39. Francis Parkman, *The Oregon Trail* (Garden City, N.Y.: Garden City Books, 1959 [1847]). His desire to see a wilderness not yet affected by man is well explained, as noted in the next chapter. Also see Roderick Nash, *Wilderness and the American Mind* (New Haven: Yale University Press, 1967), 98-100.

40. Frederick C. Selous, *A Hunter's Wanderings in Africa* (London: Macmillan, 1911).

41. Theodore Roosevelt, *Hunting Trips of a Ranchman: Sketches of Sport on the Northern Cattle Plains* (New York: G.P. Putnam's Sons, 1885).

42. Theodore Roosevelt, *African Game Trails: An Account of the African Wanderings of an American Hunter-Naturalist* (New York: Charles Scribner's Sons, 1919), vii-x. Also see Cameron, 49-60, regarding Roosevelt's enormous safari, and its influence on later safaris.

43. For example, "The low culture of many of the savage tribes, especially of the hunting tribes, substantially reproduces the conditions of life in Europe as it was led by our ancestors ages before the dawn of anything that could be called civilization." Roosevelt, *African Game Trails*, 2-3.

44. Theodore Roosevelt, *The Winning of the West* (New York: The Current Literature Publishing Co., 1905).

45.   The problem offered by the natives bore no resemblance to that offered by the presence of our tribes of horse Indians, few in numbers and incredibly formidable in war. The natives of East Africa are numerous, many of them are agricultural or pastoral peoples after their own fashion; and even the bravest of them, the warlike Masai, are in no way formidable as our Indians were formidable when they went on the warpath

Roosevelt, *African Game Trails*, 34-35.

Over most of Africa the problem for the white man is to govern, with wisdom and firmness, and when necessary with severity, but always with an eye single to their own interests and development, the black and brown races

Roosevelt, *African Game Trails*, 104-5.

46. Martin Johnson, *Safari: A Saga of the African Blue* (New York: G. P. Putnam's Sons, 1928), 4. Also see Cameron, 89-92, for a useful resume of the Johnsons' career in Africa.
47. Martin Johnson, *Safari*, 4.
48. C. A. W. Guggisberg, *Early Wildlife Photographers* (New York: Taplinger Publishers, 1977), 11-22, 31-50.
49. Ibid., 50-60.
50. Steven Ohrn and Rebecca Riley, eds., *Africa from Real to Reel* (Waltham, Mass.: African Studies Association, 1976), 87.
51. Martin Johnson, *Safari*, 57, 58-59.
52. Ibid., 60.
53. Peter Matthiessen, *Wildlife in America* (New York: Viking Press, 1959), *At Play in the Fields of the Lord* (New York: Random House, 1965), *Under the Mountain Wall* (New York: Viking Press, 1962) and *The Tree Where Man Was Born; The African Experience* (New York: Dutton and Co., 1972).
54. Matthiessen, *The Tree Where Man Was Born*, 23.
55. Ibid., 232-33.
56. Peter Matthieseen, *Sand Rivers* (New York: The Viking Press, 1981), 133-34.
57. Ibid., 188.
58. Ibid., 205.
59. Peter Matthiessen, *African Silences* (New York: Random House, 1990).
60. Edward Hoagland, *African Calliope: A Journey to the Sudan* (New York: Random House, 1978), 55. Others of Hoagland's work include, *Notes from the Century Before: A Journal from British Columbia* (New York: Random House, 1969) and *Red Wolves and Black Bears* (New York: Random House, 1976). Also see *The Edward Hoagland Reader* (New York: Vintage Books, 1979).
61. Hoagland, *African Calliope*, 56.
62. Ibid., 91.
63. Ibid., 179.
64. Alex Shoumatoff, *In Southern Light: Trekking Through Zaire and the Amazon* (New York: Vintage Books, 1990), 145.
65. Ibid., 146.
66. Alex Shoumatoff, *African Madness* (New York: Vintage Books, 1990), vii.

67. Ibid., 117.
68. Ibid., 34-35.
69. Claude Levi-Strauss, *Tristes Tropiques* (New York: Atheneum, 1974), 38.
70. Michael Jackson, *Barawa, and the Ways Birds Fly in the Sky* (Washington, D.C., Smithsonian Institution Press, 1986).
71. W. E. B. Du Bois, *Dusk of Dawn: An Essay Toward An Autobiography of a Race Concept* (New York: Harcourt, Brace and Co., 1940), viii.
72. Ibid., 117, 127.

6

Dark and Violent Mystery: Africa in American Fiction

Throughout this century few literary phenomena have been more striking than the fashionable rodomontade of Joseph Conrad and especially of his masterpiece *Heart of Darkness*.[1] This has been expressed in the huge outpouring of critical works in recent decades, nearly all of which promise new insights and fresh interpretations of this powerful novella, written, as Karin Hansson points out, as an archetypal quest (the mythic voyager searching amid the darkness of Hades).[2] As a consequence the western literary vision of Africa has been increasingly conceptualized in terms of its narrative and its themes, and *Heart of Darkness* has provided a brooding backdrop to nearly every analysis of every European or American novel written about Africa. This is unfortunate since Conrad's celebrated work (whatever its merits as an "English" novel) is neither central to the American literary experience nor especially influential in the development of the genre of Africa-related fiction produced by Americans. The novella is variously condemned as a racist tract,[3] praised as a radical attack on the imperialist assumptions of its time,[4] glorified as the first genuine work of modernism,[5] shredded as a Darwinian fairy tale,[6] flayed as a dishonest and failed vision of the primitive,[7] condemned as a typical work of Eurocentric hegemonism,[8] and lauded as one of the more extraordinary and sensitive works of twentieth-century literature.[9] In the meantime its actual place has become absurdly exaggerated.

There can be no doubt, of course, that *Heart of Darkness*, by its very title and its theme (the evil inherent in men which is unleashed by exploitative imperialism at its worst) provides a convenient frame for much of the literature covered here. Conrad made Africa a special place, an appropriate backdrop to his portrait of evil in the person of Kurtz. His revelations of dark unmentionable deeds performed in dark places by the impersonal forces of colonialism set the stage.

179

As many have noted, Conrad's unforgettable description of the "Congo" landscape became fixed forever in our consciousness. Traveling into that vast forest, was, he wrote,

> like travelling back to the earliest beginnings of the world, when vegetation rioted on the earth and the big trees were kings. An empty stream, a great silence, an impenetrable forest. The air was warm, thick, heavy, sluggish. There was no joy in the brilliance of sunshine. The long stretches of the waterway ran on, deserted, into the gloom of overshadowed distances. On silvery banks hippos and alligators [sic] sunned themselves side by side. The broadening waters flowed through a mob of wooded islands; you lost your way on the river as you would a desert . . . this stillness of life did not in the least resemble a peace. It was the stillness of an implacable force brooding over an inscrutable intention. It looked at you with a vengeful aspect.[10]

This was written a good decade before Africa became the exotic playground of the rich, the retreat of expatriates, the romantic place of escape from the crowded metropole. This was long before the "Winds of Change," and the Peace Corps, and the "novel" idea that Africa was the perfect place for wandering Americans to work out their personal sense of mission. And it was decades before American writers had experimented with the idea that Africa might provide the existential setting for western man's personal quest (an odyssey of idiosyncratic conscience like that of Bellow's Henderson). Certainly, by the early 1940s the more consciously "literary" figures—like Orson Welles when he produced a radio drama based on *Heart of Darkness*—were directly influenced by Conrad and the themes of his great work. Nonetheless, the typical American novel of Africa was far less complicated.

As a starting point, therefore, we must shift from Conrad's inimitable prose to the turgid romanticism of that most popular of early American hacks, Edgar Rice Burroughs, author of *Tarzan of the Apes* and other sequels of the ape-man and his adventures. It is in works of this sort that we find the basic symbolic conventions most perfectly expressed.[11] As for animals:

> From the dark shadows of the mighty forest came the wild calls of savage beasts—the deep roar of the lion, and, occasionally the shrill scream of the panther.

And, as for humans:

> All wore strange protruding girdles of dried grass about their hips and many were loaded with brass and copper

anklets, armlets and bracelets. Around many a dusky neck hung curiously coiled brands of wire, while several were further ornamented by huge nose rings.[12]

Despite the vulgar assumption that the Tarzan novels (twenty-three in all) are British, perhaps because the ape-man is himself a British Lord (Greystoke), they are deeply American in several respects. Not only was author Burroughs American through-and-through; his derivative character is not essentially distinct from many a frontier hero in American romances. Tarzan, in his challenging energy, his resourcefulness, his rugged individualism, is a recognizable cousin to Natty Bummpo, or Hondo. In fact, Burroughs deliberately sets the Tarzan adventures in an imaginary Africa which re-creates many of the conditions of a romanticized American frontier. The setting of jungle and swamp (and occasional savanna or "veld") through which Tarzan swings or strides with virile confidence, may at first seem totally alien to the familiar "western" setting. It is superficially akin to Conrad's vegetation in riot, but filled with apes and leopards, elephants and crocs, and it is replete with "tribes" both noble and ignoble (as in the fiction of Cooper, Bird, Grey, and Guthrie), some of whom struggle to maintain ancient and sometimes admirable ways. It is isolated—if barely so—from the effete influences of urban life, which Tarzan invariably despises, and it is altogether wild and primitive, at least in the early Tarzan novels. In short, it is a perfect image of the primeval. In this respect Burrough's Africa reflects the conventions about Africa that echo through Roosevelt's *African Game Trails*, written in the same decade as the first Tarzan novel, and through so many of the hunter-traveler books on Africa alluded to in the previous chapter.

Burrough's Tarzan novels, however, deserve some attention as creative works in their own right. In the 1990s we like to sneer at all things popular, vulgar, successful, and, above all, anything obviously "macho" and upbeat. Nevertheless, within the context of the era, the Tarzan saga clearly reflected a pervasive American vision of life, particularly within a wild and savage setting, especially regarding the "other." It is important to note that Burroughs penned the first Tarzan novel before World War I, a solid decade before Modernism and its celebration of impotence and lost innocence had captured the day, and that virtually all of the other novels in the series were written (and filmed in scores of loosely adapted variations) within the next two decades.

It is true that the Tarzan novels, as works of adventure-romance, generally recapitulate a tired formula: the altogether Caucasian hero who must use his wits and brawn to dominate (and even subdue) all that is wild and dangerous in nature, while of course serving as an agent of hereditary (racial) nobility amid scenes of barbaric splendor. Still, having his hero raised neither by cultivated but adventurous parents (as in Rider Haggard's formula novels) nor by simple but honest yeoman (as in the works of James Fenimore Cooper), but in the wildest jungle by man's closest cousins, the great apes, Burroughs, borrowing from Kipling's *Mowgli*, went that romanticist one better. He made Tarzan completely and unabashedly superior: only in part because of his genetic (English) heritage, but especially because the animal in him is dominant. Indeed as one reads the opening chapters of the first, and in many respects by far the best, novel, *Tarzan of the Apes*, one quickly recognizes that instinctive natural man which Americans claimed to honor and admire. And, if (as scores of critics have unnecessarily pointed out) Tarzan possesses intellect far beyond anything possible given the environment of his upbringing (and understood in the "feral child" literature), he also possesses the untrammeled innocence of one wholly outside civilization.

The racist elements in Burrough's work are so blatant that they hardly require comment. Tarzan (white, of English descent) only needs the tools of literacy, which he avidly acquires on his own, in order to assert an unquestioned dominance over all the Africans about him. His physical powers combined with his innate intellect have already made him dominant over the apes, as well as the other animals of the forest. In the first Tarzan novel he kills several of the local Africans: one to avenge the death of his ape "mother" Kala, and others simply because they encounter him. He only resists eating the first of these victims because a revulsion to the idea wells up in Tarzan's mind, "All he knew was that he could not eat the flesh of this black man, and thus hereditary instinct, ages old, usurped the functions of his untaught mind."[13] Because his own skin is lighter, and because he has found photos and other indications in the forest refuge built by his parents before they died, he knows that the local blacks are not of his "kind." When he finally encounters whites (in a chapter entitled "His Own Kind") Tarzan feels an immediate kinship: "somehow intuitively, he liked the young man (Clayton) and the two old men, and for the girl (Jane Porter) he had a strange longing which he scarcely understood."[14] All this only underlines Tarzan's innate and heroic nature, especially within the familiar norms of the central figure of the classic frontier adventure. Like the protagonist of hundreds of American frontier novels (including most "westerns"), Tarzan, too, was a "mixture of maturity and innocence, of experience and purity, of shyness and latent violence."[15]

Despite the self-evident American underpinnings to his work, Burroughs—as his first novel met unprecedented success and as he re-created his hero in scores of serial adventures to satisfy the escapist cravings of his millions of fans—was clearly influenced by other popular romances set in Africa. One can hardly read a Haggard work (*King Solomon's Mines, She, Alan Quatermain*) without noticing obvious borrowings, particularly in the plotting of the adventure tales themselves. Tarzan, like Quatermain, stumbles unsuspecting on semi-barbarous remnants of ancient civilizations "lost" amid the thoroughly savage Africans. He finds riches unheard of in lost cities, hidden within unknown volcanic caldera or beyond the reach of impenetrable swamps, or protected amid encircling warlike tribes. Like the heroes of Haggard's fantasies, Tarzan encounters civilizations, or the remnants thereof, with direct connections to ancient Classical civilizations (Rome, Phoenicia, Egypt, etc.). These, of course, are isolated or "planted" in darkest Africa, having little or no influence on the native Africans around them. In this respect Burroughs appears to have accepted the popular European assumption of the time that any ancient ruins found in sub-Saharan Africa had to be the product of some lost Roman legion or otherwise intrusive ancient European people. Great Zimbabwe, the undoubted inspiration for much of Haggard's fantasy, was surely so for Burroughs. Furthermore, like Quatermain and other Haggard heroes, Tarzan acts decisively to protect and defend all that is "good" among the native peoples, especially anything not sullied by outside contact with the West, and he opposes all that is "bad," especially when it is the product of corrupt Europeans. In this respect the Tarzan novels replicate the paradox within Haggard's works. Burroughs often condemns the worst sorts of colonialist exploitation (and these are defined in terms that seem to be derived from King Leopold's rape of the Congo). Haggard, writing somewhat earlier, found noble savages abused either by fiendish whites (or fiendish "half-civilized" blacks) and his heroes act accordingly. Of course, unlike the untutored Tarzan, Quatermain is a gentleman by birth, a perfect Victorian adventurer equally capable of reciting popular poetry and shooting elephants. By contrast, however, Tarzan remains—in all the novels, even after he has seen American and European civilization—the quintessence of primitive power. He has never been corrupted, even in the most benign way, by the evils of effete and literate society. Quatermain is, on the other hand, the Victorian man-of-action, hunter, explorer, equally at home in the midst of unexplored Africa as well as the board room. Nevertheless, Tarzan is a brother to the noble British wanderer in his "noblesse oblige." He is the friend of deserving Africans—this becomes especially clear in the later novels—while he is the implacable enemy of anyone (Africans included) who exploits Africans. His code might seem inconsistent—behind his race-consciousness he acts protectively of abused peoples. Actually it is not. His is the code of the new American Empire (and the newest phase of the not-so-new British one). This is Kipling's code of the White Man's Burden, and the obligation to protect the "lesser breeds" which goes with it.[16]

One could spin this endlessly, showing other affinities between Tarzan and various heroes of Victorian literature, especially within the category of so-called "racist romance," or proving further how Burroughs used the formulaic "western," or how Tarzan represents a patriarchal and racist mindset common to the time. Our central point, which bears repeating here, is not merely that Burroughs was influenced by the predominant ethos of his time, but rather that Burroughs' vision of Africa was derived from the widely popularized works which had already fixed these symbolic conventions in the American consciousness. For example, if Burroughs did not actually read anthropology, he was certainly familiar with the simplified *ouevre* printed in periodicals of the time. The Tarzan books are full of oversimplified ideas derived from Social Darwinism.[17] Tarzan himself, like the "better type" of Anglo-Saxon, was presented as the superior product of long-term social as well as physical evolution. Therefore, despite his wild upbringing, he would remain, at base, superior to any "natives" within that same "jungle" environment. This was mixed somewhat contrarily with a kind of Boasian relativism which seemed to assume that the minds of savages were entirely influenced by their environment.[18]

Therefore, the idea of having Tarzan raised, Mowgli-like, by great apes was, of course, intuitively brilliant on Burroughs' part, and it assured the ongoing success of the Tarzan epic. In Burrough's day, although virtually everyone was aware of Darwin's idea that humanity might have risen from something like the great apes, Darwin's theory was still *risque*. Even if one rejected this theory on religious grounds it lingered in the background of these novels. One did not, for example, have to accept that humans were so descended to accept the exciting idea that ape "society" approximated human society in a crude manner. Burroughs could fictionalize "tribes" of apes, with an ape "king" and wild ape dancing (drawing from the human record), and thereby underline the distinction between civilized man and primitive man. He could, on the other hand, celebrate all that is wild, powerful, dangerous, and "noble" in mankind by making Tarzan the embodiment of two contradictory ideals: the heroic male who is the product of long "upward" progress (through heredity *and* social change) and the primeval animal as yet untamed. At a time when a celebration of things primitive was gaining ground at least as fast as the study of things refined (and therefore civilized), Tarzan was the perfect foil. Americans reading this stuff could imagine themselves in Tarzan's (or Jane's) world without much strain. Kipling's *Mowgli* was a far more distant figure, especially for the typical American reader, for whom the British *Raj* was a greater stretch.

Burrough's particular view of Africa presents a problem of another sort. Clearly, if he were to be raised by great apes, Tarzan had to be placed in Africa. Borneo, or adjacent regions in which orangutans lived, would obviously not do. Africa, as Burroughs' understood the continent, was the perfect setting for a variety of other reasons. First, Africa was still the least explored (least "known") region of the globe, with scores of remote societies living what westerners thought were entirely savage lives. In such a setting Tarzan could encounter savagery not only among wild animals but also among humans. His adventures, therefore, could go one better than Cooper's Deerslayer. Even more important, Africa sheltered the largest remaining wilderness on earth (few then viewed the Amazon as a comparable wilderness), where large game ran free and where the impact of industrial technology was felt only at the periphery. Also, even as Burroughs wrote, Africa's "Edenic" image was being disseminated by popular travelers, hunters, and naturalists like Theodore Roosevelt, the Akeleys, and the Martins. Then, as now, a novelist would not be daunted by the unpleasant reality that this "Eden" was undergoing rapid and fundamental change. Finally, and no matter how contradictory to the above, was the characteristic imagery of lost cities and lost kingdoms, based on Africa's scarcely known (though genuine) historical past, but widely attributed to intrusions by external agents of civilization. We cannot know for sure whether these came consciously or unconsciously to Burroughs, but the Tarzan novels provide endless evidence that he knew how to use them.

Some readers might wonder why a pulp novelist like Edgar Rice Burroughs is given so much attention when some of America's greatest writers were also turning to Africa. As we shall see, his vastly popular formulaic novels were not the only works that echoed the symbolic conventions of the time. It may be true, as Gore Vidal has written, that the Tarzan novels were popular—and remain so—largely because they feed a fantasy not for sex, but for "power, for the ability to dominate one's environment through physical strength,"[19] but surely it is also true that they resound to this day because of the *kind* of adventure they offer.

Here we must pause. Historians believe that history itself is in large part the illumination of shadows cast by an uncertain record. The fictional version of reality—though it is obviously illuminated by imagination as much as it is based on fact—is especially subject to the mindset of the author. Ideology and bias clearly mark the bulk of the novels and stories that frame any era, even in the best of circumstances. It is equally clear that the better (and certainly the more popular) writers of any generation have considerable influence in shaping attitudes. It is partly for this reason that the versions of reality framed within fictional works remain seductive to the historian, especially to the historian who attempts—as we do here—a cross-disciplinary synthesis. The works of American writers who have chosen to make Africa their subject, setting, or object are illuminating in themselves. When examined for the conventions which shape them, the more subtle effects of such works, over time, are profiled against a sometimes disturbing backdrop. As often as not, what seems to be crystal clear on the surface (this is especially so in a vivid novel such as Robert Ruark's *Something of Value*) winds up being considerably distorted. This skewed vision— cast on the walls of Plato's mythic cave—is so seemingly lifelike that it seems a perfect reflection.

But of course it is not. The creation itself is a more accurate mirror of its author's perceptions, his own dimly perceived shadows. Sometimes the particular prism through which a writer scopes his creation is blatant in its coloration. A work like Michael Crichton's *Congo* poses few problems in this regard. Though published in 1980 it is an emanation akin to the works of Edgar Rice Burroughs sixty years before. Its ethnocentrism and its stereotypes are so familiar that we hardly raise our eyebrows.

What, then, of the works of our better writers who have taken on the grand and complex continent of Africa within these past eight decades or so? They too have obviously been influenced by these same deeply rooted conventions. Is it surprising that to a large degree (with some notable exceptions) this remains so regardless of the literary sophistication of the authors?

Though it is a big order to illustrate this, nevertheless, let us return briefly to the conventions, noted early in this book: to the idea of Africa as a mysterious place of jungle, mountain, and plain, mostly unfamiliar or unknown even decades after everything has been "explored" time and again; the idea of Africa as a zoological Eden of infinite variety replete with primordial flora, fauna, and, above all, primitive people (a human museum of the picturesque and the exotic); and the image of Africa as a distant staging point for episodes of adventure and discovery, which replicates in some respects the role once played in American literature by the American West, the setting of the legendary "quest," and to quote the bard, the "footra for the World and Worldlings base . . . [the] Africa [of] Golden Joys."[20] Even the casual reader, perhaps unaware of the uses of imagery in which these conventions are rooted, will understand how these conjure familiar scenes of darkness, savagery, barbarism, of evolutionary stasis, and all the dawning echoes of lost places within that "Pleistocene" landscape, while at the same time conjuring images of escape, exoticism, purity (the unsullied noble savage is African as well as Amerindian), renewal, and, of course, romance.

It bears repeating that conventions of this sort are very powerful, whether they loom in the unconscious or intrude consciously into a work of fiction. We may find it easy to accept that Burroughs shaped his writings to fit preconceived images of the Dark Continent, fulfilling his reader's fantasies as well as satisfying his own. We can place a portly T. R. raising his gun to blaze away at a charging hippo just before it reaches his canoe (albeit backed up by dead-shot guides). He is the big-game hunter *par excellence* and we cannot expect him to witness another Africa. He found what he sought. Edgar Rice Burroughs, as we have seen, also framed his Africa within the familiar tradition. We might find it relatively easy to accept that a writer of thrillers, like Crichton, would play to the audience which expects these conventions. Indeed, to challenge them might affect sales. But it is more difficult to accept the fact that such conventions have strongly influenced the works of such gifted authors as Ernest Hemingway, Alex Haley, Alice Walker, and Saul Bellow.

No doubt some of what follows will ring a familiar note. Scholars who know the work of Marion Berghahn, *Images of Africa in Black American Literature*, or Patrick Brantlinger, *Rule of Darkness: British Literature and Imperialism, 1830-1914*, will find influences here.[21] Few could ignore that timely essay in the sociology of knowledge by Dorothy Hammond and Alta Jablow, *The Africa That Never Was*, or G. D. Killam's *Africa in English Fiction 1874-1939*.[22] These, taken together, put English writing on Africa in perspective. Abdul R. JanMohamed's *Manichean Aesthetics: The Politics of Literature in Colonial Africa*, is essential as is George Shepperson's trenchant essay *Africa in American History and Literature*.[23] In the former we see a clear enunciation of the influence of political values (especially colonial ones) on writers, and in the latter readers will at once recognize the ahistorical, undeveloped spirit associated with Africa, a place dominated by nature, which has persisted so long, especially in American writing.

It is important that we remember that these conventions are symbolic in the Jungian sense, that is, held for the most part at the level of emotion, felt rather than known, like the archetypal "other" considered earlier in this book, the strange unknown "other" whom we all fear beneath the cognitive level. As such, these conventions are contradictory in themselves. Like other deeply rooted and largely irrational motifs common to the great myths—so brilliantly explicated in the works of Joseph Campbell—they can be both "negative" and "positive."[24] That is why, as we have seen in previous chapters, they crop up so frequently in the texts of some of our finest ethnographers. That is why they appear so often in the works of some of our most perceptive writers.

We have already shown how these images appear across the genres. They are abundantly evident in the early journalistic work of Henry Morton Stanley. Perhaps no one before or since has more vividly presented these notions, curiously apposite and opposite, of Africa and Africans. In Stanley we find the full panoply of dark and secret rites, gloomy forests, cannibalism, untrammeled primitivism, and unspeakable lusts (the very paradigm for Conrad's *Heart of Darkness* and Kurtz's doom). Here too is the stalwart African prince of noble mien (Kazembe), the lovely maiden unspoiled by the material things of this world, and the pure and teeming landscape of indescribable beauty, the wilderness of test and quest, where a real man can prove himself. In fact, Stanley's self-congratulatory accounts of his greatest expeditions are—even a century after he wrote—so unabashedly heroic in tone that a contemporary American writer, Peter Forbath, felt moved to entitle his biographical novel of Stanley *The Last Hero*.[25] An essential premise of this novel is the idea that Stanley, like his intrepid predecessors Livingstone, Burton, and Speke (the latter two apotheosized in the recent film *Mountains of the Moon*), represented an inimitable Victorian type who breasted the unknown through sheer will, winning through against the most savage of opponents and against all odds, even against the snobbishness of his class conscious countrymen. Needless to say, presented as it is in the mode of late-twentieth-century neo-romanticism (yet, with highly "naturalistic" description) this novel reads rather like Stanley's own somewhat turgid but highly readable prose, wherein one adventure follows another. Whatever else he was, Stanley was an effective writer who knew his audience.

Exactly how racist Stanley was has long been the source of debate. Jeremy Bernstein has argued, in a critical essay in *The New Yorker*, that Stanley was less racist than many of his milder-mannered contemporaries.[26] That Stanley was certain of his mission no one disputes. Forbath's novel certainly re-creates the sense of Stanley's Africa, a world inhabited by self-assured adventurers who are willing to plunge, in almost total ignorance of what to expect, into the depths of Africa's greatest rainforest, the unexplored Ituri. In the pages of *The Last Hero* we have the "old" Africa resurrected with a vengeance. Here is the enormous expedition, ostensibly sent to relieve a beleaguered Emin Pasha, emerging emaciated and decimated from a Darwinistic struggle only to discover that its object, the enigmatic Pasha, is, with his garrison at Equatoria, in far better shape than Stanley's devastated column. Even more interestingly, the man does not particularly want to be rescued. Then there is the matter of the legendary rear column which, of course, provides the factual basis for the horror of Kurtz's degradation in Conrad's *Heart of Darkness.*

The historian, of course, knows all this from Stanley's famous *In Darkest Africa,* which runs to two volumes. What makes Forbath's fiction noteworthy, at least in this context, is not only its psychological portrait of a driven man—not unlike the Richard F. Burton of Fawn Brodie's *The Devil Drives*—who must challenge everything and everyone to prove himself worthy, but rather its unabashed resurrection of an Africa seen through its hero's eyes. Those who have read the best biographies of Stanley will recognize in Forbath's novel a view of Africa that dominated the mindset of Stanley's time. A careless reader might not realize that this mindset remains very much alive.

It is in Stanley's writings that we also see the germ of the idea—later popularized by Theodore Roosevelt, Carl and Mary Jobe Akeley, Edgar Rice Burroughs, Martin and Osa Johnson, Ernest Hemingway, and Robert Ruark—that only the unspoiled African is truly noble, and that any African, male or female, who is western-ized to any degree is corrupted because of it. This is a theme which reverberates in most conventional fiction but plays itself out as well in more sophisticated works. Clearly, it owes much to a similar theme regarding the Amerindian in American literature. Also in Stanley we find the purest expression of the similar convention, repeated hundreds of times by later writers, that those parts of Africa where man's hand is least evident are purest and best, and that, as Mary Jobe Akeley put it, the native peoples are essentially overgrown children whose faithfulness "diminishes in proportion to [their] years of contact with white men."[27] All the irony is here too, and the contradiction. Stanley firmly believed, for example, that Africans could be "saved" through the good graces of missionary efforts like those of his hero David Livingstone (whose explorations paradoxically often made things worse for indigenous peoples), and through the careful process of colonial administration. Contradic-tory as they are, these ideas coexisted in the minds of those who perpetrated them.

By the time Ernest Hemingway traveled to Africa in 1933 the expectations and the mindset concerning the continent were firmly in place. The great, and already famous writer was thirty-four years old at the time and already somewhat overbearing; deep flaws in his seemingly splendid personality—perhaps not fully evident to the friends of his youth—were beginning to show. The veneer of confident sportsman which he wore like a badge must have been painfully thin to those closest to him, since his works on Africa are extraordinarily revealing on this score. Indeed, if Hemingway's considerable body of writing on Africa is any guide, the East African landscape influenced him much as it affected Roosevelt twenty-five years before. Here is Hemingway describing a group of Masai in *Green Hills of Africa* as "The first truly light-hearted happy people I have seen in Africa." Highlighted in brilliant opposition to a "theatrical" tracker and gun-bearer on Hemingway's safari, a charlatan of pretentious poses whom Hemingway (referring to the great Victorian actor) scornfully gives the nickname "David Garrick," these Masai seemed pristine in their unaffected simplicity. They "had that attitude . . . you get only in the best of the English, the best of the Hungarians and the very best Spaniards; the thing that used to be the most clear distinction of nobility when there was nobility."[28] Though, to Hemingway's credit, his African scenes avoid the cant and hypocrisy common to that era, he cannot avoid an egregious addition regarding this so-called "attitude." "It is," he writes, "an ignorant attitude and the people who have it do not survive, but very few pleasanter things happen to you than the encountering of it."[29]

It is especially fascinating that Hemingway saw Africa as the perfect stage for the working out of his personal code, which might be summed up as follows: life is paradox, and ultimately unfathomable, but in the face of this unpleasant fact, one must strive for unity with nature through a relentless struggle, "always toughening the body, mind, and spirit," so as to overcome obstacles to this unity.[30] For Hemingway, of course, the only way to this unity was through self-discipline and love. Death might win, indeed must win, but there was some triumph in the struggle (not against nature, but within it) and in the act of living itself. On the one hand, this might seem a relentless code, demanding an acceptance of reality at its most harsh, with no concessions to sentiment. It seems to be a rigorous outdoorsman's philosophy, muscular and questing. On the other hand, however, this code requires a kind of abandonment (as in the act of love) to the most primitive impulses and the wildest environs. It is no accident that outdoors-oriented folk who have experienced the catharsis of a wilderness experience (where an unstated emotion completely overwhelms reason) tend to read and treasure the best of Hemingway's stories all their lives. It therefore comes as no surprise to read, in *Green Hills of Africa*, the following paean:

> I loved the country so that I was happy as you are after you have been with a woman that you really love, when, empty, you feel it welling up again and there it is and you

can never have it all and yet what there is, now, you can have, and you want more and more, to have, and be, and live in, to possess now again for always, for that long sudden-ended always; making time stand still.[31]

Clearly, for Hemingway, Africa was one of those places (Northern Michigan and Northwestern Spain were others) one could love unstintingly, but, in the case of Africa, with full awareness of its capriciousness. Like a woman, for Hemingway, Africa was paradox and contradiction, but also unconquerable, and seductive beyond knowing. In some respects, therefore, the writer himself, scorning everything romantic, entered fully into the romance that was Africa in his mind.

This may explain why *Green Hills*, of all Hemingway's work on Africa, may ironically be his most positive, perhaps his most "authentic." Compared to the short stories written in the same period, "The Short Happy Life of Francis Macomber" and "The Snows of Kilimanjaro," both of which are brooding works, *Green Hills* is almost celebratory.[32] Almost nowhere in Hemingway's lifetime of writing do we find his incipient romanticism so unleashed, his simple love of nature so openly and joyfully expressed, his hatred of his own age (and its excesses) so righteously advanced.

> A continent ages quickly once we come. The natives live in harmony with it. But the foreigner destroys, cuts down the trees, drains the water, so that the water supply is altered and in a short time the soil, once the sod is turned under, is cropped out and, next, it starts to blow away as it has blown away in every old country and as I have seen it start to blow in Canada. The earth gets tired of being exploited. A country wears out quickly unless man puts back in it all his residue and that of all his beasts.
>
> I knew a good country when I saw one. Here there was game, plenty of birds, and I liked the natives. Here I could shoot and fish. That, and writing, and reading, and seeing pictures was all I cared about doing.[33]

Ironies abound, of course. Hemingway saw Africa as a place of escape from the very things that civilization had wrought, and as a place to act out his personal quest. In his writing so vividly about wild Africa, Hemingway, like many anti-romantic modernists who were pessimistic about western society, reinforced the romantic view of Africa already well-advanced by previous American visitors. Even the undercurrent of death and violence in the African short stories is enclosed (or bounded) by the magnificence of the setting. "Macomber" and "Snows" represent Hemingway at the height of his powers. Anthologized endlessly, analyzed *ad infinitum*, required reading in hundreds of colleges and universities, they will probably remain forever, in the literature of the West, indeed in the structure of our thoughts, as representative not only of Hemingway (and of his view of life) but of Africa itself. Anyone who has read either of these stories is liable to be carried into that dark and violent world, redolent of the mythic place of danger and death that goes back to Stanley, indeed far beyond; to the Africa of beautiful but deadly places (death lurks behind the glorious wilderness), where white males face dire challenges (sometimes from women), where women are essentially helpless, and where animals in all their glory and abundance are there to be stalked and killed.

To further illustrate this, a closer look at the basic narrative in "The Short Happy Life of Francis Macomber" reveals the dichotomy in Hemingway's Africa. In a landscape which otherwise provides the most perfect of all tests for a man, where the white man can resurrect something of the primeval power that he has "lost" by living in civilized society, such a man can still be undermined, emasculated, even killed. This end might come from fear itself, from the weakness in character that Hemingway most despised, the lack of physical courage. Worse yet it might come at the hands of a woman. An underlying message is clear enough: amid such danger, confronted by such challenges, a woman does not and cannot belong. In "Macomber" the hunt is most emphatically a masculine pursuit. Although, in Hemingway's ethos there are women who can and do hunt (P. O. M. of *Green Hills*, actually Hemingway's second wife Pauline, is certainly an example), they nevertheless know their place. The homicidal, cheating bitch of "Macomber" conforms to the unspoken hunter's code, "bring no women along." Africa, in this view, is not a place for white women, no more for Hemingway than it was for Stanley.

The truth, of course, is that Hemingway traveled often with women (his successive wives) and frequently hunted and fished with all of them. A man reared in a house full of women, he was actually never comfortable away from them. He was in reality not the kind of man who liked to go off alone, even to hunt, or to go off with one male buddy for a long period. We know that during his African travels he met the formidable Beryl Markham. He admired her, and praised her writing, and one can readily imagine him on safari with such a woman. Nevertheless, true to his public persona, his exterior code, his literary image, he could never write such a woman into his works on Africa.

A final comment on Hemingway is necessary. In *Green Hills*, unlike his fiction on Africa, Hemingway was able to liberate himself—at least in part—from the symbolic conventions; thus he could

*Ernest and Pauline Hemingway with
Ernest's lion, Serengeti Plain, Jan., 1934.*

Bob Ruark, the one-shot bwana, the mighty simba slayer.

write about Africans as real human beings. Several of the porters and guides on this extended safari are affectionately drawn, fully human, ranging the gamut. M'Cola is immortalized forever in the pages of *Green Hills* (essentially a safari book) as wise, ancient, knowledgeable, humorous, and brave. "Garrick" is in every way the opposite, but he, too, is immortalized, as real to the reader as "Pop" or P. O. M., perhaps more so. The irony is that these two Africans contributed in many ways to a developing set of stereotypes that was to dominate much of the literature on Africa. Hemingway's portraits might have been real enough, but in time they too became one-dimensional stereotypes in and of themselves.

But, of course, Hemingway, though he looms larger in his influence than any other American writer who turned to Africa, was hardly alone in his fascination. The post-war era of global conflict and cold war found Americans turning to Africa, as well as to other lesser-known regions, for confirmation of their world view. Novels of adventure mixed with historical "realism" found a ready market. Certainly, at least in popular consciousness, no American writer at mid-century produced "African" novels of wider appeal than Robert Ruark in his best-sellers *Something of Value* (1955) and *Uhuru* (1962).[34] Partly because of his "Hemingwayesque" posturing—especially his preoccupation with big-game hunting—and partly because he chose the "Mau Mau" uprising and its immediate aftermath as the subject for these two famous works, Ruark has long been dismissed as either a racist, or superficial, or both. The first charge seems justified, the second is not. Ruark was relentless in his portrayal of the worst excesses of the Mau Mau—"cows with their teats hacked off and strangled cats and disemboweled women, and menstrual fluid mixed with human sperm and animal dung and stewed brains for the oathing"[35]—and he seemed to revel in descriptions of African barbarism. The following opinion of the African, voiced by Peter McKenzie, the protagonist of *Something of Value*, is typical.

> He doesn't understand tomorrow, and he forgets yesterday, because he's got no sense of time. Time means absolutely nothing to him . . . . The best job you can give the average African is a waiting job. He needs starting to do anything specific, but he won't know when to stop if its white man's orders.

> In the African make-up there is really no such thing as love, kindness, or gratitude, as we know it, because they have lived all their lives, and their ancestor's lives in an atmosphere of terror and violence. There is no proper "love" between man and woman, because the woman is bought for goats and used as a beast of burden.[36]

While it is not fair to assume that Ruark himself held such views, his repeated attention to this white settler's viewpoint assumes a ready identification with it on the typical reader's part. Certainly most American readers of the period had little means of seeing beyond. Nevertheless, it is true, as John D. Chick has pointed out, that Ruark made a deliberate attempt to write dramatized history in these two novels, both of which are ambitious fictional explorations of "the most violent explosion of racial violence to have occurred under British rule in Africa."[37] Chick's point, however, is valid only as far as it goes. Ruark's white settlers in both novels are thoroughly unattractive people, alienated from the bulk of the native peoples who inhabit the land, and equally alienated from the "meddlesome" government of their homeland, which, in their view, undermines white rule in Kenya.[38] Also, though he accepted the common view that Mau Mau lacked any real justification (beyond acknowledging that the Kikuyu, among others, had had their lands stolen from them by the white settlers), Ruark displayed real indignation at the suffering of Africans during Mau Mau.

> The killing of the innocent, by both sides, and the slaughter of native police, and the massacre of the Athegani turned a brisk harrow in the loam of resentment. The native shanti towns of Nairobi had been dynamited and burned, leaving thousands without homes. In one year 150,000 Kikuyu were arrested. Sixty-five thousand were released, mostly to unemployment. The others were tried, sentenced and either jailed in the majority or in the minority hanged.
>
> Mau Mau's political direction shifted to purely criminal hands, where first only its implementation had been handed to thugs. The face of Kenya wore an expression of sullen fear, for the Kikuyu men and women were being—and many more would be—relocated from Nairobi and other towns and shipped up North to detention camps; some were being transported to islands in the Indian Ocean; some were being penned in hastily thrown up detention camps for screening. City business lost or was forced to discharge, for expediency, most of its clever Kikuyu help.[39]

Likewise, he did not hesitate to savage the British in Kenya for their arrogance and insensitivity. Nonetheless, try as he might, this American novelist could not come close to the historian's goal of objectivity. Clearly, to Ruark, British rule in Kenya, if not the white settlers themselves (however misguided), represented an island of civilization amid a savage sea.

Interestingly—and this is a point few critics seem to have noticed—Ruark was capable of creating self-guided African characters who went far beyond the stereotyped conventions which circumscribed most novels written by whites during that era. Joyce Cary, for example, the celebrated English novelist (*Assia Saved*, 1931; *An American Visitor*, 1934; *The African Witch*, 1936; and *Mister Johnson*, 1939) had been so successful in his satiric condemnation of colonial ineptitude (in all the above novels) that, as JanMohamed has pointed out in *Manichean Aesthetics*, his essential disdain for Africa and Africans was neglected for decades.[40] Robert Ruark, apparently, has quite the opposite problem. His preoccupation with violence (especially if perpetrated by Africans under the influence of the Mau Mau "oathing" ceremonies) is so obvious and belabored that his strengths as a novelist (already established in earlier works like *The Old Man and the Boy*) have been downplayed. For example, Ruark's Kimani, the Kikuyu antagonist in *Something of Value*, is no comic figure like Cary's Johnson, who mimics whites in a desperate attempt at becoming "civilized." Kimani, relentless, driven, committed, and resourceful, is superior in leadership to Jeff Newton, the racist child of privilege, and, throughout the unfolding story of terror and violence, he is a worthy adversary to the equally implacable and embittered Peter McKenzie. Though Kimani is clearly portrayed as having retrogressed to the side of barbarism, his behavior is scarcely less barbaric than that of McKenzie, who slays him in single combat at the end of the novel. It seems that McKenzie, when he takes Kimani's child with him after their terrible struggle, is intended also as a symbol of regression. In Ruark's view Africa brought out the savage in both. One is, therefore, forced to disagree with Chick on his point that these two Ruark novels, *Something of Value* and *Uhuru*, stand outside that well-known school, the "veneer-of-civilization-over-primitive-soul" which so dominates novels of Africa by whites even to this day.

So where do we place Ruark? Clearly, though his books were hugely successful, he was no hack writer looking for easy sales. The exhaustive detail in both these novels, presented as background to the major characters as well as to the "emergency" itself, belies the charge of superficiality. It seems undeniable that a clear identification with the mythic American frontier—here Africa is again the surrogate—colors Ruark's work. Africans in Ruark's novels are sometimes noble (like the "noble red man" of frontier Americana) and sometimes ignoble. For all their dedication to tradition they are essentially xenophobic, even atavistic, like so many Amerindians in American fiction. None therefore, including Kimani, has the essential coherence necessary to the well-realized character. One can identify, however reluctantly, with the driven Peter McKenzie in *Something of Value*. His own humanity is threatened by his obsessive compulsion to eradicate Mau Mau. He is a recognizable type, familiar to Europeans, and almost stereotypical in the American novel of the frontier: the kind of man, misguided by violence done his own people, who lives only to destroy the "savages" and all they stand for. His type is common in American fiction from the era of James Montgomery Bird and James Fenimore Cooper to Paul Horgan and A. B. Guthrie. Kimani, on other hand, is not so easy to identify with; indeed, as the story unfolds, he becomes more and more distant. Once he leaves the known boundaries of the McKenzie estate, where he and Peter had grown up together almost as brothers, once he strikes out on his own and joins Mau Mau (via its horrendously-depicted oaths and terrible demands), he has drifted into barbarism. Ruark was well acquainted with the white community; thus the validity of Chick's observation that Ruark portrayed that settler community with exceptional accuracy. Unfortunately, and obviously, he knew few Africans with the intimacy necessary to the novelist. This inevitably mars Ruark's work, undermining his own stated objectives so thoroughly that he was blinded to his failure. Despite his attempt to portray a factual reality, to reveal a truth (phrases he uses in the respective forwards of *Something of Value* and *Uhuru*), Ruark was thoroughly captivated by the romantic Africa of old. For all their alleged "realism" his African novels almost perfectly conform to what JanMohamed calls the "racial romance."

One cannot easily dismiss this writer, however. Even at midcentury Ruark was one of the few American writers to have actually lived in Africa long enough to write novels "of" Africa with any degree of verisimilitude. Though he could not match Hemingway (or Isak Dinesen for that matter) in his descriptions of wild nature, Ruark could be eloquent when describing the changing (dying) wilderness of East Africa, "the dry river beds where the sandgrouse flighted in to take their tiny, delicate sips at precise hours of morning and dusk; where the elephants came to tusk up the sand. . . ."[41] Nonetheless, Ruark, the obsessive hunter, could produce almost pornographic depictions of trophy "kills" in his safari-narrative *Use Enough Gun*. At its best, on the other hand, Ruark's work conveys a certain power beyond the superficial escapism of the typical adventure romance. Ironically, this is notably so when he plays to the theme of romance, i.e., that of the pioneering community (whites) whose very success has created that which they most despise: a sterile, stunted culture of nay-sayers and reactionaries. Strangely, though he seems to have known this (how else could he have described it?), the note of nostalgia remains predominant to the end. In Africa Ruark found (too late) only echoes of what once was, or at least what he dreamed, Africa had been. For him, too, it was that Manichean Eden: once pure, potentially renewing, its people spoiled by what the white man had brought.

During this era of the late fifties and early sixties, when so many Americans first encountered Africa, Gerald Hanley, an already established American expatriate writer with connections to Hemingway, deeply involved in the safari world of East Africa, wrote several novels on Africa. His titles, *The Year of the Lion* (1954), *Drinkers of Darkness* (1955), and *Gilligan's Last Elephant* (also titled *The Last Safari*)[42] published in 1962, give away a good deal of Hanley's concerns. Hanley, an experienced hunter himself, had honed the safari-oriented prose of that era, and had imbibed the ambiance of midcentury East Africa; the paradise of sun-baked plains and forested mountain, portrayed (as in Hemingway) in essentially nostalgic terms, a place where the disenchanted western man could escape the vulgar materialism of home and recover an elemental spirit known only to the savage. *The Last Safari* features a white American hunter named Gilligan, already fifty-seven years old as the story begins, tough and quarrelsome, a hater of cities and all things civilized (also a victim, in classical Hemingway style, of women). Gilligan somewhat disagreeably takes as a client a rich American, Muller, who wants, above all else, to prove himself against this African bush that Gilligan knows so well. The narrative revolves around the developing contest between these two—the older, wiser, but world-weary white hunter, and the equally tough, cynical, manipulative, domineering rich bastard—as they attempt to track down and kill an enormous ancient elephant in the arid reaches of Kenya's north. In the end Gilligan meets death with fortitude, his back broken by a young bull (symbolic companion to the old bull they hunt). The old, great beast escapes, while the self-indulgent Muller, having failed to wear the older man down, also survives. Dying, a delirious Gilligan, thinking he is speaking to Muller, confesses (although he is actually speaking to his guide Jama), "I wasted my bloody life,"

> That's what I did. Don't tell me about elephants or any nonsense like that. I was good for years until you came along. But you can have it all Muller, I had the best of it, though, saw it when it was new and all fine and not messed up. The park keepers are feeding the lions on slices of cold zebra in the game reserves and the Masai have to look on. The lions know they're safe and the Masai know they can't kill the lions, and the will has gone on both sides. I've seen it, I tell you. You can have it, all of it. You mean to tell me that's any use to me, that kind of thing? I tell you for the last time you can have it.[43]

But of course, we know that Gilligan has triumphed, for Hemingway has taught us so well that we know that code as well as we know the pledge of allegiance. He will return to the barren earth he has taken as his own, while Muller will return to his crowded, overpopulated, greedy urban world, having really proved nothing. He may be, like Gilligan, the best kind of tough American (the Hemingway kind), but "he felt he had not proved himself, had been talked into retreat by a black man with no conception of the bitterness, he, Muller, felt. And then again, Jama might know. Might."[44]

Readers, familiar with this theme in so many works—by no means confined to male writers, since even in Dinesen's *Out of Africa* the men are more infatuated with the hunt than with the women who love them—may not pause to think beyond this trope: of quest, contest, trial, and apotheosis in nature. It is a theme filled with the nostalgia for an Africa, which, in these works, seems to exist for whites only.

Africans in such works, certainly in Hanley, are symbols of the savage land. Hanley's Somali guide, Jama, stubborn and brave, also possesses the virtue of simplicity. He is at one with the land: like the elephant, he personifies everything contrary to civilization. If not the stock figure of most popular British fiction (the devoted factotum, silent, obedient, loyal), Jama is very much akin to Hemingway's M'Cola or, for that matter, akin to Cooper's Uncas or Chingachgook, the noble savage incarnate. In this regard, Hanley was at least able to stretch the familiar convention, which made the white man (or woman) the parent and the African a child, to a relationship of something like rough equality. Leatherstocking and his red companions share their adventures; one is never servant to the other. Perhaps this is because few Americans (outside the South), even the rich, have experienced a servant class who "know their place," who bow and scrape—even in humorous ways—to their "betters," as do the servants of the British society of caste and class, recapitulated in fiction for three centuries and more. The observation made by de Tocqueville early in the nineteenth century about the behavior of Americans of all classes certainly holds true in the middle of the twentieth. American novelists are more inclined, even when writing within the conventions outlined in this book, to see Africans as counterparts. They may be rendered, as in Ruark's works, as opposites, as mirrors held up to the savagery in "civilized" folk, but they are rarely subservient. The "Gunga Din" type common in British novels from Kipling on is a rare sort in American fiction, with the exception of romances of the "old South" and slavery.

One of the more celebrated novels of Africa published near mid-century is *Return to Laughter* (1954) by Elenore Smith Bowen (the *nom de plum* of anthropologist Laura Bohannan). A beautifully written and loving—but unrelenting—portrait of a remote people, based on her work among the Tiv of Nigeria, as seen through the eyes of a young woman anthropologist, *Return to Laughter* powerfully depicts the intricate network of kith and kin among a people as much threatened by their seemingly benign environment as they are sustained by it.[45] No reader with experience of rural African verities— the life and death struggle against endemic disease, the power of witchcraft and negating myth, the tyranny of provincial ignorance— would be surprised by Bohannan's unfolding and tragic story. Here, with none of the posturing of a Ruark, without the distancing of a Hemingway, and without a hint of romanticism, is an Africa of people: the massive, good-hearted Ikpoom whose natural sensitivity cannot overcome his fears, the devious and unscrupulous Kako who will betray his own wife to preserve his power, the exuberant child, Accident, who is a born survivor, Yabo, aged, drunken, but enormously clever, and the beloved Amara whose death in childbirth (attributed to witchcraft at Yabo's hands) bereaves everyone. Few novels written by an outsider are so revealingly subtle in unraveling the web of family relationships, the intricate force of tribal custom (in courtship, marriage, childbirth, disease, healing, and death), or the complex interactions between the sexes. Re-reading *Return to Laughter* thirty years after one's first encounter only underlines its magic. Bohannan has captured the inherent drama of real human beings struggling within the confines of their seemingly luxurious forest environment (which hides so many evils, mostly in the form of invisible microbes which are incomprehensible to the impoverished peasant cultivators), trying to achieve a minimum of security, to protect and nurture love, and to allay the terrors of the unknown. This is especially poignant as "modernization," as it was then called, begins to affect the villagers' daily lives.

In some respects *Return to Laughter* reminds one of Chinua Achebe's equally relentless portrait of his own people in his 1958 classic *Things Fall Apart*, when the outside world—represented by British colonialism about a half century earlier—intrudes with shattering impact. Such comparisons are difficult, needless to say, for no matter how observant, no matter how sensitive, no matter how well-honed her ethnographic antennae, Bohannan the American scientist cannot view her subjects from inside out, as Achebe can. As observer, even when language is mastered, she can only become familiar. For the Tiv she is "other," no matter how keen her urge to comprehend, or to share in compassion. For her, despite friendships cultivated (especially with the doomed Amara) and pain and laughter shared, the Tiv remain essentially benighted. Ultimately, as she admits, the author could not bridge the gulf between them. Near the end of the novel when the protagonist is infuriated by the seeming callousness of the villagers, she writes,

> Ikpoom was a good man by nature, but he was a savage. They were all savages.
>
> It was not just to blame them, but I could no longer be charmed by them. The lush vegetation covered a harsh ground; the vine-draped groves of the streams were haunts of disease and poisonous fungi. Nature had given this land a warm beauty to cover its cold, selfish indifference to the struggles of those who lived upon it. Man is not nice about means of survival. The land could fascinate, but in that fascination there could be little affection. The people seemed to me as the land. At first acquaintance they had laughter, a proud bearing, and a grace of speech and movement. Underneath? Whether it was their nature or their circumstances, today they seemed harsh and cruel.[46]

To be sure, Bohannan goes on to explain, in one of the more eloquent and candid passages in either fictional or ethnographic literature, that the alleged kindness and compassion of the West (her own culture) was largely "a luxury born of our ability to spare help and resources,"[47] yet she senses that she cannot abandon that luxury, which for her has become "a moral obligation." Her unwillingness to laugh at misery is too deeply rooted. She can no more easily abandon her values than she can abandon her identity. What she can do, and ultimately does, is to recognize among these people the saving grace of laughter.

After reading scores of novels about Africa, the bulk of which—though they reinforce our point—are not worthy of note, one turns with pleasure to the works of writers like Bohannan who at least make an attempt to bridge the gulf between cultures, to those who through a combination of experience and artistic imagination seek to fuse with the observed society, whether it be the Tiv, the Mandinka in Haley's *Roots*, the fictional Wariri in Bellow's *Henderson the Rain King*, or the fictional BaNare in Duggan's *Lovers of the African Night*. To thrust beyond the stereotypes of "natives" who are so often portrayed as half-developed at best, or unfathomable at worst, is a worthy goal. Whether any American writer, black or white, has yet succeeded is another question. Too often the attempt seems false (as in Ruark's novels), with echoes of the voyeur in it. Sometimes, and here it seems Bohannan is a notable exception, it takes the form of elevating the "primitive" for its own sake. This, at least in contemporary fiction, is the literary equivalent of certain anthropologists' celebration of all things exotic, different, primitive, as yet unspoiled by the blight of western culture;

a neo-Rousseauanism only recently subjected to the critique it deserves.

Roots, by far the most famous of novels by a black American, unquestionably remains the most ambitious work of popular American fiction which openly attempts to objectify Africans. As critics have long since pointed out, Alex Haley largely succeeds in directly challenging many of the negative stereotypes about Africa, and he is especially successful in his portrait of an African world—that of Kunta Kinte and his family—which goes far beyond the conventional non-civilized versions. This is in striking contrast, for example, to the work of an earlier black American novelist, George Schuyler, whose novel *Slaves Today* recapitulates the standard conventions. Haley's characterizations early in *Roots*—before Kunta is captured and sold into slavery in America—are especially effective in this regard. Omoro and Binta, Kunta's parents, and the "slave" and storyteller, Nyo Boto, are thoroughly believable and likable characters, developed fully in their interactions with Kunta and his siblings and age-mates. Here, perhaps more notably than in any other part of his rambling novel, is the strength of Haley's work. Even as the action shifts to Virginia and to the generations of slaves whose struggles constitute its greater part, one is held by the powerful heritage which bolsters Kunta, and which makes him different from the other slaves. Kunta prevails, and his offspring benefit, precisely because of his *identity* as an African, the very attribute which both white and slave society, in colonial America, would deny.

Haley does a great service, therefore, in presenting his fictionalized, if somewhat idealized portraits of real Africans in an African setting, coping as people cope with genuine life-and-death situations. Kunta's experience of his *kafo* (age grade), for example, surely goes a long way toward illustrating an aspect of African society which otherwise seems available only in the dense tomes of ethnography. Likewise Haley's detailed descriptions of farming, foods, husbandry, rituals, and rites within a traditional West African context is worth a dozen lectures.

Nonetheless, and partly because of this, large segments of *Roots* are didactic, turgid, and to one familiar with African lifestyles, rather forced. Much of the African section of this novel is made up of laborious (and sometimes questionable) extrapolations from contemporary Mandinka culture in modern-day Gambia, where Haley did a part of his research. And, though the interior life of Kunta's family is triumphantly believable—Haley's well-honed narrative skills are most telling both here and in later segments in Virginia—many of the traditional symbolic conventions loom large, sometimes where least expected. Kunta, for example, growing up within a well-populated region of the upper Gambia, fully agriculturalized for perhaps two millennia, has several stereotypical confrontations with wild animals, including a leopard, lions, hyenas, and a herd of elephants. While one can scarcely argue that this is not possible, (the youth David confronted a lion in Biblical Israel three or four thousand years after agriculture was established there) these episodes in *Roots* are, like David and the lion, perfectly mythic in content and purpose. In such a highly organized, deeply rooted, well-settled agricultural society as that which nurtured Kunta Kinte, a confrontation with dangerous wild beasts would be about as common as it would be in Chaucer's England or Thoreau's New England. Here Haley is characteristically American. That is, unlike a contemporary African novelist—such as Camara Laye (*L'enfant noir, Le regard du roi*)—who might treat the wilderness and its flora and fauna in a quite distinct and African mythic form, Haley sees the African wilderness exactly as Americans (black and white) see their wilderness, partly as a place of confrontation with nature, partly as a place for spiritual communion, and partly as a backdrop to romantic episodes of hunting and survival.

Perhaps most interesting to the historian is Haley's apparently deliberate stereotyping of the *toubab* (whites), as seen through African eyes in the middle of the eighteenth century. This is perfectly expressed by the *kitango* (instructor) of Kunta's *kafo*.

> Even worse than toubob's money is that he lies for nothing and he cheats with method, as naturally as he breathes. That's what gives him the advantage over us.[48]

Obviously, in a conscious effort to turn the tables, Haley uses many of the same negatives when describing the *toubab* as one encounters in eighteenth- and nineteenth-century white European or American narratives, which purported to describe Africa. However annoying this may be to the sensibilities of whites, this is an effective twist and, if nothing else, might force some who hold to the classic paradigms to reappraise their own values. The idea is hardly original with Haley, of course. Many African writers, including Peter Abrahams, Chinua Achebe, and Ngugi wa Thiong'o, had previously reversed the standard images; and some of the best of them have indeed shown how the negative image of the "other" is hardly confined to those of "colonial" mentality.[49] Nevertheless, few Americans read African literature, in part because of its unfamiliarity, and in part because African writers—for obvious reasons—do not produce their works within the standard and expected paradigms.

In a sense, with some judicious borrowing from the images of the better African writers, and with some use of the modes of anthropological fiction, this is what Haley has done. Yet *Roots* is a thoroughgoing American novel. It is either consciously or unconsciously a novel whose focus is America. In Haley's creation Africa is backdrop, background, and place of origin. Yet, for all its "authenticity," Africa remains exotic. Its landscapes possess much of the same mysterious allure that captivated earlier generations of writers (whether white or black), and its peoples possess a pristine sense of values and an unsullied sense of place quite alien to most Americans. Only the noblest Amerindians (at least in American literature) possess such untrammeled virtues, and only when they have remained unspoiled by the white man's civilization. This is the Eden, then, from which Kunta and all his enslaved brothers and sisters have sprung. In Haley's vision Africa is a place where even slavery—presented as if it existed in only one benign domestic form—is muted by custom, its evils allayed by the fact that it is confined to Africa. The stark comparison between the almost gentle systems of slavery described among Kunta's Mandinka kinsfolk and the brutality and harshness of the system into which he is sold in North America—after his capture by raiding whites, abetted in their action by a few African *slatees*—is deliberate and unforgettable. To the historian it is also misleading. Few readers, moved by Kunta's plight, would possess the requisite knowledge of Africa's several systems of bondage (including some which might be as socially and psychologically benign as that described in *Roots*) to make a balanced judgment. Slavery, as it existed among the Mandinka and their neighbors in the Senegambia in the mid-eighteenth century, is fairly well-documented, and chattels were certainly common.[50] Clearly, among peoples with similar customs there were ameliorating circumstances, and clearly the fact that Africans enslaved by Africans were of the same color is a telling point emphasized by every serious historian of Africa for four decades. Nonetheless, the complete integration of the former slave Nyo Boto into the daily life of Kunta's family, though possible, represents a deliberate process of selection on the part of the author. It is what is left out that is important. For example, the conspicuous absence of any further examples of how bondage among Kunta's people worked (or how it might affect a relatively well-born youth like Kunta) can only be taken as evidence that the author is presenting the domestic system of slavery in idealized form.[51] In the final analysis, by turning the standard stereotypes on their heads, and by creating an obverse series of images whereby blame can easily be laid to the unmitigated evil of whites, Haley risks the accusation that he is romanticizing Africa.

Among the most popular of African American writers, hardly comparable to Haley for obvious reasons, but significant nonetheless, was the historical novelist Frank Yerby, whose potboiler formula novels (*The Vixens, Jarrett's Jade, Fairoaks*, and many more) entertained millions of readers in the 1940s, 1950s, and 1960s. Yerby was briefly in the news following the 1971 publication of his best-seller, *The Dahomean*, when many of his readers (a sizable number of whom were white Southerners) expressed surprise that he was not white. Several of Yerby's earlier novels, set primarily in the antebellum South, had vivid African scenes in them, but none were as ambitious in attempting to construct an African setting as *The Dahomean*. According to Yerby, this novel was based loosely "so far as its historical sociological aspects are concerned"[52] on Melville Herskovits' classic *Dahomey: An Ancient West African Kingdom*. Unfortunately, all resemblance to anything Herskovits produced ends there. Colorful, violent, explicit, *The Dahomean* fits all the requisites of the genre, with adventure centermost. Amazons, lust, bloodshed, slavery, sadism, witchcraft, armies on the march, it is all there in abundance. The consequence, in spite of Yerby's intent to shed light on a traditional African kingdom at the height of its power, is to underscore the symbolic conventions. The picture of a West African kingdom in all its barbarous nineteenth-century splendor, despite some memorable characters (Nyasanu and Nyaunu the star-crossed lovers, Kpadunu the sorcerer, Alogba the Amazon, King Gezo himself), is presented here entirely within the classic format. Yerby was one of the better formula writers of his time, and in this novel he did not waste his skills. For example, regarding the prevalence of magico-religious beliefs which dominated much of Dahomean life, Yerby has Kpadunu explain,

> People are—lonely, desperate, hurt, afraid, and . . . we sorcerers, and the diviners, and the priests of all the various cults, give them hope. And by the same method, we speak loudly and confidentially about things which by their very nature mankind does not nor cannot know. Repeating over and over again words like magic, charms, *su du du's*, tabu, spirits, ghosts, gods, until almost we convince ourselves that they mean something, which they don't.[53]

Even in the 1930s the Herskovits's would have been jolted by such a cynical revelation on the part of a religious figure like Kpadunu. Sad to say Yerby gives himself away in scores of similar passages, which are obviously designed to appeal to his late-twentieth-century readers. He constantly titillates us with bloody rituals, violent sex, and sadism, and then attempts, rather lamely, to explain these away. Any pretense of enlightening his readers about

typical African stereotypes is suborned here to the purple prosody
that makes such works the ultimate in escapism. The alleged historicity of *The Dahomean*, like so many other historical novels, is, to
paraphrase Henry Ford, "bunk." Frankly one can find little distinction between Yerby's work and that of writers such as Edgar Rice
Burroughs of an earlier generation, or Wilbur Smith of a later one.
These novels appear to be boiled in the same dark pot.

A final comment on Yerby is needed. One can hardly read *The
Dahomean* without some admiration for the central character
Nyasanu. He is heroic in every respect: powerful, kind, firm but
gentle, capable of unleashed but righteous violence only when pro-
voked, steadfast and brave. Once more in a novel of Africa we find
the American frontier hero resurrected in full panoply. Nevertheless, any connection between the engaging Nyasanu and the Africa
he allegedly represents is purely coincidental.

Alice Walker's 1982 prize-winning novel *The Color Purple* presents a disturbing question in this regard. Unlike Haley, or even
Yerby, Walker makes no attempt to recreate an historical past in
Africa; rather she treats Africa (via Nettie's letters to Celie) as a
mythic place, its images presented via a melange of narratives
which come to the reader in bits and pieces in Nellie's words. To
some these oral vignettes may serve to underline Nettie's alienation
from a racist America and her attempt to rediscover a larger
humanity for herself in Africa; but to the scholar, or even to a
reader vaguely familiar with Africa, this melange can be confusing,
and even contradictory. The Doris Baines story, for example, told
on shipboard to Nettie, is blatantly ahistorical, and, in part, inco-
herent. Granted, its rambling humor is in keeping with oral literature of this sort, but as narrative it cannot stand up to systematic
scrutiny. Equally typical is Walker's fictional version of "DuBoyce's"
(W. E. B. Du Bois') reaction to Aunt Theodosia's tale about the
Congo.

> Madame, he said, when Aunt Theodosia finished her story
> and flashed her famous medals around the room, do you
> realize King Leopold cut off the hands of workers who, in the
> opinion of his plantation overseers, did not fulfill their rub-
> ber quota? Rather than cherish that medal, Madame, you
> should regard it as a symbol of your unwilling complicity
> with this despot who worked to death and brutalized and
> eventually exterminated thousands and thousands of
> African peoples.[54]

The use of the plural for African people(s) might, in speech,
represent a rhetorical device, hyperbole used to make a telling
point. Likewise the implication that King Leopold himself gave

orders to cut off the hands of Africans who failed to fulfill the rubber quota. Though Leopold's culpability, thoroughly documented in the work of Roger Casement, Edmund Morel, and Mark Twain, has never been in doubt, he never set foot in Africa. No one knows (and we shall probably never know) how many Africans died as a direct or indirect result of Leopold's misrule in his "personal" colony; some estimates range into the hundreds of thousands.[55] Still, the implication that whole peoples were exterminated is misleading.

Perhaps it is unfair to judge any writer, particularly one whose work, like Walker's, is closely akin to fable, by a strict historical standard (that is, to demand accuracy as to background). Many of the greatest, including Shakespeare, played unabashedly to convenient myths of their time (the ascendancy of the Tudor's, for example, with its assumption that the last Plantagenets were evil incarnate), but it is incumbent on historians to say so, whether we are speaking about Shakespeare or some lesser figure. The impressions of Africa conveyed in *The Color Purple* are no doubt intended to be mythical in content as well as in tone, but that does not mean they should be confused, for one moment, with anything real.

In fairness it should be noted that Walker never claimed that her mythical vision of Africa is consciously based on the historical. Indeed, in the afterword to her more recent novel, *Possessing the Secret of Joy*, she notes that "I do not know from what part of Africa my African ancestors came, and so I claim the continent. I suppose I have created Olinka as my village and the Olinkans as one of my ancient, ancestral tribal peoples."[56] Nevertheless, *Secret of Joy* represents a major departure in her approach to the continent. Here, Africa is at the heart of the narrative, and the symbolic conventions which loom so large in *The Color Purple* are re-examined. Olinka seems no less real for being an abstraction, indeed, it becomes a prime example of a literary creation whose reality forces the reader to think beyond the commonplace. Walker's thematic focus in *Secret of Joy* is sharp and unyielding, and she pursues her central issue—the problem of female circumcision—with a relentless intensity.

Whatever one may think about this novel as literature or social commentary, it stands out as a book which took considerable moral courage to write. Clearly in the decade since the appearance of *The Color Purple*, Walker took pains to look closely—and with uncompromising honesty—at a well-known aspect of African "tradition" that had been all-too-often glossed over, rationalized, and sometimes excused in the ethnographic literature, a widespread custom which, in Walker's view, is simply inexcusable and tragic. Walker's view is emphatically a "western" one, more specifically an American one, despite the compelling detail of life in Olinka. In this respect *Secret of Joy* is best understood as a feminist statement (its African setting secondary to the larger issue of women's' rights and the struggle of women to control their own destiny). But it does not follow that the African setting is secondary to the narrative in this extraordinary work.

Secret of Joy is loosely tied to *The Color Purple* through its major character, Tashi. Tashi is the African wife of Adam; Adam is the son of Celie, whose story is the focus of Walker's earlier (and widely celebrated) novel. Celie's sister, Nettie, a missionary, had taken Adam and his sister Olivia to Africa, to Olinka, where he met his African bride. The couple spent some time in America, but Tashi grew restless: her people were in the midst of an anti-colonial struggle and she wanted to play a part. She was also anxious to strengthen her cultural bond with the motherland, so when she decided to return to Olinka and cast her lot with the rebellion, Tashi also chose to submit to a rite of passage which was expected of all Olinka women—circumcision. Thus, when she reached the camp of the freedom fighters she willingly submitted to the knife of M'Lissa, the woman who was honored as the chief practitioner of this sacred ritual, a ritual whose importance had been reaffirmed and championed by the "progressive" (male) leader of the national liberation movement. As Tashi began her physical recovery from this act of mutilation she soon discovered her tragic mistake: she learned that this valued "tradition" was a terrible and inexcusable punishment which no woman should be expected to bear. When her legs were finally unbound and she was able to "walk a few steps . . . she noticed [that] her own proud walk had become a shuffle."

> It now took a quarter of an hour for her to pee. Her menstrual periods lasted ten days. She was incapacitated by cramps nearly half the month. There were premenstrual cramps: cramps caused by the near impossibility of flow passing through so tiny an aperture as M'Lissa had left, after fastening together the raw sides of Tashi's vagina with a couple of thorns and inserting a straw so that in healing, the traumatized flesh might not grow together, shutting the opening completely; cramps caused by the residual flow that could not find its way out, was not reabsorbed into her body, and had nowhere to go. There was the odor, too, of soured blood, which no amount of scrubbing, until we got to America, ever washed off.[57]

Her physical recovery was difficult enough, but her quest for inner peace proved to be an ordeal of years rather than months. In spare but powerful prose, Walker recounts Tashi's continuing struggle to come to terms with this permanent violation of her body and spirit. Tashi journeys to Switzerland for psychoanalysis, but her therapist, the "old man" (Carl Jung, in all but name), cannot find the key to defusing her pain. She goes on to bear a son who is mildly retarded, a condition she attributes to the trauma of his birth and the nature of her mutilation. If this were not enough, she plunges into a deepening spiral of despair and jealousy as Adam fathers a healthy son by another woman, a Frenchwoman who has never suffered the attentions of a rusty knife. Finally, she can bear no more, and in middle age she returns to Africa to confront the architect of her agony: M'Lissa, the old woman who has since become a national hero "for her role during the wars of liberation . . . and for her unfailing adherence to the ancient customs and traditions of the Olinka state."[58] Tashi has not come to this old woman's "shrine" to pay homage, however. Instead, she has come to end her torment by committing a "crime against the state." She murders M'Lissa, and becomes the subject of a showtrial whose verdict is a foregone conclusion.

Beyond her condemnation of an ancient rite of passage, Walker's vision of independent Olinka is unremittingly harsh. Adam retains an outsider's perspective on events in Olinka. When he returns to this African nation during Tashi's imprisonment, he becomes

> morbidly interested in this country's problems as they are revealed by inept and corrupt journalists. All the credible journalists have by now been beaten into silence, bought off, murdered, or chased into exile. The ones that are left have but one function: tell the people lies that flatter the president. In every edition of the two remaining papers there is a huge photograph of him: roundfaced, chuckleheaded, beaming like an evil moon. He is president for life, and that is that. The people are reminded over and over of his exploits as a youth against the white colonialists. They are told how, daily, he fights the neo-imperialists, who are still intent on stealing our country from them. They are told how frugally he husbands their dwindling resources and of how, during the latest interminable drought, he permits the lawn of his palace to be watered but once a week. Of course it is practically the only lawn in Olinka. . . .[59]

In a similar vein, Pierre, Adam's son by the Frenchwoman, Lisette, explains to his half-brother, Benny, that, while the impending execution of Tashi might be difficult to understand, Benny could

> Look at it this way. In the year nine hundred and twelve the people of Olinka had a stupid leader who put people to death by hanging. Now their stupid leader puts them to

death by shooting. Now he is driven everywhere in a Mer-
cedes. In nine hundred and twelve he was carried on the
shoulders of four strong slaves everywhere he went. You
see?

From her prison cell, Tashi can hear daily demonstrations in the
street below. Olivia informs her that what she is witnessing is "the
cultural fundamentalists and Muslim fanatics attacking women
who've traveled from all parts of the country" to support her cause.
"They kick them. They swing at them with clubs, bruising the
women's skins and breaking bones."[61] Apparently, women who do
not conform with tradition are seen as the enemy, and Tashi herself
has become the archenemy in the country of her birth. As for that
distant nation which she has accepted as her homeland, a country
she will never see again, she has this to say to M'Lissa in their final
encounter when the old woman asks her to describe "what an
American looks like":

> An American, I said sighing, but understanding my love of
> my adopted country perhaps for the first time: an American
> looks like a wounded person whose wound is hidden from
> others, and sometimes from herself. An American looks like
> me.[62]

In the final analysis, having effectively built on the success of her
earlier work, Walker's *Possessing the Secret of Joy* is a fine example
of creative growth. Some might argue that the condemnation of
female circumcision, seen throughout this work as a barbarous custom, is, in itself, playing to the symbolic conventions, especially
those which paint Africa as a place of dark and bloody rites. This
would be a mistake, however, for the condemnation and the uncompromising honesty which lies at the core of this work is balanced by
a sensitive narrative wherein the evils of colonialism, and the struggle for independence, are seen within the context of a local culture,
one which comes to life, one which recreates a believable world. In
this sense, as perhaps in few examples in contemporary American
fiction, Walker's transformation is all the more remarkable.

Another recent novel by an African American, widely praised if
less widely read, is Charles Johnson's *Middle Passage* (1990), the
chronicle of a former slave named Rutherford Calhoun and his
adventures (c. 1830) on a slave ship out of New Orleans which visits the West African coast and returns via the infamous middle passage with a load of slaves.[63] These include several "Allmuseri"—a
mysterious, gifted magician tribe from a mythical place called Ban-
galang—who join in a ship-board rebellion to overthrow the terrible

(but brilliant) Captain Falcon. The idea is marvelous, the fashionable resort to magic and fantasy (also on board in a special crate is an African "god" of vague but awesome powers) is fun, the dialogue sparkling, and certainly the characters are original. Johnson's inventive range of non-stereotypical characters (whose color does not in any way determine quality) is exceptional. In this respect, as in the means by which Rutherford discovers himself, the novel is triumphant. All this—on the level of metaphor and in terms of puncturing racist stereotypes—is marvelous.

Unfortunately the story itself is so contrived, and bears so little resemblance to reality, as to try the patience of the most determined reader. Apparently Johnson, playing as he does to metaphor and myth, intent as he is to turn the old racist metaphors around, does not want his work to bear the slightest resemblance to the so-called historical novel of the type made famous by writers such as Yerby. One can understand why. Such works, in their bogus historicity, reinforce all that is empty and wrong within the conventional framework. Nonetheless, any reader looking for Africa in this work, even for a semblance of Africa as the birthplace of so much that is noteworthy, will come away disappointed.

Some readers might object here, or at least question the inclusion of novels like *Roots*, *The Color Purple*, and *Middle Passage*, in this analysis. It is true that none of these works is properly a novel of or about Africa, in the way that *Henderson the Rain King* is, or *The Last Hero*, for that matter. Furthermore, these three must be understood as novels within a distinct category because they are written by African Americans. The ambivalence of American blacks toward Africa—well documented in such non-fiction as Richard Wright's *Black Power*, W. E. B. Du Bois' *Dusk of Dawn*, and David Jenkin's *Black Zion*—is a case in point.[64] Reality is less important, clearly, than image. Despite the ebb and flow of literary trends, African American novelists when they deal with Africa at all (and a surprisingly small number have attempted to do so) typically enter another realm of myth. The tendency is to make liberal use of the positive symbolic conventions, which, in the negative version, they disparage.

Saul Bellow is hardly the sort one might expect to fall into any "convention." Indeed, looking at his novel, *Henderson the Rain King*, one is struck by the fact that its African scenes and characters—though penned in the mid 1950s when most Americans still conceived of Africa as Tarzan's lair—are remarkable for their inventiveness. In much of *Henderson* the reader follows the protagonist into a cultural universe quite distinct from the expected mumbo-jumboland, a place where Africans view the posturing Henderson with wry amusement. Indeed, the Africans in this novel are paragons of sensibility compared to Henderson himself, a grown man given to adolescent dreams.

One writer has gone so far as to claim that the entire novel is a deliberate refutation of the "nihilistic Romanticism" as best expressed in Conrad's *Heart of Darkness*.[65] At face value there may be something to this, since *Henderson* is certainly anti-romantic in spirit and in its satiric treatment of Henderson's adventures, and, like all of Bellow's work, filled with dark humor and numerous examples of life's absurdities. Surely Bellow's work (including many of his other novels, especially *Seize the Day, Herzog,* and *Mr. Sammler's Planet*) represents a gifted writer's sardonic vision, an open disdain for the overtly romantic. Yet in *Henderson,* beneath the dark humor, is a powerful celebration of life, even of hope. It therefore seems to this writer unfair and reductionistic to use such a comparison, especially with an allegedly nihilistic Conrad.

Among the more telling analyses of Bellow's *Henderson* is a recent insight, provided by David Anderson, who argues that Henderson's picaresque quest is about "the serious business of myth, the serious business through which Henderson, like Hemingway moves larger than life, creating at the same time, like Hemingway, a myth in which he can survive."[66] It is surely correct, as Anderson notes, that Hemingway's Africa is the Africa of wonder which so thoroughly captivated America at midcentury, when "Papa" Hemingway emerged from a second plane crash, alive, larger-than-life. This is the Africa of new beginnings, the Africa of potential renewal. Jaded, aging, half-mad, Bellow's Henderson, intrepid anti-hero though he is, writes back to Lily, "The experience in Africa has been tremendous. It has been tough, it has been perilous, it has been something! But I've matured twenty years in twenty days."[67] Evidently Bellow's Africa, though not outwardly romanticized as in the novels of lesser contemporaries, represents for Henderson (a character who is very likely based, as Anderson has pointed out, directly on Hemingway) the place of salvation, the setting where he, heretofore lost, can complete his quest and become "King of the Rain." In short, Africa is exactly the place where Henderson can find himself.[68]Therefore, while *Henderson The Rain King* may be overtly anti-romantic, it has a mythic center, romantic in the classic sense that renewal and resurrection is possible. In Henderson's own words, his African journey is a demonstration that no matter how awful the modern world, no matter how heavily he is saddled with ennui, "reality is not all darkness and . . . men can see the light."[69] Bellow was already an accomplished writer, even at this early stage of his career. He understood that he must not fall into the trap of stereotypes. Nonetheless, it is *in* Henderson's opposing stereotypical African abominations among the Wariri to the romantic nobility of the Wariri King, Dahfu, that he finds a kind of apotheosis. Earlier in the novel we see Henderson's adventures among the comically innocent Arnewi, a people who seem to embody the childhood of humanity—like the idealized "primitives" of certain fashionable anthropologists. He moves on, of course, to meet the brilliant Dahfu, and thus his comic redemption. But how can we miss this centrality: this old theme of Africa as primordial renewer, a place whose darkness hides an Eden. Though Bellow's *Henderson* is a wonderful realization of the renewing power of creative humor few readers would argue that it succeeds on this level alone. It seems equally apparent to this writer that it also succeeds because Bellow finds for Henderson the mythic Africa of romantic hope, even of renewal.[70] No doubt, in creating Henderson, and in constructing the story of his quest, Bellow was fully aware of these paradigms (he had, after all, been briefly a student of Herskovits at Chicago). Nonetheless, in this superb novel, certainly ranking among the best American novels of its time, Africa's classic mythic purpose is served.

Little-known in its time but significant for its irreverence is another 1954 novel, *White Hunter, Black Heart* by Peter Viertel, who had written the screenplay based on the C. S. Forester novel for John Huston's famous production, *The African Queen*, in 1951-52. Though the film itself—despite powerful performances by Hepburn (as the prim Rose Sayer) and Bogart (as the hard-drinking Charlie Alnut)—absurdly reinforces the usual stereotypes of an Africa devoid of Africans, Viertel's novel is less easily categorized. Apparently the experience of filmmaking in Zaire with the egocentric Huston had a profound effect on Viertel (as it did on Hepburn, who later wrote a book about the experience) and his thinly-disguised account of Huston, despite the latter's posturing and womanizing is gripping stuff from start to finish. Quickly one discovers that, though Viertel was disgusted by the director's narcissism, he was also bemused by Huston's uncompromising vision and his adherence to a masculine code right out of Hemingway. This contradiction produces a dual conflict in *White Hunter, Black Heart*, revealed both within the director's paradoxical character, and within a traditional Africa where man and beast alike are seen as mere pawns in the white man's game. What might have become just another psychological profile of undisciplined genius is thus all the more revealing for its portrait of unrestricted machismo within a traditional African setting, where the great man, sick of the *ennui* of Hollywood, must prove himself by killing an elephant. The director wants this so badly, "testing my strength and my wits" against the greatest of all beasts, that he is willing to risk the completion of the film itself, even his own life and the lives of others.[71] In the end, willful to the last, the Huston character (effectively played in the recent movie version by Clint Eastwood) is attending the funeral of his African guide, senselessly killed by a charging elephant while setting up an incredibly dangerous hunt, when the surviving relatives begin to chant a song in Swahili. Wondering at what seems to be a note of anger in the singing, the director, somewhat chastened now that life has been lost, asks for a response. "White hunter, black heart," comes the translation. How better to sum up western arrogance, epitomized in the flawed character of Hollywood's most flamboyant and gifted maverick? Apparently, to Viertel, it was doubly absurd that a man like Huston—a man whose "noblesse oblige" was so keen that in defense of a hapless African servant he took a terrible beating at the hands of a sadistic British hotel-keeper—could countenance such behavior in himself.

Any watershed is hard to define, especially in literature. Nonetheless, a new era of American fiction dealing with Africa began around 1960 with the "New Frontier" of Kennedy, with the Peace Corps, with the burgeoning Civil Rights movement, and with the Vietnam War (and the anti-war movement) which shaped the next decades. Certainly this generation, born too late to participate in World War II, experienced Africa very differently than the generation of Hemingway, or Hanley, Ruark, Viertel, or even Bohannan, and *very* differently from such British novelists as Joyce Cary, Elspeth Huxley, or even Graham Greene. True, a few American writers born since the 1930s might—like Michael Crichton and Peter Forbath—continue within the old paradigms, but any list of novels written about Africa by Americans from the late sixties on must include those of Paul Theroux and Philip Caputo, not to mention W. T. Tyler, Maria Thomas, William Duggan, Norman Rush, and John Updike (of a slightly older generation), all of whom have written significant fiction on Africa.

The more recent works which have depicted Africa entirely within the symbolic conventions fall rather easily into the categories noted previously: the classic adventure tale, often with overtones of the typical American frontier novel whereby an intrepid hero must win out against a savage wilderness, while beset by savage beasts or savage peoples; and the neo-romantic novel often involving a protagonist who travels in Africa on a personal quest wherein he ultimately finds himself, either through identification with a primitive people (who, despite their "uncivilized" nature, have lessons to teach) or via a regeneration through nature whereby the protagonist learns how empty is his urban society and how vital and alive is the wilderness of Africa. Most safari novels fall into this category. A far more important category, though less popular, is the tragic—or tragi-comic—novel of existential disillusionment and despair wherein the protagonist is forced by his experience in Africa to learn tough lessons about life, death, love, disease, war, and man's inhumanity to man. In many of these novels the central character is typically a naive, self-indulgent, suburbanized American, frequently a Peace Corps volunteer, health worker, naturalist, or field worker. Sometimes the story centers around an arrogant soldier, diplomat, or adventurer, and occasionally an academic, whose very innocence about the real world brings disorder and even death. Writers such as Paul Theroux, William Duggan, W. T. Tyler, and Maria Thomas, again come to mind. It is obviously difficult to classify some of these, especially the work of Philip Caputo. *Horn of Africa*, as we shall see, is not essentially a novel of or about Africa (though its setting in the Horn is certainly no accident and he portrays the Eritrean conflict well and faithfully.)

In several respects Michael Crichton's novel *Congo* (1980) reestablishes the archetype of the African adventure tale, with overtones of sci-fi and popular science. Here—perhaps never more perfectly rendered since Burroughs set his pen to the Tarzan epic—is the unreconstructed Africa of yore recreated for the generation of yuppies.[72] Crichton, apparently having traveled enough in Africa to describe the immense Ituri rainforest with some verisimilitude, nonetheless titillates his readers with the news that deep in that jungle there are still peoples who will resort to cannibalism when threatened by external forces they cannot understand. Just to make sure the reader gets the point, Crichton has one of his characters, named Captain Charles Munro, explain to the skeptical scientists that a local tribe, fictionalized as the *Kigani*, has just eaten an entire family. When one of the scientists näively says "We should consider ourselves lucky. We're probably among the last people in the world to see such things," Munro replies, "I doubt it . . . Old habits die hard."[73]

Crichton fans, aware of the popular science behind so many of his thrillers (*The Andromeda Strain, Jurassic Park*, and *Eaters of the Dead*, the latter of which also includes cannibal scenes) are liable to be bemused by Crichton's striking portrait of Zaire's remote interior, the perfect setting for his tale of unexpected primate evolution (an unknown ape species of high intelligence and awful violence, far closer to man than anything hitherto unknown) and pseudo-scientific meddling—a rather transparent retelling of H. G. Well's science-fiction classic *The Island of Dr. Moreau* (1896). One might argue that *Congo* is less a novel of Africa (or about Africa) than it is a sci-fi thriller rather deliberately set amid the most savage of places imaginable to its readers. The Amazon, otherwise remote, will clearly not do since it harbors no apes. Where else but Africa could *Congo*'s author assume that his readers would come to the adventure primed and ready? One might wonder why this could still be true in 1980, after three quarters of a century of scholarship. But certainly, at this point, after the successful reprinting, beginning in the 1960s, of the complete Tarzan series, after the successful reissuing of Rider Haggard's works a century after their first appearance, after the worshipful popularization of the exploits of the great nineteenth-century explorers (Forbath's *The Last Hero*, Harrison's *Mountains of the Moon*), after the huge success of books on the great apes by Jane Goodall and Dian Fossey, after *Nova* made Colin Turnbull's excellent work on the Ituri pygmies known to every schoolchild, and after George Lukas brings us an exciting new television series called the "Young Indiana Jones Chronicles," much of which is filmed in Africa, no one should be surprised that the symbolic conventions, buttressed and reinforced, remain intact.

Any fair criticism of such a work does not depend on "proving" or falsifying the darker images which Crichton uses to such effect. Indeed Crichton takes pains to produce evidence of cases of cannibalism in Zaire's remote northeast, especially during the terrible period of the Congolese Civil War in the 1960s. He also cites a writer who lived in a cannibal village in the fifties. Some years ago Milan Kalous produced evidence that Sierra Leone's legendary Leopard and Alligator societies which flourished in the nineteenth century had continued to engage in ritual cannibalism well into this century, at least on a limited scale.[74] Many scholars wondered, however, about the purpose of Kalous' research. The point, of course, is not that such practices existed, or even that in some cases they persist. One can produce evidence that Native Americans engaged in cannibalism. One can reasonably surmise that Tacitus was correct when he attributed human sacrifice to the Druids of ancient Britain. It is known that ritual murder is a common rite-of-passage into certain American street gangs. One can show that female newborns have been murdered in contemporary China. Few would conclude that any of these cases should be seen as typical of the culture or continent in question. Yet, in *Congo*, as in most novels of this kind, Africa is implicitly equated with savagery.

There are many other works in this vein, most of them hardly worthy of note. Yerby would fit in some respects, as would Wilbur Smith, the Rhodesian whose earlier novels celebrate a colonial world view, and who, in his most recent novel, *Elephant Song*, offers an unintentionally comical synthesis of enlightened mercenary violence and kindergarten environmentalism. Africa, because of its powerful associations, is bound to provide the background and setting to thrillers of all kinds, as it has in this case, and it seems unlikely that the market will die out in the near future. Just as that enduring image of the wild Indian who comes howling over the next hill—or sneaking through the dark woods—will provide background for many a western to come, so unfortunately will Africa's mysterious jungles continue to provide dusky savages and dark rites as a backdrop to fantasyland adventures.

Another "adventure" tale, though in striking juxtaposition to Crichton's work, is the 1980 novel *Water Music* by T. Coraghessan Boyle, a hilarious bawdy romp through late eighteenth-century England and the unknown regions of the upper Niger in company with Mungo Park, Scottish explorer extraordinaire. Boyle's *tour de force*, a deliberate imitation in late-twentieth-century consciousness of the picaresque English novel of Mungo Park's own era (the 1790s and early 1800s), owes more to that form than it does to any of our well-trod categories. Park is more the foil for Boyle's "deliberately anachronistic" invention than he is a "real" historical character. Nonetheless, the novel succeeds in capturing the mood of an era, and more than succeeds in recapitulating the mixture of disdain and fascination that Europeans of that era (as well as our own) held toward Africa. During Park's second, ill-fated expedition of 1805-1806 to trace the course of the Niger to its mouth, we find Mungo, having lost a dozen men to disease, lamenting the setbacks and trials in his tent somewhere near Boontokooran, buoyed only by the indomitable humor and spirit of Johnson, his black "factotum" and guide.

> That's the worst of it: the thievery. The rest Mungo could live with—man against nature and all that—but this unremitting assault by the natives—the very people who would most benefit by his opening the region to British trade—it's exasperating, heartbreaking. Instead of looking on each successive village with relief, as a place of refuge and respite, the explorer has come to dread the approach to any civilized area. The word has gone out: the coffle is dummula-fong, fair game. Up and down the road, from Doogikotta to Kandy, the rumor flies like something on wings: a party of white men is on the way, men so debilitated they can hardly hold up their weapons or drive their asses laden with beads and gold and things so exotic that no names exist for them in the Mandingo tongue.[75]

Johnson, portrayed in the novel as a well-traveled literate man (quite the opposite of the typical "factotum" of explorer literature), provides a counterpoint throughout the novel to Park's brave but redundant arrogance. At one point earlier in the novel we read part of a page Park has written in his journal about his discovery of the Niger, flowing *eastward*, and especially his account of the local ruler, Mansong of Bambarra.

> We were greeted with a warmth and civility that made our hearts glad after grappling so long with inanition and the merciless depredations of the desert Moor. . . . There were open courtyards in the Iberian style, flowing fountains and exotic gardens laden with every sort of fruit and bud imaginable. We were led through a succession of these courtyards to the inner sanctum itself, where Mansong awaited us.
>
> The potentate was a big-boned man of cheerful countenance, seated on a golden throne and surrounded by his fierce elite guard, savages built like racehorses and standing six and a half or seven feet from the ground. I made my obeisance, and then presented him with the gifts I had carried from England.

Johnson however, responds with spirit, providing the reader with a corrective that is both comic and timely.

> "But this is the purest of bullshit," says Johnson, handing the slip of paper back to the explorer. "A distortion and lie. About the only thing that's accurate is the seven-foot guards. And the cash."

Ruminating on this, Park replies, "Exactly," he says, folding up the scrap of paper and working it under his hatband.

> "Can you imagine how unutterably dull it would be if I stuck strictly to the bare facts—without a hint of embellishment? The good citizens of London and Edinburgh don't want to read about the misery and wretchedness and thirty-seven slaves disemboweled, old boy—their lives are grim enough as it is. No, they want a little glamor, a touch of the exotic and the out-of-the-way. And what's the harm of giving it to them?"[76]

Such a novel, though it is chock full of the stuff of adventure, hardly plays to the symbolic conventions. Park's escapades, like those of unlucky and ill-fated Ned, a parallel character throughout the novel who escapes the awful slums of London to join Park on the second expedition, need no romantic embellishment. Indeed, London is seen through Ned's eyes as a place of unrelieved barbarism. For one of Ned's class, Africa is a step up. The tone of irony, the ribald humor, the terrible conditions of life, the waste and greed, all underline the absurdity of the story itself. In *Water Music*, Africa is ultimately no different than other places, except that it is unknown to the Europeans. Boyle's successful attempt to represent the African point of view in this novel, also succeeds in illustrating the European view of the time. The author, in an

"Apologia," admits to much invention in the reconstruction of the history behind this work: "the impetus . . . is principally aesthetic rather than scholarly." This seems altogether accurate. Nonetheless, *Water Music* is completely different in tone and purpose from the neo-romantic potboiler like Wilbur Smith's *Elephant Song*, or even Peter Forbath's *The Last Hero*. One might as well label Thomas Berger's satiric masterpiece *Little Big Man* a "western" as to classify Boyle's novel in this fashion.

To return to Forbath it is clear that *The Last Hero*, certainly the best historical novel about Henry M. Stanley, and one of the best on the era of exploration, is neo-romantic from first to last despite its naturalistic scenes of death and horror. It may seem incongruous but this is a significant work because it so accurately reconstructs the awful conditions of the infamous "Emin Pasha Relief Expedition" which Stanley led up the Zaire (Congo) River through the Ituri forest to Lake Albert, and then to Zanzibar, in 1887-88. Forbath is a seasoned writer and the book is an excellent read, especially interesting for its painstaking characterizations and background. In its investigation of psychological conflict—especially on the part of Stanley and of the doomed Barttelot of the "rear column"—it is altogether contemporary, a post-modern book of the 1980s. The sophistication of detail provided by the author so as to underscore motivation, family, and personal history, and the thoroughly believable dialogue, elevate *The Last Hero* far above the typical work in this genre. It is not the kind of book a Rider Haggard could have written, though it is emphatically a work *about* the late Victorian "scramble" for Africa, nor is it the kind of book a Hanley or a Huxley might have written, of an Africa preserved in amber. The overtones are romantic—because the subject lends itself to the romantic—but Forbath brings a contemporary insight to the conflicts of that era.

Forbath does, however, play brilliantly on the symbolic conventions, especially the negative images of the vast Congo basin, portrayed as a realm of darkness as hellish as anything in Conrad. Some of the physical description is memorable, and Forbath uses comparison very effectively. Tippu Tib's great slave-catching headquarters, fictionalized as "Stingatini," is, for example, described as a beautiful town full of lush gardens, minarets and a domed mosque, handsome whitewashed villas up to two stories high, miles of lush plantations of sweet potatoes, rice, onions, maize, and bananas, orchards of lime and mango, and a thriving grand bazaar. At first it seems almost a paradise compared to the crude "native" town, Yambuyu, where the people live in sullen fear and poverty.[77] But Forbath has set up the reader with all this luxury for Tippu Tib's Stingatini harbors evil. There, Barttelot (whom Forbath presents as a character in the mold of Conrad's Kurtz) is seduced and lost. At a crucial point in the novel, Troup, another character left with the rear column, has traveled up to Stingatini to "rescue" Barttelot, only to find him besotted and dissipated.

> He looked at the unconscious Barttelot. Food like this, hashish, women, gardens in luxuriant bloom, courtyards with tinkling fountains, nights and days spinning away undifferentiated except by dreams—Stanley knew about such Arabian seductions and had warned against them.[78]

Though Barttelot recovers something of his upper-crust discipline, it is too late. The Victorian gentleman—something the iron-willed Stanley most emphatically is not—has succumbed to all the decadence. The "beautiful soldier" whom even Stanley had admired—much decorated in war, witty, handsome, gracious—has revealed himself a fool, worse yet, a brutal African-hating martinet, rotten inside. His death, after his fall, comes almost as an anticlimax.

This is a novel Conrad might have enjoyed. What would Stanley have thought of it? Or Tippu Tib? Stanley certainly would have enjoyed the portrait of himself as the larger-than-life, heroically-determined *Bula Matari*, "Breaker of Rocks," resilient and resourceful, but he would have hated the insight into his temperament, his tortured Victorian sexuality, his driven urge to prove himself to his social superiors. One suspects that Chinua Achebe, the great Nigerian novelist, who considers Conrad's work racist and condescending, would feel much the same about this work. It is certainly not conducive to a more generous view of Africa. The point, however, is that Forbath is faithful to the genre; he tells the story as if we today need to understand all of Stanley's brutality and will, energy and violence, relentless waste and huge ego, and above all his overwhelming drive. Implicit is the idea that Stanley cannot be simply dismissed as another "bloody racist." The novel is a portrait of a man at variance with our era, as well as at odds with most of the Africans (by no means all) that he encountered. More importantly, he was at odds with virtually all the weaker Europeans (especially the British) around him. We cannot know for sure whether Forbath has it right. It does seem likely that he is close to the target, however, regarding Barttelot (Kurtz), a type thoroughly corrupted by the Africa of that time, just as Stanley's brutal power fed on everything that "darkest" Africa at its worst could throw at him.

There is, however, fiction of quite another sort, works which often challenge the symbolic conventions of six decades. These works, while often satiric or ironic in tone are notable for their revelatory content. They are, if not known to a large American public, works which are fully representative of the best American writing in the final decades of the century. The most prolific of these, Paul Theroux probably has the most extensive African experience. He was a Peace Corps volunteer in Malawi in 1963-65, was expelled from the Peace Corps—and deported from Malawi—for alleged association with "revolutionaries" who attempted to overthrow the Banda regime, and he taught for several years more in Uganda, where he married, met V. S. Naipaul, and in 1967 published *Waldo*, his first novel. In subsequent years, living in Singapore and then near London from which he ventured to write his famous travelogues (*The Great Railway Bazaar, The Old Patagonian Express, The Kingdom by the Sea*, and *Ride The Iron Rooster*), Theroux produced three novels set largely in Africa: *Fong and the Indians* (1968), *Girls at Play* (1969), and *Jungle Lovers* (1971) plus one with substantial portions set there, *My Secret History* (1989).[79]

Admittedly, an analysis of these within any category is exceedingly difficult, perhaps impossible. Theroux, born and educated in America, is American in the way that T. S. Eliot was American, or perhaps Henry James, an expatriate of mid-Atlantic sensibilities whose life and work have been increasingly centered in England and the world, not America. Though one could argue that *Saint Jack* (1974), *O-Zone* (1986), and especially his masterpiece, *The Mosquito Coast* (1982), are American works through and through, Theroux's African novels sometimes seem rather distanced, emblematic not so much of any American experience in Africa, but rather as odd and ironic windows on strange and isolated lives in a cosmopolitan but dreary world of empty routines and desperate days, where no one is at home. Anyone familiar with the detached comic tone of the British writer William Boyd, especially in *The Ice Cream War* (1982) and *A Good Man in Africa* (1972) will recognize similarities here, especially in the sardonic and cynical view of black and white alike, whenever they come into contact.[80] The main characters of *Girls at Play*, Miss Poole and Heather Monkhouse, are single British women, feuding amid an alien environment—quite hostile now that the Empire has gone—both trying to connect with something, with someone. As always, Theroux's insights are pointed: Miss Poole

> felt exactly the same about Africans [as she did her pets].
> She had fed them and they responded in a manner that was
> both savage and innocent. Their undirected savagery was
> occasional, always inspired by people who wanted to change
> them.[81]

How could such a woman link in any real way with Africans? Theroux, the keenest of observers, sees this clearly. Later in the novel we meet the young American Peace Corps volunteer, B. J. Lebow, naive, generous, innocent (the kind of innocent who is capable of doing evil out of sheer ignorance), who challenges the two Brits—considering them contemptible racists—with her schoolgirl idealism. Exasperated, Heather shoots back,

> They're savages, pure and simple. When you realize that, as I did—and I was just like you B. J., when I arrived, full of idealism and let's give the chaps a fair chance—when you realize that, you're content and you stop fighting people's battles for them. You wait and see. You'll change.[82]

Alas, B. J., in her ignorance, sets the stage for violence. She is raped by an African whom she trusts, and responding in horror and confusion, she drowns. Shortly thereafter Miss Poole is dismissed from her post as headmistress and Heather, her replacement, is hacked to death by Rose, Miss Poole's sullen albino servant. From the pointless mental warfare between the two English schoolmarms to the chaos in nature and the disorder in society which this novel unravels, like some terrible nightmare, is one grotesque vignette after the other. The novel is brilliant, without a doubt, and deeply unsettling. One critic has suggested that Theroaux developed a liking for Africa during his long stay in Malawi and Uganda. It is very difficult to find anything of the sort in these works, but then, it is hard to find a "liking" for anyone, anyplace, anything, in Theroux, and this includes anything he writes about his native country as well. *Girls at Play*, a prime example of his early fiction, replete with luminous detail of landscape and scalpel-sharp dissections of personality is not the work of one charmed by Africa. The idea is alien to Theroux's anti-romantic sensibilities. He has been often praised for his honesty as a writer, and this seems fair, but sometimes his work takes on a misanthropic tone so harsh that one recoils.

In this regard, a long passage from Theroux's erotic, often exotic, very funny, and presumably autobiographical novel, *My Secret History*, which contains extensive African scenes, is revealing. Here, the main character, Andre Parent, is listening to Jenny, his bride-to-be, who is complaining about the changes their love affair has made in her life, and the control she has surrendered to him:

"I can learn [to drive the African roads]. I've driven in Africa. I speak Swahili," she said. "I'm not stupid. I have an Oxford degree—and you made me quit my job."

Later,

> Now I'm just like all these expatriate wives I used to pity
> and despise. I'm a memsahib—you made me a memsahib. I
> stay home and wait for you.

After some further grievances, where Jenny complains that she
had originally come to teach Africans, Parent explodes,

> Teaching Africans what? How to speak English. How to do
> Math. That's ridiculous. I'm sick of doing it—sick of hearing
> about it. Half the students here are married and have fami-
> lies, and they pretend they're schoolboys. They say they
> want to go abroad and study. They're lying—they want to
> get out and never come back. They hate their lives. They
> want a ticket to England or America. They hate farming.
> They want to wear suits and neckties. Those girls you were
> teaching will all end up in a village pounding corn in a
> wooden mortar. They'll have ten kids each and a drunken
> husband. What is the point of teaching anything here except
> farming?[83]

When Parent claims, against Jenny's charge that he dislikes
Africans, that "the only friends I've had for more than four years
here have been Africans—and some Indians" the disclaimer seems
hollow. His relationships with Africans (and Indians) are, like those
with the British or other whites, largely superficial, constrained by
a distant reserve which seems more British than American. Parent
literally drips with scorn when Jenny mentions an allusion he had
made earlier to the "bare-assed Karamojong."

> That's perfect. Pretend you don't see their dongs. Pretend
> this is a real city. Pretend they don't kill each other. Pre-
> tend they don't envy and hate you. Pretend you're not
> white. Pretend they're not staring at your tits. Pretend your
> teaching is helping the country. Pretend you're not here to
> have a grand old time in the bush. Pretend that in a few
> years there's going to be a big improvement in Uganda. Pre-
> tend the president is not a total asshole as well as a mur-
> derer, a torturer—.[84]

As in many of Theroux's travel books, the reader needs a pause, a
long breath. At times one is inclined to agree with such trenchant
observations: "yes . . . no doubt it is like that; he's right." But it is
all so relentless. Humor there is aplenty, but very little of the
redemptive humor of a Bellow, or a Boyle. One is reminded, in
Theroux's portraits of whites in Africa, of the unpleasant portraits

of meddling whites in the works of Graham Greene, especially in his 1961 novel of central Africa, *A Burnt-Out Case* and in his 1948 work, *The Heart of the Matter*, set in Sierra Leone during the War years.[85] Greene's whites are typically well-meaning but disconnected, absurdly misplaced visionaries; burnt-out cases filled with malaise; or cynical unregenerate reactionaries. Theroux's Africans range the gamut, but they, like Greene's, have little power to act, or if they do, they act within corrupt hierarchies (remnants of colonial bureaucracies) or within irrational tribal patterns, caught up in violence they cannot control. Perhaps this represents a new, or at least revived, stereotype which makes Africans into pawns of forces that cannot contain, or understand.

Some of Theroux's characters remind one of the star-crossed characters in the excellent novel by Ronald Hardy, *Rivers of Darkness* (1979); the tale of several World Health Organization workers (Dr. Harry Lynd, a Scottish physician, Annie Yeomans, an English nurse) caught up in the revolution in Mozambique in the 1970s. They, too, mean well and labor with great energy to help the Africans around them, but despite their dedication to eradicating river blindness, and the aid they provide to a revolutionary named Santarem, in the end they have virtually no positive impact, if not a negative impact, on the horrific conditions of disease and war that surround them.[86]

It is arguable that this kind of sensibility, poststructuralist and postmodernist "discourse" theories aside, has dominated the vision of contemporary "expatriate" writers whatever their nationality. Though Africa, in many of Theroux's works, may no longer be the "heart" of darkness, it is still the Africa of irrational forces which no westerner can fully comprehend, and Africans, as in the past, are victims of forces beyond their control. Assuredly a man of this terrible century, Theroux cannot escape those themes that any serious twentieth-century artist is bound to reflect. The "killing fields" of Southeast Asia, the murderous decimations of Central and South America, the fratricides and genocides of Europe, might have removed Africa from its former "centrality" as an abode of darkness. Still, Conrad would surely recognize in the works of Theroux that same darkness beneath that thrumming exterior. In the final analysis (despite the combative tone of almost-hope that springs repeatedly from failure in his magnificent novel, *The Mosquito Coast*) Paul Theroux' works, and particularly his novels of Africa, share a great deal with that prescient Polish genius whom Theroux himself has openly admired since his career began. What Theroux seems to have found in Africa, amid all the drama and melodrama, absurdity, hilarity, and struggle, is that same heart of darkness.

Finally, there are several American novels of contemporary Africa, typically filled with sardonic disillusionment, which seem to represent an extension of the genre within the U.S. and the larger world. Among the best of these is *Lovers of the African Night*, by William Duggan, a sequel to *The Great Thirst*. This 1987 novel set in Southern Africa (Kalahariland, in Botswana) from the Second World War to the 1980s, chronicles the lives of several generations of resourceful "BaNare" women (from Ata Four all the way back to Ata One) whose primary role is to serve the BaNare men in the rural town of Naring, just across the border from South Africa. Many of these men are itinerant laborers who work on short-term (annual) contracts in South African cities, living in strictly segregated "locations" and returning periodically to Botswana. Which, of course, is where the women come in. This chronicle of a family of prostitutes might seem, at first glance, a strange way to tell the story of an abused extended clan who live not only on a geographical (political) border but also at the margins of traditional and industrial society. But Duggan makes it work somehow, mostly through a controlled bare-bones prose.

> Winter was the season for court cases, weddings, council meetings, funerals and feasts, when all the BaNare were back from their fields and eager for the company of Naring. The oldest among them refused to die in summer, alone in their fields with no one there. If they felt death coming on, they would sit down and conserve their remaining breath until winter, when they could die in Naring with everyone watching.[87]

Duggan's prose, though entirely distinct in content, is reminiscent of the spare but evocative narratives of Michigan novelist Jim Harrison (*Dalva*, *Farmer*, *Sundog*, etc.), whose works chronicle mid-American scenes, or, if they include an occasional episode in Mexico or Europe, are set in the heartland. In Duggan's African works there is a similar capacity to encapsulate decades into a trenchant paragraph, and to convey a sense of personal loss (if not nostalgia) amid chaotic events. Certain characters act with courage, but they are not heroes in the classic sense. It is enough if they survive. In *Lovers of the African Night*, young Kanye, the son of Ata Four, wounded (and photographed) while defying guns with rocks at the bloody Sharptown massacre, witness to the slaughter of innocents, separated from his lover, Claire Vlei, returns crippled to his mother's shop at the end of the story:

> As for Kanye himself, he worked for his mother, driving the truck, counting money and crates. At night he sat with

the customers, discussing the news of the week, awaiting that miraculous day when his knee would heal and his face would no longer be famous. Whenever a stranger mentioned South Africa, Kanye sat down at his table and spoke the words that pained his mother, an echo of her own: echo of herself:

"Did you come from South Africa?" said Kanye. "Did you see Claire Vlei?"[88]

Duggan's work, like that of Norman Rush, W. T. Tyler, and perhaps the best of the lot, Maria Thomas, is also distinguished by a distancing of writer and object that is very typical of a weary and cynical era, these final years of the twentieth century. In most of these novels absurdity reigns amid chaos or near-chaos (no traditional "home" remains intact, no village is unviolated, no family is unbroken), and one paradox after the other is revealed. For example, in *Whites*, a collection of short stories by Norman Rush, another American who has experience in Botswana and southern Africa, we are introduced to a strange region of the mind (framed by a dry desert scape, treeless, and lonely), where the gulf between whites and Africans never seems deeper. In one story, "Near Pala," two British couples, driving across the desert on an indescribably bad road in a Land Rover, commence to talk about Africans. Nan, somewhat "liberal" and well-meaning, is loudly trying to care about the poverty-stricken people. First she takes on her cynical husband Gareth, as well as soft-spoken Tess and the other husband Tom, whenever they breathe a word of scorn or disdain, which they frequently do.

Tom said, "We put in the roads and they don't maintain them, do they? They think a road is a thing like your fingernail—chip it and it will grow back. Well, they're wrong, aren't they?"

Nan said, "It's unfair. We bring in all these metal and plastic things and bottles that don't decay. In the old times, they could leave anything about and it was organic—it would decay or be eaten. Even as it is, the goats eat a lot of the plastic. Look at the courtyards, Tess. They are as neat as you like. They sweep them morning and evening."

"Yes, everything goes into the lane," Gareth said.[89]

As the story unfolds, deep in the desert amid a terrible drought, driving at speed through a region where they cannot stop without bogging the vehicle in deep ruts, they come upon distant figures who emerge as "Bushies" (!Kung)—apparently a mother carrying an infant, and two daughters, who are uncharacteristically begging for water. Nan insists they stop (they have water bottles) but Gareth refuses, grinding on, ignoring Nan's almost hysterical pleas. Nan throws a water bottle out and Gareth stops the Land Rover suddenly,

> "One of us must collect the water bottle." Gareth says, and when Tom starts to do so he stops him.
> "One of us must collect the bottle" Gareth said again.[90]

With this command, apparently, the proper order has been restored, at least amongst these four Britishers within the confines of a Land Rover. In such works, clearly, Africa is no longer the mere playground for expatriates that it was in the time of Hemingway, Ruark, and the newly fashionable Paul Bowles.[91] Yet, when we look hard at the novels themselves, especially at their language, we find that Africa remains different, distinct, even unique. It may be a place (*the* place if the writer is seeking Eden) where terrible weakness is unveiled, where mankind is allegedly at its worst, a place where one struggles fruitlessly for personal integrity or meaning, where contradictions reign, but it is also the same Africa which in the end challenges the outsider, where the very environment itself is personified. Certainly, in these stories by Norman Rush, this is so, and Rush's acclaimed novel, *Mating*, which won the National Book Award in 1991, is a larger extension of this essential idea, that Africa "is a stage on which the individual weaknesses of Europeans—Americans—who venture there emerge in their most dramatic form.[92]

What, then, do we make of John Updike's exceptional 1978 novel, *The Coup*, a work in which Africa is not so much a world apart as it is a contemporary extension of an American region of mind peculiar to Updike himself? This is not to say that the fictional "Kush," portrayed in Updike's inimitable prose is not recognizable as African:

> Kush is a land of delicate, delectable emptiness, named for a vanished kingdom, the progeny of Kush, son of Ham, grandson of Noah.[93]

Updike has done his reading: has traveled in the interior "Soudan" and knows its reaches across the dry savannah, now encroached upon by desert sand, overpopulated, overgrazed, overused for millennia. As he puts it: "The last elephant north of the Grionde [river] gave up its life and its ivory in 1959, with a bellow that still reverberates."[94] His portrait of a land beset by hunger and drought, yet full of ancient vitality, is drawn by its President,

Colonel Hakim Felix Ellellôu. The President is a Muslim intellectual, born in 1933 of the "rape of a Salu woman by a Nubian
raider," a veteran of Dienbienphu (a mere sergeant then), who later
emerged from the shadows of anti-colonial resistance (in Algeria
and elsewhere) to inherit power in the recently independent state
of Kush. Though a place only loosely connected to an ancient
(largely fictional) kingdom of that name, Kush's King still holds
nominal powers. Ellellôu's view is literate, informed, sardonic,
often bitter. He can be tender, violent, brutal, and compassionate.
The American reader may also find him judgmental. Of an arrogant American, soon to become the victim of a Tuareg mob, immo-
lated atop a huge pile of contraband smuggled in under CIA
auspices, Ellellôu says,

> I felt I knew this man well. As is common in his swollen
> country, he was monstrously tall, with hands of many
> knuckles and fingernails the width of five-lu. His age was
> not easy to estimate; the premature gray and show-me
> squint of these Yankees is muddled in with their something
> eternally puerile, awkward, winning, and hopeful. They
> want, these sons of the simultaneously most expansionist
> and most avowedly idealistic of power aggregations, to have
> things both ways: to eat both the chicken and the egg, to be
> both triumphant and coddled, to seem both shrewd and
> ingenuous.[95]

Ellellôu knows whereof he speaks (that is, Updike knows the
appropriate words to put in his mouth), since he understands
America too, or fancies that he does; one of his wives, daughter of a
Tutsi chief, had been educated in a small black Alabama college
and speaks idiomatic American. Ellellôu had been educated there
himself, at a college in Wisconsin (before he took Islam seriously
and renounced the mindless materialism of the West), and his
experience there—like Nkrumah's—has forever affected him; he
hates that "land of devils," capitalist, secular America, with the pas-
sion that only a former lover can hold. But he had a lover there as
well, whom, we later discover, is his shuttered second wife, held in
purdah, in near-secret, the "Muffled One," Candice, shrewish and
bitchy beyond belief. "Don't give me this Kismet crap," she rails at
one point, "I knew you when you couldn't tell the Koran from the
Sears Roebuck Catalogue."[96] Candy is the incarnation of the mindless American (maybe barely believable as a real person, certainly
overblown). At least in his relations with women, particularly American women, Ellellôu possesses ambivalence. His ruthless lieutenant, Ezena, has none. The latter's tirades (of equal parts vitriol
and brilliance) against America and all things American are back-

drop to the unfolding drama of this novel; what indeed must the President do with the American Klipspringer, and his many-strings-attached aid package?

Not surprisingly, the American aid comes at the price of Ellellôu's office; he is undermined and overthrown, hides, attempts a comeback, and ends up with his American-educated Watutsi wife in exile in France. Ellellôu is unquestionably one of Updike's more memorable characters, in some ways a triumphant *tour de force* of creative imagination. Admittedly, everything is irony in *The Coup*, and Updike characteristically succeeds in mowing down one stereotype after another in the course of his narrative. Surely, however, there are many readers who have known Africa, and who have seen dictators and military men come and go (few, if any, quite so erudite as the fictional Ellellôu), in places somewhat less fantastic than Updike's Kush, who must wonder at the Africa Updike has recreated here—an Africa not without certain romantic embellishments.

Unromantic in the extreme is *Horn of Africa* by Philip Caputo, a horrifying novel of war at its worst. Caputo is without doubt one of the best American writers whose works span America's conflicts from Vietnam to the Gulf War, an international reporter of first rank, a novelist of undisputed power. *A Rumor of War*, his 1977 memoir, based on his shattering experience as a Marine Lieutenant in Vietnam in 1965-1966, stands almost twenty years after its publication as the best of its kind, head and shoulders above hundreds since published.[97] *Horn of Africa*, which appeared in 1980, is Caputo's tale of mercenary warfare in the crucible of violence which has torn Eritrea for much of the past three decades.[98] In many ways, this violent, fascinating story is a psychological portrait of a certain kind of international mercenary not uncommon in our world. Jeremy Nordstrand is a Nietzchean monster, super-trained, a sociopath honed to kill, American-made but uncontained by any nationality, unconstrained by any moral code, a man spawned by this bloody age, cunning, powerful, uncompromising, murderous, savage to the core, a modern barbarian machine, an engine of destruction and death, who has chosen an old African war to act out his murderous passions.

> Jeremy Nordstrand was a miracle of human genetics. Nature had designed him for survival, like a shark. Unable to bear the thought of the ambush taking place without him, he issued a general call-up of his body's natural defenses. They too obeyed unquestioningly his implacable will, closed ranks, and fought to repel the alien disease that had invaded him. . . . [Soon] he was able to walk about, though unsteadily; he could look into the light, though he still had

to wear sunglasses. He had literally commanded himself to recover, and I was afraid he would on time, and had no idea of what I would do if he did.[99]

What he does is lead men who are almost as hard as himself into oblivion. Gage, the narrator, survives, but he has discovered a capacity for barbarism inside himself, peeled down to that essential savagery that lurks beneath the veneer of civility, which in the end makes him a victim too. Caputo's view of humanity is harsh and uncompromising.

Of course the place is not accidental. This "old" African war in Africa's Horn whose origins reach back into the Middle Ages (when Muslim and Christian fought across the Abyssinian escarpments for slaves, booty, and power), had been transformed in the 1960s into an extension of the "Cold War" between East and West, into the kind of bloodbath that only external governments (like the U.S. and the U.S.S.R.) could support, with massive infusions of "military aid," advisors, mercenaries, and the hypo-technology of late-twentieth-century militarism. Africa's Horn (once called "the Hell-hole of creation" by a European traveler) provides the elemental setting, its scorched black rock, dusty plains, hellish winds, its ancient feuds, and the infusion of all the worst that modern weapons and modern ideologies can bring, all these provide the stage for this acting out, a horrific *anabasis* without reprieve. In one sense, therefore, Africa is almost incidental to Caputo's unrelenting narration, to its meaningless climax, when Nordstrand (along with the strangely loyal Osman, and the misguided Englishman, Moody) meets his much-deserved end. Nonetheless, as he penned this gritty tale, Caputo must have been aware that Africa has long been imaged as a place where civility and honor, decency and compassion, loyalty and virtue, and all the trappings of rational legalism are stripped away by events. On one level, therefore, *because* it is set in Africa and not in some other equally war-torn region (Beirut is the primary setting for Caputo's equally brutal and compelling novel, *Del Corso's Gallery*), *Horn* is another almost Conradian work. Internecine war, corruption, famine, the corrosive influence of power politics (especially via American and Soviet intrigue) eventually reduce the characters to the most elemental level. Another heart of darkness is unveiled. Yet, on another level, Africa for Caputo is more of a backdrop to this tale of violence (and of the incipient capacity for evil in all mankind) than it is intrinsic to it. Caputo, the Vietnam veteran, who has dauntlessly reported nearly every war since (his career, chronicled in his 1991 autobiography *Means of Escape*[100]) could have set this particular story in any of a dozen places— Afghanistan, Iran, Lebanon, Southeast Asia, Nicaragua, El Salvador, the Philippines, Indonesia, Eastern Europe, and yes, inside the U.S. itself—without losing an iota of its power.

Of course this does not mean that readers, expecting the images that Africa evokes to be fulfilled, do not look to those negative images themselves. Africa, as revealed in this novel, will unfortunately not disappoint them.

The final work considered here, a haunting novel by Maria Thomas, *Antonia Saw the Oryx First* (1987), like all works of art, is difficult to classify.[101] Maria Thomas is the pen name of the late Roberta Warrick, who was killed with her husband in a tragic plane crash in Ethiopia in 1989 that also took the lives of U.S. Congressman Mickey Leland and his entourage. Thomas's book is emphatically a novel of Africa, literally brimming with portraits and pictures which could only be African. Like Theroux (though the comparison ends there) Warrick also had long experience in Africa, beginning with Peace Corps service in Ethiopia in 1971, followed by extensive residence in Nigeria, Tanzania, Kenya, and Liberia.

The story in itself is unusual, even unexpected, especially when one has grown accustomed to formula escapist works, neo-romantic quest stories, or even the cynical exposé within a well-worn realism which seems to find new shape in Africa in every decade. Basically the story revolves around two distinct characters; as different as two humans could possibly be, yet akin in spirit. Antonia is a Tanzanian-born white American (the child of a coffee planter and his conventional mid-American spouse), working as a physician in a run-down hospital in contemporary Dar es Salaam. At first Antonia seems to be the typical African-born expatriate: she has white friends, like her sometime lover Brian McGeorge (he is Kenyan-born), who survive and even thrive on a combination of practical cynicism and existential cleverness, shifting and paring conscience, manipulating their way. Another (also a sometime lover) is the ex Peace Corps volunteer, Ted Armstrong, a man "perpetually pissed off" because "he couldn't *believe*—even after ten years—that something as profound as this idea of going with a gift of technology was going to fail."[102] Antonia, we discover, not only lives in a quite "unsuitable" African suburb, she is also estranged from her African husband, Paul Luenga, brilliant, Harvard educated, reformist and even revolutionary in his views, yet irrevocably linked to his past. She has left him because he cannot, in fact, reconcile himself to what she represents in his eyes:

> The beginning of anger like his was a kind of self-hate, because he had been Westernized. That made the wedge that his family widened. Behind the tolerance and the good-natured banter [laughing as he tried to skin a goat] they were only waiting. . . .

Even though they let her [Antonia] help cook and serve the food, taught her how to prepare tea their way . . . all the time they were holding interviews with Helen's father [the father of Paul's African wife] without saying a word to either of them.[103]

Once a man of vast hope, Paul has become angry over the years, and disaffected, hating the exploitative Western world and blaming whites for Africa's manifold problems, and Antonia, forced to deal with him regularly because he is a physician in the same hospital, watches with pain as his once inspired anger turns to bitterness. Antonia is more than typically sensitive to nuances of race and culture, especially to the nuances of cross-cultural and inter-racial love in a modern African setting. She is especially sensitive to this in part because her mother, who had fled to America after the death of her father, truly hates Africa and Africans, endlessly warning her daughter about "them." Antonia, on the contrary, can imagine no other place to live; though she seems unaware of this, she is wedded to Africa every bit as firmly as is Paul.

The other major character is Esther Moro, ex-prostitute, semi-literate, once a "bush" girl who has suffered physical abuse (genital mutilation with a broken bottle) at the hands of a Greek sailor. Though terribly threatened, she is possessed of a kind of resilience that surpasses understanding. She meets Antonia when the latter treats her awful wounds, and the two gradually become close. It is a moving story indeed, though related entirely without sentimentality. Esther, deeply engaged with others, empathic, compassionate, influenced by memories of her illiterate father who had worked as a helper in a rural clinic, soon discovers in herself an inborn capacity to heal. Though she attempts to link this gift, expressed via traditional African modes (a laying on of hands, a ritual-based process connected to a spirit world) with modern technology and the scientific base of modern medicine which she stands in awe of, Esther cannot do so. Around her things are breaking down. No avenue is available, not through modern education, nor through the dying traditional way. It is clear that somehow she must find another way and she seems to think she can. She can interpret dreams and draw on nature.

Esther also has her love, Nkosi, a man seemingly unsuited to her, a black South African poet, exiled, a revolutionary seeking peace, uncomfortable with his own anger, who had sought another world as a photographer in Sweden and England, but returned to another African country. He finds a kind of peace in kindly Esther, but recurrent bilharzia and malaria, contracted in his guerrilla career, have knocked him down and in the end, despite all that Esther can do, or Antonia with her western medicine, he dies.

In the end, though the two women have touched one another at a level beyond speech, they cannot remain linked. We know that Antonia will have to return to America, where (though educated there, though her mother lives there) she has nothing. She too will be exiled.

Throughout this extraordinary novel there is an ineffable tone of sadness and loss, yet, it must be said, this is not nostalgia for the Lost Eden of the romantic Africa we have come to know so well. The Africa of Maria Thomas is far more than that. The Africa we see in *Antonia Saw the Oryx First*, as in "The Jiru Road" and other stories published in the posthumous *African Visas*, is an Africa seen from within rather than from without.[104] To be sure it is an Africa rent by misuse and abuse, torn by history, wrenched by racial and ethnic rivalry, but these are felt as background only. In *Antonia* they frame the human story, told on a human scale of small events, seen from an earthly perspective, felt in the bones of women, known through the daily routines of Esther Moro and Antonia Redmond who seemed so entirely different.

Perhaps in the final analysis there is hope that is revealed in art, especially the novelist's art. Hemingway, though he could not escape the paradigms or conventions of an Africa which he could only see with a hunter's eye, was captured by Africa perhaps more than by any "place" he ever saw, or even any place he ever lived. His posthumous novel *Garden of Eden*, strange in its sexual triad (modern beyond its time in that sense), forced in the telling, nevertheless has at its heart a memory of Africa, revealed in the novel being written by David, the main character, an Africa which, for this character, is home.[105]

Likewise, beyond the siren call of romantic legends and nostalgia for times gone by (the era of the white hunter, the white highlands, the time when Africans were servants, helpers, shadows, supporters, extras), beyond the purely physical, that brilliant and luminous environment which has so affected American writers, beyond even the resurrected frontier with all its images of Edens lost (or found), Africa has proved to be a special place for Americans, a place— obviously—they can identify with. The best of our writers, it is clear, have found that continent irresistible. It is a good bet that this will not change, no matter what new and unexpected comes out of Africa.

Notes

1. Joseph Conrad, *Heart of Darkness* (New York: New American Library, 1980 [1902]).
2. Karin Hansson, "Two Journeys into the Country of the Mind: Joseph Conrad's *Heart of Darkness* and Saul Bellow's *Henderson the Rain King*, in ed. Mirko Jurak, *Cross Cultural Studies* (Ljubljana: Unce delavnice, Ljubljana, 1989), 435.
3. Chinua Achebe, "An Image of Africa: Racism in Conrad's 'Heart of Darkness,'" *The Massachusetts Review* 18, no. 4 (Winter 1977): 782-94.
4. Anthony Fothergill, *Heart of Darnkess* (Philadelphia: Open University Press, 1989).
5. Martin Green, *Dreams of Adventure, Deeds of Empire* (New York: Basic Books, 1979), 297-319.
6. Allan Hunter, *Joseph Conrad and the Ethics of Darwinism* (London: Croon Helm, 1983).
7. Marianna Torgovnick, *Gone Primitive: Savage Intellects, Modern Lives* (Chicago: University of Chicago Press, 1990). Torgovnick's savaging of Conrad (141-58) represents a fashionable version of contemporary textual criticism, whereby the practical opposite of what one reads *in the text* of the novel itself is alleged through clever deconstruction and quotes taken out-of-context.
8. Edward Said, *Orientalism* (New York: Vintage Books, 1979).
9. Among those who see *Heart of Darkness* as central to a new kind of twentieth-century literature is V. S. Naipaul. See "Conrad's Darkness," in ed. Robert D. Hammer, *Joseph Conrad: Third World Perspectives* (Washington, D.C.: Three Continents Press, 1990), 189-200.
10. Conrad, 102-103.
11. Edgar Rice Burroughs, *Tarzan of the Apes* (New York: New American Library, 1990 [1912]).
12. Ibid., 29, 96.
13. Ibid., 94.
14. Ibid., 136.
15. John G. Cawelti, *Adventure, Mystery, and Romance: Formula Stories as Art and Popular Culture* (Chicago: University of Chicago Press, 1976), 233.
16. Albert Memmi, *The Colonizer and the Colonized* (Boston: The Beacon Press, 1967) is a superb philosophical study of the paternalistic mentality of the colonizer and its impact on those colonized. There are, of course, scores of works on the essential racism behind this paternalism. From a psychological viewpoint the best works are Franz Fanon, *Peau noire, masques blancs* (Paris: Seuil, 1952) and his later work, *Les Damnes de la terre* (Paris: Maspero, 1961).
17. Herbert Spencer, *Principles of Sociology*, 3 vols. (London: D. Appleton and Co., 1898-1899) was the basis of the mistaken idea that social evolution had followed a path parallel, if not identical to, biological evolution.
18. Franz Boas, especially *The Mind of Primitive Man* (New York: MacMillan, 1938), directly challenged the idea (equally popular among scientists of

his day) that the differences between human groups could be categorized according to superior and inferior attributes and that these reflected a hereditary process.

19. Gore Vidal, "Tarzan Revisited," an Introduction to the Signet Classic Edition of *Tarzan of the Apes* (New York: Signet Books, 1990), 10.

20. William Shakespeare, *Henry IV, Part II* (Dubuque, Iowa: W. C. Brown, 1971).

21. Marion Berghahn, *Images of Africa in Black American Literature* (Totowa, N.J.: Rowman and Littlefield, 1977); Patrick Brantlinger, *Rule of Darkness: British Literature and Imperialism 1830-1914* (Ithaca, N.Y.: Cornell University Press, 1988).

22. Dorothy Hammand and Alta Jablow, *The Africa That Never Was: Four Generations of British Writing About Africa* (New York: Twayne Publishers, 1983); G. D. Killam, *Africa in English Fiction 1874-1939* (Ibadan, Nigeria: Ibadan University Press, 1968).

23. Abdul R. JanMohamed, *Manichean Aesthetics: The Politics of Literature in Colonial Africa* (Amherst: University of Massachusetts Press, 1983); George Shepperson, *Africa in American History and Literature* (Oxford, Oxford University Press, 1979).

24. Joseph Campbell, *The Masks of God*, 4 vols. (New York: Penguin Books, 1969).

25. Peter Forbath, *The Last Hero* (New York: Simon and Schuster, 1988).

26. Jeremy Bernstein, "The Dark Continent of Henry Stanley," *The New Yorker* (31 December 1990): 93-107.

27. Mary Jobe Akeley, *Carl Akeley's Africa* (New York: Cornwell Press, 1929), 35.

28. Ernest Hemingway, *Green Hills of Africa* (New York: Scribners, 1956 [1935]), 151, 152.

29. Ibid., 152.

30. Robert W. Lewis, "Vivienne de Watteville, Hemingway's Companion on Kilimanjaro," in John M. Howell, *Hemingway's African Stories: The Stories, Their Sources, Their Critics* (New York: Scribners, 1969), 101-9.

31. Hemingway, *Greens Hills*, 49.

32. See, Kenneth M. Cameron, *Into Africa: The Story of the East African Safari* (London: Constable and Co., 1990), 93-94, for an interesting analysis of Hemingway's African works and their influence on the whole idea of the African safari. Also see Bartle Bull, *Safari: A Chronicle of Adventure* (London: Viking, 1988), 275-83.

33. Hemingway, *Green Hills*, 194.

34. Robert Ruark, *Something of Value* (Garden City, N.Y.: Doubleday and Co., 1955) and *Uhuru* (New York: McGraw Hill, 1962). Also see, Ruark, *Use Enough Gun* (London: Hamish Hamilton, 1966).

35. Ruark, *Uhuru*, 190.

36. Ruark, *Something of Value*, 202.

37. John D. Chick, "The World of the White: European Alienation in the Novels of Robert Ruark," in ed. Paul F. Nursey-Bray, *Aspects of African Identity: Five Essays* (Makerere, Uganda: Makerere Institute of Social Research, 1973), 81.

38. Ibid., 80-81.
39. Ruark, *Something of Value*, 488.
40. Joyce Cary's *Mister Johnson* (New York: New Directions, 1989 [1939]). This novel, along with *Assia Saved* (London: Michael Joseph, 1952 [1931]), *An American Visitor* (London: Michael Joseph, 1952 [1932]) and *The African Witch* (London: Michael Joseph, 1951 [1936]), established Cary as one of the more sensitive British writers of the immediate pre-war era. Cary's satiric condemnation of British colonialist ineptitude and misrule and his ironic (also comic) portraits of Africans as victims, tended for decades to hide the fact that Cary disdained Africa and Africans. Though it might be going to far to categorize his work among the "racist romance" of the time, according to Abdul R. JanMohamed it is obvious to any careful reader of his work that Cary neither liked nor admired Africans. Further analysis is available in Jonah Raskin, *The Mythology of Imperialism* (New York: Random House, 1971), especially the chapter entitled "Mr. Johnson On the Road," 294-309.
41. Ruark, *Uhuru*, 9.
42. Gerald Hanley, *Gilligan's Last Elephant* (Greenwich, Conn.: Fawcett Gold Medal Books, 1962). This is also entitled *The Last Safari* in later American editions.
43. Ibid., 184.
44. Ibid., 192.
45. Elenore Smith Bowen, *Return to Laughter* (Garden City, N.Y.: Doubleday and Co., 1964 [1954]).
46. Ibid, 230.
47. Ibid., 231.
48. Alex Haley, *Roots* (Garden City, N.Y.: Doubleday and Co., 1976), 121.
49. Peter Abrahams, *Mine Boy* (London: Longmans, 1946), *Tell Freedom* (New York: Knopf, 1954) and *Wild Conquest* (London: Faber and Faber, 1961). Chinua Achebe, *Things Fall Apart* (London: Heinemann, 1958), *No Longer at Ease* (New York: I. Obolensky, 1961) and *Girls at War* (Garden City, N.Y.: Doubleday and Co., 1973). Ngugi wa Thiong'o, *A Grain of Wheat* (London: Heinemann, 1967) and *The River Between* (London: Heinemann, 1965).
50. Igor Kopytoff and Suzanne Meirs, eds., *Slavery in Africa: Historical and Anthropological Perspectives* (Madison: University of Wisconsin Press, 1977), especially chapter 13 by Martin A. Klein, 335-63.
51. Claude Meillassoux, ed., *L'esclavage en Afrique precoloniale* (Paris: F. Maspero, 1975), remains the best single account for this region of Africa.
52. Frank Yerby, *The Dahomean* (New York: Dell, 1971).
53. Ibid., 152.
54. Alice Walker, *The Color Purple* (New York: Washington Square Press, 1982), 210.
55. Edmund Morel, *Red Rubber* (London: T. Fisher Unwin, 1906); Mark Twain, *King Leopold's Soliloquy* (Boston: P.R. Warren Co., 1905); Ruth Slade, *King Leopold's Congo* (New York: Oxford University Press, 1962).

56. Alice Walker, *Possessing the Secret of Joy* (New York: Harcourt Brace Jovanovich, 1992), 283.

57. Ibid., 64.

58. Ibid., 147.

59. Ibid., 194.

60. Ibid., 193.

61. Ibid., 191.

62. Ibid., 208.

63. Charles Johnson, *Middle Passage* (New York: Atheneum, 1990).

64. Richard Wright, *Black Power* (New York: Harper, 1954); W. E. B. Du Bois, *Dusk of Dawn: An Essay Toward An Autobiography of a Race Concept* (New York: Harcourt, Brace and Co., 1940); David Jenkins, *Black Zion: Africa, Imagined and Real, as Seen by Today's Blacks* (New York: Harcourt Brace Jovanovich, 1975).

65. Daniel Majdiak, "The Romantic Self and *Henderson the Rain King*," in ed. Harry R. Garvin, *Makers of the Twentieth Century Novel* (Lewisburg, Pa.: Bucknell University Press, 1977), 276-89. Majdiak's focus is on renewal and resurrection in Bellow's novel, worked out, he claims, according to Wordsworth's terms (283). The African "setting"—as a place where Henderson can work out his salvation—is all-important in this regard, since *Henderson* is not a romantic work. Regarding Conrad, see the excellent analysis by Jonah Raskin in Jonah Raskin, *The Mythology of Imperialism* (New York: Random House, 1971), 126-205.

66. David A. Anderson, "Hemingway and Henderson in the High Savannahs, or Two Midwestern Moderns and the Myth of Africa," *MidAmerica* 15 (May 1988): 98.

67. Saul Bellow, *Henderson the Rain King* (New York: Fawcett, 1969 [1958]), 282.

68. Ibid., 283-86.

69. Ibid., 283.

70. Hansson, 435-444. Hansson's investigation of the legend of the Holy Grail, as well as other quest literature, is especially interesting as applied to Bellow's novel. For Henderson, clearly, Africa's Manichean nature—the Kingdom of Light versus the Kingdom of Darkness—is all important. What makes Bellow's novel exceptional, if not unique, is its deliberate use of "brightest" Africa rather than "darkest" Africa at a time when the latter still dominated western literature.

71. Peter Viertel, *White Hunter, Black Heart* (London: W. H. Allen, 1954), 76.

72. Michael Crichton, *Congo* (New York: Alfred A Knopf, 1980).

73. Ibid., 161.

74. Milan Kalous, *Cannibals and Tonga Players of Sierra Leone* (Trentham, New Zealand: Wright and Carman, 1974).

75. T. Coraghessan Boyle, *Water Music* (New York: Penguin Books, 1981), 352.

76. Ibid., 121.

77. Peter Forbath, *The Last Hero* (New York: Simon and Schuster, 1988), 584.

78. Ibid., 250.

79. Samuel Coale, *Paul Theroux* (Boston: Twayne Publishers, 1987). Coale covers Theroux' work up through the publication of *O'Zone* in 1986. Coale accuses Theroux of a kind of "double-edged romanticism that . . . parallels America's own cultural contradictions" (138), yet on the whole he sees a dark vision in the body of his fiction, a "Jamesian confrontation between American innocence and a darker, more mysterious landscape" beneath the brilliant focus on the individual, the inner self, however deluded. It is hard to argue with this, yet the earlier "African" novels, in this writer's view, emphasize images of hopelessness, decay, and darkness, more akin to Conrad than to any American writer who comes to mind.

80. William Boyd, *An Ice Cream War* (London: Hanish Hamilton, 1982) and *A Good Man in Africa* (New York: William Morrow, 1982).

81. Paul Theroux, *Girls at Play* (London: Hamish Hamilton, 1978 [1969]), 40.

82. Ibid., 90.

83. Theroux, *My Secret History* (New York: Ballantine Books, 1989), 301-302.

84. Ibid., 303.

85. Graham Greene, *A Burnt-Out Case* (New York: The Viking Press, 1961) and *The Heart of the Matter* (New York: The Viking Press, 1948).

86. Ronald Hardy, *Rivers of Darkness* (New York: Putnam's Sons, 1979).

87. William Duggan, *Lovers of the African Night* (New York: Delacourt Press, 1987), 40. This novel is the sequel to *The Great Thirst* (London: Hutchinson and Co., 1985).

88. Duggan, *Lovers*, 226.

89. Norman Rush, *Whites* (New York: Alfred A Knopf, 1986), 19-20.

90. Ibid., 30-31.

91. Paul Bowles, *The Sheltering Sky* (New York: New Directions, 1948).

92. Norman Rush, *Mating* (New York: Alfred A Knopf, 1991).

93. John Updike, *The Coup* (New York: Penguin, 1980 [1978]), 10.

94. Ibid., 11.

95. Ibid., 37.

96. Ibid., 104.

97. Philip Caputo, *A Rumor of War* (New York: Ballantine Books, 1977).

98. Philip Caputo, *Horn of Africa* (New York: Dell, 1980).

99. Ibid., 486.

100. Philip Caputo, *Means of Escape* (New York: Harper Collins, 1991).

101. Maria Thomas, *Antonia Saw the Oryx First* (London: Serpent's Tail, 1988 [1987]).

102. Ibid., 125.

103. Ibid., 133.

104. Maria Thomas, *African Visas* (New York: Soho Press, 1991).

105. Ernest Hemingway, *The Garden of Eden* (New York: Scribners, 1986).

7

Visions of the Homeland: The African American Response 1880-1930

In 1852, the Reverend F. Freeman, a white abolitionist, published a book entitled *Africa's Redemption: The Salvation of our Country*. Freeman was no flaming radical, and he certainly was no John Brown. Indeed, he argued that "if slavery is to be brought to an end in our land, in a way that shall be honorable and not destructive of our national existence, it must be by the consent of the south." Freeman had no doubt of the alternative: he was convinced that "a dissolution of the Union and civil war, perhaps a servile war also, would be the inevitable consequence of any coercion on the part of the non-slaveholding states."[1] Like many of his fellow abolitionists—especially those of his own color—Freeman was an advocate of "colonization," a process of emancipation which would be closely followed by the removal of the newly freed slaves to Africa. The foundation of such a strategy had been laid with the creation of Liberia in the 1820s, and a limited program of repatriation had been under way for the past several decades. Unfortunately, for many white Americans, a fervent desire for abolition was not always linked to a fervent desire for the meaningful integration of African Americans into the wider society and economy. Colonization provided an attractive program for those numerous opponents of slavery who were deeply concerned with the "race question" since it seemed to offer a convenient solution to a host of problems, from unemployment to the franchise to miscegenation, which were bound to follow from "the day of Jubilee."

Abolitionist writing had its patterns and conventions, and most extended treatises on this subject contained a reasoned defense of the "Negro" and his intellect and capabilities, a discourse which sometimes went beyond the African American to specifically embrace the African himself. Freeman's work stands out as a detailed case in point.

The book consists of a sequence of fictional conversations between Mr. Lovegood, "a beloved and respected father" and the type of "authority to which a dutiful and affectionate child loves to refer for information and advice," and his inquisitive children, "Caroline, a lovely and interesting girl of sixteen [and] Henry, a sprightly and intelligent boy, who was next to his sister . . . in age."[2] Early on in the first "conversation," the following exchange ensues:

> "Why, Pa, you surprise me. You certainly do not mean to be understood that Africans have ever been distinguished for genius and intellectual attainments?"
>
> "I do, my daughter, as strange as it may seem. Africa, unhappy Africa, is now degraded, and wherever are her sons and daughters, they are reproached and trampled underfoot; but among her children stand immortalized in history a long list of names, as honorable, for aught I know, as any nation upon earth can produce."
>
> This, C. professed, was to her a new idea; and Henry, who admitted that he had "always thought the Africans a much injured people," and who protested that he felt "very little respect for those people who sometimes place the Africans on a level with *baboons*," acknowledged "that the idea of literature and science associated with an African name" was as novel to him as it was to Caroline.[3]

In the next several chapters, the enlightened Mr. Lovegood went on to develop the outlines of this startling idea for his precocious and remarkably attentive children. Central to his argument was a possibility, indeed a probability, which Freeman's alter ego elaborated on at length in a detailed footnote:

> It may greatly startle some who have heard of "the fame of Egypt's wisdom—of the gigantic size of her eternal pyramids—the splendor of her twenty-thousand cities—of Thebes with her hundred gates and superb palaces and temples—of the wisdom of her law and policy . . ." to be told that "Egypt—ancient, renowned, victorious Egypt, the mother of science and arts, both ancient and modern, was *inhabited by negroes*—that Egyptians *were in fact black and curly-headed*," especially if they have been accustomed to think with a distinguished governor of the south, that God has "stamped inferiority and slavery on the negroes' brow."[4]

"Lovegood" cited a range of authorities from Herodotus to the French Orientalist Volney to make his case, and while he acknowledged that "there are, indeed, slight shades of variety which distinguish all the different tribes of Africa," this was ultimately irrelevant since "however diversified may be the different tribes, there can be no doubt of their common origin as descendants of Ham."[5] This was only part of the story, however, since the glory of these "Cushites" or "Ethiopians" had reached far beyond their ancient land, and Lovegood made sure that his "dear children" were fully alert to the truth that "that very light which long since blazed before the world in Greece and Rome, and which now rises to its noonday splendor under the auspices of Christianity, in Europe and America . . . was kindled on the dark shores of Africa."[6] No doubt the planter aristocracy and their intellectual apologists, who displayed a devoted if shallow allegiance to the classical tradition in their architecture, in their letters, and even in their political economy, were deeply disturbed by the specter raised by Freeman and his fellow abolitionists. The very possibility that their human capital, the flesh and blood and sinew of their "Peculiar Institution," the Africans who were working in their fields, wetnursing their babies, and living in squalor under their benevolent despotism might actually be the sons or daughters (or at least the cousins) of Ancient Egypt, the descendants of the mentors of Plato, Aristotle, and Caesar, was an idea that must have been unsettling. While this abstract notion was not compelling enough to create a rush toward emancipation, it must have given the more literate and sophisticated slaveholders at least a momentary pause.

African American intellectuals were deeply divided on the issue of colonization both before and after the Civil War. Some saw this issue as a diversion from their primary struggle on the domestic front, and argued that their people had paid an enormous price for the right to live in freedom and dignity in the New World. They realized that the end of slavery would merely be the first step on this journey, and though the road ahead promised to be a long and trying one, they were not prepared to forsake this struggle and "go back" to an Africa which they had never even seen. Others, however, saw no real future for the black man in a racist America and argued that the return of even a portion of the diaspora would reinvigorate the mother continent and provide a haven and a homeland which might, in its own time, refute the skeptics and emerge as a significant power in its own right. On both sides of this debate, however, there was little evidence that contemporary African cultures were viewed with nostalgia or admiration, and little explicit sentiment that they should be allowed to persist on their own terms. Africa was not seen as a storehouse of models for African Americans: instead, "Africa's redemption" was regarded as the fundamental duty of its enlightened children across the ocean. There were pronounced differences over how this transformation of the continent could best be achieved. Some argued that this project should be an exclusively black enterprise, while others were willing to accept a substantial, even dominant presence on the part of Europeans and white Americans. There were optimists who thought that this vision could be realized by a handful of missionaries and educators, while there were those who continued to see a need for wholesale colonization, whether by African Americans or other "civilized" pioneers. Most agreed, however, that since "Ethiopia was stretching out her hands unto God," as the Bible had predicted, the time had surely come to provide for her deliverance.

Throughout their long ordeal American slaves had preserved a fond and positive vision of their African motherland, and the recollections of first generation slaves had been passed down to their descendants in the form of a vibrant oral tradition. This legacy was clearly a significant one: indeed, some scholars have argued that these memories and the popular culture which they helped to support provided an important basis for black political thought and action in the nineteenth century and beyond.[7] At the same time, however, there were strong countervailing forces which tended to push African American intellectuals away from this tradition and encouraged them to embrace an appraisal of the continent which was more consistent with the white American norm. More often than not those talented young blacks who struggled to become clergymen or teachers would make their passage through white religious or educational institutions, or through "Negro" schools and institutes which were heavily reliant on white sponsorship and direction: this was especially true in the decades before the Civil War. Under these conditions, it is not surprising that the attitude of the black intelligentsia toward African society and culture was ambivalent at best.

The writings and career of Alexander Crummell, a prominent black clergymen who was deeply concerned with Africa's future, provide an interesting example of these formative influences at work. His father, "Boston Crummell, an oysterman of New York, is reported to have claimed descent from the Temne chiefs of West Africa in the region that is now Sierra Leone." The younger Crummell later recalled "his father's 'burning love of home, his vivid remembrance of scenes and travels with his [own] father into the interior, and his wide acquaintance with divers tribes and customs.'"[8] Alexander also developed an abiding interest in Africa and her people, but it took a very different form from the childhood memories of his father. After overcoming a host of obstacles he finally achieved an important personal goal in 1844 when he was ordained as a priest in the Episcopal church. Four years later he traveled to England, and in 1853 he graduated from Queens College, Cambridge University. Rather than stay in England or return

to America he decided to serve in Liberia as a pastor and a missionary, and he was well on the way to becoming an ardent convert to
the cause of colonization. Like other African American intellectuals
(such as Martin Delaney and Henry Highland Garnet) he was coming to regard this strategy as an increasingly attractive solution to
the dilemma of his people. As Wilson Moses has noted, these influential figures and other supporters of the "African Civilization"
movement were every bit as militant as those black abolitionists,
such as Frederick Douglass, who argued that the future of the
African American should rightfully, and logically, be in America:

> The civilizationists began to question the feasibility of dig-
> ging in for the seemingly interminable fight against Ameri-
> can prejudice. Their nationalism was immediatist; their
> antislavery was implicitly gradualist. . . . The Delaneys, the
> Garnets, and the Crummells believed that only by putting
> first things first could the black race vindicate its claims to
> equality, and force the proud Anglo-Saxon to acknowledge
> its rights. They came to view Douglass's antislavery
> approach as utopian. Their first priority was to establish a
> black national power, which must serve as the necessary
> base for the struggle against slavery and prejudice.[9]

In the case of Crummell—and other black thinkers with a comparable education and mindset—this objective was linked to an image of
Africa which was sadly familiar in the wider American culture. In a
letter written in 1860 during his stay in Liberia (and later published
under the title "The Relations and Duties of Free Colored Men in
America to Africa") Crummell stated his position in a characteristically direct fashion:

> Africa lies low and is wretched. She is the maimed and crip-
> pled arm of humanity. Her great powers are wasted. Disloca-
> tion and anguish have reached every joint. Her condition in
> every point calls for succor—moral, social, domestic, political,
> commercial, and intellectual . . . Africa is the victim of her
> heterogeneous idolatries. Africa is wasting away beneath the
> accretions of civil and moral miseries. Darkness covers the
> land, and gross darkness the people. Great social evils univer-
> sally prevail. Confidence and security are destroyed. Licen-
> tiousness abounds everywhere. Moloch rules and reigns
> throughout the whole continent, and by the ordeal of Sassy-
> wood, Fetiches, human sacrifices, and devil-worship, is
> devouring men, women, and little children.[10]

Crummell did not see these conditions as entirely the fault of the
Africans themselves. He was uncompromising in his condemnation

of the Atlantic slave trade and, while this enterprise had largely ended, he passionately insisted that its devastating effects were still being felt throughout the continent; and he was equally vigorous in denouncing the contemporary trade in alcohol and firearms. At the core of the problem, however, was a crying need for spiritual and intellectual uplift, and he was convinced that it was the duty of his fellow African Americans to assume the burden of this imposing "civilizing mission." In his eyes, "to wrest a continent from ruin; to bless and animate millions of torpid and benighted souls; to destroy the power of the devil in his strong-holds, and to usher therein light, knowledge, blessedness . . . is, without doubt, a work which not only commands the powers of the noblest men, but is worthy [of] the presence and the zeal of angels." There was no need to wait for supernatural intervention, however, since it was "just this work which now claims and calls for the interest and activity of the sons of Africa" who had been cruelly torn from their homeland.[11]

It would be a serious distortion to think that Crummell's analysis was rooted in a notion of black racial inferiority. In his excellent biography, Wilson Moses points out that "Crummell and his black contemporaries . . . shared with Americans and Europeans an inflated idea of the triumphs of nineteenth-century civilization." A unilineal version of cultural evolution did not have to be linked to race: indeed, "the fact that Europeans were further along in the process of civilization did not mean that they had been more intelligent, inventive, or creative, merely that they had *submitted* earlier to the divine and natural law and were now carried along in the current of inevitable progress."[12] Nevertheless, while he had great hope for the future of the continent, he did not see the Africans achieving their destiny without the guiding hand of their more civilized brethren. As Moses observes, Crummell was convinced that

> History moved with a purpose: the pattern could be discerned. . . . The simultaneous Christianization and civilization of black Americans under Anglo-American auspices was clear evidence they were on the progressive road to a new stage in civilization. As for the ability of Africans to develop a culture on their own terms, he was indeed pessimistic, and indeed, like most conservative Christians, he had a pessimistic view of primitive humanity. All good in the world came from submission to Christian institutions, which must first have evolved up to a certain standard, namely modern Protestanism.[13]

Unlike some of his contemporaries, Crummell had little to say about the glories of the African past or Ancient Egypt. In 1850, the London *Christian Observer* published a piece of Biblical commentary in

which he offered a revised (and somewhat more benign) interpretation of the Hamitic hypothesis. In "The Negro Race Not Under A
Curse: An Examination of Genesis IX.25" he maintained that the
curse on the sons of Ham was limited to Canaan and did not apply
to Cush, "the eldest, and undoubtedly the most distinguished, of all
the sons," who "appears to have been the great progenitor of the
Negro race." Accordingly, he was able to conclude that "this curse,
in its significance and locality, is altogether Asiatic, and not
African."[14] Nevertheless, while Moses maintains that "like most people possessed by a sense of national history, Crummell was susceptible to the need for identification with symbols of ancient splendor,"[15]
it does not seem that his enthusiasm extended to the cultural and
political legacy of ancient Egypt. In fact, his Biblical orientation had
led him in quite a different direction. From a moral and compassionate standpoint there was little which merited celebration in the long,
dark age before the coming of Christ, and, as Moses noted, for
Crummell

> reflecting on ancient history brought to mind "the murder-
> ous exploits of a Sesostris or a Shiskah; and the remains of
> its high and unequalled art [which] are the obelisks and the
> urns, commemorative of bloody conquerers—or the frowning
> pyramids, upon whose walls are the hieroglyphic
> representations of war, conquest, and slavery."[16]

Still, an exclusive claim to the civilization of ancient Egypt provided
the writer and polemicist with a powerful rhetorical instrument. It
should not be surprising that a number of black clergymen, activists,
and authors made good use of it in proclaiming the merits and destiny
of their people. For those who were schooled in the Christian tradition
it provided a means of demonstrating the capabilities, indeed the
genius, of "the Negro" while avoiding an invidious comparison with the
"primitive" tribes and cultures of the African interior. Admittedly, by
invoking the "revised" Hamitic hypothesis and other scriptural devices
they were able to assert, in a general and abstract fashion, the unity
and indivisibility of all African peoples. Realistically, however, at a
more immediate and concrete level, by linking themselves to Egypt
they were also delinking themselves from their West African heritage
and distancing themselves from the host of racist and reductionistic
associations that went with it. Thus, for some African American
intellectuals, the emphasis on Egypt served as a useful means of
resolving a threatening intellectual contradiction.

On the other hand, there were alternative approaches to this
problem of origins which seemed to exacerbate these conceptual
tensions rather than reduce them. In his perceptive essay on

"Afro-Americans in Search of Africa: The Scholar's Dilemma," Elliot Skinner considers the work of George Washington Williams, whom he describes as "the first professional Afro-American historian." In 1883, Williams published *The History of the Negro Race in America*, and he devoted part of this work to the African past and the role of Africans in world history. As Skinner points out, Williams "stated that his chapters on Africa were intended to 'explain and explode two erroneous ideas—the curse of Canaan, and the theory that the Negro is a distinct species—that were educated into our white countrymen during the long and starless night of the bondage of the Negro.'"[17] At the same time, however, Williams advanced a theory of his own which was less than complementary toward the people of West Africa (and, in the short term, at least, less than favorable to African Americans themselves). Skinner points out that

> Williams had a curious theory about the degeneration of the Negro race. He believed that the antiquity of the true Negro race is beyond dispute and that the "importance and worth of the Negro have given him a place in all the histories of Egypt, Greece, and Rome. . . ." In contrast, the contemporary Negro type was the result of degradation of the genuine Negro caused by a migration over mountain terraces in numerous waves from an abundant and unknown source into malarial West African districts. Williams concluded that the "weaker tribes" of Africa were the chief source of supply of Negro slaves for the United States.[18]

Through this formula, Williams was able to divorce the glories of the African past from an African present which he, and most other Americans, both black and white, found less than attractive. His theory also had the advantage of predicting a brighter future for his people. Whatever its horrors, "slavery did cure the Negro of his idolatry," and Williams was confident that now that the freedman was "an American citizen 'he is likely to move over to an extreme rationalism.'"[19] Thus, his ultimate message was reassuring: with proper guidance, there was no reason why Africa and Africans could not assume—or reassume—a distinguished place among the peoples and nations of the world.

The notion that Africa was in need of spiritual (and material) redemption, and the related conviction that the children of the diaspora were God's chosen instrument for accomplishing this task, were ideas which still retained their appeal and force at the turn of the century. In December 1895, the Stewart Missionary Foundation for Africa of the Gammon Theological Seminary sponsored a "Congress on Africa" at the Cotton States Exposition in Atlanta. While the nominal organizers of this conference were white, Booker T. Washington, who delivered a famous speech, played an important role behind the scenes, and this meeting attracted a number of prominent black clerics who voiced their opinions on the future of the continent. An elderly Alexander Crummell, clearly disillusioned with the results of the colonization movement he had done so much to encourage, made a plea for the training and deployment of indigenous missionaries since he was now convinced that this tactic was the most effective means of bringing the continent to God.[20] His basic assessment of African culture was no more positive than it had been in the earlier stages of his career. In one of his addresses in Atlanta he argued that it was not enough to win an African to the faith and simply leave him in the "rude, crude, half-animal condition in which the missionary first found him"; instead, duty and humanity decreed that "this man-child [was] to be reconstructed." In the process, "all the childishness of inheritance [was] gradually to be taken out of his brain, and all the barbarism of ages [was] to be eliminated from his constitution."[21]

In sharp contrast to Crummell, Bishop Henry McNeal Turner of the African Methodist Episcopal Church issued an impassioned call for colonization. Turner can be accurately described as a militant; as Carol A. Page has noted, he was "an arch-critic of U.S. imperialism and racism" and "the editor of perhaps the most combative black American newspaper then in existence, the *Voice of Missions.* Through the *Voice*, the bishop disseminated his views on the need for the international solidarity of blacks, the efficacy of assertive and concerted action to redress their common grievances, and the necessity for defensive violence."[22] In the final analysis, however, his assumptions about Africa and Africans were every bit as patronizing and paternalistic as those of Crummell. A critical posture on racism and colonialism did not prevent him from suggesting that the hand of God had been behind the African slave trade:

> The white slave purchaser went to the shores of that continent and bought our ancestors from their African masters. The bulk who were brought to this country were the children of parents who had been in slavery a thousand years . . . the argument often advanced, that the white man went to Africa and stole us, is not true. They bought us out of a slavery that still exists over a large portion of that continent. For there are millions and millions of slaves in Africa today. Thus the superior African sent us, and the white man brought us, and we remained in slavery as long as it was necessary to learn that a God . . . made the world and controls it, and that that Supreme Being could be sought and found by the exercise of faith in His only begotten son.[23]

While there were variations in emphasis and strategy, the other black speakers at this congress also called for a dramatic transformation of the African social order. There was general agreement that the spread of Christianity and the introduction of "civilization" should proceed hand in hand and a basic confidence that African cultures, indeed the Africans themselves, could be reshaped along acceptable western lines. Several delegates (including Crummell) saw European colonialism as a positive force which should be encouraged, while others argued that African Americans should play the leading role in the renewal of their homeland. When the glories of ancient Egypt were invoked it was not to argue for their direct and substantive connection with modern African culture. Instead, the point was made that the civilized world owed a substantial debt to its original African tutors, and that the time had come for repayment in kind through a significant transfer of guidance, education, and technology. Also, the achievements of the Pharaohs were offered as convincing proof that the black man was fully capable of receiving (and, in fact, originating) a form of culture higher than that which he was presently able to display.

For John Smyth, the editor of *The Reformer* of Richmond, Virginia and the former U.S. Minister to Liberia, the heritage of Egypt was an important source of black pride. He insisted to the delegates in Atlanta that "the Negro[es] of the Americas and the Antilles" were

> the descendants of those races whose moral elevation and mental ripeness in the morning of time manifested themselves in the conception and execution of those wonders of the ages, the pyramids. . . . These ruins have seen other civilizations in their dawn, their noontide, and will, notwithstanding the vandalism of the Caucasian, continue beyond his day. Those perished peoples of Africa furnished Europe with letters, science and arts, although we, their lineal heirs, by the selfishness, greed, and ingratitude of the Caucasian, have been denied, until within the century, the title of human beings.[24]

Nevertheless, despite this eloquent assertion of black achievement and white rapacity, Smyth, a supporter of Liberia and the colonization movement, was also able to assert that "Africa fears not the invasion of her shores by Europe and the rightful acquisition of her territory, and no Negro who knows Africa regards the European's advent there as a menace to the progress and advancement of her races, except when they bring with them rum and firearms."[25] Another black conferee, M. C. B. Mason of the Freedmen's Aid and Southern Education Society, noted that while Africa was "robed in superstition and buried in ignorance today, she was not always thus. She was once the cradle of civilization, the mistress in [sic] the arts and sciences."[26] Moreover, Mason predicted a wonderful future for the Christian Africa which was soon, and sure, to emerge:

> Thy idols shall be broken, thy idolatrous temples destroyed, thy people transformed, and Jesus the Christ shall reign throughout thy borders. Christian churches shall adorn thy hills and Christian school-houses abound in thy valleys. The rattling steam engine and the rumbling car of commerce shall be heard in all thy borders. . . . Thy wonderful resources shall supply the world, thy storehouses once more feed the famished nations, and thy land become an asylum for the poor and oppressed of all mankind."[27]

These views were echoed by E. W. S. Hammond, editor of the *Southwestern Christian Advocate* of New Orleans. Hammond noted Africa's honored role in the Bible, and he maintained that "the Christian world owes to Africa its highest and best forms and types of . . . civilization." In order to "break those chains which error and superstition forged," he called for the mobilization of an army of Christian soldiers which would "push its victories from ocean to ocean," and he envisioned "an unbroken line of Christian workers stretching from the Cape of Good Hope to Egypt; thence to Sierra Leone and Liberia; thence onward victoriously and gloriously to the Soudan and the Congo State."[28] The message here was fairly consistent: while all of these participants in the Atlanta conference displayed a deep and genuine concern for the future of the continent, in none of their addresses was there any indication that there was much in African culture which was worthy of preserving. The consensus was that African practices and ideals were not to be emulated; instead, they were to be upgraded and transformed according to the guiding light of western civilization.

Although the number of African Americans who actually served as missionaries was small, their evangelical presence was felt in areas as diverse as Liberia, South Africa, and the Belgian Congo. Like their white brethren, they soon discovered that their message would not always be received in the manner it was intended—either by the Africans themselves or by their colonial overlords. Both mainline denominations and black churches and mission boards sent African American pastors to the continent, and the directors of Tuskegee Institute (Booker T. Washington and his successor Robert R. Moton) mounted a fairly substantial effort of their own:

> Tuskegee . . . played a significant, though ambiguous, "missionary" role as a model for black educational systems

throughout colonial Africa. . . . Tuskegee received an endless stream of educators, politicians, philanthropists, and missionaries from around the world who wanted to discover the secrets of the Tuskegee ideal. Tuskegee students visited and worked in different parts of colonial Africa. . . . By 1935, when Moton resigned, the scale and scope of Afro-American missionary contact with Africa had grown, but the underlying motivations remained constant, the idea of religious regeneration and modernization along western lines.[29]

On more than one occasion, black missionary efforts became a source of anxiety for colonial administrators who feared that their ultimate objectives might be political rather than spiritual. In South Africa, the activities of the African Methodist Episcopal Church attracted the suspicion of a paranoid assortment of clergymen, editors, and bureaucrats. Without any convincing evidence, these white observers concluded that the A.M.E. pastors were seeking to establish a beachhead for African American immigration as a preliminary to the overthrow of European rule. In fact, the Africans who attended their services were far more assertive than the A.M.E. ministers themselves. As Page has demonstrated, these American messengers were "cautious, conservative in temperament, and petit bourgeois in orientation," dedicated to the cause of African "improvement" and the Tuskegee ethic of self-help, and concerned that their mission might be "endangered by some reckless act or statement on their part or on the part of their subordinates."[30] The South African establishment had nothing to fear, at least in the short run: these Christian soldiers were hardly the forward party of racial revolt and violent insurrection.

It should not be thought, however, that all black missionaries were entirely apolitical. While some African Americans—including Alexander Crummell—had praised the Belgian King Leopold for his grandiose intentions in the Congo, others had expressed a healthy skepticism which proved to be fully justified. When William Henry Sheppard arrived in the Belgian Congo in 1890 to spread the Word on behalf of the Southern Presbyterian church, this black Virginian was not immune from making "the common missionary observations on 'spiritual darkness' and 'moral gloom.'"[31] However, he soon developed a more positive and diversified assessment of the peoples within his parish and an increasing unease with the policies and actions of their colonial masters. As rumors (and evidence) of Belgian misgovernment began to mount, Sheppard's superiors commissioned him to launch an investigation in his area of operations, Kasai province. He soon discovered that "a more exploitative system could hardly be devised," and when the Belgians failed to take effective action, his detailed indictment "caused the Presbyterian

Mission Board to appeal to the U.S Department of State, to protest directly to King Leopold," and "the expose became internationally famous."[32] For Sheppard, the release of this report was the beginning of an extended crusade against the calculated brutality of the "Congo Free State." According to Walter L. Williams,

> The black missionary . . . continued his campaign so relentlessly that the concessionaire Kasai Company took him to court in 1909 for libel. Sheppard's "crime" consisted of writing an article in the mission newspaper which traced the decline of the Bakuba society. Before the coming of the Europeans, he wrote, the Bakuba farmed their own lands and they were prosperous. However, with the entry of the Kasai Company the people were forced to work for the whites making rubber. The cash wages they received, after taxes, were too meager to buy the goods they needed but no longer had time to produce for themselves. . . . After proving the truth of his statements Sheppard was found not guilty.[33]

Thus, while most African Americans continued to regard Africa as a land in need of salvation and redemption, an increasing number began to voice their conviction that European colonialism was not a desirable (or even acceptable) method of assuring the welfare of their homeland. Moreover, among those fortunate members of the black intelligentsia who were able to travel to the continent of their ancestors, a growing political consciousness was often matched by a basic curiosity about the African past. Sheppard was no exception to this pattern, and it was not unusual when, in an address to the students of Hampton Institute in 1893, he ended his speech by speculating on the reasons for "Bakuba [cultural] superiority," suggesting that "'Perhaps they got their civilization from the Egyptians—or the Egyptians theirs from the Bakuba!'"[34] At the turn of the century this theme was still a popular one, and ancient Egypt remained a useful rhetorical device for explaining all things African—just as Africa was regularly summoned forth as a convenient and appealing means of explaining all things Egyptian.

During the same period that Du Bois and Woodson were helping to define a more scholarly approach to Africa, a less rigorous genre of African American commentary was also making its presence felt. This popular, or "folk" tradition had emerged from the abolitionist and evangelical discourse of the previous century and it continued to hold the field against the more secular and rational voices which were fighting to make themselves heard. The significant popularity of these works, which reached its peak in the 1920s and 1930s, is easy to understand. By any measure the social and economic plight of the African American was a difficult one and, as Elliott P. Skinner has pointed out, "the black masses, largely uninterested in the nuances of history or culture, praised these works and their authors whom they viewed as helping the cause. This admiration not only pleased the lay writer on African affairs, and fortified the tradition of lay authorship, but persuaded young people to do likewise."[35] Unfortunately, the intellectual consequences of this trend were far from salutary, and many of these authors

> did not attempt to master the techniques of either historio-graphy or of the social sciences. They often cited as fact the ideas of early white writers which had been disproved by later white scholars. It sufficed for these black writers that the works cited supported their predilections, and books began to appear that were factually and theoretically unsound. Unfortunately, the black lay writers on African subjects were unable to learn from their mistakes because their work was ignored by white scholars and black scholars who read their work seldom said anything for fear that any critical appraisal would be misinterpreted as joining the "enemy camp."[36]

That sense would only make slow and gradual inroads against non-sense should not be surprising. The same state of affairs existed within the sphere of white American writing on Africa, albeit for a different set of cultural and historical reasons. The dramatic rhetoric of Stanley, Roosevelt, and Burroughs remained far more appealing than the measured scholarship of Boas and Herskovits, and, for their part, African Americans had a more compelling reason for creating an Africa that was a servant of their aspirations and their dreams.

The vision of the African past which emerged from these popular tracts was firmly rooted in Biblical scripture and physically centered on Ethiopia and Egypt. Some of these works, such as Augustus J. Bell's *The Wooly Hair Man of the Ancient South*, seemed to derive their appeal from the basic obscurity of their argument and the impenetrable mystery of their sources. The title page of this undated book proclaimed that it was designed to "help the poor black man in his struggle," and further described its contents as "the Media or Key to 'Bell's Ethnical Encyclopedia', disclosing much of value as collected from a very ancient writing called 'The Key of the Treasure of Knowledge.'"[37] Through a highly convoluted chain of reasoning he attempted to establish the textual and historical importance of ancient Ethiopia, and he suggested that the publication of a certain, missing version of the Ethiopian Bible could have an immediate, concrete, and decisive impact on the status of black people everywhere.

I traced it from London to this country in 1840 when it fell into the hands of one of our great scholars which [sic] I want to buy if it can be sold. If we can buy this book or the other spoken of on my Circular, our side of the race question will be practically settled. And from these we shall be able to "represent a proper standard of character, intelligence, intellect and morality. . . ." Whether a Porter on a railway, or a Police on the street, we will have fair pay that will put us on our feet; whether a soldier on the guard-post, or in battle on the field, or a sailor on the sea coast, we will have a square deal.[38]

If Bell's expectations were rooted in the mystical, the Rev. John William Norris took a more consciously historical approach in his assessment of *The Ethiopian's Place in History and his Contribution to the World's Civilization*, a volume published in 1916. Norris was clear and direct in stating his intentions: he declared that "I want the boys and girls of my race to see behind them a wonderful ancestry."[39] Like other authors in this genre, Norris adopted an absolute and unilineal notion of cultural diffusion, tracing the spread of "civilization" from point to point with a level of confidence which was highly remarkable in light of the obvious absence of method and evidence. In his estimation, some basic historical truths had been lost through a conspiracy of silence and distortion:

> Superficial criticism, guided by local and temporary prejudices, has attempted to deny the intimate relations of the Negro with the great and historic races of Egypt and Ethiopia. But no one who has travelled in Northeastern Africa or among the ruins of the banks of the Nile, will for a moment doubt that there was the connection; not of accident or of adventitious circumstances, but of consanguinity between the races of inner Africa of the present day and the ancient Egyptians and Ethiopians.[40]

Since Norris was certain that Greece and Rome had built their cultures on this African foundation, and then, in turn, passed these crucial achievements on to the rest of Europe, it was not surprising that western intellectuals were reluctant to acknowledge their enormous debt. It was "a known fact that modern civilization is only the reproduction of an ancient civilization; and that civilization was the product of [the] Hamitic or Negro brain." Moreover, since "the white man has never conceived civilization," it was not especially remarkable that he was in no particular hurry to make this failure known to a world which had generally come to accept his claims of racial superiority.[41] Norris was sending a clear and uncompromising message which was designed to raise the morale of his brothers and sisters, and its lack of accuracy and precision in no way detracted from its basic emotional power.

In 1922, Dr. J. E. Blayechettai, a self-proclaimed "prince" of Abyssinia, made his contribution to this argument in a work entitled *The Pen of an African*. Blayechettai claimed to have been born in the city of Choa (Shoa: which is actually an Ethiopian province), and he also insisted that, in his youth, he had been taken prisoner by the "Dervish tribe" (an apparent reference to the Mahdist movement, which had not been organized on a "tribal" or ethnic basis).[42] According to his account, after escaping from captivity Blayechettai met an Englishman who agreed to send him overseas and sponsor his education. He emerged from King's College in 1909 with a proper British schooling and the vocation of a missionary and after a series of adventures in the service of his calling he arrived in the United States, where he traveled throughout the South and West on a lecture tour of black churches. It is possible that Blayechettai was, in fact, an Ethiopian, but much of his story is dubious, and a tendency toward inaccuracy and overstatement does not inspire confidence in the accuracy of his autobiography.

In his inspirational speeches, the Rev. Dr. Blayechettai stressed two basic themes: the need for Africa to come to Christ and the crucial historical role of Ethiopia as the cradle of civilization. The "prince" was heartened by the fact that "the stones, the wood, the gold, and the huge tusks of elephants that were once handled by the nimble fingers of chiefs and kings [and] molded and worshipped for their Gods, are converting into commerce," and he enthusiastically proclaimed to his audiences that "before the Gospel of the Son of God, the stupid gods of Africa are falling."[43] While there had been "a powerful dark race on this earth thousands of years before the coming of Christ," they had fallen from grace because "their civilization was too high, and they thought they could live without God, and God turned his back on them."[44] Thus, the solution to the African dilemma was obvious to the reverend: the continent's ancient prominence would be restored in all its glory if its people turned to Christ.

Blayechettai also subscribed to a model of cultural diffusion which was every bit as unambiguous as that of Norris. The major point of difference was his firm conviction that Egypt owed its greatness to the original genius of Ethiopia:

> It has been said that civilization went up the Nile, but the underground temples that have been unearthed a year ago, is [sic] proving to the world that civilization came down the Nile. The Ethiopians were the first people to throw the flashlight of knowledge upon the shores of Egypt. Egypt handed

it to Babylon, Babylon handed it to Greece, Greece handed it to Rome, and Rome handed it down to the western world.[45]

Undoubtedly, Blayechettai's claim to be an African prince lent an air of authenticity to his historical and philosophical speculations, and the published testimonies in the front of his book which vouch for his effectiveness as a speaker suggest that he frequently made a strong impression on his audiences. This is understandable, since his message had an obvious and immediate appeal for a people who faced a relentless daily struggle against racism and economic hardship. Reduced to its essentials, his oratory offered them nothing less than the vision of a glorious past and the prospect of a brighter and more inspiring future.

Edward A. Johnson offered a comparable array of ideas in his amateur analysis of *Adam vs. Ape-Man and Ethiopia*, published in 1931. Johnson derived his spurious authority from a different source than Blayechattai: the frontispiece announced that the author was the holder of an "LL. D." and a "former member of the New York Legislature," an interesting set of qualifications for an aspiring Egyptologist. Johnson announced that his goal was "to prove that the early Ethiopian blacks who inhabited what is now Southern Egypt were not only the first people to evolve, but also, the first to have a recognizable civilization" and, like Blayechettai, he lamented the fact that "what the Ethiopians accomplished, has always been accredited to the Egyptians."[46] Admittedly, recent archaeological finds in the borderlands of Ethiopia have lent an element of plausibility to his geographic notion of human evolution. On the other hand, Johnson, for obvious reasons of logic and chronology, was totally unable to establish any credible or direct link between the origin of man and the first appearance of a "higher civilization." Still, he insisted on the cultural and intellectual primacy of his "Microbian Ethiopians," and he maintained that "their ancient abode or location is suitable to our theory of 'Diffusion' which we maintain sprang [sic] in the South and from there advanced step by step along the Nile and diffused throughout the world."[47] Johnson also offered his version of what was, by then, the standard litany of these works:

> it would only seem logical to presume that since man evolved in the north-east section of Africa he was the first to form himself into a social state and from there diffuse his culture throughout the world. And this is just exactly what happened, for Lower Egypt got her knowledge from these black men. She in turn passed it on to India and Greece. India and Greece passed it on to Rome. The Romans under their Emperors passed their knowledge of science and art on to the Helvetians, Aquitani, Gauls, and Britons.[48]

Nowhere in these postulated chains of influence is there any acknowledgment of prior knowledge or capacity on the part of the recipient peoples. History is reduced to an exalted relay race in which the passing of a cultural baton results in an instant and absolute transformation from a state of barbarism to a state of civilization; and central to this process is the notion that human achievement has only one source, a source which is as predictable as the course of the Nile itself.

While this line of analysis was already well established, it became an article of faith for a considerable portion of the African American intelligentsia during the 1920s and 1930s. Highly respected clergymen such as the Reverend Adam Clayton Powell, the pastor of New York City's Abyssinian Baptist Church, argued the virtue of its premises from the bastion of their pulpit. Powell (as quoted here by Johnson) had no doubt of the hereditary relationship between black Americans and Ancient Egyptians:

> No Colored man can go to Egypt and study the past and present achievements of its people without being proud that he is a Colored man, for the Egyptians are undoubtedly a Colored people. The features of all the pictures that are in the tombs, pyramids and galleries of the old Egyptians are Negroid. . . . Except for the red fezes on their heads and their Arabic language, I met people in every town and country place in the land of Ham who reminded me of every Colored person I had seen in America. If these men and women would put on our clothes and walk through Harlem without talking, a Philadelphia lawyer could not tell them from Colored Americans.[49]

Of all the African American writers of this period who sought to restore their people's place in history, perhaps none was more widely read in the black community than Joel Augustus Rogers. His more popular works, such as the *World's Great Men of Color*, were still in demand in the 1960s when they were reissued to provide an ample and accessible body of evidence which could be deployed in the struggle for "Black Pride." While much of his work was seriously flawed, his life and labors are deserving of respect, and his long career tells us much about the trials of the self-taught black intellectual in the first half of twentieth century. As W. Paul Coates has noted, his road was not an easy one. While his books and syndicated columns in African American newspapers attracted a large black audience

> he was largely ignored by many members of the white and black academic community. His approach to history was

regarded as too subjective, too emotional, and diminished by errors of fact. Lacking a formal degree and rejected by academia, Rogers found publishers were unwilling to publish his works. He was further frustrated by the lack of interest publishers displayed in producing works of black history, especially those portraying Blacks in a positive light. Unable to find a publisher, Rogers was forced time and time again to solicit money from friends and supporters to help him self-publish and distribute his numerous works.[50]

At one point, Rogers discussed some of the factors which had encouraged him to embark upon his intellectual odyssey. As a young man, he became convinced that the portrait of Africa he was gradually constructing from white sources was a grossly misleading one, and this was a prominent reason for his growing curiosity.

> There were . . . the books on Africa, "darkest Africa," by Stanley, and works by missionaries in which Africans were painted either as faithful dogs or horrible savages. Occasionally, I heard a newly returned missionary from Africa, who, at a Sunday morning service, would paint a most pitiable picture of what he called "the heathen" . . . when I did go to Africa I saw natives who lived better than a large number of whites in Europe, especially England and Italy. . . . As for the poorer Blacks, I venture to say that their huts of grass, sticks, and clay, were no worse than the slums I saw in the East End of London.[51]

Rogers responded to this image of Africa through a strategy of biography, but his selection process was not especially notable for its lucidity or consistency of vision. Prominence and notoriety were the primary criteria for inclusion, and there is little evidence of any guiding moral or political agenda. Some of the candidates were predictable, and their presence echoed a familiar theme. The first figure discussed in the *World's Great Men of Color* is "Imhotep: God of Medicine, Prince of Peace and the First Christ." Rogers confidently noted that "when Egyptian civilization crossed the Mediterranean to become the foundation of Greek culture, the teachings of Imhotep were also absorbed there, but as the Greeks were wont to assert that they were the originators of everything, Imhotep was forgotten for thousands of years"[52] in favor of Hippocrates. The book also included brief sketches of Hatshepsut, Thotmes III [sic], Akhenaton, and Cleopatra, entries which further reflected his basic assumption. To be fair, however, Rogers' notion of "men of color" was fairly flexible, and it potentially encompassed any historical celebrity who was not of European origin. Among the notables discussed in the Asian section of this collection were "Ibn

Saud, King of Saudi Arabia," "Malik Andeel, Sultan of Bengal, India" and "Eugene Chen, Dynamic Statesman of China." A favorable assessment might hold that the prescient author had anticipated the notion of the "Third World," while a less favorable estimate might suggest an overly casual approach in defining the premises of his biographical project. In any event, he seemed to share a cardinal assumption with white racists of every type and description: the notion that the slightest trace of African ancestry made the subject a "Negro," or a "black man," or an "African." Inevitably, ideologies of race—whether affirmative or disparaging in intent, and however complex their superficial trappings—always, at some point in their development, lend themselves to the most simplistic forms of classification and analysis.

Some of Rogers' distinguished men of color were the holders of rather dubious credentials. For example, he was able to describe Tippu Tib, one of the major slavetraders of East and Central Africa, as the "trailblazer for the great explorers of Africa," making full recourse to the very symbolic conventions he had condemned in the process of detailing his feats.

> Starting from the island of Zanzibar, his birthplace, Tippoo Tib crossed Africa by way of Lake Tanganyika, up through the vast stretch of what is now the Belgian Congo. The journey took him eleven years during which he traversed territory no one from the outer world had ever penetrated before. He fought his way through the primeval forest, forced himself into the lands of the tribes and defeated chief after chief until he was master of a territory as large as Western Europe.[53]

Rogers did admit that Tippu Tib "was a great instrument of evil. He brought immense suffering to the primitive people of Central Africa,"[54] but, strangely enough, this damning characterization did not debar him from a seat among the illustrious members of his "race."

This unfortunate absence of critical criteria was apparent in his other works as well. In *Your History: From the Beginnings of Time to the Present*, a book which consisted of line drawings backed up by brief descriptive captions, Rogers singled out some equally improbable figures for his gallery of thumbnail commentaries. Included in his roster of notables was "Edward Barter, an English mulatto who was the leading slave-trader of West Africa" (the author noted that "In the early 1700s, he exercised greater power on the coast than the three leading English traders together;")[55] "John Ormond, a Negro known as 'Mungo John' and 'Mulatto Trader' [who] was the principal slave-trader in West Africa in the late 1700s;"[56] and "Don Antonio Mingo, mulatto, king of Ouerre, West Africa, [who] was one of the richest slave traders in 1644."[57] Certainly, Rogers did nothing to reinforce the notion that the Atlantic slave trade was entirely a European venture. Some of his entries were even more whimsical, such as

> John Indian and Tituba, two West Indian Negro slaves [who] were the originators of the great witchcraft scare of Salem, Mass. in 1692. Experts in palmistry, fortune-telling, magic, second sight and incantations, the two played on the superstitions of some of even the most learned white people until the latter thought they saw witches everywhere. 19 white persons were hanged and 53 tortured as a result.[58]

Thus, far from being scapegoats and victims, these black New Englanders were portrayed as the masterminds of a particularly ingenious slave revolt, an unusual interpretation which was not without an intrinsic appeal for an audience in search of a positive and usable past.

In retrospect it is all too easy to dismiss Rogers, but his approach to history was both popular and influential, whatever its programmatic defects. His books were the type of publication which were passed from hand to hand by readers who were anxious for a glimpse of their own past, readers who had a burning curiosity and little in the way of alternative (and accessible) sources through which they could satisfy it. At one level, his inspirational vignettes became a kind of oral history in and of themselves, a collection of secondary legends which became steadily more imposing as they continued to circulate by word of mouth. Undoubtedly, for many young African Americans, Rogers was a singular and reassuring voice who offered an exciting message: the notion that they did, indeed, have a distinguished history which was well worth learning about.

It is not surprising that Rogers became an early and ardent follower of another champion of the "Negro" cause, a fellow Jamaican who arrived in Harlem in 1916 with the dramatic vision of a black imperial renaissance. By 1920 Marcus Garvey and his Universal Negro Improvement Association had become a force to reckon with in black communities throughout the United States and the Caribbean; by 1925, however, the movement was in ruins and its leader was nearing the end of a series of legal battles which would result in his deportation (and, some would argue, his disgrace). Historians and polemicists have given us many different Marcus Garveys, and the irony is that there is an element of truth in all of them. By turns, the man can be seen as the father of

modern Pan-Africanism; the pragmatic advocate of black capitalism; the unprincipled confidence artist and incompetent administrator; the unfortunate victim of political persecution (at the hands
of the U.S. Department of Justice); the physically unimpressive
activist whose charismatic leadership attracted a following throughout the African diaspora; and the outspoken defender of black civil
rights who could sit down and discuss matters of mutual interest
with the Grand Wizard of the Ku Klux Klan. While his career was a
welter of stunning contradictions, he cannot be denied credit for his
one basic accomplishment: the creation of a truly secular "Back-to-
Africa" movement which attracted global attention and posed a
vague but unsettling challenge to the colonial order, a challenge
which did not go unnoticed in the capitals of Europe.

If one is to judge by its literature and its oratory, the Universal
Negro Improvement Association had one overriding objective: the
establishment of an "independent" African state under its own
political stewardship. This hypothetical nation would provide an
outpost for an advance guard of the diaspora, and it would also
serve as a beachhead for the eventual liberation of the entire continent. In the broadest sense, this territory would function as a com-
monwealth in which Africans and African American immigrants
would share and prosper alike. In reality, however, it was clear who
would hold the commanding heights of political and economic
power: the dedicated footsoldiers of the U.N.I.A. led by the "Provisional President of Africa" himself, Marcus Garvey.

Garvey himself was not a "liberal" or a "socialist." Instead he
was, quite unabashedly, a capitalist and an imperialist. He was
convinced that the time had come for the children of the diaspora
to become participants in the great game of empire rather than its
victims. He held to a sort of cultural and political Darwinism which
suggested that the day of the European had passed and the day of
the black man, the African throughout the world, had arrived. At
one level this process might almost be regarded as a cyclical one
since he was confident of the ultimate source of all the great
empires of the past. In a 1925 publication he argued, in relation to
the attitudes of white racists, that "their arrogance is but skin deep
and an assumption that has no foundation in morals or in law":

> when we were embracing the arts and sciences on the banks
> of the Nile their ancestors were still drinking human blood
> and eating out of the skulls of their conquered dead; when
> our civilization had reached the noonday of progress they
> were still running naked and sleeping in holes and caves
> with rats, bats, and other insects and animals. . . . The world
> today is indebted to us for the benefits of civilization. They
> stole our arts and sciences from Africa. Then why should we

be ashamed of ourselves? Their modern improvements are but *duplicates* of a grander civilization that we reflected thousands of years ago . . . to be resurrected and reintroduced by the intelligence of our generation and our posterity.[59]

This theme remained constant, and Garvey continued to echo it even after his deportation from the United States and the virtual collapse of the U.N.I.A. suggested that the black millennium was not at hand. In February, 1928, he assured an audience in Kingston, Jamaica that "we are gradually laying the foundation of Africa's new imperialism that we hope shall last longer than Rome's, Greece's, France's, Germany's or any of the existing empires of today. We hope it shall last longer because of our better and superior knowledge of what it takes to make a nation, to make an empire and to hold it."[60] Although his own political empire lay in ruins, he was confident that history and evolutionary logic would eventually vindicate his optimistic predictions. He told his black audience in Kingston that

> thousands of years ago the world looked to your fathers, and to mine, for leadership in the higher arts, in the higher works and in the higher culture of civilization. You were the torchbearers, the advanced guard of all that was worthwhile in the world. Evolutionarily you lost your place; and you reverted back to a state of inertia, inactivity, a state of laxity, a state of almost savagery and barbarism and cannibalism—out of which through the same laws of evolution you are gradually emerging. . . . No group has ever permanently held the world.[61]

The image of Africa betrayed in statements such as this is ambiguous, even patronizing, and it helps explain the difficulties which Garvey (and the U.N.I.A.) had in their dealings with the homeland. While "Mother Africa" had her own "civilized" and advanced elites, it seemed to be assumed that the preponderance of leadership in government, in trade, and in the arts and sciences would come from the diaspora. In this respect, Garvey had not gone beyond the thinking of intellectuals like Crummell (and the participants at the Atlanta conference of 1895), who subscribed to the notion that Africa, and Africans, should be regenerated and transformed in accordance with the standards of a "higher" (i.e., European) civilization. These sentiments were regularly echoed by followers such as Duse Mohammad Ali, a journalist whom Garvey had enlisted for the U.N.I.A. and its newspaper *The Negro World*. Ali expressed a positive perspective on the "Negro," but his position on the African was more problematical:

The Negro was the mother of nations, even black Egypt was the cradle of civilization passed away [sic] and he was driven forth, for the most part, to dwell in the primeval forest of Africa to remain mentally fallow for a period until his mental rejuvenation should have been complete. The time is at hand. The Negro is doing and has done all that the European can and is doing.[62]

In the final analysis, it is clear that Garvey, and the black intellectuals who supported his cause, regarded traditional African cultures as essentially static and backward. Their rhetoric implied that African history since the passing of ancient Egypt had amounted to little more than the long night of the "Negro," a darkness from which he was just emerging with the assistance of enlightened elements from the diaspora—in particular, the Universal Negro Improvement Association. This mindset should not have been surprising given the guiding principles of the movement. While the U.N.I.A. Manifesto of 1917 included a call to "strengthen the imperialism of independent African states," a more secular and militant position than was common at the time, it also proclaimed its intention "to assist in civilizing the backward tribes of Africa" and "promote a conscientious Christian worship among the native tribes of Africa,"[63] objectives which echoed the agenda of the black churchmen who had met in Atlanta several decades earlier. The call for "African redemption" was as strong and pronounced as it had ever been, and while Garvey championed the notion of "Africa for the Africans" and took an uncompromising stand against European colonialism, a more accurate slogan for his political crusade would have been "Africa for the diaspora."

Despite this orientation, the U.N.I.A. was able to attract a surprising level of support in certain parts of Africa, particularly in the British colonies and especially among the educated and urbanized members of the middle class who were beginning to chafe under the restraints of racial barriers and foreign rule. Not surprisingly, African Garveyites—and Garveyites in Africa—tended to stress the anti-European and anti-colonial aspects of their program in preference to the emigrationist and transformationist messages, which, for most potential recruits, were decidedly less appealing. In the most complete published collection of documents on this movement, an appendix listing the locations of U.N.I.A. divisions worldwide makes reference to six chapters in South Africa and two in Southwest Africa (Namibia), three chapters in Sierra Leone, two chapters each in Liberia and the Gold Coast (Ghana), and a single unit in Basutoland (Lesotho).[64] The more aggressive parts of its platform had an obvious attraction in South Africa, where racial

oppression was becoming more intensive and systematic. C. Boyd
James has noted that

> Within the continent of Africa, and apart from Liberia, Gar-
> veyism seemingly had its widest mass appeal in South
> Africa. South Africa housed approximately nine UNIA divi-
> sions in Cape Town, Pretoria, Johannesburg, and other
> remote enclaves. The pages of the *Negro World* are replete
> with news from Black South Africa. . . . Factors other than
> the UNIA spirit of resistance and redemption contributed to
> South African restlessness: the vast number of West Indian
> militants who settled along Cape Town waterfronts employed
> as stevedores, shipwrights, and foremen, like others before
> them, brought with them the anti-colonial spirit.[65]

While the influence of Garveyism in South Africa was centered in
the urban areas, it also extended to certain rural regions such as
the Transkei where "one Wellington Butelezi offered his tribesmen
membership badges costing 2s. 6d. and promised the resurgence of
his people's past glories. He told his following that American Blacks
would arrive from the air to liberate them from the whites,"[66] a formula which his modern namesake seems to have reversed (at least
in term of its racial essentials).

Perhaps the most significant chapter in West Africa was in
Lagos, Nigeria, and far from being radical or incendiary, the stated
objectives of this organization were remarkably conservative and
bourgeois: its avowed goals were to "assist in civilizing the backward tribes of Nigeria," "establish technical and industrial institutions for boys and girls," and "conduct local and commercial and
industrial enterprises on corporative lines . . . (in compliance with
our loyalty to the Crown)."[67] There was little here that was threatening or subversive: indeed, it appeared that Garveyism had provided
a vehicle for a local businessman's club rather than a militant
forum for Pan-Africanist sentiment. On the other hand, it is somewhat misleading to measure the nature and impact of Garveyism in
Africa by the formal rhetoric of its widely scattered and politically
vulnerable urban associations. Its actual influence was probably
more extensive and more informal, as Jomo Kenyatta suggested to
C. L. R. James:

> In 1921, Kenya nationalists unable to read would gather
> round a reader of Garvey's newspaper, the *Negro World*, and
> listen to an article two or three times. Then they would run
> various ways through the forest carefully to repeat the
> whole, which they had memorized, to Africans hungry for
> some doctrine which lifted them from the servile conscious-
> ness in which Africans lived.[68]

While this statement reflects Kenyatta's flair for appealing to the symbolic conventions (and his liberal British audience) it accurately conveys the broader reach of Garvey's anti-colonial message. The U.N.I.A.'s plea for action was also heard and considered by African nationalist leaders, especially within the British sphere of control. As Rupert Lewis has noted, Harry Thuku, the Kenyan activist and "secretary of the East African Association, had corresponded with Garvey," and "when Thuku was arrested in March 1922 and twenty-five Africans protesting his detention were shot dead . . . Garvey organized a massive protest meeting in New York where the massacre was denounced and a protest lodged with the Colonial Office."[69] This meeting would have been duly noted in the *Negro World* which would, if we accept Kenyatta's statement, have eventually made its way back to Nairobi with its declaration of outrage and political solidarity. Such a process cannot be quantified, and its actual significance is equally difficult to estimate in more abstract terms, but it suggests a circuit of ideas and emotions which should not be casually dismissed.

All this considered, there is another side to Garvey's Pan-Africanism which is notably less impressive. One perceptive African American provided this telling vignette of the U.N.I.A. and the grandiose ambitions of its leader:

> It was upon the tenth of August, in High Harlem of Manhattan Island. . . . There was a long, low, unfinished church basement, roofed over. A little, fat black man, ugly but with intelligent eyes and big head, was seated on a plank platform beside a "throne," dressed in a military uniform of the gayest mid-Victorian type, heavy with gold lace, epaulets, plume and sword. Beside him were "potentates," and before him knelt a succession of several colored gentlemen. These in the presence of a thousand or more applauding dark spectators were duly "knighted" and raised to the "peerage" as knight-commanders and dukes of Uganda and the Niger. . . . What did it all mean? A casual observer might have mistaken it for the dress rehearsal of a new comic opera and looked instinctively for Bert Williams and Miller and Lyles.[70]

This scathing appraisal was provided by W. E. B. Du Bois, one of the harshest critics of Garvey, a man whom Garvey would ultimately describe as "purely and simply a white man's nigger."[71] The antipathy between these two men was intense, and by the mid-1920s the "Provisional President of Africa" was blaming Du Bois' personal intervention (and Harvey Firestone and his plantation project) for the ignominious failure of the U.N.I.A. effort in Liberia. By any standard, however, this accusation was seriously misplaced:

Garvey's assumptions and methods were sufficiently flawed on their own to assure the collapse of his primary initiative in Africa. The Jamaican visionary tended to forget that Liberia was a sovereign state with a ruling elite which was extremely jealous of its prerogatives, and it did not matter whether the party which sought to preempt them was white or black, European or "African." The Liberian administration of President Charles King had initially agreed to accept a program of U.N.I.A. settlement, but by June 1924 his Secretary of State, Edwin Barclay, informed the shipping company that was bringing these colonists to Monrovia that "the government of Liberia has decided that no member of the movement known as the Garvey movement will be permitted to enter the Republic."[72] With this pronouncement, the U.N.I.A. initiative in this West African nation effectively came to an end.

The reasons for this reversal of policy are not hard to ascertain. Garvey's suggestion that Liberia could serve as a springboard for the military liberation of Africa did nothing to reassure a government which shared a set of ill-defined borders with British and French colonies: provocative statements by Garvey and his followers only deepened the risk to Liberian independence. Beyond this, Garvey's serious belief in his own "provisional" authority over Liberia, indeed, over the entire continent, was bound to lead to a political showdown which he had no chance of winning. One particular episode underscores the sense of make-believe which was inherent in Garvey's idiosyncratic notion of *realpolitik*. In the hope of furthering his relations with the Liberian government, he had arranged for the "election" of Gabriel Johnson, the mayor of Monrovia, to the position of "Supreme Potentate" of the U.N.I.A. (an essentially meaningless post for all its rhetorical splendor). Unfortunately, this conciliatory gesture did not produce the desired practical result.

> the election of an African as Supreme Potentate would be insufficient to cement UNIA-Liberian diplomatic relations. Indeed, the new status and privileges afford[ed] the Monrovia Mayor from the courtiers across the Atlantic . . . incurred the jealousy and wrath of President King and his cabinet. . . . [These attitudes] played themselves out in an incident during an official state banquet for Liberian dignitaries in the winter of 1920. One Dr. Cassell, President of Liberia College, proposed a toast to "Supreme Potentate Johnson, the first Negro in the World." In his wrath and disgust, President King, to the amazement of all present, lifted his glass and toasted to the "health of the mayor of Monrovia."[73]

Aside from his presumption of eminent political domain over the entire continent, Garvey's notion of a "civilizing mission" did not sit well with African elites (whether "traditional" or contemporary). Prince Madanikan Deniyi of Lagos was not alone when he complained to an African American audience in the *Chicago Defender* that Garvey and his followers "behaved as though Africa was 'a continent of savages who would mildly acquiesce in having our civilization forced upon them and give up to us, because we are black.'"[74] That "Garvey's Pan-Africanism stemmed from the elite tradition of ambition and uplift, not the mass desire for land" can be seen in a statement by the U.N.I.A.'s vice-president, William Sherrill, who affirmed in the *Negro World* in 1924 that his organization "is not a 'Back to Africa' movement, it is a movement to redeem Africa.'"[75] Even if Garvey's impossible dream had somehow been realized in a political sense, these two sets of elites—one from the diaspora, and one that was indigenous—would inevitably have come into conflict. As C. Boyd James has pointed out, "the UNIA, like white imperialist[s], harbored a historical view of Africa seeing the latter as uncivilized, backward, and in need of Christianity, God, western law, education, politics and economics." This intellectual shortcoming was compounded by the fact that

> the timing of Garvey's program coincided with the emergence and development of a new West African elite whose objective and plans for Africa were directly antagonistic to Garvey's and the UNIA . . . those personalities, themselves, though sympathetic to Garvey's racial economic efforts in Harlem, were, in no way, prone to tolerate his racial programs and propaganda within the African mode of operation . . . in the end, persistent attempts to promote Garveyism would have eventuated into antagonisms sufficient to generate intra-racial or class wars between both groups with the eventual deportation of the UNIA from Africa.[76]

In the final analysis, Garvey and the U.N.I.A. were firmly rooted in the African American (and Afro-Caribbean) tradition that the ancestral homeland, however sacred and cherished, stood in dire need of salvation and improvement, and that its children overseas should, with their cultural advantages and abilities, take the lead and willingly serve as the forward agents of its redemption.

With the demise of Garveyism (and the coming of the Great Depression), black activism quickly diverged into a number of different channels: any semblance (or pretension) of a unified mass movement was gone. "Among the more radical [of these] movements was the Lost-Found Nation of Islam. During the summer of 1930, a small, earnest brown-skinned man who usually went by the name of Wallace Fard arrived in Detroit. . . . Fard claimed to be a prophet from Arabia who had come to the United States to help black Americans discover their dual African and Islamic heritage. He told his listeners that they, not whites, were the chosen people."[77] In all likelihood, Fard had derived the idea of appropriating and modifying Islam from another African American entrepreneur who had achieved a certain degree of success. According to C. Eric Lincoln,

> About 1913, a forty-seven-year-old North Carolina Negro named Timothy Drew established a "Moorish Science Temple" in Newark, New Jersey. From this seed grew a movement that, at its peak, had established temples in Detroit, Harlem, Chicago, Pittsburgh, Philadelphia and in numerous cities across the south. Membership may have been as high as twenty or thirty thousand during the lifetime of "the Prophet."[78]

In its early years, the "Lost-Found Nation of Islam" did not begin to approach Nobel Drew Ali's "Moorish Temple" in terms of its geographical range or its membership. Better times were in the offing, however. While Fard's basement meetings only attracted a handful of followers, among them was a young migrant from Georgia named Elijah Poole. Poole was receptive to Fard's messianic message for a number of reasons. His father had not only been a "hardworking sharecropper" but a Baptist preacher as well, a legacy which left his son with a heightened sensitivity to the power of scripture and the pulpit; and he had moved to Detroit in 1923 from Macon, Georgia after the "one thing [he] dreaded most came to pass: one of his white employers [had] physically accosted him,"[79] an incident which made him especially eager to embrace the call for black dignity and self-assertion. Poole, who soon changed his name to Elijah Muhammad, would follow in Fard's footsteps as the leader of the "Nation of Islam" and, after moving its base of operations to Chicago, he gradually developed the "Black Muslim" movement into a highly visible and vocal presence in the African American communities of the urban north and Midwest.

The creed invented by Fard and developed by Elijah Muhammad bore virtually no resemblance to orthodox Islam. On the one hand, like the prophet Muhammad himself, his black American namesake took the disparate threads of a great religious tradition and a melange of popular beliefs and practices and knit them into a distinctive ideology that was direct and accessible. On the other hand, the founder of Islam offered a message that was distinguished by its universalism, while the visionary from Chicago defined a formula that was notable for its particularism, a particularism which was grounded in one overriding factor: race. While the Nation of Islam proclaimed an absolute and undivided world view that was not without its popular appeal, it also espoused a mythological version of evolution and history which held little attraction for the black intelligentsia. As Malu Halasa has explained it:

> according to Fard, the world was initially ruled by members of a Black race who were known as the original men. Theirs was a highly advanced civilization. . . . Some of the original men settled in Arabia and became known as the tribe of Shabazz. They lived in peace, worshipping Allah from the holy city of Mecca, until evil entered the world in the form of a mad scientist named Yacub. Full of pride, Yacub broke the laws of Islam and was exiled from Mecca. His heart set on vengeance, he applied his knowledge of genetics to create a race of immoral men, the white devils. The whites caused endless trouble for the blacks until they were herded together and exiled to the cold wasteland of Europe. Allah then sent his black prophets Moses and Jesus to convert the white devils to Islam. Instead, the whites distorted the prophet's teachings and founded the blasphemous religions of Judaism and Christianity.[80]

As a corollary to this argument, Elijah Muhammad and his followers maintained that "the so-called Negro in America is a blood-descendant of the Original Man . . . 'the descendants of the Asian Black Nation and of the tribe of Shabazz.'" Moreover, by dint of the same logic, it was assumed that "all so-called Negroes are Muslims, whether they know it or not."[81] The primacy of "the tribe of Shabazz" and its location in Mecca, along with the "Asian" identity of these mythical forebears, suggest that Africa did not play a central role in the "Nation's" unusual version of black history.

As a matter of fact, within this dramatic and imaginative framework, the role of Africa—and Africans—can best be described as ambiguous. In sharp contrast to Garveyism, the Black Muslim movement showed little sustained interest in the realities and future of sub-Saharan Africa. As Elijah Muhammad put it in 1959, as several dozen colonies stood on the brink of independence, "We must realize that the black man in Africa is our brother [but] our central responsibility is with the black man here in the wilderness of North America. For us to expend our energies pleading for the cause of Africa is like a blind man pleading that his fellow blind man be given eyes while he continues to stumble in darkness."[82] Nevertheless, the publications of the "nation," in particular its official newspaper *Muhammad Speaks*, paid great attention to one continuing story which was unfolding on the continent: the archaeological quest for human origins in East Africa.

Why this interest in a scientific issue on the part of a movement which was essentially anti-intellectual? The answer is simple: the evidence from sites such as Olduvai Gorge was accepted as convincing proof that the "original man" was, in fact, a black man, an interpretation which was consistent with the Nation's myth of creation. The revelation of this fact was seen as crucially important, and in May 1962 *Muhammad Speaks* reported that a massive conspiracy existed to keep this truth from coming to light. A front page story with a banner headline claimed that "unknown to the general public, a group of American scientists, historians, Egyptologists, entologists, zoologists, biochemists, anthropologists, and historians [sic] have long been engaged in a super-secret project to further propagandize so-called 'white supremacy' by officially establishing earth's 'Original Man' as white."[83] The fellow travelers who had shown a "deep interest" in this project—institutions such as "Harvard University, the Smithsonian Institution . . . the Ford Foundation and various other colleges [and] museums"—were determined to ignore "the complete failure of all other historical efforts to find a single black cave man," and by so doing to create "a hypothetical picture of caucasian supremacy over all mankind."[84] The article elaborated on the "characteristic hairy bodies" of the white race which supposedly demonstrated an especially close evolutionary relationship with monkeys, apes and gorillas, juxtaposing this analysis with L. S. B. Leakey's recent discovery of two pieces of jaw and a tooth at his Kenyan research site. Surely, this find was definitive evidence that the "smooth, non-hairy skinned black man"[85]— the "Original Man"—predated the hirsute creations of the demented Yacub by millions and millions of years (a theory which Leakey himself, unfortunately, was not asked to comment on).

Two years later, another announcement by Leakey prompted the Black Muslim newspaper to return to this subject once more in an article entitled "After the Africans Came the Cave Dwellers." To illustrate their point, the editors ran a photo of a diorama in the Field Museum of Natural History in Chicago which portrayed "a Neanderthal family found on Gibralter 70,000 years ago." The caption noted that these creatures, "for years exemplified in textbooks as mankind's 'earliest ancestors,' must now be relegated to the realm of some of man's backward newcomers."[86] On another occasion, Elijah Muhammad also cited a remarkable piece of "behavioral evidence" in defense of his particular version of human evolution and world history: the sartorial practices of the "hippies" of the 1960s and early 1970s. As he put it, "you see some of the white people rehearsing the cave days of their fathers, and they are not ashamed to do so. They come out with long, straggly hair as their fathers did. . . . This is Allah (God) forcing the white man to bear Him Witness that they were really once the cave man."[87] Thus, in his final years—Muhammad died in 1975—the self-proclaimed "Messenger of Allah" turned to Africa for evidence to buttress the racial (and racist) theories he had begun to develop as early as the 1930s.

Nevertheless, while the evidence from East Africa was useful for substantiating the myth of the "Original Man," this did not translate into a broader enthusiasm for the traditional—and contemporary non-Muslim—cultures of the continent. *Muhammad Speaks* would gladly point to the woeful deficiencies of the prehistoric "white man who lived in caves, of bleak, rocky, barren European wastelands, while [the] black man was building earth's first civilization in [the] verdant, fruitful Valley of the Nile."[88] The official position became much more ambivalent, however, when the discussion moved from the ancient to the modern, and the geographical focus shifted from Egypt to the countries south of the Sahara. Although he did not dwell on the subject, Elijah Muhammad was openly critical of those millions of Africans who had not accepted Islam, and he sometimes resorted to the crudest form of negative stereotyping in order to make his point. From his perspective, the material achievement of these cultures was sadly inadequate: speaking of African American poverty in the rural south, he noted that "these are the worst living conditions of human beings that could even be in [sic] the jungles of Africa where they do not have sawmills or brick kilns to saw timber into lumber and to mold bricks."[89] His judgments were even harsher when it came to assessing the cultural and moral position of the people in the homeland. Quite simply, he was appalled by the idea that non-Muslim Africans could be seen as a model for African Americans. On one occasion he lamented the fact that

> For nearly forty years I have been preaching to the Black man in America that we should accept our own; and instead of the Black man going to the decent side of his own, he goes back seeking traditional Africa, and the way they did in jungle life and the way you see in some parts of uncivilized Africa today. They are not using barber's tools, shears and razors to keep themselves looking dignified as a civilized people should look. The Black man in America accepts the jungle life, thinking that they would get the love of Black Africa. Black Brother and Black sister, wearing savage dress and hair-styles will not get you the love of Africa. The dignified people of Africa are either Muslim or educated Christians. But Africa today does not want Christianity.[90]

For the leader of the "Nation of Islam," the symbolic conventions concerning Africa had a definite polemical use: the "primitives" of "Darkest Africa" who had not embraced the one true faith could be usefully contrasted with those "civilized" descendants of the "Original Man" who had. Ironically, Muhammad's Baptist background is instructive here: in the final analysis, his basic assumptions about Africa were remarkably similar to those of the black American clergy who were his primary ideological rivals.

Without a doubt, there existed a special relationship—emotional, spiritual, intellectual and increasingly, political—between African Americans and the mother continent. The ravages of slavery had not obliterated the historical memory—details had been lost, but this loss of personal particulars had rendered the abstract idea of Africa all the more powerful and compelling. Nevertheless, with the passing of slavery the culture and ideology of black America was increasingly influenced by the values of the cultural mainstream, a force which dominated the realm of the printed word and set the standard for "appropriate" black behavior and attitudes, standards which were the basis for survival and success in the wider society. The rhetoric of Protestant Christianity, accepted in the slave days as the stairway to salvation and deliverance, assumed a more secular dimension as the freedmen entered a brave and perilous new world. It should not be surprising that educated black opinionmakers in postbellum America called for the transformation and "redemption" of the African homeland. In most cases they had been taught that spiritual conversion, moral reform, and the habit of industriousness were the key to their own prosperity, and they had no reason to doubt that the same formula applied with equal logic to the plight of their African brothers. This helps to explain why the African American vision of sub-Saharan Africa during this period was not, on balance, a positive or celebratory one. It also helps to explain why black clergymen and intellectuals turned toward Egypt and, to a lesser extent, toward Ethiopia for their model of cultural achievement. This tendency cannot be seen as entirely affirmative: at one level it reveals the extent to which the predominantly negative vision of Africa had made a significant impact on the black community. The Egypt of the pharaohs could be safely embraced since it was effectively distant, in terms of time and space, from the realities of contemporary Africa. A rhetorical assertion of ancient glory posed no threat to the evangelical idea that *modern* Africa should be remade and given the benefits of Christianity and "civilization," an idea which had become firmly rooted in the Protestant faith (and ethic) of black America during the decades after emancipation.

By 1920, a small but inspired group of black scholars had taken the lead in establishing Africa as a serious academic subject. Carter Woodson and W. E. B. Du Bois, no less than Franz Boas and

Melville Herskovits, had demonstrated that the people and history of the continent embodied a legacy which was much more complex and substantial than had been previously acknowledged. At this point, the African American approach to the homeland began to diverge into two reasonably distinct, if not entirely autonomous, tendencies. As Elliott Skinner has suggested, an empirical and intellectual orientation to Africa and its problems was challenged, and often overshadowed, by a more populist and mythical perspective which was designed to engender pride and, in some cases, to serve as a practical basis for organization and mobilization within the black community. Today, some might argue that these strategies have been adequately reconciled, or maintain that the basic conceptual differences which they represent have no meaningful impact on the contemporary image of Africa. For others, however, this issue continues to be both real and problematic.

Empirical and intellectual orientations notwithstanding, in most societies folklore acts to reinforce family traditions, to maintain significant mythologies of how things were, and especially to link those who have moved or migrated. In the U.S. the connection to the "old country," so folklorist Richard Dorson tells us, is especially important for immigrants and other groups whose roots seem shallow. "Obscured Americans," to use another phrase from Dorson, often reveal a great deal about their feelings toward the dominant society in their lore. Everyone has heard of the atrocity tales of the days of slavery which proliferate among African Americans.[91] While they accurately convey a more general truth, it is not surprising that few of these can be substantiated, or that some fly directly in the face of documented history. A major tributary of African American folklore, for example, gives the impression that many thousands of heroic men and women escaped north (indeed it would seem that nearly every black family claims at least one ancestor who did so), when, in fact, only a tiny proportion did so. Such folklore, like the tale of the ubiquitous Polish Count who seems to have sired half the population of Americans of Polish descent, takes on a "legendary hue" all its own. It serves another creative purpose.

When one understands this phenomenon as part of a myth-making process, much of the fabricated "history" told from person-to-person among African Americans as among other marginalized Americans can be seen as a necessary counter-myth, a fully human response, an effort to balance things out. Like the hyperbolic myth of our frontier—erected and sustained in part because of the guilt that lurks beneath official justifications for the extermination of the Native Americans—such a myth can take on great force. It can influence the intellectual as well as the everyday gossip, the professor as well as the local *raconteur*.

Some of the figures covered in this chapter clearly succumbed to the blandishments of the counter-myth. Reacting against the image painted by whites of the barbarism of Africa (especially of West Africa) whence had come ninety-nine percent of slaves in America, they sought heroic images, great empires, lost cities. Africa, of course, had its share of these, as the better scholars were well aware. Africa, therefore, could become not only the homeland, it could become the place of salvation.

Serious African American scholars, more aware of the implicit dangers in any counter-myth (especially when put forth for an ideological purpose), therefore sought alternative explanations for the racist interpretations which bombarded Americans of all colors, every day, every year. They, too, embraced Egypt—although they stressed cultural rather than racial factors—but, in the final analysis, they were less concerned with the Nile than the Niger. Carter G. Woodson was one of these pioneers. Determined not to allow the most destructive images to go unchallenged, he organized the Association for Negro Life and History in Chicago in 1915, also in that same year taking on the editorship of *The Journal of Negro History*, its major organ.[92] Though the Association's major purpose was to research and preserve historical and sociological data on Negro life in America, and above all to publish the results of that research in the *Journal*, Woodson never lost sight of Africa's significance for people of color. To that end, when he published his widely-read book, *The Negro in Our History*, in 1923 (publication having been held up since 1917 because of wartime printing expenses), the opening chapter, "The Negro in Africa," contained an excellent précis of the best scholarship then available, whether produced by black or white, on African history.

It is well to remember that African history, as such, had not yet found acceptance in the 1920s, even as a subsection in the official histories of empire. Nevertheless, Woodson was undeterred. Like his contemporary, Du Bois, he pointed out the obvious:

> Since most historians in this field know next to nothing about the Negroes in Africa prior to their enslavement, it will be profitable to give their situation in that land at least a cursory examination.[93]

Africa, he continued, possessed "peculiar" geographic conditions that acted to separate large regions one from the other, a circumstance that, over the millennia, affected people in profound ways, and that influenced profoundly the achievements of Africans in all their variety. It is noteworthy that Woodson, like W. E. B. Du Bois, did not play down the negatives, such as the extent of slavery within Africa, but rather he sought ethnographic and environmental explanations, free from the idea of race as determinant. He had already perused the works of Boas, and even those of the West African scholar Casely-Hayford (whose *Ethiopia Unbound* provided one of the most powerful correctives to white racist views in vogue at that time), and he fully understood that a huge gap persisted in the popular imagination between a perceived "type" of African and the undeniable achievements of Africans across the centuries. He also challenged directly the idea that black Africans were in some special way distinct from other Africans. He recognized, like Boas, that categorization by racial characteristics alone (on the premise that the extremes of any geographical variation represented some kind of "pure" human type) would play into racists' hands.[94]

Though we can only guess what Woodson might have thought about the pronouncements of such blatant racists-in-reverse as Leonard Jeffries and others who have recently promoted a new theory of biological superiority (the *herrenvolk* turned upside down), we can be sure that he saw Africa as a complicated mix of peoples and cultures. Later in *The Negro in Our History* he argued that the presence of the Negro in the U.S., the very mix of peoples that made up the nation, was a good thing. He celebrated ethnic and racial diversity before the term came into use. Furthermore, reading his work today one is struck by its freedom from cant. The following passage on Africa is a case in point.

> In the north the controlling forces centered for some centuries in Egypt, which, though commonly regarded as a country of Asiatic civilization, was, like other parts of Africa, molded in this crucible of cultures. It was a land of mixed breeds or persons comparable to Negroes passing in this country as people of color. When these people were in ascendance, the great nations of the Mediterranean world, like the Greeks, the Italians, and the Carthaginians, came into contact with them and were thereby influenced to the extent that investigators contend that the civilizations of southern Europe had African rather than European origin.[95]

Like many African American scholars Woodson unabashedly sought Egyptian origins for higher civilization. He believed, with many European scholars of that time, that the ancient Nile civilization was by far the greatest influence in the rise of later Mediterranean and European high culture. Egypt's influence, undoubtedly profound (stretching back through millennia), was, to Woodson, simply and overwhelmingly obvious. There it was, the great river debouching into the Mediterranean, carrying with its African waters an array of practices, ideas, inventions, and beliefs.

Where a white traveler in Egypt might point up the paintings on tombs and monuments which reveal slaves, sometimes blacks from Kush, being led by a reddish or yellow-hued Pharaoh, an African or African American might point to a similar painting of Asiatic slaves being subdued by a darker Pharaoh. Where a European-trained architect trying to comprehend the origins of the great colonnades and column-supported temples of Greece or Rome might look to near Asia for earlier models, an African American might look to Luxor or Karnak on the Nile. Clearly, one's interpretation was colored by experience, and by expectation. Clearly, Woodson was justified in attempting to restore the balance.

As we have explained above this was not a new idea. Nevertheless, as presented by Woodson, the concept of Egypt as the seedbed of high civilization in the West was neatly connected to the idea that Egypt was, because of its geographical location, and above all because of its mixed people, an African land. This was the kind of argument that in our era black and white alike can accept without discomfort on either part, though in Woodson's time it was provocative. It put the idea that civilizations borrow from one another, and learn from each other, back at the center, rather than allowing race to dominate. Without denying the Asian influence or the Asian component, not to mention the problematic North African component in Egypt's "racial" composition, Woodson emphasized non-racial factors. In doing so he helped shift the emphasis—at least among African American historians—away from the invidious counter-myth. If European racists wanted to argue theories of supremacy based on dubious genetic indices, Woodson's approach would challenge the entire foundation of that theory; like Boas, like Casely-Hayford, like Blyden and Du Bois, he would look to culture.

A final comment on Woodson, one of the more effective writers of his era, is in order. He understood back in the 1920s what few seem to understand today: that race and color do not necessarily equate with culture, in either direction. If he sometimes repeated the standard view of that era, that Africans were somehow less "civilized" as one moved south in that continent, he saw this as the product of the natural environment. If he was somewhat inconsistent regarding the connection between African "society" and widespread abuses like slavery, he took pains to point out that slavery had been the bane of American life, too, indeed of American civilization, right from its birth. His contribution to a revised history was conscious of race (indeed it represented a positive counter-balance to contemporary white supremacist literature) without being "race-conscious" in the classic sense. He spoke to, and for, blacks, yet he did not claim to speak to blacks exclusively.

W. E. B. Du Bois, premiere among African American scholars and writers of this century, took a similar tack in his many works, although as he grew older and more bitter his counterattack took on something of a crusade. Like Woodson, Du Bois looked first to Egypt, a place he equated with ancient Ethiopia, a place he deeply believed to be "by blood and by cultural development a part of the history of Africa and Negro Africa."[96] He found it absurd and insulting that the African component of Egypt, especially its cultural origins in the pre-dynastic past, was so blatantly downplayed or ignored by modern white historians. Like Blyden, whom he quoted, Du Bois could not look at the Sphinx at Giza without seeing "the African or Negro type with 'expanded nostril,'" nor could he countenance the fashion in which historians had "cut the history of the Nile Valley entirely away from the history of Africa."[97] Later in life Du Bois, building on the same concept, went a step further. He wrote in *The World and Africa* that "The Egyptians . . . regarded themselves as Africans. The Greeks," he continued "looked upon Egypt as part of Africa not only geographically but culturally, and every fact of history and anthropology proves that the Egyptians were an African people varying no more from other African peoples than groups like the Scandinavians vary from other Europeans."[98] In our era this might seem unduly argumentative, but it must be realized that Du Bois rejected any "science" of genetic determinism, and, like Woodson, Boas, Hansberry, Herskovits and others who sought non-racist explanations, he saw no contradiction when he went on to say, regarding the people of Pyramid period,

> These [mixed stocks] are the people portrayed in such magnificent works of art of the Pyramid period as the sphinxes of Gizeh and the Louvre, and they are no doubt representative of a considerable part of the population of the Ancient Kingdom.[99]

His purpose was not to counter the claims of racial supremacy coming out of Europe—which reached an especially virulent extreme in Nazi Germany—with an equally dubious claim of Negro superiority; it was rather to point out that the admixture of people which made up Ancient Egypt would be close indeed to the mix that constituted African Americans, indeed nearly all peoples of African descent in the Americas. True, he took some pleasure in linking Ancient Egyptian religion to the "animism" of the African forest,[100] and he gloried in the lack of evidence that Egyptians possessed race consciousness in the modern sense: "The separation of human beings by color seemed to have had less importance among the Egyptians than the separation by cultural status."[101] He seemed aware, therefore, that his own emphasis on color, if not on race, in elevating Egypt once more to primacy in the origin of civilization in the West, and in centering that culture in Africa rather than in the Middle East, represented an ironic twist. Du Bois sought "Negroid" traits and influences among the Ancient Egyptians not to promote racism, but rather to counter the pretense, so widely accepted throughout most of his life, that Egypt, somehow, was not a part of Africa, that somehow it was white.

But what of the rest of Africa, then, especially those parts not directly influenced or ruled by Egypt at one time or the other? Did Woodson and Du Bois, like Elijah Muhammed, simply ignore the vast coast of Guinea, the endless Sudan, the great Zaire basin so large it could contain most of Europe, the complicated south, the savannahs and mountains of the East? The answer, of course, is that they did not. Woodson, for example, wrote summaries of the kingdoms of Ghana and Songhai, Ashanti and Dahomey, and he carefully examined ancient and modern systems of slavery, slavery among Christians and Muslims, slavery among fifteenth- and sixteenth-century Europeans, and then he placed the African systems of slavery, and the slave trade, above all, within this larger context.[102] Interestingly, his estimate of ten million Africans "expatriated" unwillingly to the Americas is very close to the current best estimates. He did not, apparently, buy into the tendency to inflate the numbers, already popular even in his day.

Du Bois, far more ideological than Woodson, sought deeper explanations for the new system of exploitation of slave labor that grew following the European Renaissance. Though he took care to point up the distinctions noted by Woodson, he linked the "doctrine of race" based on economic gain with the rising elite which benefited from the Commercial Revolution of the sixteenth century. In doing so, like Eric Williams he saw a direct process of cause and effect: "The African slave trade of the sixteenth and seventeenth centuries gave birth to the Industrial Revolution of the eighteenth and nineteenth."[103] Explaining the fact that Africans thus became goods was, for Du Bois, not enough. He also sought a rational explanation for that terrible question, "Why did they submit?" His answer, backed by dense pages of solid scholarship representing a lifetime of work, is worth quoting,

> Negroes were physically no weaker than others, if as weak; they were no more submissive. Slavery as an institution is as old as humanity; but never before the Renaissance was the wealth and well-being of so many powerful and intelligent men made squarely dependent not on labor itself but on the buying of that labor. And never before nor

since have so many million workers been so helpless before the mass might and concentrated power of greed, helped on by that Industrial Revolution which black slavery began in the sixteenth century and helped to culmination in the nineteenth.[104]

In the 1990s when the controversy over the "gift" of the Nile civilization often polarizes scholars, one camp reacting to the other's exaggerated claims, it is important to understand the simple fact that the solid, intellectual approach to Africa represented by Woodson and Du Bois early in this century provided a practical baseline for honest historical debate. Suffice it to say here that in matters of such import to education, to the self-image of millions of African Americans, and to the continuing education of the majority of Americans (of whatever creed or color) who tend to look upon Africa as a place of darkness, there is no substitute for careful scholarship.

Notes[105]

1. F. Freeman, *Africa's Redemption: The Salvation of our Country* (Detroit: Negro History Press, c. 1969 [1852]), 147.
2. Ibid., 13.
3. Ibid., 16.
4. Ibid., 28-29.
5. Ibid., 30.
6. Ibid., 34.
7. Wilson Jeremiah Moses, *Alexander Crummell: A Study of Civilization and Discontent* (New York: Oxford University Press, 1989), 9.
8. Ibid., 11-12.
9. Ibid., 128.
10. Alexander Crummell, "The Relations and Duty of Free Colored Men in America to Africa," in Alexander Crummell, *The Future of Africa* (New York: Negro Universities Press, 1969 [1862]), 219-20.
11. Ibid., 280.
12. Moses, 7.
13. Ibid., 138.
14. Alexander Crummell, "The Negro Race Not Under A Curse: An Examination of Genesis IX.25," in Alexander Crummell, *The Future of Africa* (New York: Negro Universities Press, 1969 [1862]), 339, 342.
15. Moses, 79.
16. Ibid., 46.
17. Elliott P. Skinner, "Afro-Americans in Search of Africa: The Scholars' Dilemma," in eds. Pearl T. Robinson and Elliott P. Skinner, *Transformation and Resiliency in Africa As Seen by Afro-American Scholars* (Washington, D.C.: Howard University Press, 1983), 11.
18. Ibid., 11-12.
19. Ibid., 12.

20. Alexander Crummell, "The Absolute Need of an Indigenous Missionary Agency in Africa," in ed. J. W. E. Bowen, *Africa and the American Negro: Addresses and Proceedings of the Congress on Africa* (Miami: Mnemosyne Publishing, 1969 [1896]), 137-42. Also see Moses, 251-54.

21. Alexander Crummell, "Civilization as a Collateral and Indispensable Instrumentality in Planting the Christian Church in Africa," in ed. J. W. E. Bowen, *Africa and the American Negro: Addresses and Proceedings of the Congress on Africa* (Miami: Mnemosyne Publishing, 1969 [1896]), 119-20.

22. Carol A. Page, "Colonial Reaction to AME Missionaries in South Africa, 1898-1910," in ed. Sylvia M. Jacobs, *Black Americans and the Missionary Movement in Africa* (Westport, Conn.: Greenwood Press, 1982), 178.

23. H. M. Turner, "Essay: The American Negro and the Fatherland," in ed. J. W. E. Bowen, *Africa and the American Negro: Addresses and Proceedings of the Congress on Africa* (Miami: Mnemosyne Publishing, 1969 [1896]), 195.

24. John H. Smyth, "The African in Africa and the African in America," in ed. J. W. E. Bowen, *Africa and the American Negro: Addresses and Proceedings of the Congress on Africa* (Miami: Mnemosyne Publishing, 1969 [1896]), 73.

25. Ibid., 81.

26. M. C. B. Mason, "The Methodist Episcopal Church and the Evangelization of Africa," in ed. J. W. E. Bowen, *Africa and the American Negro: Addresses and Proceedings of the Congress on Africa* (Miami: Mnemosyne Publishing, 1969 [1896]), 143.

27. Ibid., 148.

28. E. W. S. Hammond, "Africa in its Relation to Christian Civilization," in ed. J. W. E. Bowen, *Africa and the American Negro: Addresses and Proceedings of the Congress on Africa* (Miami: Mnemosyne Publishing, 1969 [1896]), 208.

29. Sylvia M. Jacobs, "The Impact of Black American Missionaries in Africa," in ed. Sylvia M. Jacobs, *Black Americans and the Missionary Movement in Africa* (Westport, Conn.: Greenwood Press, 1982), 221-22. For a more detailed examination of this issue, see Manning Marable, "Ambiguous Legacy: Tuskegee's 'Missionary' Impulse and Africa during the Moton Administration, 1915-1935," in the same volume.

30. Page, 186.

31. Walter L. Williams, "William Henry Sheppard, Afro-American Missionary in the Congo, 1890-1910," in ed. Sylvia M. Jacobs, *Black Americans and the Missionary Movement in Africa* (Westport, Conn.: Greenwood Press, 1982), 138.

32. Ibid., 147.

33. Ibid., 147-48.

34. Ibid., 143.

35. Skinner, "Afro-Americans in Search of Africa," 15-16.

36. Ibid., 15.

37. Augustus J. Bell, *The Wooly Hair Man of the Ancient South and a Digest of Facts from the Original Languages* (New York: LBS Archival Products, 1989).

38. Ibid., 21.
39. Rev. John William Norris, *The Ethiopian's Place in History and his Contribution to the World's Civilization* (Baltimore: The Afro-American Co., 1916), 17.
40. Ibid., 5.
41. Ibid., 10.
42. J. E. Blayechettai, *The Pen of an African* (n.p.: c. 1922), 19-20.
43. Ibid., Introduction.
44. Ibid., 38.
45. Ibid., 35-36.
46. Edward A. Johnson, *Adam vs. Ape-Man and Ethiopia* (New York: J.J. Little and Ives Co., 1931), 272.
47. Ibid., 273.
48. Ibid., 124.
49. Ibid., 277-78.
50. W. Paul Coates, "Publisher's Note," in J. A. Rogers, *Your History: From the Beginnings of Time to the Present* (Baltimore: Black Classics Press, 1983). Also see the valuable biographical sketch by W. Burghardt Turner, "Joel Augustus Rogers: An Afro American Historian," *The Negro History Bulletin* (February 1972): 34-38.
51. Joel A. Rogers, *World's Great Men of Color* (New York: J. A. Rogers and Future Press, 1947), 1: ix.
52. Ibid. 1: 2.
53. Ibid. 1: 191.
54. Ibid. 1: 196.
55. J. A. Rogers, *Your History: From the Beginnings of Time to the Present* (Baltimore: Black Classics Press, 1983), 1.
56. Ibid., 8.
57. Ibid., 5.
58. Ibid., 6.
59. Marcus Garvey, "African Fundamentalism," in ed. John Henrik Clarke, *Marcus Garvey and the Vision of Africa* (New York: Vintage Books, 1974), 157.
60. Marcus Garvey, "Speech by Marcus Garvey: Kingston, 5 February 1928," in ed. Robert A. Hill, *The Marcus Garvey and Universal Negro Improvement Association Papers* (Berkeley: University of California Press, 1990), 7: 127.
61. Ibid., 126.
62. Duse Mohammed Ali quoted in C. Boyd James, "Primitives on the Move: Some Historical Articulations of Garvey and Garveyism, 1887-1927," Ph.D. diss., University of California, Los Angeles, 1982, 270.
63. Richard B. Moore, "The Critics and Opponents of Marcus Garvey," in ed. John Henrik Clarke, *Marcus Garvey and the Vision of Africa* (New York: Vintage Books, 1974), 213-14.
64. Appendix 10: "Locations of UNIA Divisions and Chapters," in ed. Robert A. Hill, *The Marcus Garvey and Universal Negro Improvement Association Papers* (Berkeley: University of California Press, 1990), 7: 986-1000.
65. James, 297-98.

66. Judith Stein, *The World of Marcus Garvey: Race and Class in Modern Society* (Baton Rouge: Louisiana State University Press, 1986), 220-21.
67. James, 303.
68. Rupert Lewis, *Marcus Garvey: Anti-Colonial Champion* (Trenton, N.J.: Africa World Press, 1988), 165.
69. Ibid., 165-66.
70. W. E. B. Du Bois, "Back to Africa," in ed. John Henrik Clarke, *Marcus Garvey and the Vision of Africa* (New York: Vintage Books, 1974), 105.
71. James, 349.
72. Ibid., 286.
73. Ibid., 232.
74. Ibid., 312.
75. Stein, 109.
76. James, 216.
77. Malu Halasa, *Elijah Muhammad* (New York: Chelsea House, 1990), 43-44.
78. C. Eric Lincoln, *The Black Muslims in America* (Boston: Beacon Press, 1961), 51.
79. Halasa, 29.
80. Ibid., 50.
81. Lincoln, 75.
82. Elijah Muhammad, *The Fall of America* (Chicago: Muhammad's Temple of Islam No. 2, 1973), 16-17.
83. "Who is the Original Man?" *Muhammad Speaks* (May 1962), 1.
84. Ibid., 1.
85. Ibid., 23.
86. "After the Africans . . . Came the Cave Dwellers: History of Man's Origin Must now be Rewritten," *Muhammad Speaks* (8 May 1964), 11.
87. Muhammad, 150.
88. "Who is the Original Man?," 23.
89. Muhammad, 79.
90. Ibid., 150.
91. Richard M. Dorson, *American Folklore and the Historian* (Chicago: University of Chicago Press, 1971), 143-44.
92. Carter G. Woodson, *The Negro in Our History* (Washington, D.C.: The Associated Publishers, 1962 [1922]), 341-42.
93. Ibid., 1.
94. Ibid., 2-5.
95. Ibid., 5-6.
96. W. E. B. Du Bois, *Black Folk Then and Now* (Millwood, N.Y.: Kraus-Thompson Organization, Ltd., 1975), 38. As Herbert Aptheker points out in his introduction, the early parts of this work appeared in *The Negro*, a small book by Du Bois, published by Henry Holt in 1915.
97. Ibid., 38.
98. W. E. B. Du Bois, *The World and Africa* (New York: The Viking Press, 1947), 98.
99. Ibid., 202.
100. Ibid., 104.

101. Ibid., 106.

102. Woodson, 9-22.

103. Du Bois, *Black Folk Then and Now*, 126-27. See Eric Williams, *Capitalism and Slavery* (Chapel Hill: The University of North Carolina Press, 1944). This important work provided a vital corrective to the predominating view at midcentury which assumed that the abolition of slavery was an entirely philanthropic endeavor. William's work, however, has since generated a lively scholarly debate on this basic issue.

104. Du Bois, *Black Folk Then and Now*, 128.

105. Several of the more obscure texts cited in this chapter can be found in the Schomberg Collection of the New York Public Library.

8

Africa Politically Corrected

For Africans and African Americans alike, the 1950s and 1960s were a time of anticipation, then triumph, and, at the end, a time of anger and disillusionment. In the United States the civil rights movement became a force to reckon with on the national scene, and from the *Brown v. Board of Education* decision by the Supreme Court in 1954 (which called for an end to "separate but equal" schools), through the sit-in and voting rights campaigns in the Deep South, to the advent and full emergence of the charismatic leadership of the Rev. Martin Luther King Jr., African Americans went from victory to victory in a moral revolution that was no less dramatic for its emphasis on legality and non-violence. In Africa, British Prime Minister Harold MacMillan's "Winds of Change" speech in 1960 admitted the wholesale onset of a process which many observers had seen coming since the renewed imperial bloodletting of the Second World War: the end of European empire in the "Third World." When the Union Jack was hauled down in Accra, Ghana in 1957 and that colony became an independent nation, it signaled a changing of the guard throughout the continent and the rapid creation of a host of new African states. In both cases, however—in Africa and in America—a period of formal and sweeping political change was not accompanied by a corresponding economic transformation, and the 1960s ended with a sense of uncertainty for black intellectuals and activists on both sides of the Atlantic. On the streets of Detroit, Harlem, and Watts, a generation of young blacks vented their rage at a dream denied, an escape from the poverty which these earlier breakthroughs had seemed to foreshadow. At the same time, in Accra, Nairobi, and the other capitals of independent Africa, the new elites enjoyed an increased prestige and authority while the rural (and urban) masses soon discovered that the trappings of independence had done nothing to better their daily lives or increase their immediate prospects for a brighter future. Perhaps it is an exaggeration to argue that the end of this era was a time of despair; it was, however, a time of reflection, reassessment, and intensified political debate both within Africa and throughout the diaspora.

For those who called for an immediate and decisive change in the black condition during the 1950s, the options for action resolved themselves into two radical alternatives. Nowhere were the differences between these two basic strategies more sharply and lucidly defined than in George Padmore's searching inquiry into the problem of *Pan-Africanism or Communism*. As James R. Hooker has pointed out, Padmore was uniquely qualified to address this question: the West Indian expatriate had been the "organising genius" (with the help of Du Bois) behind the Fifth Pan-African Congress in Manchester, England in 1945, which brought together such future African statesmen as Jomo Kenyatta and Kwame Nkrumah. And, earlier in his career, Padmore had risen "to become the foremost black figure in the Communist International—the Comintern—culminating in his . . . appointment as a colonel in the Red Army."[1] While Padmore acknowledged that there was a considerable element of truth in the Marxist analysis of history and economy, he made it absolutely clear that "if there is one thing which events in Africa, no less than in Asia, have demonstrated in the post-war years, it is that colonial peoples are resentful of the attitude of Europeans, of both Communist and anti-Communist persuasion, that they alone possess the knowledge and experience necessary to guide the advancement of dependent peoples."[2] On the basis of political experience, Padmore concluded that it made no sense to link the future of Africa to the twists and turns of the self-interested policies of the Soviet Union. Instead, he called for a program which "rejects the unbridled system of monopoly capitalism of the West no less than the political and cultural totalitarianism of the east," and a philosophy which "identifies itself with the neutral camp, opposed to all forms of oppression and racial chauvinism."[3] In short, he opted for an idealistic vision of Pan-Africanism, a principled approach which

> seeks the attainment of the government of Africans by Africans for Africans, with respect for racial and religious minorities who desire to live in Africa on a basis of equality with the black majority. Economically and socially, Pan-Africanism subscribes to the fundamental objectives of Democratic Socialism, with state control of the basic means of production and distribution. It stands for the liberty of the subject within the law and endorses the Fundamental Declaration of Human Rights, with emphasis upon the Four Freedoms.[4]

In presenting his arguments in *Pan-Africanism or Communism*, Padmore was anxious to allay the fears of white Europeans and Americans who thought that the African independence movement (and the struggle for civil rights in the United States) were simply subordinate branches of the "international Marxist-Leninist conspiracy." The more paranoid among his audience had nothing to worry about, however, since sporadic Communist efforts to win the sympathy of black America had been both comically presumptuous and utterly maladroit. As Padmore explained it, an early effort by the young American party—to penetrate the Garvey movement—had resulted in a total fiasco:

> the Provisional President of Africa proved more than a match for the Communists. Armed with an acid tongue and a sharp pen, Garvey turned upon the infiltrators and ejected them lock, stock, and barrel. He then took the offensive right into the Communist ranks by inciting his fanatical disciples to break up Communist street-corner meetings in Harlem. Negro members were denounced as "Red Uncle Toms" and "traitors to the black race," for Garvey's racialism made him intolerant of any kind of co-operation with white radicals.[5]

Apparently, the nucleus of this Communist "insurgency" consisted of the former members of another black nationalist group known as the "African Blood Brotherhood." This organization had been founded by Cyril Briggs, a West Indian immigrant and the editor of the New York *Amsterdam News*. "While Garvey was coming up with his grandiose plan for a Negro state in Africa, Briggs countered it with the view that the 'race problem' could be solved by setting up an independent Negro nation on American territory. . . . He suggested locating the 'colored autonomous state' in the West, either in the states of Washington, Oregon, and Idaho, or, as he thought preferable, in California and Nevada." Garvey and Briggs became bitter enemies, and the Brotherhood emerged in a new guise in 1921 as "the first Negro contingent for the American Communist movement, which had been founded two years earlier."[6] This was the first quixotic attempt by the Communist movement to attract African American support, but events would prove that it would not be the last.

Not content with this setback, nor deterred by the collapse of several African American "front" organizations in the years that followed, the party eventually seized on an equally impractical strategy for attracting black support. The plan itself—and the identity of its author—can best be described as bizarre. According to Padmore

> It was . . . decided that since Marcus Garvey had rallied
> popular support by promising to establish a "National
> Home" for blacks in Africa, the American Communists
> should go one better and offer the American Negroes a state
> of their own in the Black Belt . . . that strip of territory in
> the heart of the southern part of the U.S.A. extending south
> and south-west from the eastern part of Virginia to the bor-
> der of Texas, in which the Negro population exceeds the
> white. . . . The blueprint of the "Black Republic" . . . was the
> brain child of a former Finnish university professor of Marx-
> ist sociology, Dr. Otto Kussinin. . . . Dr. Kussinin, a member
> of the Faculty of Red Professors, was at the time one of the
> secretaries of the Comintern.[7]

The absurdity of this initiative was obvious to any casual observer
of the American political scene. Nevertheless, in the late 1920s this
fantastic scheme was "with Stalin's blessing . . . imposed upon the
American party. Those who rejected Kussinin's thesis were expelled
as 'right-wing deviationists.' Among the victims of this purge were
many of the most intelligent Negroes."[8] Ironically, Stalin's most
implacable foe within the international Communist movement also
eagerly embraced this idea. Indeed, "the most tenacious advocate of
Negro 'self-determination' . . . was Leon Trotsky. In 1933, he
advised his reluctant American followers to support the Negroes'
right 'to separate a piece of land for themselves'" and he even "held
out the possibility that the Negroes might well get to the 'proletar-
ian dictatorship' ahead of the white workers through the medium of
self-determination."[9] Obviously, in this case—as in so many others—the yawning chasm between theory and practice, and the possible and the impossible, was totally lost on these invincible
"warriors of the dialectic."

After the announcement of this "proposal" to the "Negro masses,"
a number of black intellectuals immediately condemned it as nothing more than an opening wedge for the type of racist and segrega-
tionist system which was gradually being imposed in South Africa,
a pathology which would reach its apogee in the 1940s with the formal adoption of "apartheid." Clearly, the creation of a "Black Homeland" on such invidious terms—in Africa *or* America—would be a
curse rather than a blessing. In addition to this clear and present
danger, the "Black Belt" initiative made no real sense from a demographic standpoint. As Theodore Draper has pointed out,

> While the Communists were discovering the Black Belt, it
> was already breaking up. About 200,000 Negroes migrated
> North annually after 1916. The number of counties in which
> Negroes comprised 50 per cent or more of the population in
> the twelve Southern states went down from 262 in 1910, to

222 in 1920, 190 in 1930, 178 in 1940, 151 in 1950, and
134 in 1960. The exodus to the North was slowed during the
depression, but it picked up momentum toward the end of
the 1930s and turned into a flood in the next two decades.[10]

Thus, while black Americans increasingly looked toward the
urban centers of the industrial north, the Communist Party continued to base its program on the dubious attractions of the rural
south. Moreover, beyond this serious conceptual problem, African
Americans had their own compelling reasons for doubting the sin-
cerity of their aspiring white comrades. As an anonymous reviewer
noted in *The Crisis* (the journal of the N.A.A.C.P.) in 1952,

> Negroes believed that a Soviet America, if one ever came to
> pass, would be run by white commissars. They saw through
> the "Black Belt" scheme as mere hokum, since it meant
> more segregation . . . being the most American of Americans
> they would have none of Communist doctrine. . . . The Negro
> masses have always been "leery" of poor whites bearing
> them gifts. And most Communist missionaries were po'
> whites in their eyes. The Negroes are very religious. God and
> the church still come first in their . . . group philosophy, and
> an atheistic foreign screed leaves them cold, when it does
> not arouse their hostility.[11]

Clearly, if the only political options open to African Americans
had been Pan-Africanism or Communism, it seems obvious what
their choice would have been. The problem was considerably more
complex, however—and the choices considerably more varied—than
Padmore's stark dichotomy would tend to suggest.

It would be misleading to argue that the majority of African
Americans had a deep and informed interest in African affairs in
the 1950s, although it seems reasonable to maintain that the
extent and intensity of this interest continued to grow as the
decade progressed. As Roger Wilkins suggested in *Foreign Policy*
magazine, the basic reason for this lack of engagement should be
painfully obvious: "there was too much business to be done with
the 'man downtown,' who hired and fired and had the power of life
and death, with the lady whose house was to be cleaned every day,
or with the welfare department. There was no time to give even a
passing thought to the Department of State."[12] In retrospect, it
should not be surprising that the daily struggle for survival took
precedence over more abstract notions such as Pan-African solidarity. There was, however, another—and even more disturbing—reason for the emotional and intellectual distance between the African
American and his ancestral homeland. In the words of Wilkins:

"What is Africa to me?" the poet asked in a hymn of praise to
the lush, rich darkness of the American Negro's past. . . . For
most blacks of my generation, who grew up in the 1930's and
1940's and came to full height—if not to maturity—in the
1950's, the answer was simple: nothing. Nothing except a
reminder of shame: irrelevant except for our need to repress
and forget it in our drive for assimilation here in America.[13]

During a period in which black Americans were forced to prove
their worthiness for full and equal citizenship—in white eyes, and
on white terms—it was understandable why many were reluctant to
embrace an Africa that was routinely described as "primitive," "savage," "backward," or, in the more neutral and academic parlance
that was beginning to take hold, "underdeveloped." The symbolic
conventions had lost none of their power, and it is easy to see why,
for an educated and ambitious young person such as Wilkins, "to
identify with the black clods of Tarzan's Africa never entered my
mind."[14]

This attitude was further reinforced by the black press, which
lacked the resources to develop an independent network of agencies
and reporters in Africa. Most of its information on the continent
was culled from "mainstream" newspapers and magazines—both
American and European—and the editors of these publications
were faced with the unenviable task of distinguishing truth from
fiction, and fact from fantasy, with no real empirical base of their
own and no effective instruments aside from their logic and their
intuition. As Martin Staniland has observed in his outstanding
study of *American Intellectuals and African Nationalists, 1955-1970*,
"At least until the late fifties, African American periodicals often
reflected both a low level of interest in Africa and a rather disdain-
ful attitude toward its inhabitants"[15]—an analysis which applies
with equal precision to the "white press" during this same period.
Given the intellectual (and informational) environment in which
these black editors functioned, it is not surprising that "expressions
of support for self-government were sometimes accompanied by
approving remarks about the distance that Africans had traveled
from primitivism."[16] Given the basic limitations on finance and per-
sonnel, the development of a totally independent perspective would
have been difficult to achieve in any case—aside from the obvious
fact that the African American press did not operate in a cultural
vacuum, free from the influence of the dominant media and the
negative stereotypes which they continued to disseminate.

As Staniland has suggested (through a series of telling examples), the image of Africa projected by the major periodicals was
often closely mirrored in the pages of their African American

counterparts. In a review of Vernon Bartlett's *Struggle for Africa* in *The Crisis* in 1954, Hugh H. Smythe noted that the author "constructively advises the black man to recognize that there can be 'little hope of genuine partnership until the Africans learn something about the nature of civilization.'"[17] Moreover, according to Smythe,

> No book is perfect. Yet so minor are the errors the author commits—"The absence of an African history must always remain a mystery" or in referring to the Union of South Africa "with so much lawlessness about, the insistence on the Pass Law is understandable"—that these defects detract not in the least from this admirable and helpful volume. Mr. Bartlett's command and insight of all he surveys is strikingly and prophetically displayed in his comment on the predicament of those fast losing control of Africa's destiny: "But at the back of all these policies is the realization that the black man is awaking from a sleep as long as history, and there is a flavor of Lilliput about our efforts to cope with him."[18]

Difficulties arose even when an author or commentator attempted to transcend the symbolic conventions. When *Ebony* offered a "photo-editorial" entitled "The Ten Biggest Lies About Africa" in 1957, the intentions were good but the ultimate result was ambiguous and patronizing. The story centered around a full-page picture of "University of Chicago student Adebisi Otudeko," an African student who is seeing his first lion "behind the bars of an American zoo." The anonymous author explained that there was little to fear from wild animals in the African bush: indeed, "the former footpaths of Old Timers are now sissy safari routes running through thousand-mile game preserves with all the comforts of Route 66." More importantly, the article stressed that "Not all Africans . . . are black, child-like 'natives' clothed in loin cloths. . . . A vast number of Africans wear western clothes. . . . The Mau Mau did not menace the entire continent . . . and although a few unenlightened brethren still practice cannibalism, there are areas where Africans firmly believe that white men eat them!" This was hardly a militant exercise in cultural revisionism: it was apparent that the objectives of the writer were far more modest. He—or she—was simply content to point out that "The Big Sleep is over. The people are awakening. And all of those tall tales about the homeland, they know now, are not necessarily so."[19]

The independence of Ghana in 1957 was a turning point for many African Americans in their relationship with the mother continent. This event, which was dramatically underscored by the march to freedom of a majority of the African colonies over the next five years, was a tangible source of inspiration for black activists involved in the American civil rights struggle: it demonstrated that victory was, indeed, a real possibility, that the "promised land" was within reach. A new level of consciousness on African affairs was definitely emerging in the black community, but, as Elliott Skinner has suggested, this transformation was far from being an overnight phenomenon:

> Ghana's Independence Day was relatively unnoticed by the majority of Americans, black and white. Among Negroes, the event was celebrated only by a handful of intellectuals and veterans of the Garvey Movement who felt not only pride, but vindication in their slogan of "loyalty to Africa." However, the veritable avalanche of new African states in 1960 and their subsequent admittance to the United Nations caught the imagination of all but the handful of Negroes who could not overcome their prejudice toward Africa.[20]

For some young Americans, however, the coming of African freedom marked a watershed in the development of their self-image and sense of self-respect. James Baldwin noted in 1961 that "At the time I was growing up, Negroes in this country were taught to be ashamed of Africa. They were taught it bluntly by being told . . . that Africa had never contributed 'anything' to civilization. Or one was taught the same lesson more obliquely, and even more effectively, by watching nearly naked, dancing, comic-opera cannibalistic savages in the movies."[21] While the damage this concept had caused was real it was not permanent, as Baldwin made clear in no uncertain terms:

> None of this is so for those who are young now. The power of the white world to control their identities was crumbling as these young Negroes were born; and by the time they were able to react to the world, Africa was on the stage of history. This could not but have an extraordinary effect on their own morale, for it meant that they were not merely the descendants of slaves in a white, Protestant, and Puritan country; they were also related to kings and princes in an ancestral homeland, far away. And this has proven to be a great antidote to the poison of self-hatred. It also signals, at last, the end of the Negro situation in this country as we have known it thus far. Any effort, from here on out, to keep the Negro in his "place" can only have the most extreme and unlucky repercussions.[22]

For Phaon Goldman, writing in the *The Negro History Bulletin* in 1960, the impact of African events on the struggle in America was direct and immediate. Goldman maintained that "the valor and sense of justice of the ancient peoples of West Africa can most clearly be seen . . . in the determined, forthright, and courageous stand for freedom now being taken by our . . . Negro youth of the South who in spite of threats, insults, and violence, stand by their right to be accorded the simple human decencies that all other people . . . get in America."[23] Moreover, in his estimation at least, the relentless pace of the African liberation drive had also sent an unmistakable message to the advocates of caution and delay on the American homefront.

> The strength of our forefathers is with us still, and make no mistake about it, the students' inspiration came from the fight for freedom now being waged all over the African continent by their brothers and sisters who recognize that the "go slow" school of moderates didn't tell the Hungarians and Tibetians [sic] to "go slow" and they don't want to hear it either.[24]

To be sure, there were some black Americans who did not share this enthusiasm for a compelling new emphasis on the African present—and past. This attitude was certainly not prompted by a sense of shame: instead, it was felt by some observers that this Afrocentric tendency performed a disservice by diverting popular attention away from the legacy of black resistance and achievement in the United States. John A. Morsell, the assistant to the Executive Secretary of the N.A.A.C.P., enunciated this position in the pages of *The Crisis*:

> Fixing on Africa as the chief symbol of Negro militancy is something of a paradox: it really implies acceptance of the derogatory stereotype of the American Negro as submissive and dependent, the passive beneficiary of a freedom bestowed upon him. Persons genuinely free of this stereotype and adequately informed as to their history might well have chosen their heroes and heroines from the American Negro's too little-known record of slave revolts, escapes, resistance to captors, abolitionist crusading, and valiant combat by tens of thousands in the Revolutionary War, the War of 1812, and the Civil War.[25]

Moreover, while the argument seems tenuous, at least one scholar has suggested that the increasing interest in "emerging" Africa among America's black bourgeoise may have been based on a sense of class, as well as racial solidarity. According to Martin Staniland, there was a growing realization among this group that "there was now an African middle-class elite with tastes and ambitions similar to their own. . . . As *Ebony* put it (in words that would have made the radicals of the sixties shudder): 'The emergence of Nkrumah and other pipe-smoking, cultivated African leaders who wear Bond Street tweeds and carry briefcases is gradually changing U.S. Negro opinions of Africa!'"[26] For those members of the black middle class who had labored hard to achieve some modest degree of prosperity, such analogies must have been both interesting and heartening. Unfortunately, the steady support of the more "traditional" members of the black middle class for the cause of African freedom was—and still is—often forgotten. For the most part, their rhetoric—the rhetoric of political moderation and non-violence, which had also been the starting point for Martin Luther King Jr.— was lost in the medley of more insistent and "revolutionary" voices which came to the forefront in the late 1960s and the early 1970s.

With the assassination of King and the wave of violence which followed in its wake a more militant approach to the issues of civil rights and economic justice at home, and African Liberation and "Third World Solidarity" abroad, assumed center stage within the black community. The call for direct and decisive action was certainly not unprecedented within the historical context of black activism—one need only consider the legacy of abolitionism, the scattered but widely celebrated (and feared) slave rebellions, and even the ambiguous legacy of Garveyism to confirm this. Nor was the call for a more aggressive strategy merely a spontaneous reaction to the momentous chain of events from Memphis (where King was assassinated), to Vietnam (where blacks assumed a disproportionate role in combat), to the political debacle of Watergate. As early as 1962, the black intellectual Harold Cruse had noted that a new sense of urgency was in the air:

> During the past fifteen years, there has been more noise in the United States about the Negro's changing status than actual changes in that status. At the same time, the social changes taking place in the colonial world—especially in Africa and Latin America—have been more revolutionary than anything the American Negro has experienced since the post-civil war period. By comparison with colored peoples elsewhere, Negroes in America have found that their own advance toward fuller freedom is lagging. And an uncomfortable awareness of that discrepancy has given rise to a new set of political and cultural values which, taken together, have come to be called "Afro-Americanism."[27]

Here was Padmore's "Pan-Africanism" painted on a broader canvas, a popular tendency which encompassed cultural as well as strictly political values, a more holistic (if also more diffuse) approach to the problem of black identity and action. A variety of different doctrines and approaches would emerge in the cauldron of the 1960s, but most who fit within Cruse's description agreed on certain general principles: the necessity for an international struggle against racism and the vestiges of colonialism and the economic empowerment of blacks (and other minorities), which was usually seen as occurring through the medium of some vaguely defined variant of socialism. Some would stress the political aspect of this mission while others would concentrate on its cultural dimension, but all would agree with Malcolm X's unequivocal estimate of the black condition: that substantial and immediate change must be brought about "by any means necessary."

Ironically, over the next several decades, a more moderate and concrete response to the problems of Africa would grow and flourish side-by-side with the more emphatic forms of "Afro-Americanism." Individual efforts, such as the work of Leon Sullivan, who helped devise a set of guidelines for American corporations in South Africa, and the presence on the international scene of prominent appointed officials such as Andrew Young and Donald McHenry (and political figures such as Jesse Jackson) would not go unnoticed in the corridors of power. When added to the collective efforts of lobbying groups such as TransAfrica and the legislative impact of the Congressional Black Caucus, this presence would ensure that an African American voice would be heard when it came to making policy on Africa. At this point it is important to stress that those who chose to work "within the system" shared many of the basic goals of those who challenged it from outside: on issues as diverse as apartheid and urban renewal there was considerable unanimity within the black community on desired ends (if not appropriate means). Still, the more insistent and uncompromising voices commanded the greatest share of public attention, and political style proved to be every bit as important as political substance. Cruse was a remarkably accurate prophet when he predicted (in 1962), with obvious ambivalence, that "with all their inadequacies, inexperience and lack of any historical sense of Negro life, the Afro-Americans are here to stay." He was confident that

> In the future they will undoubtedly make a lot of noise in militant demonstrations, cultivate beards and sport their Negroid hair in various degrees of *la mode au naturel*, and tend to be cultish with African and Arab-style dress. . . . Already, they have a pantheon of modern heroes—Lumumba, Kwame Nkrumah, Sekou Toure in Africa; Fidel Castro in Latin America; Robert Williams in the south; and Mao Tse-tung in China. These men seem heroic to the Afro-Americans not because of their political philosophy, but because they were either former colonials who have achieved

complete independence, or because, like Malcolm X, they
have dared to look the white community in the face and say:
"We don't think your civilization is worth the effort of any
black man to try to integrate into it."[28]

The death of King created a crisis in moderate leadership which
was never fully resolved. Among younger African Americans, his
very murder confirmed the suspicion that his philosophy and tactics were no longer sufficient for the challenge at hand. The torch
had passed to a new generation which had little patience with
compromise and delay, a generation which had raised the rallying
cry of "black power" and gone well beyond the more modest objectives of its predecessors.

At the center of all this was Malcolm X, a man who grew in intellectual stature toward the end of his life and achieved his greatest
influence—as a symbol and icon of resistance—after his death. Malcolm's profound impact on black political consciousness in the late
1960s was underscored by another prominent militant, Eldridge
Cleaver:

> Malcolm X, as far as Afro-America is concerned, is the father
> of revolutionary Black nationalism. After he separated from
> the Nation of Islam and repudiated the leadership of Elijah
> Muhammad, Malcolm came to Africa, and he traveled all over
> the continent. Egypt, Ethiopia, Tanzania, Ghana, Nigeria, the
> Ivory Coast, were all stops on his itinerary. The black world
> burst fully upon him during this sojourn . . . Afro-Americans,
> following the new direction of Malcolm X, became Africanized
> overnight . . . Malcolm emphasized our African heritage,
> insisting that we must become connected with Africa, even
> though he offed the "Back to Africa" concept. He also empha-
> sized that we must resort to armed struggle and fight for our
> freedom.[29]

As Cleaver has suggested, the break with Elijah Muhammad was
critical for several reasons. Most importantly, it allowed Malcolm X
to openly espouse a more sophisticated analysis of events and freed
him from his mentor's fantastic racial mythology, an ideology which
had little real attraction for educated and sophisticated young
blacks. Retaining the essential message of the end of white
supremacy, he was able to dispense with the notion of "evil scientists" and prehistoric Islam which undermined the credibility of his
basic argument. Although his concept of an "Organization of Afro-
American Unity" (modeled on its African counterpart) came to
naught, it suggested the exciting possibility of a "Black United
Front" in the United States, a joining together of a host of national
and community organizations in pursuit of a common goal.[30] This

idea did not necessarily represent the final stage in his intellectual evolution, however, since there is reason to believe that he had already begun to develop a broader and more optimistic vision of the future. The consequences of Malcolm's personal and emotional growth after his trip to Mecca and his participation in the *Hajj*—a seminal experience which led him to question the basis of *any* ideology which was rooted in a racial or ethnic consciousness—were never fully realized. This was not only due to his untimely death: realistically, it is also obvious that, even had he lived, this potential direction would have had little appeal for a generation of activists who were determined to organize the struggle along strictly racial lines.

When one thinks of the black "revolutionary" spirit which reached its full maturity in the late 1960s, the group which most readily comes to mind is the Black Panthers, or, to cite its original name, the "Black Panther Party for Self-Defense." This organization was formed in Oakland, California in 1966 by two junior college students, Huey Newton and Bobby Seale. At Merritt College "they took their first step toward nationalist political activity by joining a local Afro-American Association, which soon proved insufficiently militant for them."[31] Several run-ins with the police inspired them to form the party and directly led to their most famous and notorious initiative, the dispatch of armed patrols which tailed patrol cars in the name of "self-defense." Ideology was another matter, however: although they issued a "Ten-Point Program" which was designed to enunciate their goals, their positions taken collectively were not especially notable for their coherence or consistency, nor for their continuity over time. As Theodore Draper has pointed out, their ideas were a "peculiar amalgam, as Trotsky would have called it, of bits and pieces from Malcolm X, Mao Tse-tung, Ernesto Che Guevara, Regis Debray, and others . . . typical of the kind of do-it-yourself Marxism-Leninism that . . . [had] recently come into vogue."[32] Central to their definition was the vision of their role as a "vanguard party," an advance guard of the "people's revolution" which would lead by action and example rather than by words. This rhetorical posture certainly had its advantages: in particular, it helped to deflect attention from their ongoing internal disputes and their continuing problem with doctrine.

Whatever else they were, the Panthers were not a "Back-to-Africa" party. Their nebulous position on the "national question" was stated in the "Ten-Point Program," which called for "'a United Nations-supervised plebiscite to be held throughout the black colony in which only black colonial subjects will be allowed to participate, for the purpose of determining the will of the black people as to their national destiny.'"[33] The "colony" which they referred to was the African American population of the United States, and it was apparent that the only "homeland" which would be acceptable in the future would be a domestic one. Newton, especially, had little patience with those who advocated an "Afrocentric" solution to African American problems, or with those who emphasized cultural values and appearances over substantive political action. As he stated:

> "Cultural nationalism deals with a return to the old culture of Africa and that [sic] we are somehow freed by identifying and returning to this culture, to the African cultural stage of the 1100's or earlier . . . we believe that it's important for us to recognize our origins and identify with the revolutionary Black people of Africa and people of color throughout the world. But as far as returning per se to the ancient customs, we don't see any necessity in this."[34]

This point was made even more forcefully by other Panther leaders. Draper refers to the blunt opinion of their "Minister of Education" George Mason Murray who "called this kind of pro-African cultural nationalism 'a fixation in a people's development like a half-formed baby,' 'reactionary and insane and counterrevolutionary', [and] 'a bourgeois-capitalist scheme to confuse the masses . . . so that they will not assault the city halls, the bank tellers, and managers, or seize control of the community schools.'"[35] Thus, if one were to agree with Murray, every African American clad in a dashiki represented a potential agent or stooge of "American imperialism and neo-colonialism" and was guilty of a serious ideological deviation.

Nevertheless, this adamant stand against the glorification of Africa did not prevent the Panthers from making good use of the symbolic conventions when it suited their purpose. One need only think of the memorable and dramatic photograph of Newton, dressed in a black beret and a black leather jacket, seated in an "African" wicker chair suitable for royalty, with a gun in one hand and a spear in the other, the modern vision of Shaka Zulu incarnate, the very symbol of assertive black masculinity and the very embodiment of the white racist's worst nightmare. Predictably, there was no attempt to reconcile this widely disseminated photo (and poster) with the official Panther position on "cultural nationalism."

For the Panthers, this was not the final word on Africa, however. By 1971, as Kathleen Rout has indicated in her excellent biography *Eldridge Cleaver*, the party had split and the faction which was led by Cleaver had begun to display a much more serious interest in the liberation struggle on the continent. In that year, Cleaver headed a Panther delegation to Congo-Brazzaville, the "People's Republic of the Congo," a trip which was chronicled in his book entitled *Revolution in the Congo.* At this time the versatile Cleaver was in the midst of his "Marxist-Leninist" phase, and he described his experience in the most turgid "revolutionary" prose he could possibly summon. Not surprisingly, he had nothing but praise for the "democratic" regime which had been founded by paratrooper captain Marien Ngouabi. Apparently, the "historic victory of the Congolese people" had done many things: and, if one is to believe Cleaver, it had even resolved the bitter conflict between political militants and cultural nationalists in the United States. By 1970, this division had assumed serious proportions.

> We understood very clearly the contradiction between our-selves and the cultural nationalists. We knew what it was about the cultural nationalists that we didn't like. We could relate to African culture. We incorporated it into our beings. We had no hangups about that. But we even stopped wear-ing dashikis and emphasizing our Africaness as part of our struggle against the cultural nationalists who had turned African culture into either a fetish or a marketable commod-ity, and at the same time completely repudiating the gun. We wanted to call people's attention to the gun.[36]

This crisis of ideas and action was soon resolved for Cleaver, however, as he experienced a shattering dialectical revelation on the road from Brazzaville. On his return he proclaimed that:

> a loud voice has risen from the heart of Africa. . . . The his-torical existence of a Marxist-Leninist nation in Africa destroys all arguments supporting the perpetuation of the contradiction between the revolutionary black nationalists and the cultural nationalists, which for several years has bottled up and stifled an unestimated amount of revolution-ary energy. This energy must again burst forth, on a higher level of consciousness, with cadres already committed to ideology, but firmly rooted in our African heritage and iden-tity. We now have an African model, The People's Republic of the Congo, which is a black nation with a Marxist-Leninist state. All arguments over the synthesis of our history, our culture, and Marxism-Leninism can now be dealt with objec-tively, because we have an example of where this has already been done successfully.[37]

Unfortunately, this schism would not be magically healed by the proclamation of an African "People's Republic," and the Ngouabi regime would not go on to distinguish itself as a "model" of political achievement or economic development. Nevertheless, the Congo—

and the symbolic conventions surrounding it—would continue to retain a powerful emotional attraction, even for a committed "scientific socialist" such as Cleaver. Ironically the Panther leader noted that "of all words, phrases, and statements connected with Africa, even more than the word 'Africa' itself, the word 'Congo' sets off some very deep vibrations in black hearts, in black souls, in black minds."[38] Indeed, for one African American traveler, at least, the "heart of darkness" had been transformed into "the mother of light."

Cleaver was not the only member of the party who developed a greater interest in Africa and its Marxist-Leninist experiments. Stokely Carmichael, a leading figure in the Student Non-Violent Coordinating Committee, went on to join the Panthers for a brief period; in time, he would change his name to Kwame Ture in honor of the West African leaders who had inspired his personal and distinctive blend of Pan-Africanism and socialism. Despite these attempts at synthesis, however, the split between the "political militants" and the "cultural nationalists" did not disappear, and it was still very much in evidence when the "movement" began to lose its energy in the early 1970s. For the most part, this dispute was conducted through a battle of words; but the potential for violence among self-proclaimed "revolutionaries" was always there, and on one occasion events took a tragic turn:

> The struggle for control of the Afro-American Studies Center at the University of California at Los Angeles went so far that two Black Panther leaders who were also students at UCLA were shot to death on January 17, 1969, in the university's Campbell Hall. . . . The murders were ascribed to a rival nationalist outfit headed by "Maulana" Ron Karenga (born Ronald Everett) who founded the organization US . . . in 1965. Information from the Panthers led to the indictment of five US members. The Panthers vowed vengeance . . . but Karenga . . . eluded them. (Karenga means "keeper of the tradition" and "Maulana" is an honorific title in Swahili). Karenga represent[ed] to the Panthers the most dangerous of the pseudo-African cultural nationalists. . . . [39]

While Karenga and his approach have endured, the Panthers could not survive the steady pressure of official harassment and the crippling internal divisions which helped to compromise their influence in the black community. Admittedly, their Marxist rhetoric and dubious posture as a "vanguard party" found a receptive audience among white radicals of the "new left." Nevertheless, the Panthers' strident call to action made no real headway within their basic constituency. Despite a growing sense of anger and frustration, the majority of African Americans rejected their apocalyptic message and continued to direct their political efforts toward more concrete and achievable goals.

While most black activists were able to agree on the general outlines of the American experience, the movement continued to suffer from the lack of a coherent historical vision of the mother continent. There was an obvious need for a positive interpretation which could help to unite the various ideological camps, a paradigm which could be embraced by Pan-Africanists, Marxists, and even liberals of a more daring persuasion, a sense of the African past which could command the support of cultural nationalist and political militant alike. The time was ripe for such a venture, and in the late 1960s a brilliant young West Indian scholar stepped forward and attempted to meet this challenge. Walter Rodney had been trained in the University of London's School of Oriental and African Studies, and his doctoral dissertation and subsequent history of the Upper Guinea Coast had been well received by the established historians of Africa. His professional credentials were impeccable but he was as much an activist as an academic, and he saw the writing of history as a "means of struggle" rather than a personal vehicle for a "bourgeois" career. Tragically, this personal involvement would lead to his untimely end: "on June 13, 1980 . . . [Rodney] became the best-known victim of a systematic campaign of assassination . . . carried out by the governing authorities of his native land, Guyana."[40] Still, his most important work, *How Europe Underdeveloped Africa*, would leave a lasting and controversial impact on the historiography of the continent. His success was not absolute, however, since his greater goal remained unfulfilled. Despite a favorable reception by intellectuals throughout the diaspora, his research failed to provide an adequate rallying point for the black left, which continued to suffer from serious divisions which could not be healed by an act of scholarship, no matter how "committed" or polemical its intent.

Rodney's analysis was thoroughly grounded in Marx's theory of economy and history. His revisions, additions, and criticisms were many, but the logic of "dialectical materialism" provided the starting point for his study of *How Europe Underdeveloped Africa*. Karl Marx had argued that mankind's social and economic development had been (and would be) realized through a series of discrete and recognizable stages, ways of life which were closely linked to the level of technology at any given time. Simply stated, mankind would pass through "primitive communism," slavery, feudalism, capitalism, and socialism on the way to its ultimate historical destiny—communism. Rodney was alert to the Eurocentric nature of Marx's vision, however, and he described a stage of African development—"communalism"—which preceded feudalism, since, in his polemical estimate, "in Africa, there were few slaves and certainly no epoch of slavery."[41] According to his scheme, the central tragedy of African history was that most of the societies on the continent had been poised to make the transition from communalism to feudalism when a potent external force—European imperialism—had intruded upon the scene and disrupted and distorted this process beyond recognition. He also maintained that, at this point, Europe had been somewhat more advanced in the course of its development, in an intermediate stage between feudalism and capitalism. Thus, Europeans were in a position to turn this advantage to their own end through the systematic exploitation of Africa and other regions of the Third World. African markets and commodities, but most of all, African labor, hastened the European transition to capitalism, a development which allowed for a more intensive exploitation of the African continent and brought about increasing social dislocation and a steadily worsening situation for its people.

This historical condition had enormous implications for the present. Rodney insisted that "underdevelopment" was a relative concept—a term which only made sense when one part of the world was contrasted to another—and he maintained that Africa had been locked into a destructive and unequal relationship with the West for several centuries. Political independence had done nothing to change this basic reality, and Africa could never truly develop, nor truly be free, until it found a way to break the bonds of this fatal economic embrace.

Up to this point, whether one accepts or rejects Rodney's interpretation largely depends on one's evaluation of Marx's theory of history. There are modifications in his scheme to account for African realities, but the Marxist method and logic are basically intact. Reams of scholarship, ranging from the brilliant and accomplished to the narrow and reductionistic, have been produced on the premise that the economic and material are indeed paramount, that this "base" of the human experience undergirds and limits and even determines the social, cultural, and intellectual "superstructure" which is built upon it. Some have argued that this theorem drastically limits the scope of effective human action and reduces man to a reflexive puppet of impersonal economic forces. In response to this objection a "revisionist school" of Marxists (following the lead of the French theoretician Louis Althusser) has argued for a greater degree of actual equality—and a *mutual* pattern of influence—between base and superstructure. The variations on this theme are infinite and the debate rages on, endlessly and earnestly, in a myriad of journals and political broadsheets.

Still, this summary does not describe the full extent of Rodney's intellectual universe. It is notable that his book was not entitled

"How Capitalism Underdeveloped Africa" but rather "How *Europe* Underdeveloped Africa," and the difference here is a crucial one for it suggests the other half of his guiding charter. If one follows Rodney, a straightforward Marxist analysis only reveals part of the picture since capitalism in the Western world soon developed a particular characteristic which made it something more than an abstract and dispassionate "mode of production." Admittedly, Rodney warned that "occasionally, it is mistakenly held that Europeans enslaved Africans for racist reasons. European planters and miners enslaved Africans for *economic* reasons, so that their labor power could be exploited."[42] At the same time, however, he was equally insistent that the Atlantic slave trade was only the first step in a more thorough and enduring process of subordination.

> It would be much too sweeping a statement to say that all racial and color prejudice in Europe derived from the enslavement of Africans and the exploitation of non-white peoples in the early centuries of international trade. There was also Anti-Semitism at an even earlier date inside Europe and there is always an element of suspicion and incomprehension when peoples of different cultures come together. However, it can be affirmed without reservation that the white racism which came to pervade the world was an integral part of the capitalist mode of production. . . . The racism of Europe was a set of generalizations and assumptions, which has no scientific basis, but were rationalized in every sphere from theology to biology.[43]

Here is where Rodney's analysis assumes its distinctive character and betrays its essential schizophrenia. By arguing that European racism was subsumed within the capitalist world system he seemed to suggest that the economic factor was still in the ascendant. Throughout his book, however, it is not entirely clear which force—the racial or the economic—is the primary determinant of action and events. The result is a divided agenda and a variety of history in which Africans are usually passive victims rather than conscious actors. Moreover, it is a history in which positive African accomplishments do occur, but always in spite of, and in defiance of, the relentless and all-pervasive grip of Eurocentric capitalism. The idea that some Africans actually benefited from this very system by turning it to their own ends—indeed, that some Africans manipulated it with consummate virtuosity and skill, and often did so at the expense of other Africans—could not be easily or comfortably accommodated within Rodney's Manichean worldview. When all was said and done he could only condemn (or apologize for) these Africans, whom he portrayed as the deliberate or unwitting fellow travelers of the European capitalist conspiracy. Referring to Africa's contemporary predicament he noted that

> The question as to who, and what, is responsible for African underdevelopment can be answered at two levels. First, the answer is that the operation of the imperialist system bears major responsibility for African economic retardation by draining African wealth and by making it impossible to develop more rapidly the resources of the continent. Second, one has to deal with those who manipulate the system and those who are either agents or witting or unwitting accomplices of the said system.[44]

Thus, in the final analysis, Rodney's undeniable talent was largely consumed by a futile and thankless exercise in intellectual gymnastics: the attempt to reconcile two distinct, and often incompatible, lines of historical analysis. Unlike Padmore, he did not see the African dilemma as a matter of *Pan-Africanism or Communism*; in fact, his magnum opus could have been subtitled *Pan Africanism and Communism* since he was determined to fashion a practical synthesis of these two ideals. In attempting this fusion Rodney walked an uncertain line between scholarship and polemic, and if the result was sometimes inconsistent and unconvincing his rhetorical offensive made a definite impression. Above all, his challenge had the positive effect of forcing historians of Africa to take a critical look at their basic assumptions and methods.

The problems with Rodney's approach are most apparent in his treatment of the Atlantic slave trade. Without naming names, he suggested a conspiracy among "western bourgeois" historians to cover up the full extent and impact of this holocaust. His argument revolved around the number of victims and the level of damage to African societies and economies. On the former point he argued that

> A recent study has suggested a figure of about ten million Africans landed alive in the Americas, the Atlantic islands, and Europe. Because it is a low figure, it is already being used by European scholars who are apologists for the capitalist system and its long record of brutality in Europe and abroad. In order to whitewash the European slave trade, they find it convenient to start by minimizing the numbers concerned. The truth is that any figure of Africans imported into the Americas which is narrowly based on surviving records is bound to be low, because there were so many people at the time who had a vested interest in smuggling slaves (and withholding data).[45]

What is one to make of this? How, by any stretch of the imagination, does an estimate of ten million victims amount to a "whitewash"? And who are the "European scholars" who are orchestrating this cover-up, and what are their ultimate motives? Since Rodney provided no footnotes (and only a "Brief Guide to Reading" at the end of each chapter) the reader has no real means of evaluating his statements. He was far more credible when he maintained that "if the low figure of ten million [is] accepted as a basis for evaluating the impact of slaving on Africa as a whole, the conclusions that could legitimately be drawn would confound those who attempt to make light of the experience of the rape of Africans from 1445 to 1870."[46] Even then, however, we are still left to guess who is "making light" of this terrible historical tragedy—and why they are doing so.

At times, Rodney tended to blur an issue by hinting at—rather than actually advancing—a false comparison. In an apparent reference to the figure of ten million, he noted that "on any basic figure of Africans landed alive in the Americas, one would have to make several extensions starting with mortality in transshipment." This obviously makes sense. He then went on to state—with equal accuracy—that many had died in the violence associated with the capture of slaves, and that "there were also numerous deaths in Africa between time of capture and time of embarkation." Thus, he rightfully concluded that "it is necessary to make some estimate as to the number of people killed and injured so as to extract the millions who were taken alive and sound." This is all well and good, but how does it invalidate the (anonymous) calculation of "ten million Africans *landed alive* in the Americas, the Atlantic islands, and Europe"?[47] While these "extensions" are perfectly logical in assessing the overall impact of the trade, he did not establish that these variables were ever included in the original figure he was so anxious to invalidate, a figure which, as his own language suggests, was strictly limited to actual imports. Thus, by implication rather than direct argument, the "scholarly conspiracy" he posits is made to seem even more nefarious than he originally suggests.

Rodney made it clear that the continent as a whole had been victimized by the slave trade. He was scornful of "certain European (including American) scholars"—whom he never named—who had (supposedly) argued that "the European slave trade was undoubtedly *a moral evil*, but it [had been] *economically good* for Africa . . . that African rulers and other persons obtained European commodities in exchange for their captives, and this was how Africans gained 'wealth.'"[48] This is a classic example of setting up a "straw man" which can be conveniently and convincingly demolished. Some, indeed, had pointed out that certain African individuals (and societies) had profited from the trade at different times, but one must search long and hard for a scholar who had suggested that this commerce had been "economically good for Africa" in any broader and significant sense. Rodney, however, was perfectly willing to reverse this claim and make an equally sweeping and dubious generalization in order to advance his case. He totally rejected the possibility that "certain African kingdoms grew strong economically and politically as a consequence of the trade with Europeans." Moreover, in assessing the progress of West African states such as Oyo, Benin, Dahomey and Ashanti he was willing to make his own interesting leap in logic. He correctly pointed out that "the fact that a given African state grew politically more powerful at the same time as it engaged in selling captives to Europeans is not automatically to be attributed to the credit of the trade in slaves," but he then proceeded to argue that

> A cholera epidemic may kill thousands in a country and yet the population increases. The increase obviously came about *in spite of* and not because of the cholera. This simple logic escapes those who speak about the European slave trade benefiting Africa. The destructive tendency of slave trading can be clearly established; and, wherever a state seemingly progressed in the epoch of slave trading, the conclusion is simply that it did so in spite of the adverse effects of a process that was more damaging than cholera. This is the picture that emerges from a detailed study of Dahomey, for instance, and in the final analysis although Dahomey did its best to expand politically and militarily while still tied to [the] slave trade, that form of economic activity seriously undermined its economic base and left it much worse off.[49]

This raises a host of interesting questions, not the least of which is whether or not Dahomey's failure to "expand politically and militarily" was directly and primarily related to its large-scale participation in the slave trade. Beyond this, however, Rodney's analysis poses a more fundamental issue. If, in fact, the slave trade had such a deleterious effect on these West African states, why did their leaders choose to, and continue to, engage in it? Were they competent political actors within their own regional sphere or nothing more than compliant dupes of the Europeans? Also, in his insistence that all Africans suffered from the trade, Rodney made no systematic distinction between the victimizers and the victims. Did the raiders suffer as extensively as the raided? Did the acquisition of firearms through this trade provide no short-term political and military advantages for the African polities which obtained them? In a sense, there is little to choose between Rodney's conception of

African political capabilities and those set forth by Henry Morton Stanley and Theodore Roosevelt. The gap between "savages" (or "barbarians") in need of tutelage and misguided and myopic victims who cannot comprehend their own best interests is far too close for comfort; the language is different, but the essential helplessness of the Africans it portrays is not.

It was not an easy task for Rodney to construct a history which stressed a positive record of African cultural and political achievement (on the one hand) and wholesale exploitation and victimization at the hands of Europeans (on the other), and the strain was especially apparent in Rodney's commentaries on particular African societies. With respect to Yorubaland (in modern-day Nigeria), Rodney noted that "numerous captives were taken in war, most of whom were sold to Europeans, so that Yorubaland became notorious as a slave-supplying region up to the 1860s. But many war prisoners were retained locally, in conditions approximating either to slavery or to serfdom, depending on whether or not they were first generation captives." He further pointed out that during this period "the division of labor among the Yoruba was extended with the rise of professional soldiers, or 'war-boys,' as they were called. The professional soldiers, who were sons of aristocrats, left farming disdainfully to prisoners and serfs—the large number of whom insured agricultural plenty."[50] Thus, by Rodney's own admission, slaveraiding, at a certain point, *did* contribute to the process of political and economic expansion. Rodney's implication, however, was that slavery and slaveraiding were acceptable and constructive instruments within a purely *African* context, and they only became problematic when they were directed toward the export trade of the Atlantic system. Indeed, Yorubaland, by these means, was well on the way to feudalism when "Ibadan's farming areas were hit by war, and Ibadan's rulers also started removing prisoners farming the land and selling them instead to Europeans. That became necessary because Ibadan needed firearms, and those only could be obtained by selling slaves. It was at that point that the undermining effect of the presence of European slave buyers on the coast became really paramount."[51]

There are some obvious problems here. If Rodney had followed this analysis to its logical conclusion he would have been bound to concede that these "European slave buyers" were a harmful force because they were disrupting an *indigenous* system of production in which slavery played a significant role. A careful examination of this case study does little to support Rodney's contention that slavery (apart from the export trade) was historically insignificant in Africa. It also says nothing about the societies which were the target of this raiding prior to the strategic emphasis on the export trade. And finally, it suggests that slaveraiding was only tantamount to "cholera" when it assumed a particularly virulent European strain. Aside from a basic and understandable (if oversimplified) demographic argument—that slaves and captives kept within the continent might contribute to its development while those who were taken out could not—there is little to recommend in Rodney's estimate of events.

In point of fact, a close examination will reveal that this type of polemical rationalization was endemic in Rodney's approach to the African past. Speaking again of Dahomey, he argued that "throughout the eighteenth and nineteenth centuries, [it] had a stagnant if not declining population, and an economy that had virtually no props other than slave exports. What Dahomey succeeded in doing in spite of all that is a tribute to the achievements of man inside the African continent."[52] In this regard, echoing Herskovits, he maintained that

> the story of the reputed savagery of Dahomey was exaggerated incredibly. The Dahomean state created such refinements as a population census; it conducted diplomacy far and wide, with all the niceties and the protocol that one usually hears of only in connection with "civilized" European states; and it built up a system of espionage and intelligence as an essential ingredient in its own security.[53]

One must pause and ask a basic question at this point: if Dahomey had developed a "population census," how could its leaders have been unaware of the demographic havoc which the slave trade was apparently causing? Furthermore, why did they continue to participate in this trade if its effects on their economy, their society, and their power base were overwhelmingly negative? Quite simply, this makes no sense. One must also question his brief analysis of "the role of the artist in Dahomean society." He justifiably praised their impressive achievements, and insisted that although "it was art that centered around royalty and noble families . . . it was also a national product and a point of identification for the people as a whole." Furthermore, and just as significantly, "particular individuals were being given the opportunity for self-discovery and self-development and of serving the society as a whole."[54] Is it not possible, however, that these artistic efforts were made possible by a surplus which had been generated, in whole or in part, by slavery and the slave trade? Moreover, if this was the case, how did the political economy of this artistic expression differ from the European case, where the proceeds from the Atlantic slave trade helped to spur the economy of the British Isles and the low countries, which in turn helped to support the commercial classes who came to play a significant role as consumers of art and as patrons of artists? Predictably, Rodney had nothing to say on this point.

Rodney was equally inconsistent when dealing with nineteenth-century South African history, in particular the career of the Zulu leader Shaka. He informed his readers that "all commentators on Shaka (both African and European) frequently compare him favorably with the 'Great Men' of European history,"[55] which raises the question of whether the "Great Men" of European history should provide the measure for African achievement. Rodney provided an overview of Shaka's extensive conquests and his role as a military innovator, but he never paused to consider a more basic question: whether a preindustrial society can develop a military emphasis which can frustrate or distort other, more constructive, lines of development. The regimented social order of Shaka's regime was a subject for special praise, and his pattern of violent conquest was explained as a benevolent enterprise, indeed, as a sort of "civilizing mission" for the neighbors of the Zulu.

> The Zulu army was more than a fighting force. It was an educational institution for the young, and an instrument for building loyalties that cut across clans and could be considered as national. . . . The enforced use of the Zulu branch of the family of Ngoni languages also worked in the direction of national consciousness. . . . Policies such as curbing the excesses of witchcraft diviners . . . and the fact that Zulu-land became free of internal struggles led to an influx of population. . . . European travelers . . . were impressed by the cleanliness . . . and they were equally struck by the social order, absence of theft, [and] sense of security . . . both the cleanliness and the security of life and property were part of Zulu life from long before, and under Shaka what was impressive was the scale on which these things extended, owing to the protective umbrella of the state.[56]

Thus, Rodney made it clear that, in European terms, Shaka "made the trains run on time"; indeed, this is precisely the type of rhetoric that one associates with laudatory accounts of Italy and Germany in the 1930s. The serious disruption and loss of life that characterized the *Mfecane*—this particular period of South African history—is glossed over in favor of heroic biography. It might better be argued that Shaka's campaigns were in part reactive or defensive in nature, as a threatening European influence was beginning to be felt at the edges of his territory; or it might also be pointed out that Shaka was not the only agent of violence in the cauldron of the *Mfecane*. Yet these complexities are ignored—along with his Marxist analytical agenda—in favor of an inspired nod in the direction of the "Great Man" approach to the writing of history. In this case, as in much of *How Europe Underdeveloped Africa*, Rodney could not effectively reconcile the conflicting elements in his guiding intellectual program. Above all, by mixing an approach which was based on the assessment of impersonal economic forces—Marxism—with a conscious racist conspiracy on the part of the West, he created a view of African history which is more notable for its contradictions than for its consistencies. For all its surface brilliance and occasional flashes of insight, his method, and the basic interpretation which flows from it, ultimately fails to convince.

In recent years, another radical spokesman has arisen to challenge the conventional wisdom (and methods) of African studies. Molefi Kete Asante—an African American scholar—has proclaimed the philosophy of "Afrocentricity," a "method" which he sees as the correct and essential means of approaching the African past and defining the African future. While he praises Rodney, whom he ranks among those special individuals who possessed a "commitment to greatness," Asante has little use for the Marxism which informed his basic analysis.[57] In his view, Marxism is a Eurocentric philosophy which "over-simplifies the significance of our history," a doctrine which overstates the importance of economics and understates the historical significance of racism. Moreover, its emphasis on class struggle is a legacy of "the values of confrontation developed from the adventures of Europeans during the terrible White Ages."[58] Instead, Afrocentricity is centered around two dominant, and loosely related, intellectual tendencies. Central to his argument is the primacy of Ancient Egypt, which he sees as primarily, or exclusively, a black African civilization; as well as the direct, absolute, and lineal forerunner of the culture of Greece and Mediterranean Europe, and thus, by extension, the mother of European civilization itself. This orientation is linked to an enthusiastic revival and advocacy of the brand of "cultural nationalism" espoused by Maulana Ron Karenga, an approach which was criticized in the past for its emphasis on style and philosophy at the expense of concrete political action. Beyond this, however, at another—and more fundamental—level, the guiding ethos of the Afrocentric project has been stated best by Asante himself in his insistence that "we rid ourselves of all fantasies except those that grow out of our own history."[59] Indeed, for the less cautious advocates of this movement, the line between fact and fantasy is an inconvenient barrier which need not trouble the determined seeker of the Afrocentric Grail.

Egypt is firmly at the center of Asante's cosmology. As a determined follower of the late Senegalese scholar Cheikh Anta Diop,[60] he is absolutely convinced that its great civilization—or "Kemet," as he calls it—was founded, sustained, developed, and dominated by people from the south: by black Africans. In his opinion, "all one has to do is to look at the murals, the engravings, and statuettes which provide abundant physical evidence of the antiquity of Egypt's Africanity. The people of ancient Egypt were no different than the African people of the United States, Brazil, Mali, Nigeria, Ethiopia, Sudan, or Zimbabwe."[61] Asante seems to be positing a sort of "feedback" model between Egypt and the rest of Africa, and his lack of precision in regard to their specific cultural relationship is the cause of some confusion. On the one hand, he argues that sub-Saharan Africa provided the effective nucleus of Kemetic civilization; while on the other, he notes that "the foundation of all African speculation in religion, art, ethics, moral customs, and aesthetics are derived from systems of knowledge found in ancient Egypt."[62] Aside from this critical ambiguity, one is left to wonder why more of the material and technological assets of the Kemetic and Mediterranean world did not travel back along the original path of diffusion and go on to take root in the vast and inviting homeland to the south.

Also, Asante is equally sure that the civilization of ancient Greece was ultimately "a gift of the Nile." In *Afrocentricity*, he asserts that "we know . . . that only one ancient civilization could be considered European in origin, Greece. And Greece itself is a product of its interactions with African civilizations,"[63] a theme he expounds on at greater length in a more recent book, *Kemet, Afrocentricity, and Knowledge*. This is a thesis which has recently been brought into the intellectual limelight by Martin Bernal's *Black Athena*, an ambitious (if highly criticized) two-volume study which reflects a lifelong interest in Egyptology on the part of this professor of government and scholar of Chinese studies at Cornell University.[64] Both Bernal, from his depth of research on the subject, and Asante, from his polemical starting point, offer a strong critique—some of it justified—of those European scholars who have for several centuries wrongfully refused to acknowledge that Egypt was, indeed, one of the constructive influences in the making of Greek civilization.

Thus, there is a genuine rationale behind Asante's historical critique. Unfortunately, however, he tends to go beyond this into the realm of speculation and conspiracy. The reality of "Egyptian influence" does not imply the wholesale transmission of a pristine and unaltered civilization across the Mediterranean: nor does it rule out a meaningful contribution from other external sources. More importantly, however, this dramatic vision of diffusionism creates another logical distortion by casually dismissing the content and creative capacity of early Greek culture itself, the culture which obviously provided the material and intellectual foundation for these later achievements. Moreover, with reference to the first major issue under debate—the notion of a basic cultural unity between Egypt and sub-Saharan Africa—Asante suggests that there was a conscious effort on the part of European opinionmakers to sever the mass of Africa from its rightful classical heritage.

> There is no great emphasis in the period prior to the eighteenth century for taking Egypt and Nubia out of Africa and making those ancient civilizations "oriental" if they could not be European. Therefore, it is obvious that the predicament of Africa, the great European commerce in human slavery, and the need to minimize the contribution of Africans in order to justify the institution of slavery meant that the European writers would deliberately falsify historical records.[65]

Conspiracy theory aside, what is the scholarly consensus regarding these basic historical questions? Most would agree that the peoples to the south (or, at least, some of them) had an appreciable, if intermittent, influence—demographic and political as well as cultural—on the civilization of ancient Egypt. Most would also agree that Egypt had a definite, if indeterminate, impact on the culture of ancient Greece. Beyond this, however, there *is* no consensus, although the more rational voices in the debate approach these questions in terms of *degrees* of influence, avoiding the temptation of sweeping claims and rhetorical absolutes. The lack of unanimity on these issues was recently described by Wyatt MacGaffey in the *Journal of African History*. MacGaffey offered this succinct (and telling) impression of a 1974 conference in Cairo on "The Peopling of Ancient Egypt and the Deciphering of the Meroitic Script," a meeting whose proceedings figured in the first two volumes of the *UNESCO General History of Africa*:

> The summary report of this conference is printed in volume II as an annex to the first chapter, in which Diop expounds his view that the ancient Egyptians were black and that their language was cognate with modern Wolof. . . . In the words of the report itself, discussion "often took the form of successive and mutually contradictory monologues" (p. 49) The majority, especially the Egyptians, disagreed with the views of Diop and Obenga. The Egyptians did not think that their ancestors were black and felt sure that movements of civilizing influence in the Nile valley went from north to south rather than the other way. The Egyptian editor of volume II attached a note to Diop's chapter referring to its controversial reception at the conference; on the other hand, in

J. Greenberg's chapter in volume I on African linguistic classification, in which he associates ancient Egypt with the Semitic languages rather than with Niger-Congo, Diop's partisans attached a similar footnote indicating that the conference had "refuted" this conclusion.[66]

This was the state of scholarly debate on this issue *before* the advent of "Afrocentricity." Now that the strictly ideological element of this discourse has been intensified, one can only imagine the "dialogue" which will take place in the conferences which follow. Unfortunately, this continuing academic exchange will probably do little to clarify the fascinating history of Egypt, not to mention that of the rest of Africa, and the passionate dispute over its origins and its contribution to the early development of Europe will likely lose none of its partisan fervor in the months and years to come.

One can see the popular appeal of the Afrocentric project. By stressing the centrality of a "classical" (and antecedent) black African culture, the history of Africa is given a sense of unity, coherence and symmetry which would not otherwise be apparent to the man on the street. Europeans have always had the reassuring image of Greece and Rome; so why shouldn't Egypt be deployed to play a similar role for Africans both on the continent and throughout the diaspora? There is a further advantage to this formulation: if the accomplishments of ancient Greece are substantially derivative from Egypt, then the African continent is not only the evolutionary home of mankind but the ultimate source of European civilization as well. Moreover, from an important practical standpoint, this ideology can contribute to a sense of pride and the development of a positive self-image for African American youth, and it offers inspiration to black people whatever their age and status. There clearly is much at stake here, and Asante insists that this vision is a cause worth fighting for; at the same time, however, his pronouncements suggest that there is a cost involved as well.

> Afrocentricity maintains intellectual vigilance as the proper posture toward all scholarship which ignores the origin of civilization in the highlands of East Africa. . . . We know because of our Afrocentric consciousness that only one ancient civilization could be considered European in origin, Greece. And Greece itself is a product of its interaction with African civilizations. Among ancient civilizations Africans gave the world, Ethiopia, Nubia, Egypt, Cush, Axum, Ghana, Mali, and Songhay. These ancient civilizations are responsible for medicine, science, the concept of monarchies and divine-kingships, and an Almighty God. . . . Our collective consciousness must question writers who use symbols and objects which do not contribute meaningfully

to our victory. . . . Afrocentric criticism must hold especially
accountable the works of African [sic], continental or diasporan. . . . The times are surely different and we must now
open the floodgates of protest against any non-Afrocentric
stances taken by writers, authors, and other intellectuals or
artists.[67]

That Asante's notion of "ancient" extends as far as the sixteenth
century A.D. is not the primary issue: the attitude toward scholarship implied by this quotation is. Throughout *Afrocentricity* there
runs the notion that an idea or a piece of scholarship or art should
be judged in terms of its practical value for his intellectual agenda.
Documents and historical studies that tend to support his version
of history are acceptable, while those which tend to refute it are
not and likely fall into the category of "deviations," which he
defines in his glossary as "any action, word, or thought which does
not adhere to the Afrocentric perspective."[68] Thus one can freely
applaud a writer who follows this approach as a maker, or codifier,
of myth; but scholarship is another matter entirely, since it
demands that ideas be evaluated with some concern for their
accuracy and not strictly on the basis of their immediate utility.

Beyond this, the call for "vigilance" gives further cause for unease:
must African American scholars and their work be judged solely in
terms of their conformity with Afrocentric doctrine? The last thing
that is needed at this point is an inquisition within the black academy. In fairness to Asante, he has stressed the importance of tolerance: on a related matter, in a short piece in *Newsweek* magazine,
he insisted that "in none of the major works of Afrocentricity has
there ever been a hint of racism, ethnocentrism, or anti-anybody.
Indeed, Afrocentricity believes that in order to have a stable society,
we must always have a society that respects difference."[69] Clearly,
then, if there is any danger in this doctrine it does not come from
Asante himself, but from what others, less scrupulous and sensitive,
might try to make of it.

One must ask a further question regarding Asante's (and
Bernal's) interpretation of history, an interpretation which has
attracted so much attention in the last several years: what is
really new here? As demonstrated in the last chapter, an African-
American discourse which places Egypt, and Biblical Ethiopia, at
the center of world events can be traced back at least as far as the
abolitionist movement. Admittedly, Asante has placed this idea
within the context of a loosely defined philosophical movement,
but in the end, the historical dimension of Afrocentricity is
remarkably derivative of a long tradition of African American writing and commentary.

The cultural focus of Afrocentricity can be directly traced to Maulana Karenga, to whom Asante gives due credit. Central to this impulse, and the philosophical grounding which accompanies it, is the notion of "Njia: The Way," a collection of guidelines on proper moral, social, and political behavior which appears as an appendix in *Afrocentricity*. The thrust of these statements is affirmative rather than adversarial, and in "Quarter One" of Njia it is stated that "The Way is not contradictory to Hinduism, Judaism, Christianity, Islam, Yoruba, or any other way of peace and power; it is complementary."[70] In addition, the related ceremony of Kwanzaa—a celebration and remembrance of African American history, culture, and sacrifice—is equally positive in its guiding approach. It remains to be seen whether this week-long event achieves a widespread following within the African American community: coming as it does in the week after Christmas, there is certainly no practical (nor intellectual) reason why black Christians would feel unable to embrace it. In its essentials, Kwanzaa is every bit as rational and appropriate as any other ethnic religious festival, even if, as the African American literary critic Henry Louis Gates Jr. reminds us, it was "invented in Los Angeles, not Lagos."[71] From an intellectual standpoint, Kwanzaa is an interesting phenomenon for a variety of reasons: not the least of which is that it stands out as a classic contemporary example of "the invention of tradition," to use the term and concept advanced by historian Eric Hobsbawm.

On another level, despite Asante's sincere disclaimers, a casual reading of *Afrocentricity* will reveal that this text is not without its historical biases. In particular, Asante is highly critical of the legacy of Islam in Africa, and there is some question whether all social and cultural expressions within the continent are considered to be equally "Afrocentric." At the beginning of the book he makes it absolutely clear that Islam (in any form) is not a desirable path for modern African Americans:

> Adoption of Islam is as contradictory to the Diasporan Afrocentricity as Christianity has been. Christianity has been dealt with admirably by other writers, notably Karenga; but Islam within the African-American community has yet to come under Afrocentric scrutiny . . . while the Nation of Islam under the leadership of Elijah Muhammad was a transitional nationalist movement, the present emphasis of Islam in America is more cultural and religious. This is a serious and perhaps tragic mistake; because apart from its historical contradictions, there exists monumental contradictions in its application. All religions rise out of the deification of someone's nationalism. Understand this and you will discern the key to our own victory.[72]

Asante then goes on to demonstrate how, in his opinion, Islam is essentially the "deification" of Arab nationalism. He does not deny its power as an ideology: as he puts it, "it is one of the most powerful tools of mind control ever created. Suppose Afrocentrism had you and the white people of Europe and the Arabs of Arabia turning heads toward the sacred forests of Oshogbo, or toward Tuskegee, or Mount Kilimanjaro?"[73] Still, its effectiveness as a creed is not a sufficient recommendation except, perhaps, for other Arabs, and Asante is concerned that Africans of the diaspora start turning *their* heads in the right direction. Also, while he argues that the Europeans have been largely responsible for the systematic misrepresentation of the African cultural heritage, they have not been alone in this act of vandalism. Asante takes pains to decry

> the complete abandonment of the classical African civilizations by the conquering Arabs from the seventh century to the eighteenth century. With limited exceptions the Arabs controlled the whole of North Africa from the first jihads out of Arabia in 641. They appeared to have little respect or appreciation for the classical civilization they found in the Nile Valley. Having destroyed the organic structure of the African society they found in Egypt, reinstituted the ban on the Egyptian language, and allowed the great ancestral holy places to lie in ruin, the Arabs created the perfect opportunity for the distortion of the African heritage of Egypt . . . the subsequent suppression of the Arabs by the Ottoman Turks and Europeans made it possible for the colonizers to dictate the terms of study of ancient Egypt, even to assume the leadership of the antiquities service.[74]

It should not be surprising, then, that Asante has serious difficulties with the scholarship of Ali Mazrui and Edward Said. While he acknowledges that Mazrui is a "rhetorician capable of handling language in an eloquent fashion," he maintains that his "cynicism about Africa colors his entire corpus."[75] Despite his African birth, Mazrui is, to Asante, "a truly Eurocentric Africanist of the genre that has been schooled in the discipline most advantageous to the advancement of a European intellectual particularism."[76] For Asante, this political scientist's formulation of a "triple heritage" for Africa—a triad consisting of traditional African belief systems, Islam, and Christianity—has been an especially destructive exercise which has tended to stress the importance of external influences on sub-Saharan Africa. As he puts it, "there is no triple heritage of Africa, there is the double legacy of Islam and Christianity impacting on the indigenous culture of the continent emerging as 'double trouble' for African expression."[77] This is not all, however: Asante hints that

there was a personal motive involved in Mazrui's intellectual position. He cryptically notes that "Mazrui, like Diop, was a Muslim. He
saw in Diop a rival for African Islamic intellectual hegemony. But
Mazrui was no match for Diop in the breadth of his knowledge and
the loyalty to African traditions as essential for African advancement."[78] Obviously, Asante was probably not an enthusiastic viewer
of Mazrui's PBS television series, nor is it likely that he worked very
hard to boost the sale of the videocassette collection which closely
followed its initial showing.

The work of Edward Said—in particular his magnum opus, *Orientalism*—is equally unattractive when viewed under the Afrocentric microscope. Asante, too, is critical of the western tendency to
demand an "artificial division of philosophical reality into Eastern
and Western spheres," but although Said "has written a provocative
account of the discourse on Orientalism he is as much a victim of
the artificial division of philosophical reality as the Westerners he
so ably criticizes."[79] As Asante sees it,

> The principal problem with Said is that he has bought into
> the invisibility of Africa and has claimed classical Africa as a
> part of the Orient, largely by relying on writers who
> expressed a hostility to Africa and Africans during the
> seventeenth, eighteenth, and nineteenth centuries. More-
> over, in trying to prove that "European culture gained in
> strength and identity by setting itself off against the Orient,"
> he followed in Europe's footsteps by misunderstanding
> Africa and misplacing a part of Africa in the Orient.[80]

That "misplaced part of Africa," of course, is Egypt; and while, for
Mazrui, the Red Sea was a historical and geological mistake, Asante
seems to prefer that it had been a vast and bottomless chasm pro-
tecting Africa from the unwanted intrusion of its Arabian neighbors. As for Said, he commits the ultimate offense from an
Afrocentric perspective: in *Orientalism*, he "claims Egypt for the Orient in much the same way the French had done in the eighteenth
century after Napoleon's invasion."[81] While Said's analysis of the
attack on the Orient which came from Europe makes good sense,
Asante's counter-argument—if placed in a broader context—provides a needed qualification since Egypt *was*, in fact, linked to
Africa as well as to the Orient, if not in the absolute and exclusivist
fashion envisioned by Asante. Indeed, it must be said that Asante
makes some valid and telling points in his evaluation of the work of
other contemporary scholars: whatever one thinks of the approach
and content of "Afrocentricity," one must fully acknowledge his considerable skills as a critic.

At times, however, his rhetoric suggests a quest for ideological purity which is less attractive. In advocating the "methodological and functional perspective" of "Afrology"—the correct and Afrocentric approach to the study of black history and black realities—he suggests that most earlier African American scholars, no matter how committed or insightful, failed to measure up to its full requirements. Thus, we are informed that

> it is popular nowadays to call up the deeds of W. E. B. Du Bois, E. Franklin Frazier, Carter G. Woodson, Benjamin Brawley, Alain Locke and other scholars as indications of a long and distinguished history in afrology. But this is to invoke the names of the ancestors amiss. They were scholars who studied our people but seldom Afrologists. This is why I have said that afrology is a crystallization of notions and methods, it is the being of what was coming to be in the perceptions and perspectives of these great men. In almost every case they were excellent historians, critics, and sociologists but not Afrologists. . . . *It is the Afrocentric method which makes Afrological study.*[82]

Given the hazy, tautological, and at times contradictory manner in which this "method" is defined in *Afrocentricity*, one must agree that the outstanding scholarship of figures such as Du Bois and Woodson does not fully qualify for the "Afrological" mantle. Aside from this, however, there are other disturbing tendencies in this work. For example, gay blacks will discover that "homosexuality is a deviation from Afrocentric thought because it makes the person evaluate his own physical needs above the teachings of national consciousness." Furthermore, Asante proclaims that "we can no longer allow our social lives to be controlled by European decadence"[83] (homosexuality, apparently, being a distinctly European phenomenon). There is hope for these individuals, however; they can be cured, since "the homosexual shall find the redemptive power of Afrocentricity to be the magnet which pulls him back to his center."[84]

On another issue—the nature of the relationship between Africans and African Americans—one detects a hint of patronization when he predicts that "as we continue to travel, the influence on continentals will be much greater than their influence on us. I speak here of contemporary, not historical, influences dictated by status, wealth, and education." Another factor affecting this process will be "the overpowering capacity of technology that distinguishes our ability to disseminate innovations."[85] There are echoes here—however remote—of pristine African villages whose humble inhabitants eagerly await the guiding hand from across the sea.

Asante may well find that African realities (and attitudes) are considerably more complex than his scenario seems to indicate. These points, if taken together, give reason for caution, since they suggest that under the banner of Afrocentricity it may well be that, as George Orwell put it, "everyone is equal but some [will be] more equal than others."

At times, Asante's observations are insightful and cogent; in certain instances, however, they are obviously less compelling. There are passages in *Afrocentricity* which can only be described as silly: for instance, in a testimony to diffusionism run rampant, we learn that "Nommo [an Afrocentric forum] is also the place where facts are disseminated, such as, 'Robin Hood is an old African celebration form [sic] Egypt once called *Hruben-Hud* which was Anglicized by the English.'"[86] One shudders to think of the semantic equivalent of the sheriff of Nottingham Forest. Other statements, both absolute and oversimplified, demand a more serious level of attention. In a discussion of the nature of language and the distortions that it can perpetuate, Asante boldly proclaims (in dramatic italics) that "*There is no such thing as a black racism against whites; racism is based on fantasy; black views of whites are based on fact.*"[87] If there is, in fact, an element of truth in this assertion, Asante does not bother to provide any explanation or evidence by way of substantiating it. On another matter, he notes that "every victory over fascism, apartheid, and racism has been won by rational fanatics who have shown their commitment to excellence."[88] He might also have pointed out that "rational fanatics" played a pivotal role in imposing these ideologies in the first place, if one can accept an oxymoron as a legitimate category of analysis.

Further on the subject of language, Asante suggests that a whole range of popular vocabulary should be consigned to the dustbin of history. For example, the "use of terms like 'minority,' 'qualified,' 'standards,' 'law and order,' and 'quality control' when dealing with interracial situations reflect a communication bias often found in white language."[89] If this is not enough, his African American readers are warned that "the use of the terms *ethnicity, disadvantaged, minority*, and *ghetto* are antithetical to our political consciousness which is indivisible from the international political struggle against racism."[90] We share Asante's concern with the problem of linguistic bias: however, if we follow his guidelines on political correctness we may all be reduced to communicating in mime. By refusing to refer to south central Los Angeles as a "ghetto," will we make a significant impact on the crisis in that community? Clearly, there is too much to be done there to argue over semantics.

Today, the image of Africa is at a crossroads. The work of scholars such as Boas, Du Bois, Herskovits and Woodson helped to show the way to a more humane, and yet more rigorous vision of the continent and its people. In the ensuing decades they have been followed by a host of scholars of all backgrounds who have attempted to view African realities with the sensitivity and seriousness they so richly deserve. One can argue endlessly over the ability of any observer, indigenous or exogenous, to present an accurate portrait of events; and one must freely admit that honest and well-intentioned observers can be led astray by their own intellectual paradigms, whatever their talents and training. More importantly, however, we need to remind ourselves that people of good faith can disagree; especially since, when they look in the mirror of the "other," they inevitably see their own reflection (even if they are often loath to acknowledge it). Fortunately, the old symbolic conventions are beginning to crumble; but there is a clear and present danger that they may be replaced by a new set of distortions, a new variety of reductionism which may ultimately prove to be every bit as destructive and pernicious as the old. There is nothing wrong with fantasy as long as it is not confused with reality; there is nothing wrong with polemic as long as it is not confused with scholarship; and there is nothing wrong with mythology as long as it is not confused with history. The lines, however, are beginning to blur in the current debate over Africa and its legacy. It is not too soon to stand up and demand that they be restored. As Africa and its diaspora enter the twenty-first century, its people, its heritage, and the rich possibilities of its future deserve nothing less.

Notes

1. Azinna Nwafor, "The Revolutionary as Historian: Padmore and Pan-Africanism," Introduction to George Padmore, *Pan-Africanism or Communism* (New York: Doubleday, 1971), xxv, xxxiv. Also see James R. Hooker, *Black Revolutionary: George Padmore's Path from Communism to Pan-Africanism* (London: Pall Mall Press, 1967).
2. George Padmore, *Pan-Africanism or Communism* (New York: Doubleday, 1971), xv.
3. Ibid., xvi.
4. Ibid., xix.
5. Ibid., 282.
6. Theodore Draper, "The Fantasy of Black Nationalism," *Commentary* (September 1969): 34-35.
7. Padmore, 284-85.
8. Ibid., 285.
9. Draper, 37.
10. Ibid., 36.
11. Anonymous, "Review of *Communism Versus the Negro* by William A. Nolan," *The Crisis* (January 1952): 59.

12. Roger Wilkins, "What Africa Means to Blacks," *Foreign Policy* (Summer 1974): 131.
13. Ibid., 130.
14. Ibid., 134.
15. Martin Staniland, *American Intellectuals and African Nationalists, 1955-1970* (New Haven: Yale University Press, 1991), 178. Also see James R. Hooker, *The Impact of African History on Afro-Americans, 1930-1945* (Buffalo: n.p., 1971).
16. Staniland, 178.
17. Hugh H. Smythe, "Review of *Struggle for Africa*, by Vernon Bartlett," *The Crisis* (May 1954): 311.
18. Ibid., 311.
19. "The Ten Biggest Lies About Africa," *Ebony* (May 1957): 58.
20. Elliott P. Skinner, "African, Afro-American, White American: A Case of Pride and Prejudice," *Freedomways* 5 (Summer 1965): 387.
21. James Baldwin, "A Negro Assays the Negro Mood," in "Man's Relation to Man: Africa's Effect on the U.S. Negro," *Current* (May 1961): 6.
22. Ibid., 7.
23. Phaon Goldman, "The Significance of African Freedom for the Negro American," *The Negro History Bulletin* (October 1960): 2, 6.
24. Ibid., 6.
25. John A. Morsell, "The Meaning of Black Nationalism," *The Crisis* (February 1962): 70-71.
26. Staniland, 193.
27. Harold Cruse, "Negro Nationalism's New Wave," in "Man's Relation to Man: The Rise of Afro-Americanism," *Current* (May 1962): 45.
28. Ibid., 47.
29. Eldridge Cleaver, *Revolution in the Congo* (London: Stage 1 and The Revolutionary Peoples' Communications Network, 1971), 5-6. Also see Kathleen Rout, *Eldridge Cleaver* (Boston: Twayne Publishers, 1991), 125-26.
30. Cleaver, 5.
31. Draper, 42.
32. Ibid., 43.
33. Ibid., 42.
34. Ibid., 43.
35. Ibid., 44.
36. Cleaver, 7.
37. Ibid., 8-9.
38. Ibid., 9.
39. Draper, 52.
40. Vincent Harding, Robert Hill, and William Strickland, "Introduction" to Walter Rodney, *How Europe Underdeveloped Africa*, rev. ed. (Washington, D.C.: Howard University Press, 1982), xi.
41. Walter Rodney, *How Europe Underdeveloped Africa*, rev. ed. (Washington, D.C.: Howard University Press, 1982), 38.
42. Ibid., 88.
43. Ibid.
44. Ibid., 27.

45. Ibid., 96.
46. Ibid., 96.
47. Ibid., 96. Italics ours.
48. Ibid., 101.
49. Ibid., 102.
50. Ibid., 117.
51. Ibid., 118.
52. Ibid., 120.
53. Ibid., 121.
54. Ibid., 121-22.
55. Ibid., 129.
56. Ibid., 131.
57. Molefi Kete Asante, *Afrocentricity* (Trenton: Africa World Press, 1988), 94.
58. Ibid., 79.
59. Ibid., 7.
60. See especially Cheikh Anta Diop, *The African Origin of Civilization: Myth or Reality* (New York: Lawrence Hill, 1974).
61. Molefi Kete Asante, *Kemet, Afrocentricity, and Knowledge* (Trenton, N.J.: Africa World Press, 1990), 58.
62. Ibid., 47.
63. Asante, *Afrocentricity*, 38-39.
64. Martin Bernal, *Black Athena: The Afroasiatic Roots of Classical Civilization*, vol. 1: *The Fabrication of Ancient Greece 1785-1985* (New Brunswick: Rutgers University Press, 1987) and vol. 2: *The Archaeological and Documentary Evidence* (New Brunswick: Rutgers University Press, 1992). Among the many reviews of this work, see the highly critical piece by Emily Vermeule (Radcliffe Professor of Classics and Fine Arts at Harvard University) entitled "The World Turned Upside Down," *The New York Review of Books* (26 March 1992): 40-43.
65. Asante, *Kemet*, 65.
66. Wyatt MacGaffey, "Review Article: Who Owns Ancient Egypt?" *Journal of African History* 32 (1991): 516.
67. Asante, *Afrocentricity*, 38-39.
68. Ibid., 121.
69. Molefi Kete Asante, "Putting Africa at the Center," *Newsweek* (23 September 1991): 46.
70. Asante, *Afrocentricity*, 109.
71. Henry Louis Gates Jr., "Beware of the New Pharaohs," *Newsweek* (23 September 1991): 47.
72. Asante, *Afrocentricity*, 2.
73. Ibid., 5.
74. Asante, *Kemet*, 61.
75. Ibid., 114.
76. Ibid., 115.
77. Ibid., 130.
78. Ibid., 114.
79. Ibid., 123.
80. Ibid., 123-24.

81. Ibid., 124.
82. Asante, *Afrocentricity*, 60.
83. Ibid., 57.
84. Ibid., 58.
85. Ibid., 68.
86. Ibid., 23.
87. Ibid., 32.
88. Ibid., 41.
89. Ibid., 100.
90. Ibid., 33.

Bibliography

Abrahams, Peter. *Down Second Avenue.* London: Longmans, 1946.

———. *Mine Boy.* London: Longmans, 1946.

———. *Tell Freedom.* New York: Knopf, 1954.

———. *Wild Conquest.* London: Faber and Faber, 1961.

Achebe, Chinua. *No Longer at Ease.* New York: I. Obolensky, 1961.

———. *Things Fall Apart.* London: Heinemann, 1967.

———. *Girls at War.* Garden City, N.Y.: Doubleday and Co., 1973.

———. "An Image of Africa: Racism in Conrad's 'Heart of Darkness.'" *The Massachusetts Review* 18, no. 4 (Winter 1977): 782-94.

———. *Hopes and Impediments: Selected Essays by Chinua Achebe.* Garden City, N.Y.: Doubleday, 1989.

Adams, Percy. *Travelers and Travel Liars, 1660-1800.* Berkeley: University of California Press, 1962.

Adelman, Gary. *Heart of Darkness: Search for the Unconscious.* Boston: Twayne Publishers, 1987.

Ahmed, Abd Elrahman Abuzayd. "'Comments on Izzud-din Amar Musa, 'Islam and Africa.'" In *The Arabs and Africa,* edited by Khair El-Din Haseeb. London: Croom Helm and Centre for Arab Unity Studies, 1985.

Ahmed, Akbar S. *Toward Islamic Anthropology: Definition, Dogma and Directions.* Herndon, Va.: International Institute of Islamic Thought, 1986.

Akeley, Carl E. *In Brightest Africa.* Garden City, N.Y.: Garden City Publishing Co., 1920.

Akeley, Carl E., and Mary Jobe Akeley. *Adventures in the African Jungle.* New York: Jr. Literary Guild, 1931.

Akeley, Mary Jobe. *Carl Akeley's Africa.* New York: Cornwell Press, 1929.

Al-Faruqi, Isma'il R. Foreword. In *Toward Islamic Anthropology: Definition, Dogma, and Directions,* by Akbar Ahmed. Herndon, Va.: International Institute of Islamic Thought, 1986.

Aldrich, Charles Roberts. *The Primitive Mind and Modern Civilization.* New York: AMS Press, 1969.

Alldridge, J. T. *The Sherbro and Its Hinterland.* London: Macmillan and Co., 1901.

Anderson, David A. "Hemingway and Henderson in the High Savannahs, or Two Midwestern Moderns and the Myth of Africa." *MidAmerica* 15 (May 1988): 84-100

Asad, Talal, ed. *Anthropology and the Colonial Encounter.* New York: Humanities Press, 1973.

Asante, Molefi Kete. *Afrocentricity.* Trenton, N.J.: Africa World Press, 1988.

———. *Kemet, Afrocentricity, and Knowledge.* Trenton, N.J.: Africa World Press, 1990.

———. "Putting Africa at the Center." *Newsweek* (23 September 1991): 46.

Baldwin James. "A Negro Assays the Negro Mood." In "Man's Relation to Man: Africa's Effect on the U.S. Negro." *Current* (May 1961): 6-7

Barnes, Sandra T. *Patrons and Power: Creating a Political Community in Metropolitan Lagos.* Manchester: Manchester University Press, 1986.

Bascom, William R. "Urbanization Among the Yoruba." *American Journal of Sociology* 60 (1955): 446-54.

———. *African Art in Cultural Perspective.* New York: Norton, 1973.

Bascom, William R., and Melville J. Herskovits, eds. *Continuity and Change in African Cultures.* Chicago: University of Chicago Press, 1959.

Baudet, Henri. *Paradise on Earth: Some Thoughts on European Images of Non-European Man.* Westport, Conn.: Greenwood Press, 1965.

Beach, Joseph Warren. *The Twentieth Century Novel: Studies in Technique.* New York: Appleton-Century-Crofts, Inc., 1960.

Beatty, Jerome. "Great White Chief of the Congo." *American Magazine* (July 1939).

Beer, William R. Introduction. In *The Tears of the White Man: Compassion as Contempt,* by Pascal Bruckner. New York: The Free Press, 1986.

Bell, Augustus J. *The Wooly Hair Man of the Ancient South And a Digest of Facts from the Original Languages.* New York: LBS Archival Products, 1989.

Bellow, Saul. *Henderson the Rain King.* New York: Fawcett, 1969.

Bennett, Norman R., ed. *Stanley's Despatches to the New York Herald 1871-1872, 1874-1877.* Boston: Boston University Press, 1970.

Berghahn, Marion. *Images of Africa in Black American Literature.* Totowa, N.J.: Rowman and Littlefield, 1977.

Berkhofer, Robert F. Jr. *The White Man's Indian.* New York: Vintage Books, 1978.

Bernal, Martin. *Black Athena: The Afroasiatic Roots of Classical Civilization.* 2 vols. New Brunswick: Rutgers University Press, 1992.

Bernstein, Jeremy. "The Dark Continent of Henry Stanley." *The New Yorker* (31 December 1990): 93-107

Bidney, David. *Theoretical Anthropology.* New York: Shocken Books, 1967.

Bieder, Robert E. *Science Encounters the Indian, 1820-1880: The Early Years of American Ethnology.* Norman: University of Oklahoma Press, 1986.

Bierman, John. *Dark Safari: The Life Behind the Legend of Henry Morton Stanley.* New York: Alfred A Knopf, 1990.

Blayechettai, J. E. *The Pen of an African.* n.p.: c. 1922.

Bloom, Harold, ed. *Alice Walker.* New York: Chelsea House Publishers, 1989.

Blyden, Edward W. *Christianity, Islam and the Negro Race.* Edinburgh: Edinburgh University Press, 1967.

Boas, Franz. "The Mental Attitude of the Educated Classes." *The Dial* (5 September 1918): 232-37.

——. "Nationalism." *The Dial* (8 March 1919): 145-48

——. *The Mind of Primitive Man.* Rev. ed. New York: Macmillan, 1938.

——. *Race, Language, and Culture.* New York: Macmillan, 1940.

Bohannan, Laura [Elenore Smith Bowen]. *Return to Laughter.* Garden City, N.Y.: Doubleday and Co., 1964.

Bowen, J. W. E., ed. *Africa and the American Negro: Addresses and Proceedings of the Congress on Africa.* Miami: Mnemosyne Publishing, 1969.

Bowles, Paul. *The Sheltering Sky.* New York: New Directions, 1948.

Boyd, William. *A Good Man in Africa.* New York: William Morrow, 1982.

——. *An Ice-Cream War.* London: Hamish Hamilton, 1982.

Boyle, T. Coraghessan. *Water Music.* New York: Penguin Books, 1981.

Brantlinger, Patrick. *Rule of Darkness: British Literature and Imperialism, 1830-1914.* Ithaca, N.Y.: Cornell University Press, 1988.

Bridgman, Herbert L. "The New British Empire of the Sudan," *The National Geographic Magazine* 17, no. 5 (May 1906): 241-67.

Brooks, Paul. *Speaking for Nature: How Literary Naturalists from Henry David Thoreau to Rachael Carson Have Shaped America.* Boston: Houghton Mifflin Co., 1980.

Bruce, James. *Travels to Discover the Source of the Nile*. 5 vols. New York: Horizon Press, 1964.

Bruckner, Pascal. *The Tears of the White Man: Compassion as Contempt*. New York: The Free Press, 1986.

Buell, Raymond Leslie. *The Native Problem in Africa*. 2 vols. New York: The Macmillan Co., 1928.

Bull, Bartle. *Safari: A Chronicle of Adventure*. London: Viking,1988.

Burn, A. R. "Introduction." *The Histories*, by Herodotus, translated by Aubrey de Selincourt. Harmondsworth, Middlesex: Penguin Books, 1972.

Burroughs, Edgar Rice. *Tarzan of the Apes*. New York: New American Library, 1990.

Cameron, Kenneth M. "Introduction." In *Chronicles of a Second African Trip*, by George Eastman. Rochester, N.Y.: Friends of the University of Rochester Libraries, 1987.

——. *Into Africa: The Story of the East African Safari*. London: Constable and Co., 1990.

Campbell, Mary B. *The Witness and the Other World: Exotic European Travel Writing, 400-1600*. Ithaca, N.Y.: Cornell University Press, 1988.

Campbell, Joseph. *The Masks of God*. 4 vols. New York: Penguin Books, 1969.

Caputo, Philip. *A Rumor of War*. New York: Ballantine Books, 1977.

——. *Del Corso's Galley*. New York: Holt, Rinehart, and Winston, 1983.

——. *Horn of Africa*. New York: Dell, 1980.

——. *Means of Escape*. New York: Harper Collins, 1991.

Cary, Joyce. *The African Witch*. London: Michael Joseph, 1951.

——. *An American Visitor*. London: Michael Joseph, 1952.

——. *Assia Saved*. London: Michael Joseph, 1952.

——. *Mister Johnson*. New York: New Directions, 1989.

Cawelti, John G. *Adventure, Mystery, and Romance: Formula Stories as Art and Popular Culture*. Chicago: University of Chicago Press, 1976.

Cheeseboro, Anthony. Interview by Dennis Hickey. East Lansing, Michigan, 4 December 1991.

Chick, John D. "The World of the White: European Alienation in the Novels of Robert Ruark." In *Aspects of Africa's Identity: Five Essays*, edited by Paul F. Nursey-Bray. Makerere, Uganda: Makerere Institute of Social Research, 1973.

Chinweizu. *The West and the Rest of Us*. New York: Random House, 1975.

Clarke, John Henrik, ed. *Marcus Garvey and the Vision of Africa*. New York: Vintage Books, 1974.

Cleaver, Eldridge. *Revolution in the Congo*. London: Stage 1 and The Revolutionary Peoples' Communications Network, 1971.

Clifford, James. *The Predicament of Culture*. Cambridge: Harvard University Press, 1988.

Clifford, James, and George E. Marcus, eds. *Writing Culture: The Poetics and Politics of Ethnography*. Berkeley: University of California Press, 1986.

Coale, Samuel. *Paul Theroux*. Boston: Twayne Publishers, 1987.

Coates, W. Paul. "Publisher's Note." In *Your History: From the Beginnings of Time to the Present*, by J. A. Rogers. Baltimore: Black Classics Press, 1983.

Conrad, Joseph. *Heart of Darkness*. New York: New American Library, 1980.

Coon, Carleton S. *The Races of Europe*. New York: The Macmillan Co., 1939.

——. *The Origin of Races*. New York: Alfred A Knopf, 1962.

——. *Racial Adaptations: A Study of Origins, Nature, and Significance of Racial Variations in Humans*. Chicago: Nelson-Hall, 1982.

Cooper, James Fenimore. *The Leather-Stocking Saga*. New York: Pantheon Books, 1954.

Cooper, Merian C., and Earnest B. Schoedsack. "Two Fighting Tribes of the Sudan." *The National Geographic Magazine* 56 (July-Dec. 1929): 465-79

Cotlow, Lewis. *In Search of the Primitive*. Boston: Little, Brown, and Co., 1966.

Crichton, Michael. *Congo*. New York: Alfred A Knopf, 1980.

The Crisis "Review of *Communism versus the Negro* by William A. Nolan." (January 1952): 59-60.

Crummell, Alexander. "The Absolute Need of an Indigenous Missionary Agency in Africa." In *Africa and the American Negro: Addresses and Proceedings of the Congress on Africa*, edited by J. W. E. Bowen. Miami: Mnemosyne Publishing, 1969.

——. "Civilization as a Collateral and Indispensable Instrumentality in Planting the Christian Church in Africa." In *Africa and the American Negro: Addresses and Proceedings of the Congress on Africa*, edited by J. W. E. Bowen. Miami: Mnemosyne Publishing, 1969.

——. *The Future of Africa*. New York: Negro Universities Press, 1969.

——. "The Negro Race Not Under A Curse: An Examination of Genesis IX.25." In *The Future of Africa*, by Alexander Crummell. New York: Negro Universities Press, 1969.

——. "The Relations and Duty of Free Colored Men in America to Africa." In *The Future of Africa*, edited by Alexander Crummell. New York: Negro Universities Press, 1969.

Cruse, Harold. "Negro Nationalism's New Wave." In "Man's Relation to Man: The Rise of Afro-Americanism." *Current* (May 1962): 45-47.

Curtin, Philip D. *The Image of Africa: British Ideas and Action, 1780-1850*. Madison: University of Wisconsin Press, 1964.

Curtin, Philip D., et. al. *African History*. Boston: Little, Brown, and Co., 1978.

Custer, Elizabeth Bacon. *Tenting on the Plains*. Norman: Oklahoma University Press, 1971.

Custer, George A. *My Life on the Plains*. New York: Sheldon, 1876.

d'Azevedo, Warren. "Some Historical Problems in the Delineation of a Central West Atlantic Region," *Annals of the New York Academy of Sciences* 96, no. 2 (1962): 512-38.

de Brazza, Pierre Paul Savorgnan. *Conferences et lettres de Pierre Savorgnan de Brazza sur se trois explorations dans l'Ouest Afrique, 1875-a-1806*. Paris: M. Dreyfous, 1887.

de Gobineau, Comte Joseph. *The Inequality of the Human Races*. 4 vols. New York: Putnam, 1915.

Degler, Carl N. *In Search of Human Nature: The Decline and Revival of Darwinism in American Social Thought*. New York: Oxford University Press, 1991.

DeVoto, Bernard. *Across the Wide Missouri*. Boston: Houghton Mifflin, Co. 1947.

The Dial "Review of *Primitive Society* by Robert H. Lowie." (November 1920): 528-33.

Diamond, Stanley, ed. *Culture in History*. New York: Columbia University Press, 1960.

———. *In Search of the Primitive: A Critique of Civilization*. New Brunswick, N.J.: Transaction Books, 1974.

Dinesen, Isak. *Out of Africa*. New York: Vintage Books, 1985.

Diop, Cheikh Anta. *The African Origin of Civilization: Myth or Reality*, translated by Mercer Cook. New York: Lawrence Hill, 1974.

Dixon, Roland B. *The Racial History of Man*. New York: Scribners, 1923.

Dorjahn, Vernon. "The Changing Political System of the Temne." *Africa* 30 (1960): 110-40.

Dorson, Richard M. *American Folklore and the Historian*. Chicago: University of Chicago Press, 1971.

Dowling, William C. *Jameson, Althusser, Marx: An Introduction to the Political Unconscious*. Ithaca, N.Y.: Cornell University Press, 1984.

Draper, Theodore. "The Fantasy of Black Nationalism," *Commentary* (September 1969): 34-35.

Droixhe, Daniel, and Klaus H. Kiefer, eds. *Images de L'African de L'Antiquité au XXE Sieclè*. Frankfurt am Main; Verlag Peter Lang, 1987.

Du Bois, W. E. B. " *The Negro*. New York: Henry Holt, 1915.
———. *Dusk of Dawn: An Essay Toward An Autobiography of a Race Concept*. New York: Harcourt, Brace and Co., 1940.
———. *The World and Africa*. New York: The Viking Press, 1947.
———. "Back to Africa." In *Marcus Garvey and the Vision of Africa*, edited by John Henrik Clarke. New York: Vintage Books, 1974.
———. *Black Folk Then and Now*. Millwood, N.Y.: Kraus-Thompson Organization, Ltd., 1975.
Duggan, William. *The Great Thirst*. London: Hutchinson and Co., 1985.
———. *Lovers of the African Night*. New York: Delacourt Press, 1987.
Duignan, Peter, and L. H. Gann. *The United States and Africa: A History*. London: Cambridge University Press, 1984.
Durkheim, Emile. *Emile Durkheim: Selections from his Work*. New York: Crowell, 1963.
Duse, Mohammed Ali. *The Negro World* in *Primitives on the Move: Some Historical Articulations of Garvey and Garveyism, 1887-1927*, by C. Boyd James. Ph.D. diss., The University of California, Los Angeles, 1982.
Eastman, George. *Chronicles of a Second African Trip*. Rochester, N.Y.: The Friends of the University of Rochester Libraries, 1987.
el Zein, Abdul Hamid M. *The Sacred Meadows: A Structural Analysis of Religious Symbolism in an East African Town*. Evanston, Ill.: Northwestern University Press, 1974.
Equiano, Olaudah. *The Interesting Narrative of the Life of Olaudah Equiano or Gustavus Vasa, The African*. London: Dawsons, 1969.
Evans-Pritchard, E. E. *Essays in Social Anthropology*. New York: Free Press of Glencoe, 1963.
———. *The Nuer*, Oxford: Oxford University Press, 1969.
Fabian, Johannes. *Time and the Other: How Anthropology Makes its Object*. New York: Columbia University Press, 1983.
Fanon, Franz. *Peau noire, masques blancs*. Paris: Seuil, 1952.
———. *Les Damnes de la terre*. Paris: Maspero, 1961.
Fitzgerald, F. Scott. *The Great Gatsby*. New York: Collier, Scribners Classic, 1986.
Forbath, Peter. *The Last Hero*. New York: Simon and Schuster, 1988.
Forde, Daryll, ed. *The Context of Belief*. Liverpool: Liverpool University Press, 1958.
———. *African Worlds*. London: Oxford University Press, 1976.
Fothergill, Anthony. *Heart of Darkness*. Philadelphia: Open University Press, 1989.

Freeman, Derek. *Margaret Mead and Samoa: The Making and Unmaking of an Anthropological Myth.* Cambridge: Harvard University Press, 1983.

Freeman, F. *Africa's Redemption: The Salvation of Our Country.* Detroit: Negro History Press, c. 1969.

Fremont, John Charles. *Report of the Exploring Expedition to the Rocky Mountains.* Washington, D.C.: Gales and Seaton, 1845.

Galbraith, John Kenneth. Introduction. In *The Theory of the Leisure Class*, by Thorstein Veblen. Boston: Houghton Mifflin, 1973.

Gallieni, Joseph Simon. *Deux campagnes au Soudan francais, 1886-1888.* Paris: Hachette, 1891.

Garvey, Marcus. "African Fundamentalism." In *Marcus Garvey and the Vision of Africa*, edited by John Henrik Clarke. New York: Vintage Books, 1974.

——. "Speech by Marcus Garvey: Kingston, 5 February, 1928." In *The Marcus Garvey and Universal Negro Improvement Association Papers*, vol. 7, edited by Robert A. Hill. Berkeley: University of California Press, 1990.

Gates, Henry Louis Jr. "Beware of the New Pharaohs," *Newsweek* (23 September 1991), 47.

Geertz, Clifford. *Works and Lives: The Anthropologist as Author.* Stanford, Ca.: Stanford University Press, 1988.

Goldman, Phaon. "The Significance of African Freedom for the Negro American." *The Negro History Bulletin* (October 1960), 2-6 passim.

Gould, Stephen J. *The Mismeasure of Man.* New York: Norton, 1981.

Green, Kathryn L. "Review of *The Arabs and Africa.*" *The African Studies Review* 32 (April 1989): 132-33.

Green, Martin. *Dreams of Adventure, Deeds of Empire.* New York: Basic Books, 1979.

Greenberg, Joseph H. *Studies In African Linguistic Classification.* New Haven, Conn.: Compass, 1955.

——. *The Languages of Africa.* Bloomington: University of Indiana Press, 1963.

——. *Languages in the Americas.* Stanford, Cal.: Stanford University Press, 1987.

Greene, Graham. *The Heart of the Matter.* New York: The Viking Press, 1948.

——. *A Burnt-Out Case.* New York: The Viking Press, 1961.

Gronniosaw, Ukawsaw. *A Narrative of the most remarkable particulars in the life of James Albert Ukawsaw Gronniousaw, An African Prince.* Millwood, N.Y.: Kraus-Thompson Organization, Ltd., 1972.

Guggisberg, C. A. W. *Early Wildlife Photographers.* New York: Taplinger Publishers, 1977.

Gunther, John. *Inside Africa.* New York: Harper and Brothers, 1955.

Halasa, Malu. *Elijah Muhammad.* New York: Chelsea House, 1990.

Haley, Alex. *Roots.* Garden City, N.Y.: Doubleday and Co., 1976.

Hall, Richard. *Stanley: An Adventurer Explored.* London: Collins, 1974.

Hammer. Robert D., ed. *Joseph Conrad: Third World Perspectives.* Washington, D.C.: Three Continents Press, 1990.

Hammond, Dorothy, and Alta Jablow. *The Africa That Never Was: Four Generations of British Writing About Africa.* New York: Twayne Publishers, 1983.

Hammond, E. W. S. "Africa in its Relation to Christian Civilization." In *Africa and the American Negro: Addresses and Proceedings of the Congress on Africa*, edited by J. W. E. Bowen. Miami: Mnemosyne Publishing, 1969.

Hanley, Gerald. *Gilligan's Last Elephant.* Greenwich, Conn.: Fawcett Gold Medal Books, 1962.

Hansson, Karin. "Two Journeys into the Country of the Mind: Joseph Conrad's *Heart of Darkness* and Saul Bellow's *Henderson the Rain King.*" In *Cross Cultural Studies*, edited by Mirko Jurak. Ljubljana, Yugoslavia: English Department, Eduard Kardel, University of Ljubljana, 1988.

Haraway, Donna. *Primate Visions: Gender, Race and Nature in the World of Modern Science.* New York: Routledge, 1989.

Harden, Blaine. *Africa: Dispatches from a Fragile Continent.* Boston: Houghton Mifflin, 1990.

Hardy, Ronald. *Rivers of Darkness.* New York: Putnam's Sons, 1979.

Harris, Marvin. *The Rise of Anthropological Theory.* New York: Crowell, 1968.

Harrison, Jim. *Farmer.* New York: The Viking Press, 1976.

——. *Sundog.* New York: Dutton, 1984.

——. *Dalva.* New York: Dutton, 1988.

Hastings, A. C. C. *Nigerian Days.* London: John Lane, 1925.

Hemingway, Ernest. *Green Hills of Africa.* New York: Scribners, 1956.

——. "The Short Happy Life of Francis Macomber." In *Hemingway's African Stories: The Stories, Their Sources, Their Critics*, edited by John M. Howell. New York: Scribner's, 1969.

——. "The Snows of Kilimanjaro." In *Hemingway's African Stories: The Stories, Their Sources, Their Critics*, edited by John M. Howell. New York: Scribner's, 1969.

——. *The Garden of Eden.* New York: Scribners, 1986.

Herodotus. *The Histories*, translated by Aubrey de Selincourt. Harmondsworth, Middlesex: Penguin Books, 1972.

Hersh, Seymour M. *The Price of Power: Kissinger in the Nixon White House.* New York: Summit Books, 1983.

Herskovits, Melville J. "A Preliminary Consideration of the Culture Areas of Africa." *American Anthropologist* 26 (1924): 50-63

——. "The Cattle Complex in East Africa." *American Anthropologist* reprint/monograph s.1: s.n. (1926).

——. *Acculturation: The Study of Culture Contact.* New York: J. J. Augustin, 1938.

——. *The Myth of the Negro Past.* New York: Harper and Row, 1941.

——. *Man and His Works.* New York: Alfred A Knopf, 1948.

——. *Franz Boas: The Science of Man in the Making.* New York: Scribners, 1953.

——. *Dahomey: An Ancient West African Kingdom*, 2 vols. Evanston, Ill.: Northwestern University Press, 1967.

Hickey, Dennis C. "Ethiopia and Great Britain: Political Conflict in the Southern Borderlands, 1916-1935." Ph.D. diss. Northwestern University, 1985.

——. "Frontier Banditry and 'Legitimate' Trade: The Moyale Cattle Market, 1913-1923." *Northeast African Studies* 8 (1986): 169-79.

Hickey, Dennis, and Kenneth C. Wylie. "Heart of Darkness or 'Mother of Light'? American Perceptions of the African Rainforest, 1920-1980." *The Centennial Review* 35, no. 2 (Spring 1991), 249-63.

Hill, Jonathan D., ed. *Rethinking History and Myth: Indigenous South American Perspectives on the Past.* Chicago: University of Illinois Press, 1988.

Hill, Robert A., ed. *The Marcus Garvey and Universal Negro Improvement Association Papers*, vol. 7. Berkeley: University of California Press, 1990.

Hoagland, Edward. *Notes from the Century Before: A Journal from British Columbia.* New York: Random House, 1969.

——. *Red Wolves and Black Bears.* New York: Random House, 1976.

——. *African Calliope: A Journey to the Sudan.* New York: Random House, 1978.

——. *The Edward Hoagland Reader.* New York: Vintage Books, 1979.

Hobsbawm, Eric J., and Terence Ranger. *The Invention of Tradition.* Cambridge: Cambridge University Press, 1983.

Hodgen, Margaret T. *Anthropology, History, and Cultural Change.* Tucson: University of Arizona Press, 1974.

Holmes, Lowell D. *Quest for the Real Samoa: The Mead/Freeman Controversy.* South Hadley, Mass.: Bergin and Garvey Publishers, 1987.

Hooker, James R. *Black Revolutionary: George Padmore's Path from Communism to Pan-Africanism.* London: Pall Mall Press, 1967.

——. *The Impact of African History on Afro-Americans, 1930-1945*, Buffalo, N.Y.: n.p., 1971.

Hopkins, Anthony G. *An Economic History of West Africa*. London: Longman, 1973.

Howard, Alan. "Big Men, Traders and Chiefs: Power, Commerce, and Spatial Change in the Sierra Leone-Guinea Plain." Ph.D. diss., University of Wisconsin, 1972.

Howell, John M. *Hemingway's African Stories: The Stories, Their Sources, Their Critics*. New York: Scribners, 1969.

Hunter, Allan. *Joseph Conrad and the Ethics of Darwinism*. London: Croon Helm, 1983.

Huxley, Elspeth. "The Challenge of Africa." In *Africa and Asia: Mapping Two Continents*, by Elspeth Huxley. London: Aldus Books, 1973.

Hyatt, Marshall. *Franz Boas, Social Activist: The Dynamics of Ethnicity*. New York: Greenwood Press, 1990.

Isaac, Barry L. "Economy, Ecology, and Analogy: The !Kung San and the Generalized Foraging Model." In *Research in Economic Anthropology: A Research Annual*. supp. 5, *Early Paleoindian Economies of Eastern North America*, edited by Kenneth B. Tankersley and Barry L. Issac. Greenwich, Conn.: JAI Press, 1990.

Isernhagen, Hartwig. "A Constitutional Inability to Say Yes: Thorstein Veblen, the Reconstruction Program of *The Dial*, and the Development of American Modernism after World War I." *REAL: The Yearbook of Research in English and American Literature* 1 (1982).

Jackson, Michael. *Latitudes of Exile*. Dunedin, U.K.: McIndoe, 1976.

———. *The Kuranko: Dimensions of Social Reality in a West African Society*. London: C. Hurst, 1977.

———. *Barawa and the Ways Birds Fly in the Sky*. Washington, D.C.: Smithsonian Institution Press, 1986.

———. *Paths Toward a Clearing*. Bloomington: Indiana University Press, 1989.

Jacobs, Sylvia M., ed. *Black Americans and the Missionary Movement in Africa*. Westport, Conn.: Greenwood Press, 1982.

———. "The Impact of Black American Missionaries in Africa." In *Black Americans and the Missionary Movement in Africa*, edited by Sylvia Jacobs. Westport, Conn.: Greenwood Press, 1982.

James, C. Boyd. "Primitives on the Move: Some Historical Articulations of Garvey and Garveyism, 1887-1927." Ph.D. diss., University of California, Los Angeles, 1982.

Jameson, Fredric. *The Political Unconscious: Narrative as a Socially Symbolic Act*. Ithaca, N.Y.: Cornell University Press, 1981.

JanMohamed, Abdul R. *Manichean Aesthetics: The Politics of Literature in Colonial Africa*. Amherst: University of Massachusetts Press, 1983.

Jenkins, David. *Black Zion: Africa, Imagined and Real, as Seen by Today's Blacks.* New York: Harcourt Brace Jovanovich, 1975.

Johnson, Charles. *Middle Passage.* New York: Atheneum, 1990.

Johnson, Douglas. "History and Prophecy Among the Nuer of the Southern Sudan." Ph.D. diss., University Microfilms, Ann Arbor, Michigan, 1980.

Johnson, Edward A. *Adam vs. Ape-Man and Ethiopia.* New York: J. J. Little and Ives, Co., 1931.

Johnson, Martin. *Safari: A Saga of the African Blue.* New York: G. P. Putnam's Sons, 1928.

——. *Congorilla.* New York: Brewer, Warren and Putnam, 1931.

Johnson, Osa. *Four Years in Paradise.* Philadelphia: Lippencott, 1941.

——. *I Married Adventure.* New York: L. B. Lippencott, 1948.

Johnson, Samuel. *The History of Rasselas, Prince of Abyssinia.* London: Oxford University Press, 1968.

Johnston, Henry Hamilton. *British Central Africa: An Attempt to Give Some Account of a Portion of the Territories under British Influence North of the Zambezi.* New York: Arnhold, 1897.

——. *The Story of My Life.* Indianapolis: Bobbs-Merrill Co., 1923.

Jones, Adam. *From Slaves to Palm Kernels.* Weisbaden, Germany: F. Steiner, 1983.

Jung, Carl G. "Forward." In *The Primitive Mind and Modern Civilization,* by Charles Roberts Aldrich. New York: AMS Press, 1969.

——. *Man and His Symbols.* Garden City, N.Y.: Doubleday and Co., 1979.

Kalous, Milan. *Cannibals and Tonga Players of Sierra Leone.* Trentham, New Zealand: Wright and Carman, 1974.

Kelly, Raymond. *The Nuer Conquest.* Ann Arbor: The University of Michigan Press, 1985.

Kenney, Nathaniel T. "The Winds of Change Stir a Continent." *The National Geographic Magazine* 118, no. 3 (Sept. 1960): 303-59.

Killam, G. D. *Africa in English Fiction 1874-1939.* Ibadan, Nigeria: Ibadan University Press, 1968.

Kipling, Rudyard. *All the Mowgli Stories.* Garden City, N.Y.: Doubleday, 1936.

——. *Rudyard Kipling's Verse, Definitive Edition.* Garden City, N.Y.: Doubleday, 1940.

Kroeber, Alfred L. "The Culture-Area and Age-Area Concepts of Clark Wissler." In *Methods in Social Science: A Case Book,* edited by Alfred Kroeber. New York: Harcourt, Brace and Co., 1931.

——. *Culture and Natural Areas of Native North America.* Berkeley: University of California Press, 1939.

Kuper, Adam. *The Invention of Primitive Society.* London: Routledge, 1988.

Lamb, David. *The Africans.* New York: Methuen, 1985.

Leakey, L. S. B. "Finding the World's Earliest Man." *The National Geographic Magazine* 118, no. 3 (Sept. 1960): 421-35.

Lee, Richard B. "What Hunters Do For a Living, or, How to Make Out on Scarce Resources." In *Man the Hunter*, edited by Richard B. Lee and Irven DeVore. Chicago: Aldine, 1968.

——. *The !Kung San: Men, Women, and Work in a Foraging Society.* Cambridge: Cambridge University Press, 1979.

Leed, Eric. J. *The Mind of the Traveler: From Gilgamesh to Global Tourism.* New York: Basic Books. Harper Collins, 1991.

Lemann, Nicholas. *The Promised Land: The Great Black Migration and How it Changed America.* New York: Alfred A Knopf, 1991.

Levi-Strauss, Claude. *The Savage Mind.* Chicago: University of Chicago Press, 1966.

——. *Tristes Tropiques.* New York: Atheneum, 1974.

Levy-Bruhl, Lucien. *Primitive Mentality.* Boston: Beacon Press, 1966.

Lewis, Bernard. *Race and Slavery in the Middle East: An Historical Enquiry.* New York: Oxford University Press, 1990.

Lewis, Robert W. "Vivienne de Watteville, Hemingway's Companion on Kilimanjaro." In *Hemingway's African Stories: The Stories, Their Sources, Their Critics*, edited by John M. Howell. New York: Scribners, 1969.

Lewis, Rupert. *Marcus Garvey: Anti-Colonial Champion.* Trenton, N.J.: Africa World Press, 1988.

Liebenow, J. Gus. *Liberia: The Quest for Democracy.* Bloomington: Indiana University Press, 1987.

Lincoln, C. Eric. *The Black Muslims in America.* Boston: Beacon Press, 1961.

Longfellow, Henry Wadsworth. *The Song of Hiawatha.* New York: Gilberton, 1949.

Lowie, Robert H. "Anthropology Put to Work." *The Dial* (15 August 1918): 98-100.

——. *Primitive Society.* New York: Boni and Liveright, 1920.

Lugard, Frederick D. *The Rise of Our East African Empire.* London: W. Blackwood and Sons, 1893.

——. *The Story of the Uganda Protectorate.* London: Marshall and Sons, 1900.

MacGaffey, Wyatt. "Review Article: Who Owns Ancient Egypt?" *Journal of African History* 32 (1991): 515-19.

Mackenzie, John M., ed. *Imperialism and Popular Culture.* Manchester: Manchester University Press, 1986.

——. "Hunting in East and Central Africa in the late 19th century with special reference to Zimbabwe." In *Sport in Africa: Essays in Social History,* edited by William J. Baker and James A. Mangan. New York: Africana Publishing Co., 1987.

———. *The Empire of Nature: Hunting, Conservation and British Imperialism.* Manchester: Manchester University Press, 1988.

MacQueen, Peter. "Return of Col. Roosevelt from the Jungle." In *Roosevelt's Thrilling Experiences in the Wilds of Africa Hunting Big Game,* edited by Marshall Everett. London: A. Hamming, c. 1910.

Mair, Lucy. *An African People in the Twentieth Century.* London: Routledge and Kegan Paul, 1965.

Majdiak, Daniel. "The Romantic Self and *Henderson the Rain King.*" In *Makers of the Twentieth Century Novel,* edited by Harry R. Garvin. Lewisburg, Pa.: Bucknell University Press, 1977.

Malinowski, Bronislaw. *Argonauts of the Western Pacific.* New York: Dutton, 1966.

Mandel, Eli. "Imagining Natives: White Perspectives on Native Peoples." In *The Native in Literature,* edited by Thomas King, Cheryl Calver and Helen Hoy. Oakville, Ontario: ECW Press, 1987.

Mannheim, Karl. *Ideology and Utopia.* New York: Harcourt, Brace, and World, 1936.

Marable, Manning. "Ambiguous Legacy: Tuskegee's 'Missionary' Impulse and Africa during the Moton Administration, 1915-1935." In *Black Americans and the Missionary Movement in Africa,* edited by Sylvia Jacobs. Westport, Conn.: Greenwood Press, 1982.

Mason, M. C. B. "The Methodist Episcopal Church and the Evangelization of Africa." In *Africa and the American Negro: Addresses and Proceedings of the Congress on Africa,* edited by J. W. E. Bowen. Miami: Mnemosyne Publishing, 1969.

Matthiessen, Peter. *Wildlife in America.* New York: Viking Press, 1959.

———. *Under the Mountain Wall.* New York: Viking Press, 1962.

———. *At Play in the Fields of the Lord.* New York: Random House, 1965.

———. *The Tree Where Man Was Born: The African Experience.* New York: Dutton and Co., 1972.

———. *The Snow Leopard.* New York: The Viking Press, 1978.

———. *Wildlife in America.* New York: Viking Press, 1959.

———. *Sand Rivers,* with photographs by Hugo van Lawick. New York: The Viking Press, 1981.

——— *African Silences.* New York: Random House, 1990.

Mauroof, Saibo Mohamed. "Elements for an Islamic Anthropology." In *Social and Natural Sciences: The Islamic Perspective,* edited by Isma'il R. Al-Faruqi and Abdullah Omar Nasseef. Jeddah, Saudi Arabia: Hodder and Stoughton and King Abdulaziz University, 1981.

Mazrui, Ali A. *The Africans: A Triple Heritage*. London: BBC Publications, 1986.

McCall, Daniel F. "The Dynamics of Urbanization in Africa." *The Annals of the American Academy of Political and Social Science* 292 (1955).

McCarthy, Michael. *Dark Continent: Africa as Seen by Americans*. Westport, Conn.: Greenwood Press, 1983.

McKinley, Edward H. *The Lure of Africa: American Interest in Tropical Africa, 1919-1939*. New York: Bobbs-Merrill Co., 1974.

Mead, Margaret. *Coming of Age in Samoa*. New York: Morrow, 1928.

———. *Cooperation and Competition Among Primitive Peoples*. New York: McGraw-Hill, 1937.

———. *Sex and Temperament in Three Primitive Societies*. New York: New American Library, 1950.

———. *Male and Female: A Study of the Sexes in a Changing World*. New York: Morrow, 1952.

Mead, Walter Russell. "Dark Continent: A Grand Grim Tour of the New Europe." *Harper's* (April 1991).

Meillassoux, Claude, ed. *L'esclavage en Afrique precoloniale*. Paris: F. Maspero, 1975.

Melville, Herman. *Typee: a peep at Polynesian life*. New York: Wiley and Putnam, 1846.

———. *Omoo: a narrative of adventures in the south seas*. New York: Harper, 1847.

Memmi, Albert. *The Colonizer and the Colonized*. Boston: The Beacon Press, 1967.

Merriam, Alan P. *The Anthropology of Music*. Evanston, Ill.: Northwestern University Press, 1964.

Miers, Suzanne, and Igor Kopytoff, eds. *Slavery in Africa*. Madison: University of Wisconsin Press, 1977.

Milbury-Steen, Sarah L. *European and African Stereotypes in Twentieth-Century Fiction*. New York: New York University Press, 1981.

Miles, Nelson. *Personal Recollections*. New York: Werner, 1896.

Miller, Christopher. *Blank Darkness: Africanist Discourse in French*. Chicago: University of Chicago Press, 1985.

Mills, Anson. *My Story*. Washington, D.C.: The author, 1918.

Minter, William. "Candid Cables: Some Reflections on U.S. Response to the Congo Rebellions, 1964." In *The Crisis in Zaire: Myths and Realities,* edited by Nzongola-Ntalaja. Trenton, N.J.: Africa World Press, 1986.

Mogen, David, Mark Busby and Paul Bryant. *The Frontier Experience and the American Dream*. College Station: Texas A. & M. University Press, 1989.

Moore, Richard B. "The Critics and Opponents of Marcus Garvey." In *Marcus Garvey and the Vision of Africa,* edited by John Henrik Clark. New York: Vintage Books, 1974.

Moorehead, Alan. *The Blue Nile.* London: Hamish Hamilton, 1960.

Morel, Edmund. *Red Rubber.* London: T. Fisher Unwin, 1906.

Morgan, Lewis Henry. *The League of the Ho-de-no-sau-nee, Iroquois.* Rochester, N.Y.: Sage and Brothers, 1951.

——. *Ancient Society: Or Researches in the Lines of Human Progress from Savagery, through Barbarism to Civilization.* New York: World Publishing Co., 1963.

Morsell, John A. "The Meaning of Black Nationalism." *The Crisis* (February 1962): 69-74.

Moses, Wilson Jeremiah. *Alexander Crummell: A Study of Civilization and Discontent.* New York: Oxford University Press, 1989.

Mudimbe, V. Y. *The Invention of Africa.* Bloomington: Indiana University Press, 1988.

Muhammad, Elijah. *The Fall of America.* Chicago: Muhammad's Temple of Islam No. 2, 1973.

Muhammad Speaks, "After the Africans . . . Came the Cave Dwellers: History of Man's Origin Must now be Rewritten," (8 May 1964.):11-12.

Muhammad Speaks, "Who is the Original Man?" May 1962, 1, 23, 28

Murdock, George Peter. "The Current Status of the World's Hunting and Gathering Peoples." In *Man the Hunter,* edited by Richard B. Lee and Irven DeVore. Chicago: Aldine, 1968.

Musa, Izzud-din Amar. "Islam and Africa." In *The Arabs and Africa,* edited by Khair El-Din Haseeb. London: Croom Helm and Centre for Arab Unity Studies, 1985.

Naipaul, V. S. "Conrad's Darkness." In *Joseph Conrad: Third World Perspectives,* edited by Robert D. Hammer. Washington, D.C.: Three Continents Press, 1990.

Nash, Roderick. *Wilderness and the American Mind.* New Haven: Yale University Press, 1967.

Ngugi wa Thiong'o. *The River Between.* London: Heinmann,1965.

——. *A Grain of Wheat.* London: Heinmann, 1967.

Norris, John William. *The Ethiopian's Place in History and his Contribution to the World's Civilization.* Baltimore: The Afro-American Co., 1916.

Nwafor, Azinna. "The Revolutionary as Historian: Padmore and Pan-Africanism." Introduction to *Pan-Africanism or Communism,* by George Padmore. New York: Doubleday, 1971.

Nzongola-Ntalaja, ed. *The Crisis in Zaire: Myths and Realities.* Trenton, N.J.: Africa World Press, 1986.

O'Connor, Richard. *The Scandalous Mr. Bennett.* Garden City, N.Y.: Doubleday and Co., 1962.

Ohrn, Steven, and Rebecca Riley, eds. *Africa From Real To Reel.* Waltham, Mass.: African Studies Association, 1976.

Pakenham, Thomas. *The Scramble for Africa.* New York: Random House, 1991.

Padmore, George. *Pan-Africanism or Communism.* New York: Doubleday, 1971.

Page, Carol A. "Colonial Reaction to AME Missionaries in South Africa, 1898-1910." In *Black Americans and the Missionary Movement in Africa,* edited by Sylvia Jacobs. Westport, Conn.: Greenwood Press, 1982.

Parkman, Francis. *The Oregon Trail.* Garden City, N.Y.: Garden City Books, 1959.

Paul, Sherman. *In Search of the Primitive: Rereading David Antin, Jerome Rothenberg, and Gary Snyder.* Baton Rouge: Louisiana State University Press, 1986.

Peters, Carl. *New Light on Dark Africa.* London: Ward, Lock and Co., 1891.

Phillips, William D. *Slaves From Roman Times to the early Translatlantic Trade.* Minneapolis: University of Minnesota Press, 1985.

Porter, Dennis. *Haunted Journeys: Desire and Transgression in European Travel Writing.* Princeton: Princeton University Press, 1991.

Pratt, Louis H., and Darnell D. Pratt, eds. *Alice Malsenior Walker: An Annotated Bibliography.* Westport, Conn.: Meckler Corp., 1988.

Putnam, Anne Eisner. "My Life with Africa's Little People." *The National Geographic Magazine* 117 (Jan.-June 1960): 269-302.

Quaife, Milo M., ed. *The Journals of Captain Meriwether Lewis, etc, kept on the expedition of western exploration, 1803-1806.* Madison: State Historical Society of Wisconsin, 1916.

Radcliffe-Brown, A. R. *Method in Social Anthropology: Selected Essays.* Chicago: University of Chicago Press, 1958.

———. *The Social Anthropology of Radcliffe-Brown.* London: Routledge and Kegan Paul, 1977.

Raleigh, Walter. *The Discoverie of the Large, Rich, and Bewtiful Empire of Guiana with A Relation of the Great and Golden City of Manoa (which the Spaniards call El Dorado . . .* London: Printed for the Hakluyt Society, 1848.

Ranger, Terence O. *Dance and Society in Eastern Africa: 1890-1970.* Berkeley: University of California Press, 1975.

———. "Missionaries, Migrants and the Manyika: The Invention of Ethnicity in Zimbabwe." In *The Creation of Tribalism in Southern Africa,* edited by LeRoy Vail. Berkeley: University of California Press, 1989.

Raskin, Jonah. *The Mythology of Imperialism.* New York: Random House, 1971.

Rodney, Walter. *How Europe Underdeveloped Africa.* Rev. ed. Washington, D.C.: Howard University Press, 1982.

Rogers, Joel A. *World's Great Men of Color,* 2 vols. New York: J. A. Rogers and Future Press, 1947.

———. *Your History: From the Beginnings of Time to the Present.* Baltimore: Black Classics Press, 1983.

Roosevelt, Theodore. *Hunting Trips of a Ranchman: Sketches of Sport on the Northern Cattle Plains.* New York: G. P. Putnam's Sons, 1885.

———. *The Winning of the West.* New York: The Current Literature Publishing Co., 1905.

———. *African Game Trails: An Account of the African Wanderings of an American Hunter-Naturalist.* New York: Charles Scribner's Sons, 1919.

Rotberg, Robert I. *A Political History of Tropical Africa.* New York: Harcourt, Brace, and World, 1965.

Rout, Kathleen. *Eldridge Cleaver.* Boston: Twayne Publishers, 1991.

Ruark, Robert. *Something of Value.* Garden City, N.Y.: Doubleday and Co., 1955.

———. *The Old Man and the Boy.* New York: Holt, 1957.

———. *Uhuru.* New York: McGraw-Hill, 1962.

———. *Use Enough Gun.* London: Hamish Hamilton, 1966.

Rush, Norman. *Whites.* New York: Alfred A Knopf, 1986.

———. *Mating.* New York: Alfred A Knopf, 1991.

Ruxton, George Frederick. *Life in the Far West.* London: Blackwood and Sons, 1849.

Sahlins, Marshall. *Stone Age Economics.* Chicago: Aldine-Atherton, 1972.

Said, Edward, W. *Orientalism.* New York: Vintage Books, 1979.

———. "Through Gringo Eyes: With Conrad in Latin America." *Harper's* (April 1988): 70-72.

———. "Yeats and Decolonization." *Nationalism, Colonialism, and Literature,* Field Day Pamphlet no. 15. Belfast: Field Day Theatre Co., 1988.

Sanders, Edith R. "The Hamitic Hypothesis: Its Origin and Functions in Time Perspective." *Journal of African History* 10, no. 4 (1969): 521-32.

Sapir, Edward. "Civilization and Culture." *The Dial* (20 September 1919): 233-36.

Sass, Louis A. "Anthropology's Native Problems." *Harper's* (May 1986): 49-75.

Schapera, Isaac. *The Khoisan Peoples of South Africa: Bushmen and Hottentots.* London: Routledge, 1930.

Schmitt, Martin F, and Dee Brown, eds. *General Crook: His Autobiography.* Norman: Oklahoma University Press, 1946.

Schneider, Harold K. "The Subsistence Role of Cattle Among the Pakot East Africa." *American Anthropologist* 59 (1957): 278-301.

Schuyler, George S. *Slaves Today*. College Park, Md.: McGrath Publishing Co., 1969.

Seligman, C. G. *Races of Africa*. London: Oxford University Press, 1930.

Selous, Frederick C. *A Hunter's Wanderings in Africa*. London: Macmillan, 1911.

Shakespeare, William. *Henry IV, Part II*. Dubuque, Iowa: W. C. Brown, 1971.

Shepperson, George. *Africa in American History and Literature*. Oxford: Oxford University Press, 1979.

Shostak, Marjorie. *Nisa: The Life and Words of a !Kung Woman*. New York: Vintage Books, 1983.

Shoumatoff, Alex. *African Madness*. New York: Vintage Books, 1990.

——. *In Southern Light: Trekking Through Zaire and the Amazon*. New York: Vintage Books, 1990.

Simpson, George Eaton. *Melville J. Herskovits*. New York: Columbia University Press, 1973.

Skinner, Elliott P. "African, Afro-American, White American: A Case of Pride and Prejudice." *Freedomways* 5 (Summer 1965): 380-95.

——. "Afro-Americans in Search of Africa: The Scholar's Dilemma." In *Transformation and Resiliency in Africa As Seen by Afro-American Scholars*, edited by Pearl T. Robinson and Elliott P. Skinner. Washington, D.C.: Howard University Press, 1983.

Slade, Ruth. *King Leopold's Congo*. London: Oxford University Press, 1962.

Smith, Henry Nash. *Virgin Land*. New York: Alfred A Knopf, 1950.

Smith, Venture. *A Narrative of the Life and Adventures of Venture*. New London, Conn.: A Descendant of Venture, 1835.

Smith, Wilbur. *Elephant Song*. London: Macmillan, 1991.

Smyth, John H. "The African in Africa and the African in America." In *Africa and the American Negro: Addresses and Proceedings of the Congress on Africa*, edited by J. W. E. Bowen. Miami: Mnemosyne Publishing, 1969.

Smythe, Hugh H. "Review of *Struggle for Africa*, by Vernon Bartlett." *The Crisis* (May 1954): 310-11.

Snow, Philip. *The Star Raft: China's Encounter with Africa*. London: Weidenfeld and Nicolson, 1988.

Spencer, Herbert. *Principles of Sociology*. 3 vols. London: D. Appleton and Co., 1898-1899.

Staniland, Martin. *American Intellectuals and African Nationalists, 1955-1970*. New Haven: Yale University Press, 1991.

Stanley, Henry Morton. *Through the Dark Continent.* 2 vols. London: Sampson, Low, Marston, Searle, and Rivington, 1878.

——. *In Darkest Africa.* 2 vols. London: Sampson, Low, Marston, Searle, and Rivington, 1890.

——. *My Early Travels and Adventures in America and Asia.* 2 vols. London: Sampson, Low, Marston and Co., 1895.

——. *How I Found Livingstone.* 2 vols. New York: Gilberton, 1954.

Stein, Judith. *The World of Marcus Garvey: Race and Class in Modern Society.* Baton Rouge: Louisiana State University Press, 1986.

Stocking, George W. Jr. *Race, Culture, and Evolution: Essays in the History of Anthropology.* New York: The Free Press, 1968.

——. ed. *The Shaping of American Anthropology 1883-1911: A Franz Boas Reader.* New York: Basic Books, 1974.

Street, Brian V. *The Savage in Literature: Representations of "Primitive" Society in English Fiction.* London: Routledge and Kegan Paul, 1975.

Strong, Richard P., ed. *The African Republic of Liberia and the Belgian Congo: Harvard African Expedition, 1926-1927.* 2 vols. Cambridge: Harvard University Press, 1930.

Sulaiman, Ibraheem. *The Islamic State and the Challenge of History: Ideals, Policies, and Operations of the Sokoto Caliphate.* London: Mansell Publishing Ltd., 1987.

Thaw, Lawrence Copeley, and Margaret Stout Thaw. "A Motor Caravan Rolls Across Sahara and Jungle Through the Realms of Dusky Potentates and the Land of Big-Lipped Women." *The National Geographic Magazine* 74 (July-Dec. 1938): 327-64.

"The Ten Biggest Lies About Africa." *Ebony* (May 1957): 58-59.

Theroux, Paul. *Jungle Lovers.* Boston: Houghton Mifflin Co., 1971.

——. *Girls at Play.* London: Hamish Hamilton, 1978.

——. *My Secret History.* New York: Ballantine Books, 1989.

Thomas, Elizabeth Marshall. *The Harmless People.* New York: Alfred A Knopf, 1959.

Thomas, Maria. *Antonia Saw the Oryx First.* London: Serpent's Tail, 1988.

——. *African Visas.* New York: Soho Press, 1991.

Thomas, Marion A. "Graham Greene Travels in Africa and Dadie Travels in Europe." *African Literature Today* 14 (1984).

Thompson, Leonard. *The Political Mythology of Apartheid.* New Haven: Yale University Press, 1985.

Torgovnick, Marianna. *Gone Primitive: Savage Intellects, Modern Lives.* Chicago: University of Chicago Press, 1990.

Tucker, Martin. *Africa in Modern Literature: A Survey of Contemporary Writing in English.* New York: Frederick Ungar Publishing Co., 1967.

Turnbull, Colin M. *The Forest People.* New York: Touchstone Books, 1968.

Turner, Frederick Jackson. "The Significance of the Frontier in American History." In *The Frontier in American History,* by Frederick Jackson Turner. New York: H. Holt and Co., 1920.

Turner, H. M. "Essay: The American Negro and the Fatherland." In *Africa and the American Negro: Addresses and Proceedings of the Congress on Africa,* edited by J. W. E. Bowen. Miami: Mnemosyne Publishing, 1969.

Turner, Victor W. *Schism and Continuity in an African Society.* Manchester: Manchester University Press, 1957.

———. *The Forest of Symbols.* Ithaca, N.Y.: Cornell University Press, 1967.

———. *On the Edge of the Bush: Anthropology as Experience.* Tucson: University of Arizona Press, 1985.

Turner, Victor, and Edward M. Broner, eds. *The Anthropology of Experience.* Chicago: University of Illinois Press, 1986.

Turner, W. Burghardt. "Joel Augustus Rogers: An Afro American Historian." *The Negro History Bulletin* (February 1972): 34-38.

Twain, Mark. *King Leopold's Soliloquy.* Boston: P. R. Warren Co., 1905.

Ungar, Sanford J. *Africa: The People and Politics of an Emerging Continent.* New York: Simon and Schuster, 1985.

Updike, John. *The Coup.* New York: Penguin, 1980.

Vail, LeRoy, ed. *The Creation of Tribalism in Southern Africa.* Berkeley: University of California Press, 1989.

Van Der Post, Laurens. *The Lost World of the Kalahari.* New York: William Morrow, 1958.

Veblen, Thorstein. "The Passing of National Frontiers." *The Dial* (25 April 1918): 387-90.

———. *An Inquiry into the Nature of Peace and the Terms of its Perpetuation.* New York: Augustus M. Kelley, 1964.

———. *The Theory of the Leisure Class.* Boston: Houghton Mifflin, 1973.

Vermeule, Emily. "The World Turned Upside Down: A Review of *Black Athena,* volume 2, by Martin Bernal." *The New York Review of Books* (26 March 1992): 40-43.

Victor, Frances Fuller. *The River of the West.* Hartford and Toledo: R. W. Bliss and Co., 1870, 40-43.

Vidal, Gore. "Tarzan Revisited." In *Tarzan of the Apes,* by Edgar Rice Burroughs. New York: Signet Books, 1990.

Viertel, Peter. *White Hunter, Black Heart.* London: W. H. Allen, 1954.

Voget, Fred W. *A History of Ethnology.* New York: Holt, Rinehart and Winston, 1975.

Walker, Alice. *The Color Purple.* New York: Washington Square Press, 1982.

——. *Possessing The Secret of Joy.* New York: Harcourt, Brace, and Jovanovich, 1992.

Wallerstein, Immanuel. *The Capitalist World Economy.* Cambridge: Cambridge University Press, 1979.

Washington, Booker T. *The Story of the Negro.* New York: P. Smith, 1940.

Weisbord, Robert G. *Ebony Kinship: Africa, Africans, and the Afro-American.* Westport, Conn.: Greenwood Press, 1973.

Wells, H. G. *The Island of Dr. Moreau.* New York: Berkely/First Publishing, 1990.

White, Leslie A. *The Evolution of Culture: The Development of Civilization to the Fall of Rome.* New York: McGraw Hill, 1959.

Wilkins, Roger. "What Africa Means to Blacks." *Foreign Policy* (Summer 1974): 130-42.

Williams, Eric. *Capitalism and Slavery.* Chapel Hill: The University of North Carolina Press, 1944.

Williams, George W. *The History of the Negro Race in America.* New York: Putnam's Sons, 1883.

Williams, Walter L. "William Henry Sheppard, Afro-American Missionary in the Congo, 1890-1910." In *Black Americans and the Missionary Movement in Africa,* by Sylvia Jacobs. Westport, Conn.: Greenwood Press, 1982.

Wilmsen, Edwin N. *Land Filled with Flies: A Political Economy of The Kalahari.* Chicago: University of Chicago Press, 1989.

Wissler, Clark. *Man and Culture.* New York: Crowell, 1923.

Wister, Owen. *The Virginian.* New York: Macmillan, 1902.

Wolf, Eric. *Europe and the People Without History.* Berkeley: University of California Press, 1982.

Wolfe, Don M. *The Image of Man in America,* 2nd ed. New York: Thomas Y. Crowell, 1970.

Woodson, Carter G. *African Background Outlined.* New York: Negro Universities Press, 1936.

——. *The Negro in Our History.* Washington, D.C.: The Associated Publishers, 1962.

Wright, Richard. *Black Power.* New York: Harper, 1954.

Wylie, Kenneth C. "The Politics of Transformation: Indirect Rule in Mendeland and Abuja, 1890-1914." Ph.D. diss., Michigan State University, 1967.

——. *The Political Kingdoms of the Temne.* New York: Africana Publishing Corp., 1977.

——. "From the Fountainheads of the Niger: Researching a Multiethnic Regional History." In *Studies in the African Diaspora: A Memorial to James R. Hooker,* edited by John P. Henderson and Harry A. Reed. Dover, Mass.: The Majority Press, 1989.

Yerby, Frank. *The Dahomean.* New York: Dell, 1971.

Index

A

abolitionism, 239-40
acculturation, 78, 82,106
Achebe, Chinua, 24, 200
Adam vs. Ape-Man and Ethiopia, 255-56
Africa: American view of, 18-19, 93-4, 98; as "Eden," 3, 22, 117, 156, 185, 204, 213; as "heart of darkness," 179-80, 215, 220, 224; as laboratory, 16; as museum of cultures, 111, 146; as naturalists paradise, 156-62; as place of redemption, 241-42, 271; as place of renewal, 190-94, 212; "Dark Continent," 7, 21, 49; idealization of, 111, 204; "myth of merrie," 31, 113; mythic and populist impressions of, 206-7, 251-72; negative images of 203, 273-78; political dismissal of, 1, 20-21; primitive, 3, 22, 59-76 passim; relation to China, 36-37; relation to Islam, 37; U.S. aid to, 39-40n.39; urbanism in, 111-12
Africa's Redemption: The Salvation of our Country, 239-41
"African Blood Brotherhood," 285
African Americans, views of Africa, 211, 239-71, 287-99; as missionaries, 249-51; folk tradition of, 251-56, 272

African Calliope, 167-68
"African civilization" movement, 243
African Game Trails, 17, 156-57, 158-59, 175n.43, 176n.45
African Madness, 170-71
The Africans: A Triple Heritage, 48
Africans, as "noble savages," 22, 36, 110-11, 189; as savages, 12-19, 135-39, 158; viewed as the "other," 29-40; stereotypes of, 21-22, 29-43
"Afro-Americanism," 291-92
Afrocentricity, 1, 38, 308-17
Afrocentricity, 309, 312, 313, 316-17
"Afrology," 316
Ahmed, Abd Elrahman Abuzayd, 50
Ahmed, Akbars, 53
Akeley, Carl, 16, 160, 161
Akeley, Mary Jobe, 16
Al-Faruqi, Isma'il R. 53
Alcheringa, 75
Aldrich, Charles Roberts, 68-70; *Primitive Mind and Modern Civilization*, 68-70
Ali, Duse Mohammad, 261
American Intellectuals and African Nationalists, 1955-1990, 288
Amerindians, 10-11, 94-96
Amin, Idi, 153-54